JAPANESE ELECTRONICS MULTINATIONALS AND STRATEGIC TRADE POLICIES

JAPAN BUSINESS AND ECONOMICS SERIES

This series provides a forum for books on the workings of Japan's economy, its business enterprises, its management practices, and its macroeconomic structure. Japan has achieved the status of a major economic world power and much can be learned from an understanding of how this has been accomplished and how it is being sustained.

The series aims to balance empirical and theoretical work. It also implicitly takes for granted that both the significant differences between Japan and other countries and the similarities between them are worth knowing about. The series will present a broad range of work on economics, politics, and systems of management, in analysing the performance of one of the major players in what may well be the largest economic region in the twenty-first century.

Japanese Electronics Multinationals and Strategic Trade Policies

RENÉ A. BELDERBOS

OXFORD · CLARENDON PRESS
1997

Oxford University Press, Great Clarendon Street, Oxford OX2 6DP
Oxford New York
Athens Auckland Bangkok Bogota Bombay
Buenos Aires Calcutta Cape Town Dar es Salaam
Delhi Florence Hong Kong Istanbul Karachi
Kuala Lumpur Madras Madrid Melbourne
Mexico City Nairobi Paris Singapore
Taipei Tokyo Toronto Warsaw
and associated companies in
Berlin Ibadan

Oxford is a trade mark of Oxford University Press

Published in the United States by
Oxford University Press Inc., New York

British Library Cataloguing in Publication Data
Data available

Library of Congress Cataloging in Publication Data
Belderbos, René.
Japanese electronics multinationals and strategic trade policies/René A. Belderbos.
p. cm.—(Japan business and economics series)
Includes bibliographical references.
1. Electronic industries—Japan. 2. International business enterprises—Japan—Management. 3. Japan—Commercial policy. 4. Competition, International. I. Title. II. Series: Japan business & economics.
HD9696.A3J32338 1997 338.8'8721381'0952—dc21 96-50048
ISBN 0–19–823332–9

1 3 5 7 9 10 8 6 4 2

Typeset by Best-set Typesetter Ltd., Hong Kong
Printed and bound in Great Britain by
Biddles Ltd, Guildford and King's Lynn

For Itzel, Tonatiuh, and Yukiko

ACKNOWLEDGEMENTS

A great number of people have contributed in one way or another to the completion of this book. Background research for the project started as early as 1989 at Erasmus University Rotterdam, where Joop Stam encouraged me to pursue my research on Japanese multinationals. I thank him and Leo Sleuwaegen for their support during the next four years during which I worked on my dissertation. Without the insights and scrutiny of Leo Sleuwaegen, this book could not have been completed. Leo Sleuwaegen is also co-author of Chapters 5 and 7, and I thank him for giving me permission to include our joint work. At Sussex University, Peter Holmes greatly helped me to increase my understanding of the inter-relationships between strategic trade policies, antidumping, and antitrust. It was his idea to analyse the implications of the Zenith Versus Matsushita antitrust case and I thank him for allowing me to use the results of our joint research in Chapter 2. I am also deeply grateful to my hosts in Japan. Ippei Yamazawa arranged for my stay at the Graduate School of Economics at Hitotsubashi University in 1989–1990 and again in 1992, and Kyoji Fukao invited me to the Institute for Economic Research of Hitotsubashi University in 1995. Their continuous support and encouragement, as well as critical comment, helped to make my fieldwork in Japan a success.

I am indebted to a number of other people who have contributed in various ways to my research in the past years. Toshihisa Nagasaka and Chuji Kikutani at the Institute for International Trade and Investment (ITI) allowed me to analyse unpublished data from the MITI surveys among Japanese multinationals, and Kyoko Imada at ITI prepared the data selections. Tetsufumi Yamakawa arranged my three month stay at the Bank of Japan in 1992 and Ryotaru Komiya provided me with the opportunity to frequent the MITI Research Institute as a visiting researcher in 1995. Hideki Yamawaki suggested that I focus my empirical research on the electronics industry, which proved to be valuable advice. Tomiko Nojima answered all my questions concerning Japanese software and databases at Hitotsubashi University. Shigeru Nishiyama helped me to translate the electronics and economics jargon from Japanese to English. Marco Furlotti and Giovanni Capanelli at Hitotsubashi University commented on my work and helped me trace relevant literature in Japan. Jeroen Potjes, Martin Carree, and Clive Jie a Joen at the Tinbergen Institute have been invaluable in discovering the errors and omissions in my work. Margaret Sharp and William Walker at the Science Policy Research Unit at the University of Sussex encouraged me to seek publication of this book. Yui Kimura was an excellent referee whose comments helped to improve the coherence of the final manuscript.

This book has also benefited from comments and suggestions on the various chapters by a number of other people: R. E. Caves, Alan Cawson, Herbert Glejser, Akira Goto, Mike Hobday, Abraham Hollander, Takeo Hoshi, Motoshige Itoh, Toshiyasu Izawa, Jeremy Kempton, Yasuhiro Kiyono, Dan Kovenock, Morio Kuninori, Eric de Laat, Charles van Marrewijk, Mitsuo Matsushita, Hiroyuki Odagiri, Keith Pavitt, Frédérique Sachwald, Mari Sako, Ulrike Schaede, Alasdair Smith, Kotaro Suzumura, Shujiro Urata, Jean-Marie Viaene, Friedl Weiss, Tadashi Yamada, and undoubtedly a number of others who hopefully will accept my apologies for not including their names in this list.

I have been provided with an excellent research environment at the institutes I have been affiliated with or hosted by in the past years. I would like to offer my gratitude to the support staff of these institutes for all the assistance I received: the Science Policy Research Unit (SPRU) at the University of Sussex, the Institute for Economic Research at Hitotsubashi University, the Tinbergen Institute at Erasmus University Rotterdam, the Research Institute of the Ministry of International Trade and Industry of Japan, and the Institute for Monetary and Economic Studies of the Bank of Japan. Finally, I gratefully acknowledge grants from the Japanese Ministry of Education (Monbusho), the Japan–German Berlin Centre, and the Matsushita International Foundation.

R.A.B.
Brighton, 30 April 1996

Chapter 1 draws heavily on work for the Institut Français des Relations Internationales (IFRI) earlier published in English as: René A. Belderbos, 1995, The Role of Investment in Europe in the Globalization Strategy of Japanese Electronics Firms, in: Frédérique Sachwald, ed., *Japanese Firms in Europe*, Harwood Academic Publishers, Luxembourg, 89–168.

Chapter 2 has appeared in slightly different form as: René A. Belderbos and Peter Holmes, 1995, An Economic Analysis of Matsushita Revisited, *Antitrust Bulletin*, 40, 825–857.

An abridged version of Chapter 5 has been published as: René A. Belderbos and Leo Sleuwaegen, 1996, Japanese Firms and the Decision to Invest Abroad: Business Groups and Regional Core Networks, *Review of Economics and Statistics*, 78, 214–220.

Early versions of chapters 1–5 and 7 have previously appeared in: René A. Belderbos, 1994, *Strategic Trade Policy and Multinational Enterprises: Essays on Trade and Investment by Japanese Electronics Firms*, Ph.D. dissertation published by Thesis Publishers, Amsterdam.

CONTENTS

ABBREVIATIONS

ASIC	application-specific integrated circuit
ASEAN	Association of South-East Asian Nations
CD player	compact disc player
CEC	Commission of the European Communities
CRT	cathode ray (television) tube
CTV	colour television
DFI	direct foreign investment
DOC	Department of Commerce (US)
DRAM	direct random access memory
EACEM	European Association of Consumer Electronics Manufacturers
EC	European Community
EFTA	European Free Trade Association
EIAJ	Electronics Industries Association of Japan
EPROM	erasable programmable read-only memory
FDD	flexible disk (microdisk) drive
FTC	Fair Trade Commission (Japan)
GATT	General Agreement on Tariffs and Trade
HDD	hard disk drive
IC	integrated circuit
ITC	International Trade Commission (US)
JETRO	Japan External Trade Organisation
LCD	liquid crystal display
LCR	local content requirement
MITI	Ministry of International Trade and Industry (Japan)
MNE	multinational enterprise
MOF	Ministry of Finance (Japan)
NAFTA	North American Free Trade Agreement
NIEs	newly industrialised economies
OEM	original equipment manufacturing [company *A* manufactures products according to the specifications of client-firm *B*, which procures the products from company *A* and sells them under its own brand name]

OMA	orderly market arrangement
PAL	phased alternative line [television transmission technology]
PBX	private branch exchange [business telephone system]
PC	personal computer
PCB	printed circuit board
R&D	research and development
UK	United Kingdom
US	United States
VCR	video cassette recorder
VER	voluntary export restraint
WTO	World Trade Organisation

Introduction

The dramatic increase in Japanese direct foreign investment (DFI) in manufacturing since 1985 has been subject of much political and economic debate which is reflected in a growing literature on the determinants and effects of Japanese overseas investments.[1] The value of Japanese DFI flows did not surpass an annual 3 billion dollars until 1985 but rose to a peak of more than 16 billion dollars in 1989 (see figure 1). This rise in DFI in North America to over 8 billion dollars in 1988–1989 was particularly steep. DFI in Europe followed, with a high in 1990 of almost 5 billion dollars, while DFI in Asia showed a more gradual increase. In the early 1990s the focus of manufacturing investment gradually shifted from the USA and the EC to Asian countries.

Several factors related to conditions in Japanese industry and the domestic and international economy have been put forward as underlying the rise in Japanese DFI in the second half of the 1980s. An important factor was the 1985 Plaza Accord, by which the Group of Seven vowed to pursue realignments of the major exchange rates. The subsequent appreciation of the yen against the dollar and, to a lesser extent, against the European currencies reduced the cost effectiveness of production for exports in Japan. At the same time, the Japanese Ministry of Finance pursued expansionary monetary and fiscal policies which sharply reduced interest rates and set stock, land, and real estate prices soaring and domestic demand booming: the 'bubble economy' was born. These developments in the Japanese economy practically reduced the financing costs of Japanese firms to zero, which eased financial constraints on expansion overseas through DFI. Moreover, the appreciation of the yen substantially increased Japanese firms' purchasing power abroad and facilitated the acquisition of foreign firms and the establishment of foreign plants.

The surge of Japanese DFI was related not only to financial factors. Underlying the expansion abroad was the growth of Japanese manufacturing firms, in particular in the automobile, electronics, and precision machinery industries, into formidable competitors on world markets. Product quality and development, manufacturing prowess, commitment to marketing and service, and also competitive price setting were fields in which Japanese firms often outperformed European and US manufacturers of longer standing. In addition, many Japanese firms had by 1985 acquired experience in overseas manufacturing and in utilising management and

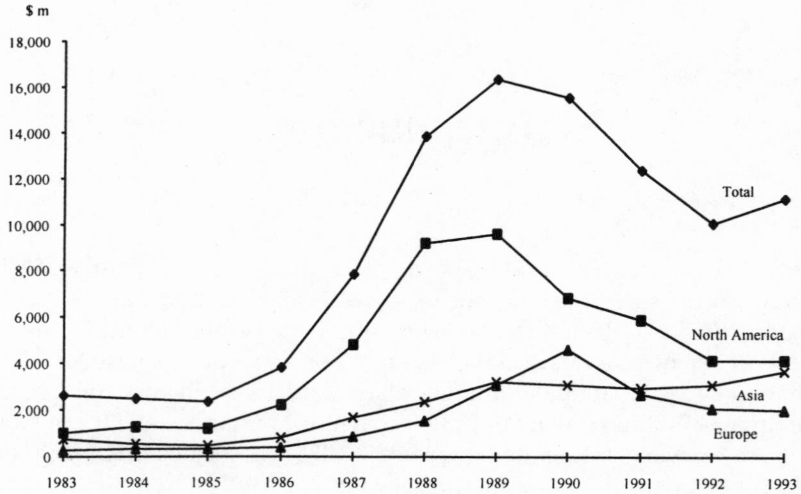

Figure I1 Japanese direct foreign investment in manufacturing industries, 1983–1993

Sources: Nihon Oukurashou (1991), Nihon Tsuushou Sangyoushou (1995).

manufacturing capabilities abroad. Japanese firms were in an excellent position to reduce their traditional reliance on exports from Japan and to expand manufacturing activities abroad.

A third factor with a major impact on Japanese manufacturing investment abroad was the rise in trade policy measures restricting Japanese exports to the United States (US) and the countries of the European Community (EC). Japan's large trade surpluses with the US and the EC gave rise to the Plaza Accord in the first place, but it also caused trade friction and increased political pressure for trade protection. Both the US government and the Commission of the European Communities, the latter since the early 1980s in charge of external trade relations of EC member states, were increasingly willing to intervene on behalf of domestic firms competing with imports from Japan. Japanese industry, through the Japanese Ministry of International Trade and Industry (MITI), was forced to negotiate voluntary export restraints (VERs) and price setting arrangements for steel (US 1985, EC 1987), machine tools (US 1987, EC 1987), cars (US 1981, EC 1987), forklift trucks (EC 1986), video tape recorders (EC 1983), and semiconductors (US 1986, EC 1989), among others.

The US government also used its Section 301 of the 1974 Trade Act to threaten Japan with tariff increases on imports if it would not act against alleged barriers to trade and investment in Japan. The negotiation of the US–Japan semiconductor trade agreement in early 1986 can be seen as a turning point in US–Japan trade relations. Apart from regulating prices of

Japanese semiconductors in the US and third countries, the agreement included a clause on a target market share of foreign firms in the Japanese market. In 1987, the US government judged that Japan was not abiding by the agreement and took the unprecedented step of imposing retaliatory tariffs of up to 100 per cent on imports of Japanese computers, colour televisions, and power tools.

Meanwhile, in the EC the year 1985 saw the publication of Lord Cockfield's White Paper on European Integration, which set the stage for the creation of the EC Internal Market by the end of 1992. The preparations for the Internal Market were accompanied by a heated debate on what the external trade barriers surrounding the Internal Market would be. Fear of the creation of 'Fortress Europe' stemmed from the political influence of the EC's southern member states, which maintained various national restrictions on Japanese imports.

Apart from negotiated export constraints and expectations of a continuous hostile environment for Japanese exporters, the 1980s were characterised by the frequent use of antidumping actions against Japanese exports. According to the 1979 GATT code on antidumping, a domestic industry may seek and obtain protection against imports if such imports are dumped (priced below the price in the country of export) and cause harm to the domestic industry. From the early 1980s, US and EC firms filed an increasing number of antidumping petitions against Japanese firms. More often than not, this led to the imposition of antidumping duties. In both the US and the EC, Japan became the most frequent target of antidumping actions among industrialised countries. The sharp appreciation of the yen compounded the threat of antidumping for Japanese firms. Japanese firms' cautious attitude towards raising export prices ('pricing to market') and their determination to maintain established overseas market positions implied that the likelihood that dumping margins calculated would be substantial increased appreciably after 1985.

The sharp increase in actual and prospective trade barriers made reliance on exports from Japan in many cases an untenable strategy and provided an important motive for overseas manufacturing investments. It had become clear that in order to compete in world markets, as an influential book by Ohmae (1985) described it, firms had to become 'insiders' in the three regions of the 'Triad' (Europe, North America, and Japan) by establishing integrated sales and manufacturing operations in each region. Becoming an 'insider' was not easy for Japanese firms. As latecomers in international production, their manufacturing operations in the US and the EC tended to emphasise assembly operations. They were often criticised for relying on imports of components from Japan, a lack of commitment to research and development (R&D) activities, and the failure to appoint local managers and grant significant autonomy to overseas subsidiaries. While these features are not uncommon for overseas operations of firms lacking experience as multinationals, it was conceivable that Japanese firms were 'different' from US and EC multinationals. For instance, the strong inter-firm linkages within Japanese industrial groups (*keiretsu*) could preclude the procurement of components and the exchange of technological know-how through ties with local firms. Such criticisms were also accompanied by actual policy measures directed against Japanese firms' overseas operations. In particular in the EC, Japanese firms have been targeted by local content rules, which required manufacturing subsidiaries to reduce their reliance on components import from Japan.

While the late 1980s were generally characterised by a rise in global protectionism, Japan was clearly the most important target of the aggressive use of trade policy instruments. On the one hand this was related to the growing strength of Japanese firms in US and EC markets. On the other hand, it was related to the perception that Japanese firms' success abroad was based on 'unfair' advantages of Japanese firms in their domestic market, where structural barriers and government policies impeded entry by foreign firms. Lack of overseas market access for US firms is ground for trade actions under Section 301 of the US Trade Act, while antidumping actions are often seen to provide some form of compensation for barriers and market characteristics that allow (Japanese) firms to maintain high prices domestically and to subsidise exports. Hence, export barriers for Japanese firms are to an important extent related to Japanese trade policies and problems of market access in Japan.

The market access question is in another intricate way related to EC and US trade policy measures. The perceived interventionist government policy in Japan and the structural barriers to foreign firms influenced the growth of an influential literature on strategic trade policy. Seminal work by Brander and Spencer (1983, 1984) and Krugman (1984), in particular, pointed out that, in oligpolistic industries where entry barriers, economies of scale, and advantages of 'learning by doing' are important, industrial and trade policies assisting domestic firms can critically alter the outcomes of rivalry in domestic firms' favour. Rather than being based on factor endowments, comparative advantage and trade patterns could be shaped by government policies. By giving domestic firms a strategic advantage in international markets, trade and industrial policy measures such as subsidies and import tariffs can increase domestic profits and wages and have the potential to increase domestic economic welfare. The advantages are all the more important if they concern a high technology or 'strategic' industry, of which the development can bring extra benefits to the economy at large in the form of technology spillovers and improved productivity in other industries.

In his seminal paper, Krugman (1984) showed that, in the presence of increasing returns to scale, protection of a domestic industry can help to promote exports. In a later study with Richard Baldwin (Baldwin and Krugman 1988) he applied a similar model to the 16K DRAM industry and concluded that the rise of Japanese firms as world market leaders could have been brought about by an artificial advantage in their home market based on import barriers. The strategic trade policy literature gave EC and US industries and policy makers and opinion leaders an unintended argument for a revival in trade and industrial policies.

The Subject of the Book

This book deals with the dramatic rise of Japanese DFI in manufacturing in the second half of the 1980s. The objective of the book is to provide insight into the determinants and effects of Japanese firms' overseas investments and in particular the relationship between overseas operations and trade policy measures. Japanese DFI and trade policies are analysed from an empirical as well as a theoretical perspective. The empirical analysis focuses on the experience of Japanese firms in the broadly defined electronics industry, leader in Japanese exports and responsible for a quarter of Japanese DFI in manufacturing.[2] The international advance of Japanese firms in this industry and the high technology character of several industry segments made Japanese electronics firms a frequent target of trade policy measures in the EC and US.

The theoretical analysis is linked to the strategic trade policy literature to examine the effects of trade policy measures in the presence of multinational firms. The analysis is in the tradition of Brander and Spencer (1984) and focuses on the welfare effects of strategic trade policies in oligpolistic industries. The models extend the existing literature and are adapted to fit the experience of Japanese firms. A first analysis deals with the kind of Japanese strategic trade policy which gave rise to concerns among EC and US policy makers. It is shown how barriers in the Japanese market can have negative repercussions on foreign industries and global competition. Two other studies deal with the effects of trade policy measures taken in the US and the EC against Japanese firms: (antidumping) duties levied on imports, and local content requirements for foreign-owned firms. The analysis in the theoretical section of the book provides insight into the rationale for trade policy measures against Japanese electronics firms and the possible consequences for resource allocation and welfare. At the same time, the results have a broader applicability to the relationship between trade policy and rivalry between multinational firms in general.

The empirical studies make use of an extensive database comprising financial, export, and DFI data for 250 Japanese electronics firms, which allows for detailed micro-level analysis of investment patterns and their determinants. In some cases, original data from MITI surveys among Japanese multinational firms could also be accessed for analysis. The electronics industry is broadly defined to include heavy electrical equipment, telecommunications equipment, household electrical goods, components and semiconductors, audio and video equipment, computers, office machines, cameras and clocks, and measuring equipment. While the role of trade policies features prominently, due attention is given to the role of firm-specific capabilities as well as to features of Japanese industrial organisation such as inter-firm linkages within *keiretsu*, without which a proper understanding of the development in Japanese DFI is impossible. Issues dealt with are the determinants of the decision to invest abroad, the effect of trade barriers on investment, the relationship between Japanese firms' DFI and exports, the response of Japanese firms to local content requirements, and the determinants of R&D activities in overseas subsidiaries.

The emphasis of the empirical analysis is on Japanese firms' activities in the EC and the US and the role of trade policies. Since Japanese firms have been confronted with different policy conditions in these two regions, comparison of trade and investment patterns often proves insightful. The most detailed analysis of Japanese firms' operations abroad focuses on distribution and manufacturing activities in the EC. The experience of Japanese firms in the EC probably provides the best example of policy driven investment.

The Organisation of the Book

The book is divided into three parts. Part I provides an overview of the major facts and factors concerning the rise in DFI by Japanese electronics firms and Japanese firms' advance in the EC in particular. It consists of one integrated essay (Chapter 1). Part II is a collection of three theoretical essays on trade policy and multinational firms (Chapters 2–4). Part III contains five empirical essays on Japanese electronics firms' DFI, exports, procurement practices, and overseas R&D (Chapters 5–9). Finally, Chapter 10 summarises the main conclusions and discusses implications.

Each chapter is essentially self-contained and can be read independently of the others. Chapter 1 should be accessible for anyone with an interest in Japanese electronics firms and EC trade policies. The chapter discusses most of the issues that are the subject of more detailed analysis in later chapters and looks ahead to the conclusions drawn there. Each of the chapters in Parts II and III treats a specific problem and connects to the existing literature on the subject. The theoretical analysis in Chapters 3 and 4 in particular is at times technical and requires a basic understanding of oligopoly theory. The empirical analysis in Chapters 5, 6, 7, and 9 uses econometric tools such as regression and logit analysis, but readers will be able to skip the limited technicalities and still gain sufficient understanding of results and implications.

Part I (Chapter 1) describes the environment in which Japanese electronics firms started their expansion abroad and provides key statistics on the growth in international operations. The focus then shifts to Japanese firms' activities in the EC. Detailed data on the growth in Japanese electronics firms' manufacturing and distribution activities are presented and characteristics of investment strategies such as the use of joint ventures and procurement activities are discussed. It is shown that investment decisions by individual Japanese firms are closely related to EC trade policies, notably antidumping actions. The chapter proceeds with a critical assessment of EC policy measures, such as antidumping, local content requirements, and rules of origin, which targeted Japanese imports and Japanese manufacturing subsidiaries in the EC. Finally, an assessment is given of the impact of Japanese DFI on the EC electronics industry.

The theoretical essays in Part II are preceded by a brief introduction to the strategic trade policy literature. Relevant terminology and concepts are introduced and the contributions in the following chapters are put into perspective. Chapter 2 then presents an analysis of rivalry in the Japanese and US colour television (CTV) industries in the 1960s and early 1970s. It is known that the Japanese CTV manufacturers formed a cartel in the Japanese market to keep prices high at a time when (cheaply priced) Japanese CTV exports made rapid inroads into the US market. This gave rise to an influential antitrust case in the US (*Matsushita* v. *Zenith*), which US CTV producers initiated in 1974 but finally lost. A model based on the stylised facts of the case shows how lack of effective competition in Japan may have harmed the interests of US industry and consumers alike, a possibility that is not taken into account in antitrust practices. Weak enforcement of antitrust laws in Japan can be seen as a 'strategic' policy supporting Japanese producers. The *Matsushita* v. *Zenith* case is important since the perceived 'unfairness' of Japanese firms' behaviour and the difficulties in applying US antitrust laws in the case gave strong impetus to the political process to strengthen US antidumping laws in the 1970s.

Chapters 3 and 4 then proceed by considering the two most important US and EC trade policy measures employed against Japanese firms: tariffs and antidumping duties, and local content rules. Chapter 3 looks at the decision to invest abroad by a foreign duopolist if a host country government imposes a duty on the firm's exports. It studies the welfare effects of such 'tariff jumping' DFI and compares them with the effects of conventional tariff policy in the absence of the DFI option. The possibility of tariff jumping DFI generally makes tariff policy less effective in assisting domestic firms. A solution to this problem may be to target the foreign multinational firm with local content rules, requiring the firm to buy more components locally for use in its host country plant. If the foreign firm's competitive edge is based partly on imported components, local content requirements can reduce the foreign firm's cost advantages *vis-à-vis* domestic firms. Chapter 4 studies the possible effects of local content rules and focuses on the situation where the host country's components industry is oligopolistic.

Part III opens with an empirical analysis of the decision by Japanese electronics firms to invest abroad and become multinational firms (Chapter 5). This analysis focuses on the role of firm-specific capabilities and the question of how membership of Japanese industrial groups (*keiretsu*) affects investment behaviour. Important differences are found in factors determining the decision to invest in South-East Asia on the one hand, and North America and Europe on the other. Chapter 6 builds on this general analysis of DFI determinants and empirically studies the role of EC and US trade policy measures in shaping Japanese DFI patterns. Specific attention is given to the differences between US and EC antidumping practices and their consequences for investment responses. The empirical results suggest a substantial impact of trade policy measures on Japanese DFI, in particular in the EC.

Chapter 7 studies one of the possible consequences of tariff-jumping DFI: a decline in exports as a result of increased local production. At the product level, examination of export and DFI patterns in the US and the EC clearly suggests that such export substitution was prevalent in the late 1980s. This is also confirmed by firm-level regression analysis of exports to Europe. Chapter 8 examines the response of Japanese firms to local content requirements targeting their US and EC manufacturing operations. The methodology is again to compare procurement behaviour of Japanese firms in the US and the EC. Evidence is found that stricter local content rules in the EC are related to higher local content levels. However, it is suggested that the measures have had only little effect on components sales by domestic EC producers. Chapter 9 concludes the empirical section of the book by examining the internationalisation of R&D activities of Japanese electronics firms using MITI survey data. Overseas R&D activities are found to be closely related to the degree of internationalisation in terms of manufacturing and sales, as well as the international experience of firms.

Finally, Chapter 10 summarises the main conclusions of the various chapters and points out broader implications of the findings.

NOTES

1. A listing confined to volumes dealing with Japanese DFI is: Sachwald (1995), Mason and Encarnation (1994), Campbell and Burton (1994), Strange (1992),

Thomsen and Nicolaides (1991), Yoshitomi (1991), Graham and Krugman (1990), Euro-JERC Research Center (1990).

2. The Japanese electronics industry was responsible for a quarter of cumulative DFI as of March 1991 (Nihon Oukurashou 1991). The electronics industry was also responsible for 27 per cent of exports to the EC and 22 per cent of exports to the US during 1991 (JETRO 1992a).

PART I

Trade Policy and the Internationalisation of Japanese Electronics Firms: *An Overview*

1

Internationalisation, Trade Policy, and the Advance in Europe

1.1 Introduction

Japan's electronics firms rank among the world's largest,[1] yet their foreign manufacturing activities have not been able to compare with those of US and European electronics firms until recently. Japanese firms' foreign involvement has long been limited to export dependence and investment in overseas distribution networks. According to a survey by the Japanese Ministry of International Trade and Industry (MITI), sales of Japanese production subsidiaries abroad amounted to 12.6 per cent of total electronics production in Japan in 1994. This foreign production ratio is only about a third of those of the US and European electronics industries a decade earlier.[2] The rapid growth in Japanese electronics firms' direct foreign investment (DFI) in manufacturing since 1985 must be seen against the background of their late internationalisation compared with their US and European counterparts.

Growth in Japanese electronics firms' DFI in the late 1980s was most pronounced in the countries of the European Community (EC). Europe's fragmented markets and cultural diversity had long prevented Japanese firms from making significant marketing inroads as in the United States. This situation has been changing markedly since 1985. The appreciation of the yen against the dollar after 1985, which was much stronger than the appreciation *vis-à-vis* European currencies, made sales growth in the US more difficult to achieve and generally led Japanese firms to shift emphasis to EC markets. This trend was reinforced by the 1985 action plan of the EC countries to create a unified Internal Market in 1993. While the prospects of improved efficiency of manufacturing and easier marketing in a unified market increased the attractiveness of the EC, the fear of protectionist walls surrounding the Internal Market (also dubbed 'fortress Europe') and a range of actual trade policy measures substantiating this fear provided an important motive for Japanese manufacturing investments.

This Chapter provides an overview of factors and facts concerning the internationalisation of Japanese electronics firms. The discussion of the broader determinants of growth in Japanese firms' global investment provides the perspective for a subsequent analysis of determinants and consequences of the advance of Japanese firms in the EC in the late 1980s. It will be shown that a close relationship exists between Japanese manufacturing investment in the EC and antidumping and other trade policies measures taken by the EC. Trade policy measures included not only duties on imports but also local content requirements and rules of origin, which affected the organisation of Japanese firms' manufacturing activities in the EC. The latter policies were among the factors that determined the gradual transformation of Japanese investment from simple duty avoidance to integrated production and specialisation of activities within the EC.

After examining the link between EC trade policies and Japanese DFI, the chapter examines the growth and characteristics of Japanese electronics firms' investments in the EC in the latter half of the 1980s and the beginning of the 1990s in detail. Based on characteristics of Japanese manufacturing activities such as procurement behaviour, R&D activities, and strategies for entry in the EC market, the effects of Japanese investments on the EC economy and electronics industry are assessed.

The plan of the chapter is as follows. The next section starts with a description of factors determining the recent trends in the internationalisation of Japanese electronics firms and provides some key figures on foreign involvement. Section 1.3 follows with a detailed account of the relationship between EC trade policy measures and Japanese electronics firms' investments in the EC. Section 1.4 presents data on Japanese electronics firms' manufacturing and distribution subsidiaries in the EC by country, product, and firm. Investment strategies in the EC are discussed by highlighting modes of entry, procurement, local content, and destination of sales, among others. The impact on the EC electronics industry is assessed in Section 1.5 and conclusions are offered in the final section.

Four appendices are attached to this chapter. Appendix 1.1 provides background information on major Japanese electronics firms' membership of *keiretsu* industrial groups. Appendix 1.2 ranks Japanese electronics firms by employment in EC manufacturing and distribution subsidiaries. Appendix 1.3 provides some key figures on the advance of Japanese firms in individual product markets in the EC, and Appendix 1.4 gives an overview of the various data sources on Japanese DFI.

Before turning to the next section, a remark concerning the definition of the electronics industry is in order. Generally, a broad definition of the electronics industry is used, covering heavy electrical equipment, telecommunications equipment, household electrical goods, components and semiconductors, audio and video equipment, computers, office machines, and measuring equipment. In a few cases, when drawing on data from surveys among Japanese MNEs conducted by MITI, the definition of the electronics industry is slightly narrower.[3] Details concerning data on Japanese DFI are given in Appendix 1.4.

1.2 The Internationalisation of Japanese Firms: an Overview

The electronics industry is one of the industries in which a clear trend towards the internationalisation of business has been observed after the world recession of the early 1980s. Developments in the 1980s can be characterised by surging R&D costs, rapidly changing technologies, shortening product life cycles, and the increasing uniformity of global consumer tastes (see Ohmae 1985). These prompted electronics firms to aim to sell on all major world markets, in order to be able to recoup R&D costs in a short time-span and to reap economies of scale. Moreover, firms had to gain a strong foothold in the major markets of the 'Triad' (Japan, Europe, and the US) to reduce their vulnerability to protectionism and exchange rate volatility, and to facilitate reliable and quick access to information on technological and market developments. In conjunction, technological developments such as flexible manufacturing techniques and advances in telecommunication facilitated transnational production and control over a globally operating company.

The need for internationalisation of business has been most distinct for Japanese electronics firms. As noted above, they were, and still are, less internationalised in terms of foreign production than their European and US competitors. Moreover, the rise in protectionism in the electronics industry has often targeted Japanese firms' exports specifically. This has induced Japanese firms to invest abroad in order to 'jump' trade barriers such as tariffs, antidumping duties, and voluntary export restraints (VERs), and to attain the status of 'insider' to alleviate threats of future protectionism. In addition, the comparative advantage for less skill-intensive production in Japan has been declining owing to the strong appreciation of the yen since 1985 and increasing labour shortages.

The underlying conditions for internationalisation through DFI were also favourable to Japanese firms. Until the 1980s, Japanese electronics firms' export successes had been based on competitive advantages which were strongly related to the home market. Japanese firms excel in the management of large scale, automated production processes producing high quality goods at low costs. Quality control through quality circles and sophisticated testing procedures, just-in-time deliveries of components through close co-operation with subcontractors, and the ability to foster the commitment of employees through lifetime employment systems are all part of the highly successful production and engineering management in Japanese companies (Franko 1983). Japanese firms had been reluctant to become multinationals because it was not evident that these firm-specific advantages could be transferred abroad successfully, since they were dependent on characteristics of the workforce and inter-firm relationships in Japan (Caves 1993). However, by the mid-1980s, the major Japanese electronics firms had gained experience in operating colour television (CTV) and video cassette recorder (VCR) manufacturing plants in the US and the EC. Japanese firms' production and management skills had proved to be, at least to a certain extent, transferable abroad.[4] Furthermore, the competitiveness of Japanese companies evolved from strengths based on production processes and management to clear technological advantages and novel products. The latter generally have much weaker links to the home market and are easier to exploit abroad (see also Dunning and Gittelman 1992 and Ozawa 1991).

Another factor influencing the internationalisation of Japanese firms is a specific trait of Japanese industrial organisation: the importance of long term business links between firms, in particular those between firms in horizontal and vertical business groups, or *keiretsu*. A basic characteristic of business practice in Japan is a flexible organisational structure involving decentralisation of responsibilities to all operatives within the firm and decentralised networking with suppliers based on various partnerships in the development and just-in-time delivery of components. It also involves long term co-operation in marketing, distribution, and R&D. This business system relies heavily on trust and informal co-operation to sustain the various inter-firm relationships (Sako 1992). The best known forms of inter-firm co-operation are the horizontal and vertical business groups. The importance of links to vertical and horizontal business groups to the largest Japanese electronics firms is illustrated in Appendix 1.1.

Horizontal business groups are large diversified groups of basically independent firms centred around a major bank and trading firm (*sougou sousha*). The major advantages derived from such membership relevant to foreign investments are a relaxation of capital constraints for foreign ventures and information exchange on foreign markets and investment conditions (Nakatani 1984, Goto 1982). Trading firms of horizontal business groups, capitalising on their long experience in doing business abroad, were instrumental in helping Japanese small and medium sized firms transfer labour intensive manufacturing activities to South-East Asia during the 1960s. The foreign plants were often set up as a joint venture between the Japanese firm, the trading firm, and a local partner (Ozawa 1979). More recently, Yamamura and Wassman (1989) found that investments in the US by member firms of horizontal business groups tend to be clustered in specific regions. It is suggested that clusters of member firms' subsidiaries in a region facilitate subsequent investment in the region by other firms of the group, through information exchange and the continuation of long term business links. Hoshi, Kashyap, and Scharfstein (1992) found that member firms of horizontal business groups are less liquidity-constrained in their investment than firms outside such groups. By the same token, long term relationships with the main bank within the horizontal business groups facilitate the financing of risky foreign ventures. Empirical analysis presented in Chapter 5 confirms that inter-firm linkages and financing within horizontal business groups have a positive influence on firms' decision to invest in South-East Asia (see also Belderbos and Sleuwaegen 1996).

Vertical business groups are groups of subcontractors, satellite firms, and trading firms around major large scale assembly type manufacturers such as Hitachi and Toyota. Here the leading or 'core' firm usually exerts control over the management of the other firms in the group. Such control is facilitated by shareholdings, financial ties, and the dispatch of managers. Aoki (1988) argues that this mode of inter-firm relationships constitutes an advantage over foreign firms in particular in industries where a large number of production steps have to be co-ordinated, such as in the electronics and car industries. The existence of long term relationships with domestic subcontractors and suppliers in Japan was an important factor in the initial reluctance of Japanese electronics firms to transfer production abroad (Caves 1993). On the other hand, once the core firm has established production subsidiaries abroad, these subsidiaries may induce subsequent foreign investments by its subcontractors. The core firm may provide subcontracting firms with information, (financial) assistance, and an exclusive market for their products, facilitating the step towards foreign production. Evidence of the importance of subcontractor relationships for DFI is provided by Head, Ries, and Swenson (1995), who show that a Japanese firm's locational choice for its manufacturing plant in the US can be explained partly by the presence of plants of member firms of the vertical business group that the firm belongs to. Chapter 5 presents further evidence that inter-firm links within vertical business groups have a positive impact on DFI by subcontractor firms.

Several other factors have also contributed to the rise in Japanese DFI. In the late 1980s, Japanese firms could command unusual amounts of liquidity and benefited from the low cost of capital resulting from record profits on the booming domestic market, low interest rates, and continuously rising stock market prices. The low cost of capital reduced the liquidity constraints on DFI, and the appreciation of the yen increased purchasing power to conduct major acquisitions (Kester 1991). In addition, since the mid-1980s, host governments in South-East Asia as well as in the US and in the EC changed their attitudes towards inward DFI to a liberal and often supportive stance. Export processing zones were set up in Malaysia, Thailand, and Taiwan, for instance, and local authorities in the US and the EC confronted with persisting unemployment were eager to attract Japanese DFI and subsidised plant establishments.

The need to internationalise business and the facilitating factors mentioned above led the larger Japanese electronics firms to embark on an internationalisation strategy which generally incorporated four features. First, firms set up assembly plants in the US and the EC for electronics goods that had been hit by import restrictions and antidumping actions. Pressure to increase the local content of goods produced in overseas Japanese plants subsequently led to an increased use of locally produced components. In general, fear of protectionism after the formation of the EC Internal Market and the North American Free Trade Area has given Japanese firms incentives to establish integrated manufacturing activities in order to become 'insiders' and to alleviate future protectionism. Such investments in the EC and the US are mainly defensive and market-oriented investments and are likely to substitute for exports (see Chapter 7 for empirical evidence).

A second type of DFI in the EC and the US concerns the acquisition of a controlling or minority stake in US and EC firms. The goal is to acquire specific technological skills, software, or access to markets. Sony's acquisitions of CBS records and Columbia Pictures, Matsushita's take-over of MCA, Toshiba's participation in Time Warner, Fujitsu's acquisition of ICL in the UK, Kyocera's acquisition of ceramic capacitor maker AVX in the US, and Ricoh's participation in Gestetner (a major distributor of office machines in Europe) are all major transactions that fit into this pattern. In addition, Japanese firms have been active acquirers of small and medium sized innovative electronics firms, in particular in the US (Genther and Dalton 1992, Yamawaki 1994).

Third, the larger Japanese firms set up so-called 'regional core networks' in South-East Asia. Regional core networks are networks of interrelated manufacturing plants making use of differences in the comparative advantages of different South-East Asian countries for labour- and skill-intensive manufacturing activities (Nakakita and Urata 1991, Gold *et al.* 1991). Regional core networks are set up to establish an efficient division of labour. Products manufactured with standardised and mature technologies, such as radios, headphone stereos, black and white televisions, and standardised parts, are produced in ASEAN countries and China where cheap but low skilled labour is relatively abundant. Products of intermediate technology such as VCRs are produced in the newly industrialised countries (NIEs), where labour is more expensive but also more skilled. High technology products and newly introduced products, such as camcorders, high-resolution VCRs, and crucial components, are manufactured in Japan, where production can be cost-effective by investments in manufacturing automation. A typical example would be labour intensive assembly of CTVs in Malaysia making use of cathode ray tubes (CRTs) and integrated circuits (ICs) from Japan, and other parts from Taiwanese affiliates (Nakakita and Urata 1991). Investments in South-East Asia are predominantly cost-oriented and are likely to lead to intra-firm, intra-industry trade between Japan and South-East Asian countries.[5]

Regional core networks provide opportunities for smaller Japanese subcontractors within vertical business groups as well as for independent component suppliers. Relocating in South-East Asia near the production sites of their Japanese client firms can lower costs and shorten delivery times. Furthermore, the client firm may offer assistance. Moreover, the Japanese government has been instrumental in promoting DFI in Asia by small and medium sized firms since the 1960s and 1970s, through tax breaks and assistance by institutions such as the Export–Import Bank of Japan. Ozawa (1979 and 1991) argues the Japan regarded (and still regards) the relocation to South-East Asia of manufacturing activities for which Japan has lost comparative advantage an indispensable part of industrial policy.

Gold *et al.* (1991) argue that regional core networks by Japanese firms in the electronics, machinery, and automobile industries are contributing to the creation of an integrated trade and investment bloc in South-East Asia. Some evidence supporting this hypothesis is provided by Urata (1992), who found that Japanese manufacturing subsidiaries are more specialised in Asian trade than Asian manufacturing industries at large, while Japanese subsidiaries are estimated to be responsible for 20 per cent of total Asian manufactured exports. The findings in Chapter 5 suggest that Japanese electronics firms are not hindered much by national borders in setting up manufacturing plants in Sough-East Asia, as distinct from setting up plants in the US and the EC. The results point to the importance of cumulative economic ties between Japan and South-East Asia and to the importance of inter-firms links within regional core networks.

Fourth, Japanese firms' internationalisation strategies have required changes in organisation and management. In the late 1980s, virtually all major electronics firms established regional headquarters in the Triad markets of the US, the EC, and Japan, and some firms assigned South-East Asia as a special region as well. These headquarters are assisting regional sales and production subsidiaries, performing functions such as dealing with government authorities, the monitoring of advertising, the co-ordination of sales and procurements, and the training of employees. The regional headquarters are also meant to show Japanese firms' commitment to become 'insiders' in the regions where they are active. In the EC, in addition, firms set up financial subsidiaries linked with these regional headquarters to procure funds at Euro-currency markets.[6] Regional headquarters in South-East Asia are usually located in Singapore and mainly are assigned the task of co-ordinating components procurement from Asian manufacturing plants for further processing and assembly in Asia, the EC, the US, or Japan. In several cases, the organisational structure of Japanese firms has been adapted more fundamentally. For instance, Matsushita Electric Industrial, the second largest Japanese electronics firm, altered its divisional structure and regrouped divisions by type of customer instead of product in 1987; in 1988 it merged with its overseas sales arm to bring control over overseas sales and manufacturing together.

1.2.1 Trends in Overseas Involvement

This section examines the trends in overseas involvement by Japanese electronics firms in the second half of the 1980s and the early 1990s. The relative importance of the EC as a market for Japanese electronics goods and as a host for Japanese investment is highlighted.

Export and DFI Figure 1.1 illustrates the trends in the Japanese electronics industry's exports and DFI to the EC and the US between 1985 and 1991.[7] Dollar denominated electronics exports to both the EC and the US have been increasing up to 1989, and the appreciation of the yen only led to a temporary slowdown in export growth in 1987. From 1989 to 1991 exports to the US declined, while exports to the EC continued their growth. Exports to the EC in 1991 reached 27 billion dollars which amounted to more than three quarters of the value of exports to the US (35 billion dollars); in 1985, exports to the EC had not reached half the value of exports to the US. Japanese electronics firms have become increasingly dependent on the EC market to absorb their exports.

The increasing importance of the EC to Japanese firms is also observable in DFI flows. DFI by Japanese electronics firms in the EC increased dramatically, from less than 100 million dollars in 1985 to 2.4 billion dollars in 1990—the first year the DFI flows to the EC were comparable to DFI flows

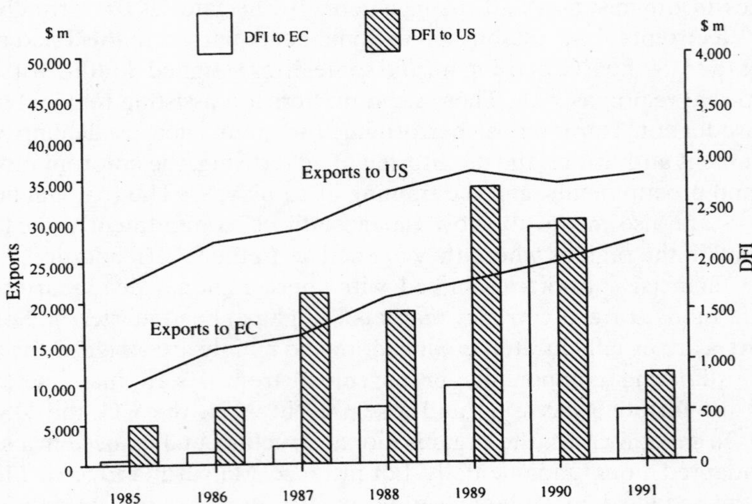

Figure 1.1 DFI and exports by the Japanese electronics industry to the EC and the US, 1985–1991

Sources: Nihon Oukurashou (1991), JETRO (1986a–1992a), Kaburagi (1992).

to the US.[8] The historical highs in DFI in 1989 and 1990 were not maintained in 1991: DFI in the EC decreased to 501 million dollars, an amount comparable to DFI in 1988; DFI in the US declined from 2.3 billion dollars in 1990 to 868 million dollars in 1991.

The DFI flows during 1989 and 1990 have been exceptional. Several major acquisitions, such as the take-over of semiconductor manufacturer AVX of the US by Kyocera and the acquisition of computer manufacturer ICL of the UK by Fujitsu, were responsible for a major share of these flows (Kaburagi 1992).[9] Such acquisitions were facilitated by the exceptionally low cost of capital for Japanese firms at the time. DFI in 1991 fell back to a level that was sustainable even under the economic conditions prevailing after 1990, characterised by falling profits and stock market prices. Indeed, recent data indicate that 1991 DFI levels were roughly preserved throughout the early 1990s.[10]

It is important to note that declines in DFI flows do not usually lead to a comparable slowdown in the growth of overseas manufacturing activities. DFI flows from Japan finance only a share of the capital requirements of foreign subsidiaries. Subsidiaries may continue to expand their activities using internally generated or locally procured funds. Hence a more accurate picture of trends in foreign involvement can be obtained by examining data on the activities of overseas manufacturing subsidiaries. This approach will be followed in the remainder of the chapter.

Export and overseas production by product Another way to read trends in overseas activities of Japanese electronics firms is to examine exports and foreign production for individual products. Figures 1.2–1.5 show that foreign production of CTVs, VCRs, microwave ovens, and compact disc (CD) players has continuously increased during the 1980s. Figure 1.2 shows a sharp decline in domestic CTV production for export in 1986 and 1987, a consequence of the steep appreciation of the yen. Foreign production rose every year, however: in 1990, roughly three quarters of CTV production for foreign markets was taking place overseas.[11] Production for exports in Japan increased again in 1990, mainly as a result of growth in the market for liquid crystal display (LCD) CTVs.

In the case of microwave ovens, by 1989 about half the foreign sales came from foreign production bases (Figure 1.3). It is noteworthy that total Japanese sales abroad have been declining since 1987, which is likely to be related to declining demand in the US and stronger competition by Korean firms. In case of VCRs, production is still largely concentrated in Japan, although foreign production reached a sizeable volume of 7.2 million units in 1990 (Figure 1.4). One reason for the relatively small share of foreign production here is that Japanese firms are relying on exports to service the US market, where there have been no import restrictions on Japanese VCRs. Foreign sales of Japanese CD players, a relatively new product, have

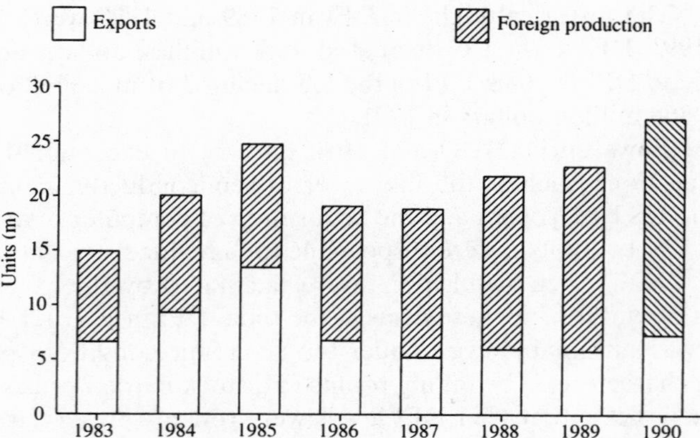

Figure 1.2 Japanese exports and foreign production, 1983–1990: CTVs
Sources: JETRO (1987a–1991a), Yano Keizai Kenkyuujo (1991a), Nihon Denshi Kikai Kougyoukai (1991b, 1992b).

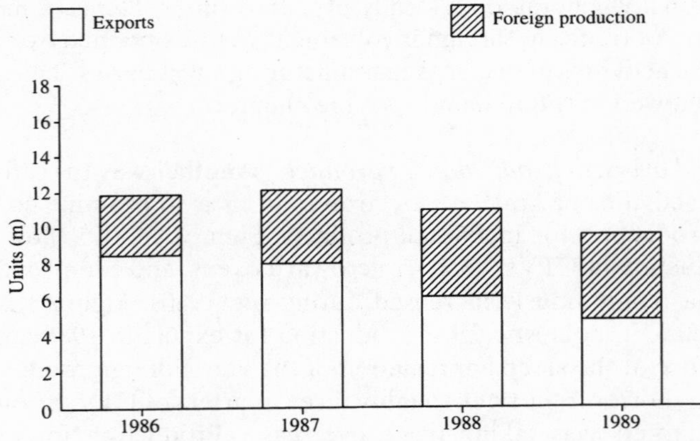

Figure 1.3 Japanese exports and foreign production, 1983–1990: microwave ovens
Sources: see Figure 1.2.

been growing rapidly since 1988 (Figure 1.5). Foreign production increased from 80,000 units in 1985 to 5.2 million units, almost a third of total sales abroad, in 1989.

DFI, exports, and licensing by Japanese electronics MNEs The results of trends in DFI and exports in the late 1980s and early 1990s are reflected in figures presented in Table 1.1, which shows some key data concerning the overseas activities of Japanese electronics firms in 1990 and 1991. The data are drawn from the MITI survey among Japanese MNEs (Nihon Tsuushou Sangyoushou 1991 and 1992). The table covers the three basic modes of foreign involvement: exports, foreign production, and licensing. The export ratio for the surveyed MNEs (given in the last column) stood at 26 per cent in 1990, while the ratio of sales by foreign production subsidiaries to domestic production was unchanged at 22 per cent in 1990–1991. In the fiscal year ending March 1990, the MNEs exported 2,127 billion yen worth of electronics goods to Europe, 27 per cent of total exports. North America absorbed 40 per cent of the MNEs' exports.

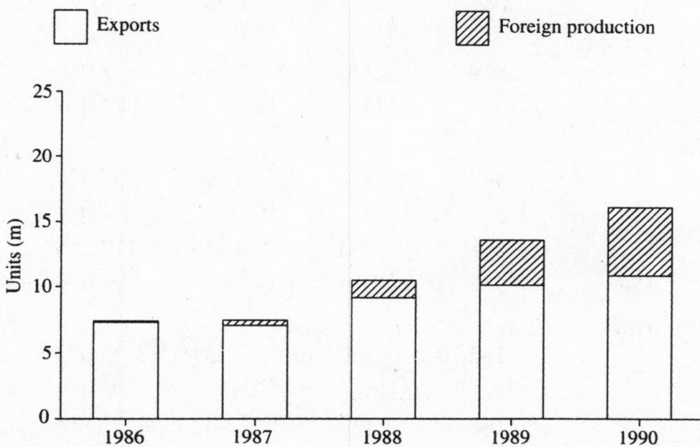

Figure 1.4 Japanese exports and foreign production, 1983–1990: VCRs
Sources: see Figure 1.2.

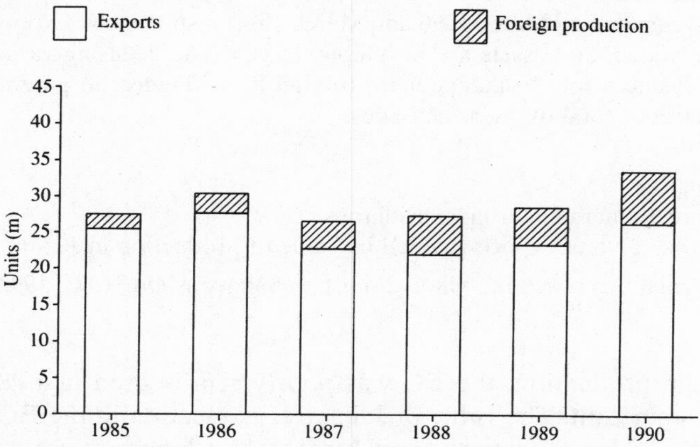

Figure 1.5 Japanese exports and foreign production, 1983–1990: CD players
Sources: see Figure 1.2.

Table 1.1 Overseas activities of Japanese electronics firms, 1990 and 1991

	EC	US	Asia	Total	Total/ Japan (%)
Exports	2,127[a]	3,150[b]	1,970	7,876	26[d]
1990	(27)	(40)	(25)	(100)	
Licensing	76[a]	118[b]	312	592	na
1990	(13)	(20)	(53)	(100)	
Foreign production[c]					
1990	1,084	3,433	1,987	6,777	22
	(16)	(51)	(29)	(100)	
1991	1,869	3,240	2,436	7,957	22
	(23)	(41)	(30)	(100)	
Employment					
1990	24,447	63,820	188,104	307,039	50
	(8)	(21)	(62)	(100)	
1991	58,861	77,996	249,043	419,215	na
	(14)	(19)	(59)	(100)	
No. of subsidiaries					
1990	112	130	353	670	na
	(17)	(19)	(53)	(100)	
1991	168	180	442	884	na
	(19)	(20)	(50)	(100)	

Notes: The figures are for the electrical machinery industry and represent the situation in March 1990 and March 1991, respectively, for the number of subsidiaries, number of licensing contracts, and employment. Exports and foreign production are for the years ending March 1990 and March 1991, respectively. Exports, foreign sales, value added, and assets are in billions of yen. The licensing variable is the number of licences sold to independent foreign firms. Figures in parentheses are regional shares in total overseas activities.

[a] Europe.

[b] North America.

[c] Sales of foreign manufacturing subsidiaries.

[d] Export ratio: value of exports divided by value of production in Japan.

Source: calculations based on Nihon Tsuushou Sangyoushou (1991, 1992).

In foreign production, the EC was poorly represented in 1990, with a share of 16 per cent. The value of Japanese production in the EC reached only half the value of exports from Japan, while Japanese production exceeded exports for North America and Asia. Clearly, Japanese firms' DFI in the EC has been lagging behind. A complete picture of market servicing in the EC and the US also requires taking into account exports from Asian subsidiaries to these regions. The available information suggests that about 15 per cent of the sales of Asian subsidiaries was directed to US and EC markets in 1990 (Nihon Tsuushou Sangyoushou 1991). Exports to the US were roughly three times exports to the EC, the latter amounting to only 70 billion yen (3 per cent of direct exports). This may be due to strict EC local content requirements in combination with antidumping actions against imports from Asian countries in the EC, which have made exports of final products and components from Asian production bases less attractive.

The pattern of overseas production by Japanese electronics firms changed markedly in 1990–1991. Japanese firms rapidly expanded production in the EC, and the EC's share in total overseas production increased to 23 per cent. The EC's growing importance in the early 1990s is even more pronounced in terms of employment, which doubled. These trends are to an important extent the result of some major acquisitions (in particular, Fujitsu's acquisition of ICL) and new ventures in the components sector (notably, a large joint venture of Matsushita and Siemens). The total number of overseas employees of the MNEs in the survey saw a sharp rise, from just over 300,000 to 419,000. The EC's share of this total increased to 14 per cent. Asian subsidiaries employed almost 60 per cent of Japanese firms' overseas employees, which also reflects the high labour intensity of production in this region.

In terms of number of subsidiaries, the EC's share increased slightly to 19 per cent (168 subsidiaries). Licensing contracts, the third mode of servicing foreign markets, are most often concluded with Asian firms, which are involved in 53 per cent of all contracts. Licensing-contracts with Asian firms provide a way of capitalising on the knowledge of standardised, low technology products which Japanese companies find difficult to manufacture competitively.

Export and DFI by individual Japanese firms Additional insight into Japanese electronics firms' overseas activities is given in Table 1.2, which presents data on sales by firms' foreign manufacturing subsidiaries as a percentage of total consolidated sales (the foreign production share[12]), export ratios, EC and US shares in exports, and the number of foreign manufacturing plants with the corresponding EC and US shares in 1989. Integrated electronics manufacturers such as Hitachi and Toshiba are least internationally involved. Both foreign production ratios (5–9 per cent) and export ratios are relatively low. Of course, by their sheer size these firms are important exporters and foreign investors. The strongest export dependence is recorded for producers of office machines and cameras and producers of audio and video products, with export ratios of 50 per cent, increasing to 70–80 per cent for some firms. Audio and video manufacturers combine export dependence with relatively high foreign production shares. The larger components manufacturers such as TDK, Alps, and Murata are internationally oriented, in terms of both exports and foreign production. Yet the smaller components manufacturers are the leaders in internationalisation in terms of foreign production: Tabuchi, Tamura, and Mitsumi produce more abroad than they export.

For the larger integrated and consumer electronics firms, exports to Europe are usually smaller than exports to the US. This reflects the traditional dependence of Japanese firms on the US market, but also the fact that the US market is larger in scale in several electronics sectors such as semiconductors. In contrast, several audio and video producers with strong brand names in Europe, such as JVC, Pioneer, Aiwa, and Akai, export more to Europe. For components manufacturers, the combined share of Europe and North America tends to be relatively small. Exports by these firms are more oriented towards Asia, in part to supply Japanese assembly plants in the region.

The information on the number of foreign manufacturing subsidiaries

Table 1.2 Foreign involvement of Japanese electronics firms, 1989

Company	Consolidated sales (bn yen)	Foreign production share (%)	Exports			Foreign subsidiaries		
			Ratio (%)	EC (%)	US (%)	No.	EC (%)	US (%)
Integrated								
Hitachi	6,401	5	25	23[b]	36[b]	17	18	12
Toshiba	3,800	9	31	30[b]	40[b]	16	31	6
Mitsubishi Electric	2,716	7	21	na	na	16	19	6
Computers, telecommunication and control equipment								
NEC	3,082	8	22	na	na	22	14	18
Fujitsu	2,387	na	18	na	na	9	22	22
Omron	372	na	15	35	45	7	29	14
Consumer, audio, video								
Matsushita	5,504	14	34	26	38	58	16	14
Sony	2,201	20	61	35[b]	39[b]	18	28	11
JVC	1,641	20	47	49	37	8	38	13
Sharp	1,258	25	48	28	41	14	29	7
Sanyo	1,255	27	32	na	na	37	14	27
Pioneer	449	30	47	44	40	3	67	0
Kenwood	157	16	53	31	49	2	50	0
Aiwa	99	15[a]	64	33	29	2	50	0
Akai	71	45	82	60	10	1	100	0

Table 1.2 (*Continued*)

Company	Consolidated sales (bn yen)	Foreign production share (%)	Exports			Foreign subsidiaries		
			Ratio (%)	EC (%)	US (%)	No.	EC (%)	US (%)
Office machines, cameras, watches								
Canon	1,106	10	74	41	48	11	27	18
Ricoh	729	na	34	na	na	5	40	20
Minolta	306	na	75	42	43	5	20	20
Brother	204	14	64	39	34	7	14	14
Components								
TDK	418	23	35	na	na	14	7	43
Alps	376	12[a]	30	24	27	12	25	25
Kyocera	338	7	45	na	na	6	50	17
Nitto Denko	191	9	15	10	23	3	33	0
Murata	243	15[a]	30	19	28	7	29	29
Mitsumi	131	29	37	4	32	12	8	0
SMK	53	11	12	23	24	5	20	0
Tamura	51	20	16	na	na	6	17	0
Tabuchi	35	40	7	69	12	3	33	0

Notes: Sales on consolidated basis: in billions of yen in fiscal year 1988 (ending March 1989); foreign production ratio: sales of foreign manufacturing subsidiaries divided by total consolidated sales (1988/1989); export ratio: exports of parent firm divided by unconsolidated sales in fiscal year 1988. See also Appendix 1.2 for a detailed overview of individual Japanese firms' operations in the EC.

[a] 1987.

[b] Share of overseas sales.

Sources: Touyou Keizai (1989a–1991a), Dempa (1990a, 1991a, 1990b), Nihon Kaihatsu Ginkou, *Kigyou Renketsu Zaimu Deita* (company reports).

had to be interpreted with care. Differences in regional markets within Europe have often compelled Japanese firms to set up more than one manufacturing subsidiary for products such as VCRs and CTVs, while in the US one large subsidiary typically sufficed. Hence, the large number of foreign production subsidiaries located in the EC relatively to the US does not imply that the scale of foreign production is larger in the EC. Several observations can be made. Most firms have set up more manufacturing subsidiaries in Asia than in developed economies: the combined share of the EC and the US in the number of subsidiaries is usually less than 50 per cent. This conforms with the data provided in Table 1.1. Another observation is that several, mostly smaller, audio and video and components manufacturers have set up manufacturing subsidiaries in the EC but not in the US. Below it will be seen that this can be partly attributed to EC trade policy measures, such as a VER restricting Japanese VCRs exports, and EC policy measures imposing local content requirements on Japanese assembly plants. The latter measures created a growing market for EC-produced components to which several Japanese components suppliers responded by setting up manufacturing plants in the EC. The next section discusses such EC trade policy measures in further detail.

1.3 Trade Policy and Japanese DFI in the EC

A most salient feature of the rise in Japanese electronics firms' DFI in the EC as well as in the US in the second half of the 1980s has been the relationship with trade policy. Specific trade policy measures such as antidumping actions and VERs have often been followed by the establishment of Japanese manufacturing plants, allowing firms to avoid duties and quantitative restrictions. This section illustrates the relationship between EC trade policy and Japanese electronics firms' investments in detail at the product and firm level. Starting with a brief discussion of the first establishment of Japanese plants in the EC in the CTV industry, investment patterns and trade policies in the 1980s and early 1990s are analysed. The role of rules of origin and local content rules affecting Japanese firms' operations is highlighted. The section concludes with an assessment of EC trade policies and antidumping in particular.

1.3.1 CTVs a and VCRs

Japanese electronics exports to the EC have been causing trade friction for almost two decades. The first major instance of such friction concerned exports of Japanese colour televisions (CTVs) in the early 1970s. Japanese CTV exports to the EC had increased rapidly, and several countries were debating the use of safeguard measures against Japanese imports. In an effort to relieve trade friction and to ensure an 'orderly working of markets', MITI in 1972 unilaterally decided to restrain CTV and CRT exports and to 'monitor' CTV prices. CTV exports to Italy, Spain, and France were already restricted by national quota, most of them set in the late 1960s when Japan joined the GATT (GATT 1988). Moreover, there were technical and contractual barriers limiting Japanese CTV sales. EC televisions worked with the PAL system, and until 1983 Japanese firms had to obtain licences to produce televisions according to this standard.[13] Licences were restricted to small size televisions and in addition contained a restrictive clause concerning the share of production that could be exported. Then, in July 1973, the UK CTV industry negotiated an industry-to-industry agreement with the Japan Electronics Industry Association restricting Japanese CTV exports to the UK. The UK was at the time the largest EC market for CTVs, with substantial growth prospects (Strange 1992).[14] As a response to these increasing impediments to exports, Sony and Matsushita started CTV assembly operations in the UK in 1974: their first manufacturing operations in Europe. In later years other Japanese firms followed, and by 1988 Japanese firms' 25 per cent market share in the EC consisted almost totally of EC-produced CTVs (CEC 1990: 12–28).

The beginning of the 1980s saw the start of a second round of trade friction over Japanese electronics exports to the EC. In 1982 Philips and Grundig, the EC producers of VCRs, marketing VCRs conforming to Philips' V-2000 standard, filed an antidumping petition against Japanese firms with the Commission of the European Communities (hereafter, the Commission).

A brief description of EC antidumping practice is in order for a proper understanding of the discussion that follows. Under the EC's antidumping law, based on the GATT antidumping code, EC firms can petition for and be granted protection against imports if there is evidence that the imports are dumped (sold below the 'normal' value of the product) and if the dumped imports are found to cause 'material' injury to the firms. Normal value can be defined either as the price in the country of export or the fully allocated production cost. Material injury is defined as 'harm which is not immaterial or inconsequential' (e.g. Destler 1992: 149) and is often indicated by a fall in profitability in the complaining industry. The Commission is the authority administering the EC antidumping system. After receiving a complaint from EC producers, the Commission carries out an antidumping investigation if the complaint is judged to be well founded. If the investigation finds dumping as well as injury, antidumping duties can be levied for a period of five years, or agreements ('undertakings') can be made with the exporting firms involved, by which these firms promise to keep prices or quantities at a certain level.[15]

Soon after the Commission received the antidumping complaint, France took recourse to administrative action to limit VCR imports, by requiring all VCR imports to be handled by the customs office of Poitiers: this became known as the 'Poitiers incident'.[16] Partly because of the pressure put on the Commission by the unilateral French action, the Commission negotiated an EC-wide VER with Japanese industry through MITI, restricting imports of Japanese VCRs and VCR kits from 1983.[17] Both the antidumping investigation and the French administrative action were cancelled in exchange.

The negotiation of the VER set the stage for a unified commercial policy in the EC with the Commission as the main actor instead of the respective national governments. It should be noted, however, that, although the Commission has broad decision making powers (among which, the power to decide on provisional antidumping duties) and is responsible for the implementation of EC antidumping rules, the individual member states through the Council of Ministers ultimately have to approve any definitive antidumping action. Until 1994, the Commission needed to convince a qualified majority of member states of the necessity to take antidumping action. A revision of EC antidumping law adopted in late 1994, just before Sweden, Finland, and Austria became members of the EC, has changed the requirement to a simple majority. Since only one antidumping case has been rejected by the Council until recently, it has been argued that the Council effectively 'rubber-stamps' the Commission's proposals (Bellis 1990: 45), allowing substantial autonomy to the Commission. However, the Commission receives member states' comments on each case through a Council of Advisers (consisting of member states' representatives) during the investigation and is obliged by law to hear the Adviser's opinions. The Commission is likely to decide on cases taking the member states' interests, as presented by the Council of Advisers, into account in order not to face defeat in the Council of Ministers vote. It is merely for convenience that antidumping actions will hereafter also be ascribed to the administrative authority, the Commission.

The antidumping petition and negotiation of the VER coincided with a wave of Japanese investments. During 1982 and 1983, JVC, Sony Matsushita, and Hitachi, the four major Japanese VCR producers at the time (Mackintosh International 1985), began VCR manufacturing operations in the EC. Two of these firms entered production by establishing joint ventures with EC firms: JVC set up a joint venture with Thorn EMI in the UK and Telefunken in Germany, and Matsushita teamed up with Bosch/Blaupunkt in Germany. While the need to be less vulnerable to trade policy measures was a major reason for these investments, the establishment of joint ventures was also part of a successful strategy by Matsushita and JVC to license VCR production to EC competitors and thereby gain an early lead for their VHS standard (Cawson *et al.* 1990).

The relationship between EC trade policy in the VCR industry and Japanese DFI is illustrated in Table 1.3, which sets out EC trade policy measures on a time scale and orders Japanese VCR manufacturing plants by the date of establishment. The table shows that other Japanese VCR manufacturers, such as Sanyo, Mitsubishi, and Toshiba, followed soon with plant establishments in 1984. All these investments, with the exception of a small second plant by Sony in France, were located in the UK and Germany. Immediately after the 'Poitiers incident', France definitely was not perceived to have a positive stance towards Japanese firms and was

Table 1.3 EC trade policy and the start of Japanese VCR manufacturing, 1982–1991

1982	83	84	85	86	87	88	89	90	91
	D VER			T		DI	PD	DD	
								Shintom G	
								Funai G	
						Matsushita Fr			
						NEC UK			
						Funai UK			
					Toshiba G				
					Matsushita Sp				
					Sharp Sp				
					Orion UK				
				Akai Fr					
				Sony Sp					
				Sanyo Sp					
				Hitachi UK					
			Sharp UK						
		Sanyo G							
		Toshiba UK							
		Sony Fr							
		Mitsubishi UK							
	Sanyo UK								
	Hitachi G								
	Matsushita G								
	JVC UK								
	Sony G								
	JVC G								
	D VER			T		DI	PD	DD	
1982	83	84	85	86	87	88	89	90	91

D = Dumping complaint filed
VER = Voluntary export restraint Japanese VCR 1983–1986
T = VER expired; EC raises tariff on VCR imports from 8% to 14%
DI = EC starts antidumping investigation
PD = Provisional duties (18%) Orion and Funai
DD = Final duty (13%) Orion, undertaking Funai

Notes: Cumulative number of plants: 24; number of investors: 13. Company name indicates the time of establishment of the company's manufacturing subsidiary or the start of manufacturing operations in an existing subsidiary; abbreviations indicate the country of establishment: UK (United Kingdom), G (Germany), Fr (France), Sp (Spain).

Sources: Yano Keizai Kenkyuujo (1989b), EACEM (1990), Watanabe (1988), Furlotti (1991), Nihon Kaihatsu Ginkou (1989), Nihon Yushutsunyuu Ginkou (1989), Kikai Shinkou Kyoukai (1989, 1992), Touyou Keizai (1993a), Bürger and Green (1991), JETRO (1993b), Nihon Boueki Shinkoukai (1985c–1992c). Updated from Belderbos (1994).

avoided. France's attitude became markedly more accommodating from 1985, however, and Akai and Matsushita established VCR plants here in 1986 and 1988, respectively.

In 1986 the VER expired,[18] but was replaced by an increase in the EC's customs tariff for VCRs from 8 to 14 per cent.[19] One year later, European producers (Philips-Grundig, Thomson, Nokia, and the JVC-Thomson joint venture J2T) filed another dumping complaint against two Japanese producers, Funai and Orion, and Korean exporters. One can discern a second wave of plant establishments around this time in Table 1.3. When in August 1988 the EC Commission decided on an 18 per cent provisional antidumping duty to be levied on VCR exports by Funai and Orion, both firms' EC plants were well in operation. Not only Funai and Orion set up VCR assembly plants, but NEC also set up its first VCR plant in the EC. In addition, several other producers set up second plants. It is conceivable that the new antidumping investigation signalled a threat of possible future trade restrictions and prompted Japanese firms to pre-empt such measures by further reducing reliance on exports. Rival South Korean firms Samsung and Goldstar also started production in the EC in 1987 in response to the antidumping action, and this will have put more pressure on Japanese firms not to stay behind. At the same time, the yen appreciation in 1986–1987 made exporting from Japan less attractive, while rapid declines in VCR prices made transport costs a relatively greater burden.

Two late investments occurred two years later in 1990. Funai started assembly of VCRs in Germany, but closed its UK assembly line, not long after it had acquired Amstrad's stake in the UK joint venture.[20] The other investment by Shintom, with Funai and Orion one of the major dedicated Japanese OEM suppliers of VCRs, was again related to antidumping. It appears that EC firms filed a complaint at the time alleging dumping of imported VCRs and singling out Shintom as the culprit. In this case, however, the EC Commission found the complaint unsubstantiated and decided not to open a formal investigation. Within two years, Shintom ceased its assembly operations in Germany to concentrate production in Singapore and Indonesia.[21]

What comes out as striking in Table 1.3 is that individual Japanese firms set up multiple plants in the EC. In 1989 there were 22 Japanese plants in operation by 12 different firms. On the one hand, this indicates that Japanese plants were mostly handling the simplest assembly and packaging tasks, so that logistics played a more important role than economies of scale in assembly. On the other hand, it reflects the fragmentation of the EC market. Fragmentation results from different technical standards (such as the SECAM video standard in France) and differences in tastes. However, other factors were probably more relevant to Japanese firms: national quotas for Japanese VCR imports, and political influences. France maintained an import licensing system for Japanese firms after the 'Poitiers incident' (GATT 1988). The need to appease the French government and to be less vulnerable to government administrative actions may have been the most important reason for Sony and Matsushita to set up an extra VCR plant in France. The plants set up in Spain are related to the fact that Spain limited Japanese VCR imports by its own national quota. Japanese firms thus opted for a country-based investment strategy rather than an EC-wide strategy. In the next section it will be seen that this began to change in the late 1980s. Japanese firms have gradually developed EC-wide strategies, and EC activities of Japanese firms have become more integrated.

1.3.2 Antidumping and Tariff Jumping DFI

The VER for Japanese VCRs was followed by an impressive range of trade policy measures against Japanese electronics exports during the 1980s and early 1990s, as illustrated by Table 1.4. The tariff for CD players was increased during a five year period,[22] and the tariff for VCRs was increased to 14 per cent in 1986, as noted above. By far the most important trade barriers have resulted from antidumping actions. The table lists 19 antidumping investigations initiated by the EC between 1982 and 1992 targeting exports of Japanese electronics firms. Some of these actions targeted Japanese manufacturing subsidiaries in South-East Asian countries. The antidumping actions cover a variety of Japanese export goods such as electronic typewriters, plain paper copiers, microwave ovens, CD players, DRAMs (dynamic random access memory chips), and audio tapes. In only one case did the Commission cancel the antidumping case without imposing any sanction against Japanese exporters. In two other cases (microwave ovens and the second CD player case) the antidumping complaint was withdrawn by the EC producers. In the other cases the EC found that Japanese firms had dumped their exports, causing injury to EC industry, and determined often substantial dumping duties to provide relief to the EC producers.

The relationship between antidumping measures and Japanese firms' investments in the EC is illustrated in Tables 1.5–1.8 for copiers, microwave ovens, CD players, and dot matrix printers. Nine copier plants were established after the initiation of the antidumping investigation in August 1985 (Table 1.5), six of which were set up before final dumping duties were levied in early 1988. Only Canon established manufacturing bases well before the antidumping action.

In the case of microwave ovens (Table 1.6) five companies started operations after the antidumping investigation was opened in December 1986. Trade friction with EC industry arose earlier and may have influenced the decisions by Sanyo and Toshiba to establish plants at an earlier date.[23] When the EC producers finally withdrew their complaint in December

1988, six Japanese firms had set up manufacturing facilities.[24] The threat of possible antidumping duties appears to have been sufficient to prompt Japanese investments. The experience Japanese firms had gained in the US must have played a role as well. A US antidumping petition against Japanese microwave ovens filed in 1979 had led the leading Japanese exporters to establish US manufacturing plants in the early 1980s (see also Section 6.2.1).

The reasons for the eventual withdrawal of the petition are unclear. To an extent, the increasing manufacturing presence of Japanese firms in the EC may have played a role. Partly as a result, the market share of Japanese imports declined very rapidly, from 50 per cent in 1986 to 20 per cent in 1988. At the same time, imports from South Korea were increasing rapidly. It may have been difficult to substantiate a claim that dumped imports were causing the injury to EC firms.[25] Philips was itself a major importer of

Table 1.4 EC trade policy targeting Japanese electronics exports, 1982–1992

Voluntary export restraint (VER)		
Period	*Products*	
1983–1986	VCRs (monitoring CTV, CRT)	
Tariffs increases		
Year	*Product*	*Tariff (%) (previously)*
1984	CD players	19[a] (9.5)
1986	VCRs	14 (8)
Antidumping		
Start investigation	*Product*	*Decision, duty (%)*
1982	VCRs	Cancelled/VER
1983	Electronics scales	1–27, undertakings
1984	Electronic typewriters	17–35
1985	Plain paper copiers	7–20
1986	Microwave ovens	Withdrawn
1987	EPROMs	94[b], undertakings
1987	Dot matrix printers	5–47
1987	SIFF printers	0–23.5
1987	CD players	8–32
1987	DRAMs	60[b], undertakings
1987	Car telephones	Cancelled
1987	VCRs	13, undertaking
1988	Small screen CTVs[c]	Duties
1989	Tungsten halogen lamps	36–47
1989	Audio tapes	2–26
1991	3.5 microdisks	6–41
1991	Aluminium capacitors	12–75
1992	CD players[c]	Withdrawn
1992	CTVs	Cancelled/duties[d]

Table 1.4 (*Continued*)

Antidumping against assembly plants		
Start investigation	*Product*	*Decision*
1987	Electronic scales	Duties/undertakings
1987	Electronic typewriters	Duties/undertakings
1988	Copiers	Duties/undertakings
1988	Printers	Duties/undertakings
1989	VCRs	—
Product-specific rules of origin		
Year	*Product*	*Requirement*
1989	ICs	Wafer etching
1989	Copiers	Major processes

[a] 16.5% in 1987 and gradually brought back to 9.5% again in 1989.
[b] 'Residual duty' for Japanese firms not involved in undertakings.
[c] Antidumping against imports from South-East Asian countries included Japanese subsidiaries.
[d] Investigation of direct imports from Japan cancelled; duties on imports from Japanese subsidiaries in South-East Asian countries.

Sources: Ishikawa (1990), National Consumer Council (1990), Van Bael and Bellis (1990), *Financial Times*, various issues, *Official Journal of the European Communities*, various issues.

microwave ovens into the EC since its main manufacturing plant was located in Sweden (Ishikawa 1990). Another factor that may have played a role is the bargaining power Japanese firms possessed because EC firms were dependent on them for licences for and supplies of magnetrons, a key component of microwave ovens.

The location of Japanese microwave oven plants shows a strong concentration in the UK. The Toshiba plant in France, the only plant outside the UK, is a joint venture with Thomson. The UK serves as a base for export to other EC countries, although the attractiveness of the UK market itself can explain the investment pattern partly. Demand for microwave ovens in the UK took off much earlier than in other EC countries, and the UK market for microwave ovens was the largest in Europe until 1989 (Euromonitor 1991).

Eleven of the 12 CD player plants (Table 1.7) in the EC were established just before or after the antidumping investigation started. Only the plant of Yamaha in France was established just after definitive duties were levied. Provisional duties of up to 34 per cent were levied in the summer of 1989, and final duties were levied in January 1990. At that time, the 11 Japanese plants had all been in operation for at least a year. In contrast, the temporary increase in the EC customs tariff to 19 per cent was not followed by

Table 1.5 EC trade policy and the start of Japanese copier manufacturing, 1974–1990

1974	84	85	86	87	88	89	90
			DI	PD DD	DIP	DDP RO	
							Sharp Fr
					Sharp UK		
					Konica G		
					Ricoh Fr		
					Canon It		
				Toshiba Fr			
				Matsushita G			
				Minolta G			
				Ricoh UK			
		Canon Fr					
Canon G							
			DI	PD DD	DIP	DDP RO	
1974	84	85	86	87	88	89	90

DI = EC starts antidumping investigation
PD = EC levies provisional duties 15.8%
DD = EC levies definitive duties 7.5%–20%
DIP = EC starts antidumping investigation against assembly plants
DDP = duties and undertakings assembled copiers
RO = EC tightens rules of origin for copiers
Notes: see Table 1.3. Cumulative number of plants: 11; number of investors: 7.
Sources: See Table 1.3.

Japanese investment. The relative importance of France as a location for Japanese plants reflects the attractiveness of the French consumer electronics market, the largest in Europe in terms of value and characterised by relatively high prices (Mackintosh International 1985), in combination with a more positive stance of the French government towards Japanese inward investments.

All dot matrix printer plants were established after the initiation of an antidumping investigation in April 1987 (Table 1.8). By the time definitive duties were levied in December 1988, 12 Japanese plants were in operation. Hitachi Koki later acquired an existing printer plant of the US firm Dataproducts Inc. in Ireland in 1990.

The above cases illustrate the strong relationship between antidumping measures and the start of Japanese manufacturing activities in the EC.

Although these are probably the most illustrative cases, a number of similar observations can be made for other products. The available evidence for electronic scales, electric typewriters, car telephones, audio tapes, tungsten halogen lamps, and microdisks is summarised in Table 1.9.

The available information again shows a relationship between antidumping and Japanese investments. In the case of electronics scales, Tokyo Electric, which was the only firm finally charged with antidumping duties, was also the only firm to set up assembly operations in response. In the case of electric typewriters, a concentration of investment is observed in 1985 and 1986, after provisional antidumping duties were levied. In these two early antidumping investigations in 1983–1984, it appears that Japanese firms opted to wait until the antidumping decision was known before deciding on a response. In subsequent cases, as shown above, the initiation of an antidumping investigation was the signal to invest.

The case of car telephones again illustrates this point. The UK subsidiary of Motorola filed a complaint in 1987 alleging that Japanese firms were dumping car telephones on the UK market. Before the antidumping investigation was cancelled, the two major exporters, Matsushita and NEC, had already set up manufacturing operations. Mitsubishi Electric had committed itself to manufacture in France around the time of the investigation but

Table 1.6 EC trade policy and the start of Japanese microwave oven manufacturing, 1984–1990

1984	85	86	87	88	89	90
			DI		W	
					Hitachi UK	
				Toshiba Fr		
				Brother UK		
				Matsushita UK		
				Sharp UK		
			Sanyo UK			
		Toshiba UK				
			DI		W	
1984	85	86	87	88	89	90

DI = EC starts antidumping investigation
W = complaint withdrawn

Notes: see Table 1.3. Cumulative number of plants: 7; number of investors: 6.

Sources: see Table 1.3.

Table 1.7 EC trade policy and the start of Japanese CD player manufacturing, 1984–1991

1984 85 86 87 88 89 90 91

T DI PD DD

Yamaha Fr
JVC Fr
Nippon Columbia G
Sharp UK
Matsushita G
JVC UK
Funai UK
Pioneer Fr
Sony Fr
Kenwood Fr
Aiwa UK
Akai Fr

T DI PD DD

1984 85 86 87 88 89 90 91

T = EC raises tariff on CD players to 19% from 9.5%
DI = EC starts antidumping investigation
PD = EC levies provisional duties
DD = EC levies definitive duties

Notes: see Table 1.3. Cumulative number of plants: 12; number of investors: 11.

Sources: see Table 1.3.

started operations later, in 1990. The car telephone case is the only antidumping case initiated against Japanese electronics firms in which the Commission found no injurious dumping. Motorola's case appears to have been weak.[26] It is important to note that the antidumping petition by Motorola was part of a worldwide battle for market share by the US company against Japanese mobile telephone producers. On behalf of Motorola, the US government put pressure on the Japanese government to increase market access for Motorola's mobile phone equipment. In the US, Motorola had filed an antidumping case in 1984 which led to the imposition of antidumping duties on imported Japanese cellular mobile telephones in 1985. Against this background, Japanese firms obviously perceived that an export-only strategy would leave them very vulnerable in the European market.

The case of tungsten halogen lamps is another standard example of the close relationship between antidumping and investment. Phoenix and Iwasaki, two of the four Japanese firms targeted by the antidumping action, set up manufacturing operations around the time the provisional duties were levied. Duties were substantial, on average about 40 per cent. None of the four Japanese firms had manufacturing operations or extensive sales networks in the EC before the antidumping case was filed, and this may explain the relatively late response of the firms compared with antidumping cases that involved major Japanese electronics firms.

The cases of audiocassette tapes and 3.5 inch microdisks are different in character because several Japanese firms had invested in EC manufacturing

Table 1.8 EC trade policy and the start of Japanese dot matrix printer manufacturing, 1987–1990

1987	88	89	90
DI	PD	DD DIP	
			Hitachi Koki Ire
		Seiko Epson Fr	
		Seikosha Fr	
	Seikosha G		
	Fujitsu Sp		
	Star UK		
	Citizin UK		
	Oki UK		
	Tokyo Electric G		
	NEC UK		
	Brother UK		
Seiko Epson UK			
Canon It			
Matsushita UK			
DI	PD	DD DIP	
1987	88	89	90

DI = EC starts antidumping investigation
PD = EC levies provisional duties
DD = EC levies definitive duties, 4.8%–47%
DIP = EC starts antidumping investigation against assembly plants

Notes: see Table 1.3. Cumulative number of plants: 14; number of investors: 12.

Sources: see Table 1.3.

Table 1.9 EC trade policy and the start of Japanese manufacturing: electronic scales, electric typewriters, car telephones, audio tapes, halogen lamps, and microdisks

Japanese firm	Country	Establishment
Electronic scales (antidumping initiated 1983.09, provisional duties 1984.03)		
Tokyo Electric[a]	Netherlands	1985.07
Tokyo Electric[a]	UK	1987
Electric typewriters (antidumping initiated 1984.03, provisional duties 1984.12)		
Canon	France	1985
Sharp	UK	1985.02
Brother	UK	1985.03
Tokyo Electric	Germany	1986.02
Kyushu Matsushita	UK	1986.08
Silver Seiko[b]	UK	na
Car telephones (antidumping initiated 1987.07, cancellation 1988.11)		
NEC	UK	1987
Mitsubishi Electric	France	1988[c]
Matsushita Graphic Communication	UK	1988.05
Audio tapes (antidumping initiated 1988.10, provisional duties 1990.10)		
Sony	France	1980.12
TDK	Germany	1986.01
Sony	Italy	1988
Hitachi Maxell	UK	1988
Fuji Photo Film	Germany	1989
TDK	Luxembourg	1989.07
Halogen lamps (antidumping initiated 1989.07, provisional duties 1990.07)		
Phoexin Electric	UK	1990
Iwasaki Electric	Belgium	1991.04
3.5 microdisks (antidumping initiated 1991.07, provisional duties 1993.04)		
Hitachi Maxell	UK	1988
Mitsubishi Chemical	Ireland	1990
Kao	Spain	1991

Notes: na = not available; Establishment = time of establishment of manufacturing subsidiary or start of manufacturing in existing subsidiaries.

[a] Tokyo Electric was the only Japanese exporter receiving an antidumping duty.
[b] Silver Seiko did not manufacture typewriters itself in the UK but consigned production to the UK firm Astec. In March 1988 it withdrew from this arrangement.
[c] Manufacturing operations did not start until the end of 1990.

Sources: see Table 1.3.

activities well before the start of the antidumping investigation. In the audiocassette tape case, the petition was filed against Japanese, South Korean, and Hong Kong exporters in October 1988. Sony had set up its audio tape plant in France well before in 1980, and had been operating a second plant in Italy since early 1988. TDK was producing the tapes in a German plant since 1986, and Hitachi Maxell had just set up its assembly plant in the UK.[27] The Japanese firms, in particular Sony, had been substituting imports for EC production. The antidumping investigation showed that Japanese firms' production of audio tapes in the EC (i.e. Sony) accounted for roughly 10 per cent of the EC market in 1985, while imports took another 60 per cent. In 1988, EC production by Japanese firms reached 20 per cent of the EC market and the import share had decreased to 50 per cent.[28] A declining market share of imports is a rather exceptional characteristic in an antidumping case: in a standard antidumping case foreign firms *increase* market share by dumping their exports. An increased market share of dumped imports is one of the factors substantiating the causation of injury to the complaining firms. In the audio tape case, Japanese firms' investments in EC manufacturing severed this link. In principle, this would make injurious dumping much harder to substantiate. However, the Commission argued, as in several later antidumping cases involving Japanese electronics firms, that, although the volume of imports had declined, imports remained an important (in this case the main) source of supply to the EC market. Since a substantial volume of imports was found dumped, it could be argued that imports were causing 'material injury' to the EC industry. In October 1990, duties of up to 26 per cent were imposed on Japanese audio tape imports.[29]

Japanese investment in the EC also had the potential of complicating antidumping actions against Japanese exporters by affecting the determination of what constitutes the EC industry ('Community industry' in the EC terminology). The EC industry is, for antidumping purposes, generally defined as all manufacturers of the product under investigation in EC member states. The definition of Community industry is important because it is used at two stages in the antidumping investigation: in determining whether the complaining EC firms are representative of the industry, and in determining whether the industry has suffered 'material injury'. Antidumping law stipulates that a complaint by EC firms can be acted upon only if the complaining firms represent a 'major proportion' of Community production. This proportion is usually interpreted as a 50 per cent share, while the firms are not considered representative if their share is less than a minimum of 25 per cent (Van Bael and Bellis 1990: 117). Antidumping law also states that the situation of the entire Community industry (not just the complainants) should be analysed to establish injury. Hence, if the share of Japanese firms' production in the EC is substantial, one could expect that it would become more difficult for EC firms to file complaints and substantiate injury. However, antidumping law allows antidumping authorities to ignore in the definition of Community industry those producers that are related to the exporters accused of dumping (Van Bael and Bellis 1990: 117–119). Thus, in the audiocassette case, the complaining firms, Agfa/BASF of Germany and Suma of France, constituted the entire 'Community industry', although production by these EC producers was not substantially greater than EC production of Japanese firms in 1988.

The implication of antidumping practice with regard to foreign firms' manufacturing operations and import decline is that Japanese firms, even if they have substantial manufacturing operations in the EC, can still be subject to antidumping actions as long as they rely on imports for part of their EC sales. The threat of antidumping duties can be fully neutralised only by shifting the lion's share of production for the EC market to factories within the EC and reducing imports to levels that cannot be alleged to harm indigenous EC producers. The response by Japanese firms in the audiocassette case was predictable: a further substitution of EC production capacity for imports. Before provisional duties were levied, TDK had set up a second manufacturing plant in Luxembourg and Fuji Photo Film was operating a plant in Germany. Although early investment did not avoid antidumping action, it did give Japanese firms the possibility to shift production to the EC rapidly and avoid paying substantial antidumping duties.

The antidumping complaint in the audiocassette case also included audiotape reels, from which audiotapes are cut. Since Japanese firms were manufacturing audiocassettes from imported tape reels, an extension of duties to reels would have hit EC assembly operations as well. Taking this threat seriously, Sony decided to integrate EC operations by establishing a tape coating plant in France (Strange 1993: 293) just after the opening of the investigation. As it happened, the Commission decided against including the tape reels in the scope of the antidumping actions. It appears that the British government had put strong pressure on the Commission to limit the scope of the action to audiocassettes. It feared negative consequences for employment at Hitachi Maxell's just established audiocassette tape plant in the UK.[30]

In the case of 3.5 inch microdisks, Hitachi Maxell was producing in the UK and Kao had just started assembly in Spain when the antidumping investigation was initiated in July 1991. Mitsubishi Chemical had acquired an Irish manufacturing facility through its take-over of the US firm Verbatim in 1990. Production of Japanese firms in the EC in 1990 accounted for roughly 12 per cent of the EC market, while the market share of imports from Japan was double that figure.[31] Similar to the audiocassette case, duties were levied, despite the fact that Japanese firms had increased production in the EC and that imports from Japan, though substantial, had been falling since 1989. The duties must have accelerated the shift to EC production, although no new assembly plants were established. The relatively small number of investments may be due to the fact that several Japanese exporters, among them Sony, TDK, and Mitsubishi Chemical, set up manufacturing operations in the US. Plant establishments in the US were concentrated in 1988–1989, the time of an US antidumping action against Japanese imports.[32] At least Sony, which operates a large plant in the US, has been reported to export to world markets from its US production base (Yano Keizai Kenkyuujo 1994a: 615).

Three products can be identified where a number of Japanese investments occurred without overt trade policy measures: videocassette tapes, facsimiles, and PCs. A list of Japanese firms' investments is provided in Table 1.10. In the case of video tapes, JVC, Sony, and Hitachi Maxell were the first companies to set up assembly operations in the EC in 1983–1984. The investments of JVC and Sony complemented VCR investments and were motivated by strategic considerations: local production of video tapes could generate a more ready acceptance of the VHS (JVC) or Betamax (Sony) standard. In 1987 Fuji Photo Film followed, and TDK established manufacturing operations in Luxembourg in 1989. With these investments, all major Japanese manufacturers had set up production capacity in the EC. In contrast with the audiocassette tape and microdisk cases, early establishment of manufacturing operations for video tapes appears to have deflected EC trade policy measures against Japanese firms. When in 1987 EC-based producers, among them BASF and Philips-Dupont Magnetics, lodged an antidumping complaint, it was against South Korean and Hong Kong firms. In 1990 a new case was opened, targeting rapidly increasing imports from China. In both cases, dumping and injury were found and duties were levied.[33] Japanese producers were not actively involved in the case but clearly benefited from protection provided by the antidumping actions.

A wave of facsimile manufacturing investments can be discerned around 1988–1989 and investments in PC manufacturing followed in 1990–1991. In the case of facsimiles, the threat of trade barriers has most evidently played a role. Although no antidumping investigation was ever initiated, several Japanese firms explicitly stated, in a survey by the Japanese Machinery Promotion Association, that their decision to invest was governed by EC antidumping actions (Kikai Shinkou Kyoukai 1989). While in the case of microwave ovens and car telephones it was the threat constituted by the antidumping investigation that induced Japanese firms to invest, in the case of facsimiles the threat that an investigation could be initiated appears to have been sufficient to induce investments. At least nine plants were set up by Japanese firms. Three of these plants were joint ventures with EC companies: Sanyo and Canon with Olivetti in Italy and Toshiba with Rhone Poulenc in France. It is conceivable that this strategy of co-operation with indigenous EC firms helped to avoid antidumping actions.[34]

Table 1.10 The start of Japanese manufacturing activity in the EC: video tapes, facsimiles, and PCs

Japanese firm	Country of investment	Establishment
Video tapes		
JVC	Germany	1983.03
Sony	France	1984
Hitachi Maxell	United Kingdom	1984.06
Fuji Photo Film	Germany	1987.03
TDK	Luxembourg	1989.07
Facsimiles		
Canon	France	1988
NEC	UK	1988.06
Ricoh	France	1988.10
Matsushita Graphic Communication	UK	1989.03
Sanyo	Italy	1989.09
Sharp	France	1989.12
Murata Machinery	Belgium	1989.12
Toshiba	France	na
Canon	Italy	na
PCs		
Toshiba	Germany	1989
Seiko Epson	UK	1990
Mitsubishi Electric	UK	1990
Fujitsu	UK	1991

Notes: na = not available; Establishment = time of establishment of manufacturing subsidiary or start of manufacturing in existing subsidiaries.
Sources: see Table 1.3.

The investments by Japanese PC producers also appear to have been influenced to an important extent by the need to pre-empt possible trade barriers (Kume and Totsuka 1991). There have been several signals that the EC was worried about the effect of (Japanese) imports on the EC PC industry. During 1987–1989 the Commission ordered surveillance of PC imports from Japan when the US levied temporary tariffs on Japanese PC imports. This was to discourage Japanese firms from export diversion to the EC. Another example is an April 1991 meeting between CEC president Delors and representatives of the EC computer industry, where the industry representatives reportedly were seeking 'high tariffs' on imported PCs (*Kyodo News*, 30 April 1991). Toshiba, market leader in the EC for laptop computers, set up a plant for laptop PCs in Germany in 1989. Seiko Epson followed with assembly operations in the UK. Mitsubishi Electric and Fujitsu entered PC production through acquisitions of UK firms Apricot Computer and ICL, respectively (see Section 1.4.2).[35]

It seems clear that, in cases where no specific trade measures were taken, Japanese investment decisions have often been governed by the fear of import barriers. The large number of Japanese plants established in the late 1980s generally reflects Japanese firms' apprehension of the much discussed 'Fortress Europe'. There was the possibility that the Internal Market to be created by the end of 1992 would have high external trade barriers resulting from the political influence of the EC's most protectionist countries. The large number of antidumping cases in 1987–1989 targeting Japanese electronics firms' exports must have given the impression that 'Fortress Europe' was indeed materialising. It had become clear that EC industry would and could count on protection via the antidumping instrument if import competition were severe. The possibility of antidumping actions and the uncertainty that this created for Japanese firms provided incentives to invest at an earlier stage. If imports could be kept small, as in case of video tapes, antidumping actions could be avoided. Bhagwati *et al.* (1987) argue that investments may also be seen as a 'quid pro quo' if there is an understanding that, provided the Japanese firms are willing to commit themselves to manufacture in the EC, trade policy measures will not be invoked. While this may have played a role in video tape and facsimile investment, the audio tape and microdisk cases suggest that commitments would need to be very substantial if Japanese firms were to succeed. These issues will be further highlighted in Section 1.3.4, which discusses the most recent antidumping actions. Before turning to recent trends, however, the role of local content requirements and rules of origins in the late 1980s is analysed below.

1.3.3 Local Content Requirements and Rules of Origin

Antidumping against Japanese imports into the EC has been an important policy factor, but not the only such factor, shaping Japanese investment patterns. Table 1.4 shows that antidumping actions were followed by two further measures: antidumping against assembly plants, and product-specific rules of origin. Both had a strong impact on Japanese firms' exports as well as on their manufacturing activity in the EC.

The extension of antidumping action against products assembled in EC plants was the response of the EC to the wave of tariff jumping investments by Japanese firms. In 1987, when it became clear that Japanese firms were attempting to avoid paying duties by investing in EC assembly plants, the EC amended its antidumping legislation to make it potentially applicable to Japanese assembly plants as well.[36] Duties could be levied on products assembled in EC plants if two conditions were met: (1) the assembly plants were set up or had increased production after the antidumping action, and (2) more than 60 per cent of components used in EC assembly were imported from the home country.

In practice, the amended antidumping law was administered as a local content rule targeting Japanese plants in the EC. The amendment has been invoked seven times, all of which involved Japanese firms.[37] All cases were finally settled through undertakings by which the Japanese firms agreed to reduce dependence on imports from Japan.[38] Although the amendment only implies that components should be sourced from 'other countries' than Japan, the Commission has at least once accepted an undertaking requiring an increase in EC local content (Bellis 1990).

The suggestion that the EC has been eager to see increased local content of Japanese plants is strengthened by the fact that local content rules had been linked to trade policy measures before. The 1983 agreement on VCRs stipulated that Japanese plants in the EC had to reach a local content of 25 per cent of value added in 1984, increasing to 45 per cent in 1985, in order for EC production not to be included in the export quota (Tyson 1992: Chapter 6, HEC Eurasia Institute 1989). Although the EC has always denied having any policy concerning the local content of foreign firms' manufacturing activities, Japanese firms would hardly have been convinced.[39]

In May 1990 a GATT panel investigation, requested by Japan to examine whether the antidumping amendment was conforming to the GATT code, ruled against the new legislation. The main reason for this was that the amendment implied that duties could be levied on EC-manufactured products that did not cross any EC-borders. This made antidumping action more akin to a trade related investment measure (illegal in the GATT code) targeting a specific group of producers in the EC, than a trade policy measure.[40] The EC has not invoked the law since, but on the other hand it has confirmed that existing undertakings would remain in force. The Commission stated that it would seek a satisfactory anti-circumvention regulation in the framework of the Uruguay Round of GATT negotiations.[41]

In the meantime, the Commission had also been accused by Japan of using rules of origin as an instrument of trade policy. In 1989 and 1990, rules of origin were tightened for copiers and integrated circuits (ICs), apparently to strengthen the effectiveness of antidumping actions, and again effectively providing strong incentives for Japanese firms to extend manufacturing operations in the EC. Rules of origin state what country of origin should be attached to a product, and gain importance when trade policy measures are country- or firm-specific, as is the case with antidumping policy or national quotas. The basic EC rule of origin, dating from 1968, takes as the country of origin of a product the country where the 'last substantial manufacturing process' is carried out. In practice, this rule is open to various interpretations by different EC national customs authorities. To ensure harmonised treatment, the EC has adopted several product-specific rules of origin. For instance, for CTVs and printed circuit boards, the definition implies that a minimum of 45 per cent of value added has to be generated in an exporting country if a product is to be considered as originating in that country.

In February 1990, a new product-specific rule of origin was accepted for copiers. This rule stipulates that a range of relatively minor manufacturing operations are not sufficient to confer origin. The new rule was directly aimed at impeding attempts of the Japanese firm Ricoh to bypass antidumping duties on copier imports from Japan by importing copiers assembled in its US plant in California.[42] Although it has been reported that Ricoh chose to integrate and extend US operations so that it could satisfy the new rule (Strange 1992: 323), the event must have given a strong signal to Japanese producers that the EC was prepared to use all the policy instruments at its disposal to discourage imports from third countries.[43]

Seven months earlier, in July 1989, a much discussed origin rule for integrated circuits had been adopted by the Commission. This rule states that the country of origin is that in which the etching of silicon wafers takes place. Previously, the 'last substantial process' rule used implied that IC assembly operations were sufficient to confer EC origin on ICs. This new rule also was targeted mainly at Japanese firms. Since 1987, Japanese IC producers had been under investigation in antidumping cases concerning DRAM and EPROM memory chips. The major Japanese IC manufacturers operated IC plants in the EC, but these plants engaged in assembly. Without the new rule of origin, EC-assembled ICs would normally be considered to be of EC origin, and antidumping duties could have been easily avoided by increasing EC assembly activities.

As it happened, no antidumping duties were levied in the DRAM and EPROM cases, although undertakings were concluded which set minimum prices for Japanese IC exports to the EC. But the rule did give Japanese firms compelling reasons to extend EC operations to include the wafer etching stage. Japanese manufacturers of products such as copiers and VCRs needed to clear local content requirements, and this led to a growing demand for ICs which could be considered of EC, or at least non-Japanese, origin. With the new rule, only ICs produced at integrated manufacturing plants could satisfy this demand. In response, all major Japanese manufacturers (NEC, Fujitsu, Hitachi, Toshiba, and Mitsubishi) announced the extension of EC operations to include wafer etching or the establishment of new integrated plants. It is estimated that cumulative investment in Japanese IC manufacturing plants in the EC amounted to 3 billion ECUs by 1991.[44]

The antidumping actions against assembly plants also led to demand for other EC-made components, such as printed circuit boards, power supply units, tuners, capacitors, magnetic heads, and the like. Such demand for EC-produced components also came from Japanese CTV producers, for whom EC origin enabled exports from bases in Germany and the UK to Spain,

Italy, and France, which maintained national quotas for CTV imports labelled 'Japanese'. In some other cases, mainly in telecommunications, European origin was necessary to receive favourable treatment under public procurement schemes (Flamm 1990).

Japanese manufacturers of electronics products (including semi-finished products such as printed circuit boards) in the EC thus have been eager to procure components of EC origin. This has been an important reason for Japanese manufacturers of electronic components to follow Japanese assembly firms in setting up EC manufacturing activities. Major Japanese components suppliers such as Alps, Murata, Tabuchi, and Tamura, which are important suppliers of components to Japanese electronics firms in Japan, set up or expanded manufacturing activities in the EC first of all to supply Japanese firms.[45] Table 1.11 witnesses the rapid increase in EC operations of Japanese components manufacturers during 1986–1991. Kyocera, which did not have any presence in the EC in 1986, became the

Table 1.11 Japanese electronic components suppliers in the EC

Company	Plant location	Products	EC employment	
			1991	1986
Kyocera/AVX	UK, G, Fr	Ceramic components, capacitors	1,866	29
Alps	UK, G, Ire	Keyboards, tuners, switches, magnetic heads	1,146	329
TDK	G, Lux	Audiocassettes, coils, magnets	1,210	180
Murata Electronic	UK, G	Condensers, filters, resistors	730	na
Tabuchi	UK	Power supply units	520	190
Munekata	UK, Ire	Plastic moulded parts	413	0
Nitto Denko	Bel	Insulating tapes	398	274
Tamura	UK	Power supply units, transformers	312	0
Mitsumi	UK, Ire	Coils, tuners, switches	234	5
SMK	UK	Keyboard switches, remote controls	178	13
Terasaki	UK	Power switch boards	160	0
Nihon CMK	Bel	Printed circuit boards	140	0
JST	UK, G, Fr	Connectors	104	0
Teikoku	Neth	Switches, resistors	40	0

Note: Letters indicate country of investment: G (Germany), Bel (Belgium), Fr (France), Ire (Ireland), Neth (Netherlands), Lux (Luxembourg).

Sources: Touyou Keizai (1987a, 1992a), Nihon Denshi Kikai Kougyoukai (1992a).

largest manufacturer in the EC among Japanese components firms through the acquisition of US-based AVX, which had substantial European operations (see also Section 1.4.3). Alps, TDK, and Murata grew rapidly by investing in greenfield plants, while a number of smaller components firms set up their first manufacturing plants in the EC.

Besides the investments of dedicated components firms, Japanese electronics assemblers increased in-house production of key components in the EC. Matsushita, for instance, chose this route more than other Japanese firms, and operates EC plants manufacturing magnetrons for microwave ovens, transformers, relays, electric motors for office equipment, and magnetic heads. It has also set up a large joint venture with Siemens in passive components. The relation between local content policy and Japanese firms' investment in EC components production has in some cases been apparent. For instance, Sony started production of optical pick-ups, a core component of CD players, in France in late 1989, in anticipation of the application of the assembly plant amendment to CD player plants. The threat of antidumping action did not materialise here because the GATT panel ruling in 1990 precluded new measures against assembly plants.

Trends in investment in the EC by company will be discussed in more detail in Section 1.4. Chapter 8 provides a more detailed analysis of EC local content regulations and Japanese firms' response, as revealed by data on EC affiliates' sales and procurement behaviour.

1.3.4 Trade Policy Trends in the 1990s

Recent trends in antidumping actions in the early 1990s on the one hand show that the use of antidumping measures against Japanese electronics imports has not been abating much. On the other hand, several antidumping actions were revoked, while the target of antidumping actions in the electronics industry has shifted to other Asian firms. The major new antidumping cases are discussed below.

Electronics scales and aluminium capacitors In 1990, EC producers petitioned for a review of the antidumping case against Japanese imports of electronic scales, as the measure was about to expire (not shown in Table 1.4). The Commission concluded that EC producers were still being injured by Japanese imports and replaced the existing duties and undertakings with higher duties (15–31.6 per cent). In addition, the Commission started an investigation into the alleged dumping of electronic weighing scales from South Korea and Singapore in 1992. This investigation resulted in the imposition of duties as well. At least two of the exporters subject to dumping duties were Japanese firms: Ishida Scale (South Korea) and Teraoka (Singapore). On top of this, the Commission started an 'anti-absorption' investigation concerning imports of scales from Japan in 1994. In accordance with a 1988 amendment to the EC antidumping law, exporters who fail to increase prices after antidumping duties are levied can be subject to further (retroactive) antidumping duties. The anticipation of renewed trade policy actions appears to have given Japanese firms new incentives to invest. Teraoka set up an assembly plant for electronic scales in the UK in 1989 (JETRO 1993b) and Ishida Scale followed suit (Denshi Keizai Kenkyuujo 1993d: 103).[46]

Two new antidumping cases were initiated in 1991 (see Table 1.4), of which the microdisk case was discussed above. The other Japanese product targeted was aluminium electrolytic capacitors. This was the first antidumping action since the DRAM and EPROM cases which concerned electronic components. (Capacitors are components used in electronics goods such as televisions, VCRs, and personal computers.) The definitive duties levied in December 1992 ranged between 12 and 75 per cent. Philips was the main complainant, while Siemens, which had transferred its condenser and capacitor manufacturing activity to a large joint venture with Matsushita, did not join the complaint.

CD players, typewriters, DOT matrix printers, and colour televisions Also in 1991, Japanese firms exporting CD players to the EC were the target of further antidumping actions. In April, Philips, the major EC producer of CD players, filed an antidumping petition against imports from South East Asian countries (Malaysia, Taiwan, and Singapore). The petition was specifically directed against exports originating from Japanese plants in those countries. Furthermore, in July Philips filed another antidumping petition against imports from Japan under the 'anti-absorption' amendment, alleging that Japanese firms had not increased prices in response to the imposition of definitive duties in 1989. These events led the Commission to start a full scale review of the case in December 1991.[47] However, in July 1993, before the Commission had reached a conclusion, Philips withdrew all outstanding petitions. The reason for this was remarkable. Philips announced that it planned to stop all production of CD players in the EC and transfer production to South-East Asia by the end of 1993. This meant there was no 'Community industry' left to protect against dumped imports. Philips itself would become an important importer of CD players into the EC. Almost ten years of protection in the form of tariffs and antidumping duties eventually resulted in a wholly Asian-owned EC CD player industry.

Similar observations can be made for the electronic typewriter industry. In 1990, the impending expiry of antidumping duties on electronic typewriters led EC firms Rank Xerox, Olivetti, and Triumph–Adler to petition for a review. This time it was the Commission that finally decided not to extend or renew duties, and antidumping measures were allowed to lapse in June 1993. The main reason for not extending antidumping measures was that two of the EC firms, of which Olivetti was one, had transferred a large part of production to South-East Asia. Production in the EC by EC firms had fallen, but this could not be attributed to imports from Japan, which did not take more than 7 per cent of the market. EC firms showed a healthy profitability on typewriter sales, and it could not be sustained that Japanese imports were causing injury to the EC industry. As in the CD player case, antidumping actions have not been very effective in keeping production by EC firms in the EC, but have instead led to substantial Japanese manufacturing activities.[48]

The third industry for which antidumping actions have not been extended is dot matrix printers. In this case, EC firms did not ask for a review and antidumping measures for Japanese imports expired in November 1993. Again, antidumping actions had resulted in sharply reduced imports from Japan and substantial Japanese production in the EC. Another factor in the lapse of antidumping protection was the rapid decline in sales of dot matrix printers. The EC market for such printers reached only 3 million units in 1993, down from 4.2 million in 1992. Dot matrix printers are being displayed by inkjet and laser printers which have rapidly come down in price.

In the above cases, growth in EC manufacturing operations in tandem with declining imports from Japan have apparently taken Japan off the list of antidumping targets. In general, the trend in the 1990s has been one of a shift in the target of antidumping actions from Japan to other South-East Asian countries (and sometimes to Japanese transplants there). The 1992 CTV case is illustrative. In July 1992, EC television producers (Philips with its related companies, Thomson, Nokia, and Seleco of Italy) alleged that colour television imports from Japan, several South-East Asian countries (Malaysia, China, South Korea, Singapore, and Thailand), and Turkey were being dumped in the EC, and they lodged an antidumping complaint. The Commission decided to investigate the complaint but only after taking Japan off the list, stressing that imports from Japan were too small to cause injury.[49] The two most important Japanese producers, Sony and Matsushita, had completed the transfer of production for EC markets to their EC plants and were not affected by the antidumping action. Other Japanese firms, such as Sharp, Sanyo, and Hitachi, which were still exporting to the EC from plants in South East Asia, subsequently announced that they would transfer all Asian production for the EC market to their EC plants as well.[50] In September 1994 the Commission imposed provisional duties, and in March 1995 definitive duties (ranging from 0 to 29.8 per cent).[51] The highest duties were imposed on South Korean firms exporting from their home country as well as from plants in other South-East Asian countries.

Antidumping against other Asian firms The first major cases against other Asian firms were the 1987 VCR case, which mainly targeted South Korean producers, and the CD player case, initiated in the same year, which involved South Korean exports as well as exports from Japan. Since then South Korean firms, but also electronics firms based in Taiwan, Hong Kong, China, and other Asian countries, have found themselves subject to an increasing number of antidumping actions. South Korean and Hong Kong firms exporting videotapes were the target of an antidumping action in 1987. In 1988 there was an antidumping action against imports of small screen televisions involving Hong Kong, South Korean, and Chinese firms. Taiwanese and Chinese firms were involved in the 1989 audiocassette tapes case. During 1990–1993, no less than eight antidumping investigations were initiated covering electronics imports from South-East Asian countries: videocassette tapes (1990, China), car radios (1990, South Korea), DRAMs (1991, South Korea), microdisks (1991, Taiwan and China), microdisks (1992, South Korea and Hong Kong), aluminium electrolytic capacitors (1993, South Korea and Taiwan), microwave ovens (1993, South Korea, China, Thailand, Malaysia), and VCRs (South Korea and Singapore, 1995). All cases against non-Japanese Asian firms resulted in the imposition of duties, except the VCR case which is still under investigation.

The 1993 microwave oven case and the 1995 VCR case best illustrate the shift in EC antidumping actions. The microwave oven antidumping petition, launched by EC producers Thomson, Moulinex, Candy (Italy), and AEG (Germany), focused mainly on exports by South Korean firms producing in their home country and in other Asian countries. Provisional duties ranging from 4.8 to 32.8 per cent were imposed in July 1995.[52] South Korean firms became a natural target for antidumping actions after Japanese firms had come to produce most of the ovens for the EC market in Europe. Imports from Japan had by 1994 declined to 5 per cent of the market, and not one Japanese firm was involved in this antidumping case.

The 1995 VCR case likewise targeted South Korean firms. In April 1995, the Commission decided to investigate a complaint filed by Philips alleging dumping of VCRs from South Korea and Singapore as well as key components of video recorders (scanners and heads) from South Korea.[53] Two features makes this a rather unique case. It is the first case since the 'screwdriver' plant cases of 1987–1989 in which existing assembly plants of Asian firms were targeted in an antidumping action. The EC had in the meantime introduced a new anti-circumvention rule in the December 1994 revision of antidumping law, based on the new post-Uruguay Round GATT code on antidumping.[54] However, application of this law may not have been very effective in this case. South Korean firms had been producing VCRs since 1987, which would make it more difficult to prove that EC assembly activities were circumventing antidumping measures on imported VCRs. More important, the new anti-circumvention rule, while maintaining the 60/

40 per cent of the value of components criterion of the 1987 amendment, also stipulates that assembly shall never be considered as circumvention if the value added of the plant exceeds 25 per cent of sales value. The South Korean plants were likely to be in reach of this threshold. Instead, inclusion of major components in the antidumping case would certainly affect VCRs assembled by South Korean firms in the European Union, since South Korean firms mainly export scanners and heads to their existing European assembly plants.[55]

A second feature of the 1995 VCR case is a rare alignment of firms. Apart from Philips, the main beneficiaries of an antidumping action would be Japanese firms, which by 1994 were producing more than 4 million units annually in the EC. In contrast, the antidumping complaint specifically targeted imports from Singapore by the other major European consumer electronics firm, Thomson.[56] Thomson, which until the end of 1991 had produced VCRs in a joint venture with JVC in Berlin, pulled out of this arrangement in 1992 and transferred production to a Singaporean joint venture with Toshiba (see also Strange 1993: 303).[57]

The recent shift in the target of antidumping actions as illustrated above reflects an increased internationalisation of production by Japanese (and recently South Korean) firms, which have relocated production to South East Asia. It also reflects the increased competitiveness and technological sophistication of Asian firms, in particular South Korean companies. Asian firms furthermore benefited from the restrictions that earlier antidumping measures had put on Japanese firms. A rapid increase in market share at the cost of Japanese and EC firms has often been the result.

Broadcasting cameras and the copier case review On the other hand, two other recent antidumping cases show that Japanese firms are not yet invulnerable to EC antidumping actions. The Commission initiated a review of the plain paper photocopier case in August 1992, after it received a petition from EC producers (Oce of Holland, Rank Xerox of the UK, and Olivetti of Italy) to impose new duties. The Commission took more than three years to examine the case (during which the existing duties remained in force) and in October 1995 found that dumped imports from Japan were still injuring EC producers. It decided to extend the existing duties for another two years and in addition widened the scope of the duties to some types of high speed copiers.

It has been reported that the Council of Ministers, which in almost all previous antidumping cases had endorsed the Commission's decisions, voted to impose duties with the smallest majority possible (eight to seven). It appears that the ministers of the new EC member states Sweden, Austria, and Finland, countries which before their entry in the EC had been target rather than initiators of antidumping actions, voted against the measure.[58] The Council's vote indicates that extension of the copier duties was controversial. Extending existing duties, determined seven years earlier, rather than imposing new duties, which would have been more suited to the changed circumstances, appears to have been a compromise solution necessary to gain a majority in the Council. The extension of duties implies that EC producers will by 1997 have enjoyed protection against Japanese imports for ten years. Two questions could be raised: whether it was imports from Japan that had been causing the injury to EC producers, and whether the existing measures had been effective. On the latter count, the evidence was not strong. The EC industry, which held 15.4 per cent of the EC market in unit terms in 1988, had seen its market share decline to 12.6 per cent by 1992. In the low-end segment of the copier market, where Japanese firms' position in strongest, Oce had virtually no production, as was the case in 1985. Olivetti, the second EC firm, was now producing all its copiers in an Italian joint venture with the major Japanese copier manufacturer Canon, while the latter firm was still subject to antidumping duties on its imports from Japan. The third and by far largest EC producer, Rank Xerox, holds a 35 per cent share of the Japanese copier market through a Japanese joint venture with Fuji Film (Yano Keizai Kenkyuujo 1994a). Thus one could well argue that there was no production to protect for the first producer, that the second did not need protection since it conspired with one of the major Japanese firms accused of the dumping, while the third firm did not need any protection given its dominant position in Japan. Moreover, the combined production of the firms had declined despite antidumping protection. In contrast, Japanese firms' production in the EC, not considered part of the 'EC industry' for antidumping purposes, had increased to 49 per cent of the EC market by 1992, while imports from Japan had declined from 38 per cent in 1988 to 26 per cent.

The Commission found evidence that Japanese firms had continued dumping practices even while the existing antidumping measures had been in effect. However, it was obvious that most of the distress of EC firms was caused by sales coming from Japanese factories in the EC, by their sheer quantity. The Commission, however, argued in the same way as in the audiocassette tape and microdisk cases: that imports covering 26 per cent of the market (in 1992) were still substantial enough to cause injury such that antidumping action was justified. The Commission could argue this because the 'material' injury criterion of the GATT antidumping code implies that the dumped imports do not have to be the principal cause of the industry's distress, they just have to contribute to the injury to an extent that is 'not insubstantial'.

It was clear that an extension of the duties was not likely to help the EC firms much since the major threat to EC firms' profitability were EC-produced Japanese copiers, and these operations could be expanded if necessary.[59] The Commission conceded that the major effect of the antidumping action had been to induce Japanese manufacturing activity in the EC:

Although the anti-dumping duties may not have been the only reason for this strongly increased Japanese production in the Community, it can hardly be doubted that they did significantly influenced this development.[60]

Before antidumping duties are levied, EC antidumping law requires that the Commission tests whether the imposition of such duties is in the 'Community interest'. This concept is not defined in detail in the law, and it has been argued that the Commission in practice equates Community interest with the interests of the complainant producers (Van Bael 1990a). In the copier case, the justification offered for extension of duties as in the Community interest was based not so much on the favourable effects on EC firms, but on the effect on Japanese inward investment. The Commission explicitly stated that expiry of the antidumping measure might lead Japanese firms to divest in the EC and shift production back to Japan or to South-East Asian countries, since cost considerations alone would probably warrant the latter transfer.

As a result, the economic advantages of producing small and relatively simple PPCs (plain paper copiers) in third countries with low labour costs, rather than in the Community where most Japanese companies produce them now, would become more alluring.[61]

The relocation of production to Asia would have a negative impact on EC employment as well as on EC suppliers of copier parts. While the Commission might well have been right in this assessment, the justification given reflects a concern of industrial policy, i.e. to develop an integrated EC copier industry aided by inward investment, rather than issues with which antidumping policy should primarily be concerned, i.e. protecting domestic industries against injurious dumping. Japanese firms, meanwhile, will again have noted that only complete relocation of production to the EC market can give them the certainty of relief from antidumping actions.

A second major case targeting Japanese exports involved television broadcasting cameras. In March 1993, the EC Commission started investigating a complaint lodged by Philips and Thomson that Japanese producers were dumping broadcasting and some professional television cameras systems in the EC. In October 1993 the Commission levied provisional duties, and in April 1994 definitive duties, ranging from 52.7 to 96.8 per cent. The Commission found dumping margins of up to 100 per cent and substantial price undercutting by Japanese firms. It accused Japanese firms of intending to drive EC firms out of an industry of crucial importance to future technological developments such as high definition television.[62]

Japanese firms as 'insiders'? Considering the extent of Japanese firms' EC production in a range of electronics industries, one could expect Japanese firms to join EC firms in antidumping petitions targeting imports by other Asian firms. A precedent was established in 1987, when the VCR joint venture of Japan Victor (JVC) and Thomson joined the dumping complaint against South Korean and two small Japanese exporters (Funai and Orion). However, the experience in recent cases shows that Japanese firms are still reluctant to use the same antidumping instrument that has been used against them so often. In none of the cases against South East Asian imports mentioned above has a Japanese firm been a complainant, although Japanese firms were in several cases beneficiaries of antidumping actions.

The 1993 microwave oven case is illustrative. Two of the complainants in the case, AEG of Germany and Thomson of France, operated a joint plant with Toshiba in France, their only production base in the EC. Toshiba, however, did not join in the petition, and, for reasons which may or may not have been related to the antidumping case, divested from the venture just after the initiation of the investigation. Toshiba and other Japanese producers may have given their tacit, informal support to the antidumping action, but Japanese firms clearly do not want to be seen as users of the antidumping instrument. They may be reluctant to be seen as acting against the interests of South-East Asian firms, because of their substantial manufacturing operations and sales in South-East Asian countries. If they can find an EC firm to do the petitioning for them, they will be able to maintain an image of championing free trade.[63] On the other hand, they may fear that use of the antidumping instrument leads to a deterioration in relations with the Commission and national governments, hurting their general interests in the EC. The behaviour of Japanese firms clearly contrasts with that of US firms such as Motorola, a petitioner in two antidumping petitions against Japanese firms. This suggests that Japanese firms may still have some way to go in reaching the status of 'insiders' in the EC.

1.3.5 Antidumping, DFI, and Industrial Policy

The analysis of the relationship between trade policy and Japanese electronics firms' investment in the EC gives strong support for the view that an important motive for manufacturing DFI by Japanese electronics firms in the EC has been to 'jump' trade barriers. The correspondence between plant establishments and trade policy measures shows that the timing of DFI has been governed by trade policy, while the evidence is suggestive that the level of investment has increased as well. This issue is addressed extensively in Chapter 6. The statistical test developed there confirms that EC antidumping as well as other trade policy measures have induced substantial additional Japanese manufacturing investment.

It is also clear that DFI has been taking place without overt trade policy measures. In some cases, such as facsimiles, the threat of import restrictions has been important, and DFI appears to have been undertaken to pre-empt trade policy measures. In general, Japanese firms have accepted the need to localise production as part of their commitment to become 'insiders' in the

EC market. It is fair to say that locational advantages of manufacturing in the EC have increased *vis-à-vis* Japan as well. Japanese firms' experience in managing manufacturing operations, the sharp appreciation of the yen, advances in automation and flexible manufacturing techniques, and the need to adapt products quickly to rapidly changing local consumer demands have made EC production more attractive. However, several of these factors have made production in South-East Asia even more attractive than production in the EC (or the US). Antidumping actions and trade policy threats may rather cause a shift of production from South-East Asia to the EC, as was clearly shown, for instance, in the 1993 CTV case.

Two issues that have not been dealt with in this chapter so far are the rationale for antidumping practice and the consequences of dumping by Japanese firms. Some would argue that antidumping measures should be considered not as trade policy measures but as mere administrative safeguards allowed by GATT to impede foreign firms from driving European firms out of the market through 'unfair' competition.[64] The main line of reasoning is that dumping by Japanese firms occurs so frequently because they are able to charge high prices in 'sanctuary markets' in Japan to which foreign firms for various reasons have no real access. Profits in Japan can be used to subsidise the advance in export markets. This as such constitutes 'unfair' competition, since EC or US firms do not have the same strategic option. Serious consequences arise if the behaviour of Japanese firms is 'predatory', i.e. intended to establish dominance in electronics industries by forcing EC and US firms to exit from the market. Once this dominance is established, Japanese firms may exploit their dominant position by charging higher prices for industrial users and consumers. Attacking the 'sanctuary markets' in Japan, for instance through a form of international competition law, would be desirable, but in the absence of international agreement about this, antidumping action is the only instrument available to deal with these problems.

The question to what extent Japanese firms have been able to use 'sanctuary markets' to sustain low prices abroad is not an easy one to answer. Indeed, there have in the past been cases of markedly higher prices for consumer electronics in Japan, which could be ascribed to the market power Japanese firms possess through their size and control over wholesaling and retailing networks in Japan (Van Marion 1992, Holmes, Belderbos, and Smith 1992). For instance, prolonged dumping of CTVs was obviously taking place in the US in the 1960s and early 1970s. Prices in Japan were substantially higher than in export markets, because the major Japanese firms prevented price competition on their home market through collusion and their control over vast networks of captive retail outlets. Informal agreements on production and prices under the auspices of the Electronics Industries Association of Japan were recorded at least until the mid-1970s.[65] Chapter 2 discusses the 1970s colour television case in more detail and argues that Japanese firms' behaviour did call for government intervention.

Since the latter half of the 1980s, a few cases have come to light of Japanese electronics firms' attempts to maintain high prices in the Japanese market. For instance, the Japan Fair Trade Commission (FTC), the government institution charged with enforcing the Japanese Anti-Monopoly Law, in March 1992 alleged that four of the major Japanese consumer electronics firms had over the previous years attempted to stop independent retailers from discounting their products too much.[66] It is not clear whether this was a concerted effort, nor whether the firms' pressure had been effective. In markets where government procurement is important, the FTC has found more evidence of collusion. In one case the FTC concluded that several Japanese electronics firms, including Sony, had pre-arranged bids to supply large liquid crystal display screens to sports stadiums. In another case, nine electrical equipment manufactures, including the three large integrated electronics firms (Hitachi, Toshiba, and Mitsubishi), were found to have engaged in bid rigging on orders from the Japan Sewage Work Agency and on orders for the construction of nuclear power plants for Japan's electric power companies (see the *Daily Yomiuru*, 9 March 1995).

In some industries that have been subject to antidumping action abroad, Japanese firms can be considered relatively shielded from (foreign) competition on their home markets. In broadcasting cameras, one of the two Japanese firms dominating the world market, Ikegami Tsushinki, historically has had a virtually captive market for its sales to Japan's national broadcaster NHK. In private telephone switching systems (private branch exchanges or PBX), subject to US antidumping duties since 1989, 66 per cent of 1993 procurements by major Japanese companies has been reported to come from other firms within the horizontal *keiretsu*.[67]

On the other hand, price competition in Japan, in particular in the consumer electronics sector, has continued to intensify in the late 1980s and 1990s. Sales of consumer electronics through manufacturer-related retailers has declined to about 50 per cent of the market, while the market share of discounters and OEM sales by general retailers has been increasing (see also Mackintosh-BIS 1991 and Dodwell 1993). As early as 1988, a joint price survey by MITI and the US Department of Commerce found that the price level in the US of a large number of Japanese electronics products was on average 10 per cent higher than prices for these products in Japan (Kokusai Kakaku Kouzou Kenkyuujo 1992). This suggests that dumping in the form of price discrimination is not a systematic characteristic of Japanese firms' business strategy at present.

There are several reasons why it can be argued that antidumping law and practice have been used not to deal with predatory pricing and the abuse of advantages derived from sanctuary markets, but rather to erect barriers to any form of foreign competition. One reason is that antidumping law disallows practices that are accepted and in line with normal business behaviour if they concern domestic transactions. Price differences between exports and domestic sales, where they are not too large, may be related to differences in market conditions such as consumer preferences and associated price elasticities. For example, considerable price differences have also been reported for consumer electronics goods in different EC member states (Holmes and Cawson 1993). Prices that are below full cost may occur as part of normal business behaviour in capital intensive, fixed cost industries in times of overcapacity. Below-cost pricing, as opposed to below-*marginal*-cost pricing, is behaviour that is in most cases acceptable by domestic anti-trust standards.[68] Hence, price discrimination and below-cost pricing are strategies open to firms in domestic (or intra-EC) transactions, but they are punishable by antidumping actions if it involves cross-border trade. There appears no real justification for the application of such different standards.[69] The broad applicability of antidumping law makes it an instrument that can be used against competitive imports rather than against anti-competitive behaviour.

A second line of argument, taken by most observers of antidumping practice, is that the frequent findings of dumping by the EC and US antidumping authorities cannot be accepted as proof that (Japanese) firms did actually engage in dumping. It is alleged that antidumping procedures are biased towards a finding of dumping (Van Bael and Bellis 1990, Hindley 1988, Finger 1992, Messerlin 1989, Eymann and Schuknecht 1992, Bell 1987). A particularly large bias occurs in EC dumping margin calculations involving the larger Japanese electronics firms, because of a calculation method the Commission uses in case the firms accused of dumping are integrated into wholesaling and retailing.[70] This specific calculation method was introduced in the 1984 electronic typewriter case, the first case targeting the large Japanese electronics firms.

In addition, it can be pointed out that the 'sanctuary market' explanation of dumping is not supported by the evidence in a number of antidumping cases involving Japanese firms. In some cases, the Commission did not use prices in Japan for comparison with export prices because the former were judged to be below full production costs (see e.g. Bell 1987). This was found to be the case, for instance, for several manufacturers of copiers and DRAMs. Below-cost pricing in Japan is distinctly different from the standard dumping case with artificially high prices in Japan and is at odds with the dumping story where profits on domestic sales subsidise exports. In some other cases, antidumping actions targeted smaller Japanese firms which lack important sales in Japan but focus almost exclusively on exports (such as Funai and Orion in VCRs). In yet two other cases, the EC producers receiving protection were actually important players in the Japanese market (Rank Xerox in copiers and Motorola in mobile phones).

In most comprehensive assessments of antidumping practice, such as

Boltuck and Litan (1991) and Finger (1992), it is concluded that antidumping measures are administered in such a way that they effectively serve as a 'safeguard clause': if a domestic industry finds itself fighting a heavy battle against increased imports, it is almost sure to find relief in antidumping.

A feature specific to the EC antidumping system as opposed to the US antidumping system is that there is an important element of policy discretion in the procedures (see Section 6.2.2). For instance, the EC has discretion in determining the level of duties (whereas in the US antidumping system duties are equal to the calculated dumping margin), and deciding whether to grant foreign importers undertakings and whether sanctions against importers are in the interest of the European Community (whereas duties apply automatically in case of dumping and injury in the US). There is evidence that the Commission has used its discretion to let the antidumping instrument deal with the 'Japan problem': the advance of Japanese firms in high technology markets of the EC, the relative weakness of EC firms, and the increasing bilateral trade deficit.

The EC has certainly used its discretionary power to disfavour Japanese firms by refusing to accept undertakings. Undertakings are less harmful for exporters since exporters do not have to pay duties and can reap extra revenues from agreed price increases. An empirical study of undertakings in EC antidumping procedures (Tharakan 1991a) found evidence of discretionary power: factors such as the state of the trade balance and the economic power of the complaining EC producers appeared to influence the decision process. An illustrative example is the case of hydraulic excavators, in which the Commission merely mentioned the 'current state of relations with Japan' to reject undertaking offers from Japanese exporters (Bellis 1990: 53). Messerlin (1989) stresses that, while the Commission has frequently allowed undertakings, it typically has not done so in cases where Japanese firms were involved. This is clearly the case for antidumping in electronics as shown in Table 1.3.[71] The major cases in which undertakings were allowed were those of DRAMs and EPROMs, where the Commission feared that price increases brought about by duties would harm EC semiconductor users. Undertakings were also preferred over new duties in the enforcement of the 'screwdriver plant' amendment, presumably because they could be instrumental in increasing the local content of Japanese manufacturing activities. In almost all other cases, the Commission rejected undertakings and imposed duties.

It also appears that the Commission has used the antidumping instrument as an instrument of industrial policy (see GATT 1993). Eymann and Schuknecht (1992), in an empirical study of EC antidumping decisions, found that antidumping duties are more likely to be levied if industrial policy considerations are in play. The role of industrial policy considerations may also become apparent by examining the Commission's reasoning why antidumping duties were deemed in the interest of the European

Community. The most illustrative case is that of DRAMs. The Commission argued that price undertakings were necessary because:

The semiconductor industry, of which DRAM production is a part, is a strategic industry in that semiconductors are a key component for the data processing, telecommunications and automotive industries. . . . A viable Community DRAM industry will provide alternative sources of supply to the Community electronics industry, thereby reducing dependence on the dominant Japanese producers of DRAMs.[72]

In other antidumping cases, similar arguments were brought forward by the Commission. In the case of copiers, the Commission was of the opinion that:

The photocopier industry will continue to form a key part in the office equipment industry as a whole and that the retention and development of the technology currently employed will be essential for the development of future reprographic products . . . a definitive antidumping duty is required to ensure the continued existence of at least certain of the remaining Community PPC (plain paper copier) producers with the consequent benefits to the Community of employment, technological expertise and local source of supply.[73]

In case of audiocassette tapes, the antidumping duties were meant to:

create conditions to allow the Community industry to increase its sale quantities, through which it could obtain economies of scale and reductions in cost, which in turn could be passed on to the consumer.[74]

The economies of scale argument for protection could have been based directly on the strategic trade policy literature (e.g. Krugman 1984). In the case of microdisks, the Commission argued:

Should this industry be forced to cease production, the Community would be rendered almost entirely dependent on third countries in a sector of growing technological importance. Moreover, this could have serious consequences for the Community manufacturers of components for 3.5 inch microdisks.[75]

It has to be recalled that the 'Community industry' in the audio tape and microdisk cases consisted of EC-owned 'indigenous' producers only. In both cases, however, Japanese firms' production in the EC had almost reached the production level of EC-owned producers. The review of the copier case resulted in an extension of duties although Japanese firms' plants produced roughly four times as much as the EC firms, and supplied almost half of the EC market (in unit terms).

On the one hand, it appears that the EC has been willing to protect troubled EC 'champions' such as Agfa/BASF, Philips, Thomson, and Olivetti against competition from Japanese and other Asian firms. The extent of protection offered by antidumping measures to some of these firms is remarkable. Philips, the Dutch consumer electronics group, was involved in no fewer than 11 out of 19 antidumping cases listed in Table 1.3, and in 16 out of 29 cases against Asian imports during 1982–1995, while Thomson of France petitioned in at least 8 cases.[76]

On the other hand, the experience with a range of antidumping actions described above (CD players, typewriters, copiers, and to a lesser extent VCRs) shows that fostering EC-owned firms by using the antidumping instrument does not necessarily create a viable EC-owned industry. What several antidumping actions have certainly fostered is a Japanese-owned EC industry. Hence at the same time antidumping actions, followed by local content requirements and stricter rules of origin, appear to have been used opportunistically to revive the EC electronics industry with Japanese plants, know-how, and components.[77] The copier case review clearly shows that the Commission considered Japanese investments in the EC, with its positive effect on growth in the EC parts industry, as the main contribution of antidumping duties to the 'Community interest'. One could interpret the Commission's decision to maintain antidumping duties as driven by this sole factor, since it was obvious that the effect on EC firms' position would be rather small.

The copier case review, and the more recent VCR case in which Philips attacked imports by Thomson, have focused attention on the effectiveness of EC antidumping policy in globalised industries and the rationale for protecting some EC producers against others. There have been calls from within the Commission, in particular since the entry of Sweden, Finland, and Austria, for a re-evaluation of the EC antidumping system and a tightening of the conditions for its use.[78] The new antidumping regulation adopted in 1994 provides for more transparent procedures which may remove a part of the bias in dumping and injury calculations (Bronckers 1995), although it is too early to tell what difference the new regulation will make in practice. More significant is the apparently increased opposition by a number of member states to the use of antidumping actions as seen in the copier case and in several other recent cases.[79] This development may put further practical restrictions on the use of EC antidumping without any formal change to antidumping law. However, some fundamental issues, such as the rationale for disallowing importing firms certain pricing behaviour, which is established and accepted practice for domestically operating firms, have not yet been addressed. It will take another round of negotiations in the World Trade Organisation (WTO) to change the basis of current antidumping practice.

1.4 Japanese Electronics Firms' DFI in the EC

This section describes patterns of Japanese electronics firms' investments in the EC by country, product group, and company. Section 1.4.1 presents a detailed picture of Japanese subsidiaries and employment in 1986 and 1990 based on a comprehensive database of Japanese affiliates in Europe. Sections 1.4.2–1.4.4 focus on specific characteristics of Japanese investments: modes of entry into the EC market (1.4.2), the adoption of pan-EC strategies (1.4.3) and the importance of Japanese investment relative to EC industry and Japanese firms' global presence (1.4.4). Finally, Section 1.4.5 looks at patterns of investment in the 1990s.

1.4.1 Manufacturing and Sales Subsidiaries in the EC in 1990

Tables 1.7–1.10 show employment and subsidiaries in the EC in 1986 and 1990 by country and product group. The figures represent the situation around May of each year. The subsidiaries are classified according to activity (manufacturing or sales[80]) and product group: consumer electronics (including microwave ovens), industrial electronics and office automation equipment, and components (including ICs). The main source of information is Touyou Keizai (1987a and 1991a), which provides a near complete listing of Japanese subsidiaries abroad.[81] Only subsidiaries in which Japanese firms hold an equity stake of more than 40 per cent are included in the tables.

Manufacturing subsidiaries Table 1.12 shows the location of Japanese electronics firms' manufacturing subsidiaries in the EC in 1990 and 1986. The total number of subsidiaries in the EC grew by 141 per cent in 1986–1990, from 70 in 1986 to 169 in 1990. The number of components subsidiaries grew by 234 per cent and surpassed the number of subsidiaries in consumer electronics in 1990. The number of subsidiaries producing industrial electronics increased by almost 200 per cent, while consumer electronics subsidiaries increased by 76 per cent. The pattern of manufacturing investment has clearly shifted from consumer electronics to industrial electronics and components in the second half of the 1980s.

The distribution over products (not shown in Table 1.12) in 1990 is closely related to EC trade policy measures, which in turn reflect to an important extent Japanese firms' export strength and competitiveness. Manufacturing plants are in operations for CTVs, VCRs, microwave ovens, CD players, car audio, audio and video tapes, typewriters, PC printers, copiers, facsimiles, car telephones, DRAMs, and various components for office automation equipment and consumer electronics (magnetrons for microwave ovens, power sources, transformers, switches, connectors, printed circuit boards, capacitors, condensers, magnetic heads for VCRs). The above list covers the larger majority of Japanese manufacturing plants in 1990.

By country, the UK is by far the most important host of Japanese DFI, attracting 38 per cent of all subsidiaries. Factors promoting investment in

Table 1.12 Japanese manufacturing subsidiaries in the EC in 1990 and 1986, by country

Country	1990				1986
	Cons	Indu	Compo	All (%)	All (%)
UK	28	13	32	64 (38)	21 (30)
Germany	4	9	16	38 (22)	23 (33)
France	15	9	7	26 (15)	6 (9)
Spain	6	2	4	9 (5)	7 (10)
Italy	3	5	3	8 (5)	1 (1)
Holland	0	4	3	6 (4)	2 (3)
Belgium	10	4	6	11 (7)	6 (9)
Ireland	0	0	6	6 (4)	4 (6)
Denmark	0	1	0	1 (1)	0 (0)
Total	66	47	77	169 (100)	70 (100)
1986 (% increase)	38 (76)	16 (193)	23 (234)	70 (141)	

Notes: Cons = consumer electronics, Indu = industrial electronics, Compo = electronic components. Multiple classification is possible if a subsidiary manufactures products in more than one product group; consequently the sum of the number of subsidiaries in cons, indu, and compo can be greater than the total number of subsidiaries. Figures represent subsidiaries with manufacturing function; these may be combined with sales functions.

Source: calculations based on Touyou Keizai (1991a, 1987a).

the UK are its large home market, the accessible English language, business attitudes and culture which are similar to those in the US, where Japanese firms have gained experience in operating manufacturing plants, and the forthcoming attitude of national and local governments, which have actively invited (and subsidised) Japanese investors. The relative attractiveness of the UK only seems to be increasing, as its share has increased by 8 percentage points since 1986. This increase is mainly caused by the UK's attractiveness for components manufacturing, arising from the large number of Japanese consumer electronics plants using these components. The UK is less dominant in industrial electronics. Well behind the UK, Germany and France host another 64 plants between them. The three largest EC markets thus received three quarters of Japanese investment.

Although the number of subsidiaries in Germany increased from 23 in 1986 to 38 in 1990, Germany's share of Japanese investment declined from 33 to 22 per cent. In contrast, France has gained considerable importance as a manufacturing base for Japanese electronics firms: in 1990 it hosted 26 subsidiaries, 15 per cent of the EC total, while investment was clearly under-represented in 1986 (9 per cent). Companies such as Hitachi and

Matsushita, the two largest Japanese electronics firms, have largely ignored France in the past because of perceived hostility and intrusiveness of the French government. Although Sony's Akio Morita also has voiced complaints about the 'administrative guidance' of the French government affecting its operations in France (Morita 1987), it has steadily increased manufacturing activity in France and currently employs 2,000 workers in manufacturing plants only. The same positive attitude can be ascribed to Canon, which operates a sophisticated copier plant in Bretagne and has recently established an R&D centre in Rennes. The French government's stance on Japanese DFI changed radically from open hostility to accommodation in 1984, when Laurent Fabius visited Tokyo and openly invited Japanese investors. Political relations were further improved upon the visit of MITI officials to France in 1986 (HEC Eurasia Institute 1989). Still, Japanese firms often cite as a major reason to invest in France the need to appease the French government and avert protectionist pressures, all the more important because the French government is seen to have a great influence on decisions taken by the EC.[82] France hosts four copier plants, but investment is mostly concentrated in consumer electronics (manufacture of VCRs and CD players). Special technical specifications for French consumer products, such as those related to the SECAM broadcasting system, play a role, and so does the attractiveness of the large French consumer electronics market.

Other European countries host the remaining quarter of Japanese subsidiaries. Belgium is relatively important (11 subsidiaries). Italy has only recently attracted Japanese investments: the number of subsidiaries increased from 1 to 8. Denmark (1 subsidiary), Greece, and Portugal (no subsidiaries) are barely considered, if at all, as locations for electronics manufacturing within the EC.

Most of the observations are strengthened by the data on employment in manufacturing subsidiaries presented in Table 1.13. The number of employees in Japanese manufacturing subsidiaries almost reached 50,000 in 1990. These figures exclude the acquisition of ICL by Fujitsu, which was finalised at the end of 1990, and a large joint venture between Siemens and Matsushita in components.[83] In terms of employment, consumer electronics is still by far the most important sector. Employment in components plants has been rising most rapidly to more than 17,000, following local content regulations and the new rule of origin for ICs, as discussed in Section 1.3.3.

The dominance of the three largest EC countries is even more pronounced in terms of employment: 79 per cent of manufacturing employment is located in the UK, Germany, and France. UK subsidiaries employ almost half the total number. Germany's share increased by 1 percentage point during 1986–1990, implying that growth in investment here was for a large part achieved by expansion of existing subsidiaries. The investment

Table 1.13 Employment in Japanese manufacturing subsidiaries in the EC in 1990 and 1986, by country

Country	1990				1986
	Cons	Indu	Compo	All (%)	All (%)
UK	15,673	2,666	10,094	22,569 (47)	4,149 (43)
Germany	3,952	1,726	3,848	9,176 (19)	1,868 (18)
France	4,805	1,630	963	6,328 (13)	482 (5)
Italy	1,120	786	0	1,236 (3)	na (na)
Spain	5,131	2,152	221	5,344 (11)	1,495 (16)
Holland	0	261	96	290 (1)	15 (0)
Belgium	388	658	959	2,005 (4)	1,268 (13)
Ireland	0	0	1,205	1,205 (2)	522 (5)
Denmark	0	160	0	160 (0)	0 (0)
Total	31,069	10,039	17,386	48,313 (100)	9,671 (100)
1986 (% increase)	6,501 (378)	886 (1,033)	3,027 (474)	9,671 (400)	

Notes: Cons = consumer electronics, Indu = industrial electronics, Compo = electronic components. Multiple classification is possible if a subsidiary manufactures products in more than one product group; consequently the sum of employment in cons, indu, and compo can be greater than total employment. Figures represent employment in subsidiaries with manufacturing function; these may be combined with sales functions. The figures for 1986 do not include manufacturing employment of Sony, Canon, Hitachi, Ricoh, JVC, Mitsubishi, and Minolta, for which no information was available. The figures for increases in employment from 1986 to 1990 are thus overestimated.

Source: calculations based on Touyou Keizai (1991a, 1987a), JETRO (1990b), Nihon Denshi Kikai Kougyoukai (1991a).

position of France improved, its employment share increasing from 5 to 13 per cent. The concentration of French employment in consumer electronics is pronounced and components manufacturing is not well represented. The other manufacturing location of importance is Spain, attracting 11 per cent of the total number of employees in 1990. However, Spain has lost some ground to the larger countries.

Distribution subsidiaries Investment in extensive distribution channels is often cited as a major strength of Japanese firms. The main Japanese electronics firms, led by Matsushita, have vertically integrated into wholesaling and retailing in Japan, controlling thousands of electronics retail shops throughout the country. In the US and the EC, Japanese firms have set up extensive distribution networks as well at the wholesale level. These networks facilitate customer services such as repair and product guarantees, they foster the brand name of the company, and they feed back information on consumer tastes and market developments. Yamawaki (1991), presents empirical evidence that investments in distribution networks in the US have enhanced the export performance of Japanese firms. In Chapter 7, similar results are found for exports to Europe by Japanese electronics manufacturers.

Tables 1.13 and 1.14 show that Japanese electronics firms expanded their distribution networks in the EC in 1986–1990. In 1990 the number of sales subsidiaries reached 416 (Table 1.14). These subsidiaries employed more than 27,000 people (Table 1.15).[84] The number of sales subsidiaries increased by 43 per cent. The increase was more pronounced for the components and industrial sectors than for consumer electronics. Sales networks for consumer electronics date from the 1960s when Sony and Matsushita established their first subsidiaries, and most networks were relatively complete in 1986. On the other hand, most Japanese component suppliers have not been active in the EC for very long and they have increased their sales efforts substantially in the second half of the 1980s.

The country distribution of the number of subsidiaries largely reflects the size of the markets in the different countries. Germany hosts the largest number of sales subsidiaries, followed by the UK and France. On the other

Table 1.14 Japanese sales subsidiaries in the EC in 1990 and 1986, by country

Country	1990				1986
	Cons	Indu	Compo	All (%)	All (%)
Uk	41	58	26	101 (24)	68 (23)
Germany	58	66	42	138 (33)	114 (39)
France	17	25	14	48 (12)	30 (10)
Spain	9	13	2	17 (4)	8 (3)
Italy	10	16	8	29 (7)	15 (5)
Holland	14	13	6	32 (8)	21 (7)
Belgium	12	15	5	26 (6)	19 (7)
Ireland	5	4	0	5 (1)	4 (1)
Denmark	8	6	2	13 (3)	9 (3)
Portugal	2	4	0	6 (1)	1 (0)
Greece	1	0	0	1 (0)	0 (0)
Total	177	226	105	416 (100)	290 (100)
1986 (% increase)	148 (20)	144 (57)	57 (84)	290 (43)	

Notes: Cons = consumer electronics, Indu = industrial electronics, Compo = electronic components. Multiple classification is possible if a subsidiary distributes products in more than one product group; consequently the sum of the number of subsidiaries in cons, indu, and compo can be greater than the total number of subsidiaries. Figures represent sales subsidiaries without any manufacturing activity.

Source: calculations based on Touyou Keizai (1991a, 1987a).

Table 1.15 Employment in Japanese sales subsidiaries in the EC in 1990 and 1986, by country

Country	1990				1986
	Cons	Indu	Compo	All (%)	All (%)
UK	6,051	5,611	1,442	8,868 (32)	5,247 (32)
Germany	5,134	4,207	1,992	9,081 (33)	5,927 (36)
France	890	2,998	307	3,802 (14)	2,899 (18)
Italy	671	966	92	1,469 (5)	648 (4)
Spain	832	892	15	1,023 (4)	172 (1)
Holland	614	1,183	181	1,531 (6)	709 (4)
Belgium	618	701	76	1,192 (4)	590 (4)
Denmark	173	151	7	264 (1)	152 (1)
Ireland	93	93	0	93 (0)	0 (0)
Portugal	91	21	0	112 (0)	9 (0)
Greece	19	0	0	19 (0)	12 (0)
Total	15,186	16,823	4,112	27,454 (100)	16,429 (100)
1986 (% increase)	9,176 (65)	9,073 (85)	1,623 (153)	16,429 (67)	

Notes: Cons = consumer electronics, Indu = industrial electronics, Compo = electronic components. Multiple classification is possible if a subsidiary distributes products in more than one product group; consequently the sum of employment in cons, indu, and compo can be greater than total employment. Figures represent employment in subsidiaries with only sales activities. Figures for both 1986 and 1990 do not include employment of Sony, Ricoh, and JVC, and Minolta, for which no information was available.

Source: calculations based on Touyou Keizai (1991a, 1987a).

hand, the smaller countries Holland and Belgium have received relatively large shares of investment in distribution owing to their geographical location, good infrastructure, and facilities for distribution centres.

In terms of employment (Table 1.15), the expansion of distribution networks is even more obvious. Employment increased by an impressive 153 per cent in the components sector, while growth in consumer electronics was 65 per cent. The distribution over countries is roughly similar to that in Table 1.14. The UK hosts comparatively large sales subsidiaries and is as important as Germany in terms of number of employees.

Data on employment and number of subsidiaries by individual firms are provided in Appendix 1.2, which lists all Japanese electronics firms employing more than 100 people in the EC by 1990. Companies are, if relevant, grouped by membership of vertical *keiretsu* company groupings.[85] The biggest investor in terms of employment is the Matsushita group. The parent firm Matsushita Electric Industrial employed more than 6,000 people in the EC in 1990. In addition, various subsidiaries of the parent firm have invested in the EC. JVC, 50 per cent owned by Matsushita but run relatively independently from its parent firm, is the largest and employs more than

2,400 in manufacturing alone. Other big investors are Sony (6,765 employees in manufacturing subsidiaries alone), Canon (nearly 8,000 employees). Toshiba (4,709), and Hitachi, NEC, Sanyo, Kyocera, and Sharp (all around 3,000 employees). Employment in sales subsidiaries is relatively high for Canon, with 6,000 employees devoted to the sales, servicing, and repair of its copiers, office machines, and cameras. Most of the large investors have increased employment in the EC rapidly over 1986–1990: Matsushita (184 per cent), Canon (110 per cent), Toshiba (84 per cent), NEC (140 per cent), and Sharp (116 per cent), for example. Towards the end of the list there is a number of (mostly small or medium-sized) Japanese firms which set up subsidiaries in the EC for the first time in 1986–1990. By 1990, investment in the EC was no longer reserved for the larger Japanese electronics firms.

Before recent trends in Japanese investment in the first half of the 1990s are discussed in Section 1.4.5, the next three sections describe particular characteristics of Japanese investment in the late 1980s and early 1990s.

1.4.2 Modes of Entry in Manufacturing

The lion's share of Japanese electronics firms' manufacturing subsidiaries in the EC are established as greenfield ventures and are wholly or majority owned. The preference for greenfield plants is related to the specific competitive advantage of Japanese firms: the ability to produce high quality products at low costs through expertise in quality control methods, production engineering, and labour management. These advantages are best transferred abroad by exercising strict control over overseas manufacturing. Investments in wholesale distribution subsidiaries (likewise mostly wholly owned) are set up to exercise control over after-sales service, spare part deliveries, repair, and marketing, which Japanese firms tend to see as critical to their market position. These have been exceptions to this general rule, though. In particular, in the late 1980s and early 1990s, joint ventures and acquisitions became a more popular mode of investment. The main joint ventures and acquisition are described below.

Joint ventures The first two manufacturing joint ventures between EC and Japanese firms concerned CTV production and were established in 1978: Hitachi and Toshiba set up joint ventures with the UK firms GEC and Rank, respectively. An earlier attempt by Hitachi to set up a greenfield plant had been called off after vigorous opposition by the UK television industry and labour unions (Cawson *et al.* 1990). The major purpose of the joint ventures was to fend off this hostility. Another important advantage of working with an existing local manufacturer was the acquisition of the right to produce CTVs for the EC market under a PAL licence. Both joint ventures eventually collapsed with the Japanese firm taking full control. The Japanese firms complained that they did not get any co-operation in introducing their efficient production and management methods. The UK side disputed the necessity of using Japanese components, and it was also argued (see e.g. van Marion 1992) that the Japanese firms wilfully let the joint ventures collapse to be able to take full control.

The next major Japanese–EC joint venture, established in 1982, also eventually ended in the Japanese firm taking control. JVC teamed up with Thorn–EMI in the UK and Telefunken in Germany to form an alliance in VCRs. It appeared a successful strategic move by JVC, which acquired access to the distribution channels (including VCR rental shops) of Thorn and Telefunken and the video software produced by EMI. This proved crucial in the battle for market share between JVC, which had developed its own VHS standard for VCRs, Sony (Betamax), and Philips (V-2000). VHS eventually became the industry standard. Thomson, the French state-owned consumer electronics firm, had opted to take part in the joint venture as well, but was blocked by the French government (Cawson *et al.* 1990). In 1984, however, it acquired Telefunken and automatically became JVC's main joint venture partner. Thorn left the venture in 1987 and since then manufacturing activities have been located in Germany and France. In Tonnerre (France) mecadecks were manufactured which were shipped to Berlin where J2T produced VCRs in one of the largest Japanese VCR plants in the EC. The VCRs were distributed separately by Thomson and JVC under their own brand names. However, in 1992 Thomson relocated its production of standard VCRs from Berlin to Singapore. Production cost considerations in the face of strong price competition from South Korean firms seems to have been the major reason for Thomson's move, rather than disagreements on management. JVC has since acquired Thomson's stake in the Berlin venture and the (reduced) output of the Berlin plant is sold only under the JVC brand.[86]

Table 1.16 lists the major joint ventures between Japanese and EC firms in the electronics industry in 1991. Until the end of 1989, the J2T joint venture was the largest with more than 1,300 employees in its two establishments. However, a much larger joint venture was established by Siemens and Matsushita in October 1989 in Germany: 5,200 employees work in a new subsidiary responsible for the manufacture, sale, and development of passive components such as capacitors and condensers. Matsushita initially held a minority stake of 35 per cent but this stake increased to 50 per cent from 1992.

Even without this major joint venture, employment in Japanese–EC joint ventures amounted to approximately 12 per cent of total employment in Japanese manufacturing subsidiaries in the EC in 1990. This percentage was substantially higher in Italy (two thirds) and, to a lesser extent, France (around a quarter). These are the two countries that have been most antagonistic to Japanese imports and investment in the past. Important objectives of the establishment of these joint ventures are to induce a more forthcoming government attitude, to secure market access, and to alleviate trade friction. Tyson (1992: Chapter 6) argues that EC firms see trade friction as an important instrument to induce Japanese firms to establish joint ventures. It was noted in Section 1.3.2 that there are indications that setting up joint ventures may have helped Japanese firms to reduce antidumping threats in the case of facsimiles. Olivetti, the firm that had successfully lodged dumping complaints against Japanese firms in printers, electric typewriters, and copiers, was by 1990 manufacturing fax machines in two joint ventures, with Canon and Sanyo. Toshiba added facsimile production to its joint venture with Rhone Poulenc in France, while Ricoh announced plans to set up a facsimile joint venture with Philips in Austria.

However, apart from the facsimile case, the evidence on the role of alliances with EC firms in reducing threats of antidumping action is mixed. On the one hand, Siemens, one of the EC's three major manufacturers of aluminium capacitors, refrained from participating in the antidumping petition against Japanese imports. Siemens' aluminium capacitor business was concentrated in the joint venture with Matsushita. On the other hand, the fact that copier production by Olivetti was concentrated in the joint venture with Canon did not withhold Olivetti from petitioning (successfully) for extension of antidumping duties on Japanese imports (including those of Canon).

It is interesting to note that there are important differences between strategies of individual Japanese firms. Matsushita, Japan's second largest electronics group and biggest investor in the EC, operates joint ventures with all major European competitors except Nokia: Siemens, Bosch, Philips, and Thomson (through JVC). On the other hand, two of the largest Japanese investors, Sony and Hitachi, do not operate any joint ventures in the EC. Sony finds strict control over manufacturing, marketing, and product design essential for its long term competitive position. Sony did become the largest investor in France, and it also set up one of the few Japanese greenfield plants in Italy.

Acquisitions Acquisitions by Japanese electronics firms in the EC were of little importance during most of the 1980s but gained importance in the early 1990s. Table 1.17 lists the major acquisitions of Japanese electronics firms in the EC, ordered by year of acquisition. The first Japanese acquisition was the take-over by Sony of the German audio manufacturer Wega in 1975. In the early 1980s there were some smaller acquisitions, including the joint venture buy-outs by Hitachi and Toshiba of their partners Rank and GEC, respectively.

Breaking with past trends, the years 1989–1992 saw a range of take-overs,

Table 1.16 Main EC–Japanese joint ventures in electronics, by country

Subsidiary name	Japanese firm (%) Partner firm (%)	Estbl	Empl (J)	Products
United Kingdom				
Lucas–Yuasa Batteries	Yuasa (50) Lucas Industries (50)	1988.08	654 (0)	Car batteries
Gooding Sanken	Sanken Electric (49) Gooding (51)	1989.10	240 (7)	Transformers, power switches
Germany				
J2T	JVC (50) Thomson (50)	1982.05	758 (1)	VCRs
MB Video	Matsushita (65) Robert Bosch (35)	1982.12	875 (14)	VCRs, CD players
Siemens–Matsushita Components	Matsushita (50) Siemens (50)	1989.10	5,448 (4)	Passive components
BT Magnet Technology	TDK (50) Robert Bosch (50)	1991	700 (2)	Ferrite magnets
France				
J2T	JVC (50) Thomson (50)	1982.03	519 (1)	Mecadecks for VCRs
Toshiba Systems	Toshiba (74) Rhone Poulenc (26)	1986.06	602 (7)	Copiers, fax
CEFEMO	Toshiba (33) Thomson (33), AEG (33)	1987.09	240 (2)	Microwave ovens

Italy				
Olivetti–Canon Industriale	Canon (50) Olivetti (50)	1987.04	642 (5)	Copiers, fax, laser printers
Olivetti–Sanyo Industrial	Sanyo (44) Olivetti (56)	1990.01	162 (1)	Fax
Sanyo Argo Clima	Sanyo (49) Elfi (51)	1991	180 (3)	Industrial airconditioners
Belgium				
Philips–Matsushita Battery	Matsushita (50) Philips (50)	1970.09	335 (1)	Lead dry batteries
Netherlands				
Noble Europe	Teikoku Tsushin (51) Philips (49)	1991.10	55 (2)	Variable resistors, switches
Luxembourg				
Teijin Dupont Films	Teijin (50) Dupont (50)	1991	150	Polyester film for audio/videocassettes

Notes: (%) = percentage capital stake, Estbl = establishment time, Empl = number of employees, (J) = number of Japanese employees. Employee figures are for 1991–1992.

Sources: Touyou Keizai (1991a–1992a), Nihon Denshi Kikai Kougyoukai (1992a), JETRO (1992b).

Table 1.17 Main European acquisitions by Japanese electronics firms

Japanese company	Target firm	Year	Cap stake	Empl 1991	Products/Activity
Acquisitions					
Sony	Wega (G)	1975	100	654	Audio, video
King Industries	Chubb Cash Registers (UK)	1983	100	230	Cash registers
Minolta	Develop Dr. Eisbein (G)	1986	83	500	Copiers
Olympus	Keymed (UK)	1987	100	510	Medical instruments
Munekata	Plastronics (Ire)	1989	100	372	Cabinets for CTV
Matsushita	Office Workstations (UK)	1989	100	65	Software
Shimadzu	Kratos Group (UK)	1989	100	290	Analytical equipment
Kyocera	AVX (US/UK)	1990	100	1,398	Passive components
Mitsubishi Chemical	Verbatim (US/Ire)	1990	100	550	Microdisks
Hoshiden	Besson (UK)	1990	100	434	Telephones, components
Mitsubishi Electric	Apricot Computers (UK)	1990	100	431	PCs, software
Sanyo	Gallenkamp Plc (UK)	1990	100	312	Measuring equipment
Ushio	Licht und Vacuum Technik (G)	1990	100	310	Electric bulbs
Advantest	Giga Instrumentation (Fr)	1990	100	90	Spectrometers
Hitachi Koki	Data Products (US/Ire)	1990	100	350	Dot printers and parts
Fujitsu	ICL (UK)	1991	80[a]	25,000	Computers
Omron	Schoenbuch Electronics (G)	1991	95	85	Sensors, switches
Fujitsu	Fulcrum Communications (UK)	1991	75[b]	570	Transmission equipment
Capital participations					
Matsushita	Loewe Opta (G)	1990	25.1	1,430	CTVs, car electronics
Ricoh	Gestetner Holding (UK)	1991	24.2	12,000	Distribution of office equipment

Joint venture buy-outs

	Joint venture	Buy-out	Set up	Empl 1991	Activity
Toshiba	Rank–Toshiba (UK)	1980	1978	na	CTVs
Hitachi	GEC–Hitachi (UK)	1983	1978	na	CTVs
Funai	Funai–Amstrad (UK)	1990	1987	116	VCRs
Tamura	Tamura Hinchley[c] (UK)	1991	1989	312	Power sources
Kenwood	Sofradore Trio–Kenwood[d] (Fr)	1991	1985	112	CD players, car stereos

Notes: Fr = France, G = Germany; Ire = Ireland; Estbl = year of acquisition; Empl = employees.

[a] The cost of acquisition was £700 m.

[b] British Telecommunications holds a 25% stake.

[c] Previously 49% owned by Cambridge Electronics.

[d] Previously 50% owned by Sofrel and Delta Dole.

Sources: Touyou Keizai (1992a), Nihon Denshi Kikai Kougyoukai (1992a), Nihon Yushutsunyuu Ginkou (1989), Burton and Saelens (1987).

two of which involved EC firms occupying a major place in EC industry. With the acquisition of AVX in the US, Kyocera acquired AVX's operations in the EC. AVX is a major producer of capacitors, among other things, and holds an EC market share of 9 per cent, equal to Siemens' and just below Philips' (CEC 1991b). The most important and ardently discussed acquisition is without doubt Fujitsu's take-over of ICL for 700 million pounds in 1991. With this acquisition, Fujitsu at once became an important player in the EC market for large computers. Less well known but also significant was Fujitsu's acquisition of the product division of Fulcrum Communications, a wholly owned transmission equipment subsidiary of British Telecommunications (BT). BT maintains a 25 per cent stake in the company. Both Kyocera and Fujitsu had a relatively small presence in the EC before, and acquisitions were a major means to reach a critical presence in the EC quickly. Mitsubishi Electric's acquisition of Apricot Computer's hardware division also falls into this category. The timing suggests that the Japanese firms found it opportune to invest before the planned completion of the Internal Market at the beginning of 1993.

Japanese firms also acquired several medium sized firms in Europe in wide-ranging areas: computer software (Matsushita's acquisition of Office Workstations), cabinets for CTVs (Munekata's acquisition of Plastronics in Ireland), components (Hoshiden-Besson and Omron-Schoenbuch), light bulbs (Ushio-Licht und Vacuum Technik), and measuring equipment (Sanyo-Gallenkamp and Adventest-Giga Instrumentation). Two more subsidiaries were acquired indirectly through take-overs of US firms. Mitsubishi chemical acquired an Irish microdisk subsidiary through the take-over of Verbatim, and Hitachi Koki acquired an Irish printer plant through its take-over of Data Products. Besides these acquisitions, joint venture buy-outs became popular again in the years 1990–1991, with Funai, Tamura, and Kenwood buying out their respective joint venture partners. In addition, there were two major capital participations by Japanese firms. Matsushita acquired a 25 per cent stake in the German CTV producer Loewe Opta, and Ricoh bought a 24 per cent stake in a major European distributor of office machines, Gestetner, to which Ricoh supplies office machines on an OEM basis.

1.4.3 EC Investment Strategies and Integration of EC Activities

In order to assess the impact of Japanese electronics firms' EC presence on the EC electronics industry, it is important to pay attention to possible EC-wide investment strategies adopted by Japanese firms and the degree of integration of EC activities. For VCRs, it was shown in Section 1.4.1 that investment in the 1980s was essentially country-specific rather than part of an EC-wide strategy. This was due mainly to national quota, rules of origin, and political factors, which kept the EC markets fragmented for Japanese firms and induced the establishment of multiple small-scale plants. A similar pattern had emerged in the 1970s in CTV production, with several firms operating plants in Germany or Spain, as well as a main plant in the UK. As late as 1989, only production at Sony's UK plant surpassed the minimum efficient scale level, estimated to be around 500,000 CTVs a year (van Marion 1992). This has been particular to CTV plants in the EC, since Japanese CTV plants in the US reached the minimum efficient scale not long after the establishment (Burton and Saelens 1987). Dunning (1986), in his survey of Japanese plants in the UK, finds no evidence of integrated EC activities in the early 1980s.

However, there is abundant evidence that Japanese electronics firms have adopted pan-European strategies and are moving towards greater integration of EC production and sales activities. Japanese firms' operations are acquiring a sufficient scale and integration to allow for a more efficient organisation of production in Europe. With locally manufactured products sufficiently 'European' to clear origin requirements, and with the movement towards the Internal Market in 1993, Japanese firms perceived fewer obstacles to intra-EC flows of final goods an components. A number of observations point to an increasing integration of EC activities. First, several firms have taken steps to rationalise VCR production in the EC towards the end of the 1980s. JVC and Thomson discontinued small scale production of VCRs in the UK in 1989 to concentrate manufacturing in Berlin. Sanyo, which operated three VCR plants in the EC, stopped production in the UK and Spain in 1987, also to concentrate production in Germany. The same focus of production in Germany has been reported for Toshiba, which quit assembly in the UK in 1989 (Sako 1992). Similar though reverse moves were taken by Sharp, which stopped production in Spain and concentrated production in the UK, and Hitachi, which closed its German plant in Germany and moved to the UK in 1993. Multiple plants are still operated by Sony and Matsushita, and in copier production (Canon, for instance, operates three copier plants in the EC), but is clearly less for later investments such as CD players (see Section 1.3.2).

Second, the major Japanese electronics firms have set up European headquarters to improve co-ordination in EC sales and procurement activities, among others. The role of these headquarters should not be overestimated, though, since the responsibility for plant investments, product lines, and the appointment of executive personnel usually still lies with the product division headquarters in Japan (Takaoka and Satake 1991: 25).

Third, developments in procurement and sales patterns of Japanese subsidiaries in the EC clearly suggest a move towards greater integration of EC activities. Table 1.18 shows the destination of sales by electronics subsidiaries in 1988, 1990, and 1993, as recorded in MITI surveys among Japanese MNEs. While the share of sales on the local market (the country hosting the plants) was a substantial 85 per cent in 1988, reflecting the persisting preference of Japanese electronics firms to concentrate manufacturing plants in the large EC countries, this share has continued to decline, to 73 per cent in 1990 and 45 per cent in 1993. Sales to other European countries have increased correspondingly and reached more than half of total sales by 1993.[87] It is also important to note that almost all production in the EC was and is for the European market, although sales to other regions has increased slightly to 4 per cent in 1993.[88]

Procurement behaviour has become more pan-European during 1988–1993 as well. Table 1.19 shows that Japanese firms in the late 1980s became less reliant on imports of components from Japan: the share of these procurements declined from 62 per cent in 1988 to 50 per cent in 1990, although

Table 1.18 Destination of sales by Japanese electronics subsidiaries in the EC, 1988–1993

	Local market (%)	Other Europe (%)	Japan (%)	Other (%)	Total (bn yen)
1988	85	14	1	0	694
1990	73	25	1	0	1,084
1993	45	51	1	3	2,085

Source: Nihon Tsuushou Sangyoushou (1990, 1991, 1994).

Table 1.19 Procurements of Japanese electronics subsidiaries in the EC by region of origin

Year	Region of origin				Total (bn yen)	% of sales
	Local (%)	Other Europe (%)	Japan (%)	Asia (%)		
1988	31	4	62	4	521	75
1990	22	22	50	4	711	66
of which: Intra-group (%)	36	77	96	71		
1993	16	28	50	6	959	45
of which: Intra-group (%)	23	79	64	72		

Source: Nihon Tsuushou Sangyoushou (1990, 1991, 1994).

it remained at this level afterwards. Local procurements (in the country of investment) have continued to decline, from 31 per cent in 1988 to 16 per cent in 1993. In contrast, procurements from EC countries other than the country of investment increased to 28 per cent in 1993 from a mere 4 per cent in 1988. Furthermore, more than three quarters of components sourced from other EC countries were supplied by subsidiaries of the same firm or affiliated firms (intra-group deliveries[89]). These figures suggest a development towards product specialisation by Japanese electronics firms' plants, with some plants located in country A specialising in components destined for an assembly plant in country B, which in turn may export to various EC countries.

The combined share of local and European procurement increased from 35 per cent in 1988 to 44 per cent in 1991 but stayed level in 1993. The data suggest a more persistent trend towards greater in-house production of components. Procurements as a percentage of sales declined from 75 per cent in 1988 to 45 per cent in 1993. These figures should be interpreted with care, however, since response rates for procurement questions in the MITI surveys vary and tend to be lower than response rates for sales variables.[90] Nevertheless, both developments imply an increasing local content ratio of EC-made Japanese electronics products. The issue of local content will be discussed at greater length in Section 1.5 and is subject of more detailed analysis in Chapter 8.

Fourth, there is evidence that a European strategy as opposed to a country perspective is already prevailing in the organisation of distribution networks of Japanese electronics firms. In Tables 1.12 and 1.13, it was shown that Belgium and Holland, countries with small national markets but enjoying a strategic geographical location in the EC, a highly developed infrastructure, and a long established position in international trade, have received a relatively large share of distribution activities. Williamson and Yamawaki (1991) analysed the determinants of the location of Japanese sales subsidiaries empirically. They found that location decisions are not much related to characteristics of national markets, but reflect the availability of physical and telecommunications infrastructure and distance to concentrations of consumers with high purchasing power. They concluded that the Japanese distribution system in Europe by 1990 was 'ready and waiting for the Internal Market'.

1.4.4 Japanese Firms' Presence in the EC in Perspective

This section attempts to put the EC activities of Japanese firms into some perspective through comparisons with sales and production figures for EC and US firms. Table 1.20 shows the EC shares in total worldwide electronics

Table 1.20 The importance of the EC market for major Japanese, EC, and US firms, 1989

Company	Electronics sales (m ECUs)			Employment ('000 persons)		
	EC	World	EC (%)	EC[a]	World	EC (%)
Japanese firms						
Hitachi	1,900	18,790	10.1	3.3	264	1.2
Matsushita	1,790	19,775	9.1	7.7	193	4.0
Sony	1,560	10,020	15.6	8.0[b]	79	10.1
Toshiba	1,360	15,080	9.0	4.7	125	3.8
NEC	910	19,820	4.6	3.1	115	2.7
Canon	859[c]	na	na	7.8	37.5	20.5
Fujitsu[d]	830	6,910	12.0	3.1	115	2.7
EC firms						
Siemens	10,050	16,830	59.7		353	
CGE Alcatel	8,000	12,000	66.7		204	
Philips	6,960	14,760	47.2		310	
Thomson	5,400	10,020	53.9		104	
Olivetti	3,570	5,880	60.7		58	
Bull	3,190	5,820	54.8		46	
Nokia	1,410	2,620	53.8		45	
US firms						
IBM	17,840	57,010	31.2	100[b]	387	25.8
DEC	3,950	11,590	34.0		121	
Hewlett Packard	3,350	10,820	31.0		87	

Notes: Electronics sales do not include sales of (heavy) electrical equipment, electric household goods, and lighting.

[a] 1990; see Appendix 1.2.

[b] Estimation.

[c] Sales of computer-related equipment and office machines.

[d] Does not include sales of the UK firm ICL, which Fujitsu acquired in 1991.

Sources: Based on CEC (1992), company reports, and Appendix 1.2.

sales and employment for major Japanese electronics firms in 1989. For comparison, world and EC electronics sales are presented for major EC and US electronics firms.[91]

The share of the EC in worldwide electronics sales varies across Japanese firms. For the biggest seller on the EC market, Hitachi, EC electronics sales represent 10 per cent of total worldwide electronics sales. Marginally smaller percentages are recorded for Matsushita and Toshiba, while NEC's EC sales amount to less than 5 per cent of global sales. Most dependent on the EC market are Sony, for which EC sales represent 15.6 per cent of global sales, and presumably Canon. The EC market was already relatively important for Fujitsu (12 per cent) in 1989; with the acquisition of ICL in 1991, it has become one of the major Japanese sellers in the EC.

The advance of Japanese firms in terms of sales has not been followed, or at least not to the same extent, by a 'localisation' of production, measured by the EC share of firms' worldwide employees. The number of people employed by Hitachi in the EC represents only a little more than 1 per cent of its total number of employees. Hitachi's manufacturing operations are still largely concentrated in Japan with the EC market mostly served by exports. Similar observations can be made for Matsushita, Toshiba, and Fujitsu, although the discrepancies between EC sales and employment shares are less pronounced. Sony and Canon are the firms that are most 'localised' in the EC. Since manufacturing employees are less well represented in Canon's employment, this leaves Sony as the only major Japanese electronics firms that has made progress in the implementation of a strategy to produce where goods are sold. It should be noted, however, that several smaller firms are at least as 'localised' as Sony. Firms such as Alps, Murata, Pioneer, and Akai have substantial manufacturing operations in the EC relative to both Japanese and other foreign manufacturing activities.

Table 1.20 also shows that EC sales of major EC firms are in general several times higher than sales by Japanese firms. Only Nokia's sales are outstripped by the top three Japanese sellers. The EC firms sell 50 to 70 per cent of their total output in the EC. This figure is roughly one third for the three major US electronics firms listed. Sales levels of DEC and Hewlett Packard are comparable to sales of EC firms such as Bull and Olivetti. The largest seller on the EC market is IBM, with sales of almost 18 billion ECUs. IBM employs an estimated 100,000 people in the EC, twice the number of all Japanese firms' employees in the EC. IBM's experience in internationalisation has resulted in a high degree of 'localisation'. It employs 26 per cent of its total number of employees in the EC, roughly comparable to its dependence on EC sales.

Although electronics sales on the EC market by major Japanese firms are relatively modest, Japanese firms have gained substantial market shares in a number of product markets. Japanese firms supply the vast majority of DRAMs in the EC,[92] and have made significant inroads in the gate array market as well. With the acquisition of ICL, Fujitsu became a major player in the market for mainframe computers. Canon holds 7 per cent of the office equipment market (CEC 1991b: 12–32) and Kyocera's acquisition of AVX launched it into the top three EC capacitor producers. Japanese firms are also the major suppliers of PC printers, copiers, microdisks, and facsimiles in the EC.

Yet the biggest advance has been in the consumer electronics market. In 1987, the EC's main producer Philips still held 15 per cent of the market, followed by Thomson of France (13 per cent), and at some distance by

Matsushita (8 per cent), Sony (6 per cent), and Hitachi (4 per cent) (Bowen 1991). Since then, Japanese producers have gained substantial ground. Japanese firms hold roughly 80 per cent of the VCR market, around a third of the CTV market, and supply virtually all camcorders. In the EC audio market, sales of Sony, Matsuhita, and Pioneer have surpassed those of former market leader Philips.

The strength of Japanese firms in consumer electronics has also been accompanied by substantial Japanese manufacturing investments in the EC, as was seen in Section 1.3. A lack of comparable data (EC manufacturing data are at the plant level while Japanese firms' data are at the subsidiary level) makes it difficult to establish precisely the extent of the Japanese manufacturing presence. Until 1989, the European Association of Consumer Electronics Manufacturers (EACEM) gathered comparable information on Japanese and European firms' plants in Europe. Table 1.21 presents the EACEM figures.[93] Japanese firms were responsible for 15 per cent of total manufacturing employment in the EC consumer electronics industry in 1989. The Japanese share in the number of plants was more than twice as high at 33 per cent, owing to the fragmentation of Japanese manufacturing activities in the EC in the 1980s. The average number of employees per Japanese plant was 328 against almost 1,000 for EC firms. This difference reflects a higher degree of integration in EC firms' plants, and also indicates that EC firms had made considerable progress towards rationalisation of EC production by 1990.[94]

Developments in the early 1990s must have led to an increased share of Japanese consumer electronics employment in the EC. As discussed above, European firms have relocated production to South-East Asia in several cases (Philips in CD players and Thomson in VCRs), while renewed antidumping threats (in CD players and CTVs mainly) have prompted Japanese firms to shift remaining production for the EC market from Japan and South-East Asia to the EC. By 1994, Japanese and Korean firms were

Table 1.21 The Japanese presence in the EC consumer electronics industry, 1989

	No. of plants	No. of employees	Employees/plant
European firms	106	105,000	991
Japanese firms	58	19,000	328
Other firms[a]	10	2,200	220
Total	174	126,200	725
Share Japanese firms	33	15	

[a] Korean and Taiwanese firms.

Sources: estimates based on CEC (1992) and EACEM (1990).

responsible for more than 70 per cent of EC output of VCRs and were left as the only producers of CD players in the EC.

For the broad electronics industry as a whole, the 1991 figure for Japanese employment, including ICL and the Matsushita–Siemens joint venture, would be roughly 80,000. This is equal to approximately 8 per cent of total manufacturing employment in the EC in 1991, although it should be noted that the Japanese employment figures include non-factory workers as well.[95] The ICL acquisition may have brought the Japanese presence in the EC almost on par with Japanese manufacturing in the US. A study by the US Department of Commerce (Genther and Dalton 1992) found that Japanese manufacturing plants provided jobs for 86,000 employees in 1990, which constituted 8 per cent of the total number of production workers in the broad US electronics industry.[96] For the audio and video production sector this percentage reached 30 per cent.

1.4.5 Recent Investment Trends

As seen in Section 1.4.2, Japanese investment during 1990–1992 showed some characteristics distinct from the pattern of investment prevalent in the 1980s. Acquisition became a popular instrument to secure access to markets ahead of the completion of the Internal Market and to complement Japanese firms' competencies. At the same time, greenfield investments took place at a lesser pace than before. It is clear that the first half of the 1990s were characterised by a much smaller growth in Japanese manufacturing than the late 1980s. The JETRO figures on manufacturing affiliates in Europe based on JETRO's yearly surveys illustrate this. In 1990, 86 Japanese-affiliated manufacturing subsidiaries were identified in the electronics assembly industry and 53 more in electronics components. In the following two years the number of assembly subsidiaries increased significantly to 112 while the number of components subsidiaries increased to 72. However, by the end of 1994, the number of assembly subsidiaries had increased by only one to 113 while the number of components subsidiaries had *declined* to 61.[97] The latter figures, however, do not imply that Japanese manufacturing activity in the EC has fallen. Lower growth (or a decline) in the number of subsidiaries often hides substantial growth in the scale of existing subsidiaries.[98] Second, subsidiary numbers may fall in the process of rationalisation and specialisation of pan-European production, as was highlighted for the VCR industry in Section 1.4.3. Loss of production capacity and employment through closure of one subsidiary may be offset to an extent by increased employment in other subsidiaries in the EC. Nevertheless, Japanese divestment from EC electronics manufacturing did become a significant phenomenon in 1992. The remainder of this section will look at some of the evidence, after discussing new investments and plant expansion programs in recent years. No comprehensive data were available, but the information does illustrate the main investment and divestment trends in the first half of the 1990s.

New investments Table 1.17 lists major and some minor Japanese investments during 1991–1995. A first observation is that the wave of (small-scale) acquisitions in 1989–1991 has not continued in more recent years. The only outright acquisition is the 1995 take-over of the Portuguese maker of telecommunications transmission and switching equipment Sistel, which gave NEC an entry into the European telecommunications market. In the same year Ricoh announced that it would increase its minority stake in Gestetner to a majority holding at a cost of 127 million pounds. In addition, Matsushita Electronics bought two cathode ray tube (CRT) factories which Nokia closed in 1994. The latter acquisition is a major new development in the European CRT industry. Until 1994, Sony was the only Japanese CRT producer in the EC. Sony produces its own Trinitron technology tubes in Bridgend, Wales, for use in its UK and other European factories. Philips and Thomson supply several European plants of Matsushita, Sanyo, and Hitachi with CRTs. Matsushita's plan to produce 2 million CRTs a year in the two German plants will inevitably reduce sales of the EC firms.

Most of the new Japanese investments concern greenfield plants. Three new manufacturing subsidiaries were established in 1991–1992 for disk drive production: YE Data set up assembly operations for flexible disk drives (FDDs) in 1991, Hitachi established a subsidiary for the manufacture of large capacity hard disk drives (HDD) in Ardon in France in the same year, and Matsushita Kotobuki set up a HDD plant in Ireland in 1992. Other greenfield plants were set up by Canon in the UK in 1991 (recycling of copying machines), Kyocera in France in 1992 (small scale assembly of inkjet printers) and by Pioneer in Portugal in 1995 (car audio manufacturing). A joint venture was established by Fuji Electrochemical and Thomson to manufacture CRT parts in France in 1995.

Probably more important in terms of employment are expansion projects of subsidiaries and plants, of which three major cases are listed in Table 1.22. Sony in 1992 decided to set up a new CTV plant in Pencoed, Wales. CTV production was transferred from the existing plant in Bridgend such that this plant could concentrate on expanding production of CRTs (about 2 million a year).[99] Two major plant expansions were announced in 1994–1995 by Japanese DRAM manufacturers in the UK, prompted by rapidly growing world and European demand for DRAMs. NEC committed itself to an extra investment of 530 million pounds in its Livingstone DRAM plant, while Fujitsu announced that its DRAM plant would be expanded and entrusted with the production of 16 megabyte DRAMs.

Table 1.22 Selected Japanese investments in the EC electronics industry, 1991–1995

Japanese company	Subsidiary name	Year	Ctry	Empl	Product	Investment type
New subsidiaries						
YE Data	YE Data UK	1991	UK	64	FDDs	Greenfield
Canon	Canon Manufacturing	1991	UK	85	Copier recycling	Greenfield
Hitachi	Hitachi Computer Products	1991	Fr	150	HDDs	Greenfield
Matsushita Kotobuki	Ireland Kotobuki Electronics	1992	Ire	217	HDDs	Greenfield
Kyocera	Kyocera Manufacturing	1992	Fr	24	Inkjet printers	Greenfield
Matsushita Electronics	na	1994	G	na	CRTs	Acquisition of 2 Nokia factories
Fuji Electrochemical	Thomson FDK France	1995	Fr	50	CRT yokes	Joint venture
Pioneer	Pioneer Electronica	1995	Por	140	Car audio	Greenfield
NEC	Sistel-Comunicacoes	1995	Por	260	Telephone switching equipment	Acquisition
Expansion of participation						
Ricoh	Gestetner Holding	1995	UK	12,000	Distribution office equipment	Majority holding (£ 127m)
Expansion existing subsidiaries						
Sony	Sony Manufacturing	1992	UK	1,860	CTVs	New plant
NEC	NEC semiconductors	1994	UK	923	DRAMs	Expansion plant (£ 530m)
Fujitsu	Fujitsu Microelectronics	1995	UK	423	DRAMs	Expansion to 16M DRAM[a]

Notes: Year = year establishment of the subsidiary, Ctry = country, Empl = number of employees in 1994, Fr = France, G = Germany, Ire = Ireland, Por = Portugal.

[a] Announced.

Sources: Denshi Keizai Kenkyuujo (1993d, 1994a, 1995), JETRO (1993b), Nihon Boueki Shinkoukai (1995c) *Financial Times* (various issues), *Nikkei Weekly* (various issues).

Divestments The main divestments of Japanese electronics firms are listed in Table 1.23. Three concern VCR assembly plants. Shintom shifted production to Batam, Indonesia, while Funai and Hitachi concentrated production in other EC plants. The plant closures do indicate a scaling back of EC assembly operations. The three firms produce mainly low-end VCRs and sales were suffering from strong competition by South Korean firms in a maturing market. Hitachi was reportedly seeking retirement for its 324 employees in Landesheim, Germany. A sharply declining market was the main reason for Star and Tokyo Electric to close dot matrix printer plants in the EC. Tokyo Electric also shifted typewriter assembly to the US, which may have been related to the expiry of antidumping measures.

In contrast, divestments by Kyocera (inkjet assembly) and YE Data (FDD assembly) took place in a growing market. Both firms had set up assembly plants only three years earlier in 1991, just before the completion of the Internal Market. The firms may have been too optimistic about growth prospects and too pessimistic about a possible rise in trade barriers for these products. Kyocera decided to move production back to Japan, YE Data to concentrate production in its plant in China. YE Data's plant was not closed but, with the help of the firm's parent, Yaskawa Electric, transformed into an assembly plant for electric inverters, while the plant also functions as a repair facility for FDDs.

Two other divestments concern manufacturing operations of EC companies acquired by Japanese firms. Advantest decided to close manufacturing operations at Giga Instrumentation, reducing employees by 60; it will instead export spectrometers from Japan. Kyocera, in a restructuring of the European manufacturing operations of AVX, closed its condenser plant in France to concentrate production in the US and elsewhere in Europe. Finally, as noted in Section 1.3.4 above, Toshiba divested from the CEFEMO joint venture manufacturing microwave ovens in 1994. This is not likely to have had any direct employment consequences.

1.5 Japanese DFI and its Impact on the EC Electronics Industry

Assessing the impact of Japanese manufacturing DFI on the EC economy in general, and on the EC electronics industry in particular, is a difficult task. Possible positive effects (such as transfer of technology) or negative effects (such as the extent to which DFI substitutes for investment by EC firms) are hard to quantify. Given structural unemployment in the EC and prolonged deficits in EC trade with Japan, public and policy debates have often focused on the effects of DFI on the trade balance and employment. Yet many economists would ague that a country's trade balance is determined by the macroeconomic balance between savings and investment.

Table 1.23 Japanese divestments in the EC electronics industry, 1992/1993/1994

Japanese company	Subsidiary name	Year	Ctry	Empl	Product	Remarks
Shintom	Shintom Deutschland	1992	G	na	VCRs	Production ceased
Hitachi	Hitachi Consumer Products	1993	G	324	VCRs	Plant closed
Funai	Funai UK	1993	UK	116	VCRs	Production ceased
Star	Star Micronics UK	1994	UK	350	Dot printers	Subsidiary dissolved
Tokyo Electric	TEC Electronics Werk	1994	G	125	Dot printers, typewriters	Production ceased
YE Data	YE Data UK	1994	UK	64	FDDs	Production ceased
Advantest	Giga Instrumentation	1994	Fr	80	Spectrum analysers	Manufacturing operations ceased
Kyocera	AVX France	1994	Fr	129	Condensers	Production ceased
Kyocera	Kyocera Manufacturing	1994	Fr	24	Inkjet printers	Production ceased
Toshiba	CEFEMO	1994	Fr	240	Microwave ovens	Stake sold to AEG-Thomson

Notes: Ctry = country, Empl = number of employees in 1992–1994, Fr = France, G = Germany.

Sources: Denshi Keizai Kenkyuujo (1993d, 1994a, 1995), JETRO (1993b), Nihon Boueki Shinkoukai (1995c), *Financial Times* (various issues), *Nikkei Weekly* (various issues).

They would emphasise that positive effects on the economy arise if foreign firms' investment increases skill levels of the labour force, introduces superior management and engineering techniques, and increases productivity. Both economists and policy makers tend to agree that DFI on balance has favourable effects on host economies.[100]

This section attempts to provide insight into the impact of Japanese DFI on the EC electronics industry by reviewing the available information on the characteristics of Japanese DFI. It will briefly discuss likely effects on EC employment and the electronics trade balance. The value added of Japanese manufacturing activities in the EC is assessed by reviewing the evidence concerning local content, procurement, and the shift from assembly to components production. The extent to which expertise and technology are diffused through the EC industry and labour force is discussed by looking at joint ventures, R&D activities, and the delegation of responsibilities to local personnel. Lastly, some remarks are made with respect to efficiency of production, consumer welfare, and the competitiveness of EC firms.

1.5.1 Employment

Japanese electronics firms have been increasing employment in the EC rapidly and have become a factor of importance in the economic landscape. As mentioned above, employment in subsidiaries with manufacturing activities probably reached 80,000 persons in 1991, which amounted to approximately 8 per cent of manufacturing employment in the EC electronics industry. Japanese investment in general has not been accompanied by increases in employment in the electronics industry, but it may have helped to stem the decline in employment which began in the early 1980s. For instance, employment in the consumer electronics industry declined from 160,000 in 1980 to 123,000 in 1988, but showed its first increase to 126,000 in 1989 (CEC 1991b) and remained stable for the next two years. After 1991, a sharp fall in consumer electronics sales in the EC was accompanied by a further drop in employment.[101] Similar observations can be made for employment in the EC components industry, which recorded an increase during 1989–1991 but a decline in the next two years. Within these broader trends, the share of employment provided by Japanese subsidiaries must have increased, while EC firms' employment, in particular in the consumer electronics industry, has declined.

For an assessment of the employment effects of Japanese DFI, however, one should look not only at mere employment figures, but also at the quality of employment. Japanese plants set up in the EC as a response to trade policy measures often limited activities to simple assembly and packaging tasks and tended to use only low-skilled labour. Recent trends towards integrated production, investments in components manufacturing, and emphasis on product design and software engineering suggest that employment provided by Japanese firms is reaching a more balanced distribution over assembly-type low-skilled and more highly skilled labour. A survey by Morris, Munday, and Wilkinson (1994) among Japanese plants in Wales found a strong trend towards increased hiring of engineers, graduates, and managers, and fewer hirings of school-leavers in the late 1980s and early 1990s. Trends in R&D and design activities are discussed below.

In addition to manufacturing employment, Japanese electronics firms provided more than 30,000 jobs in their distribution subsidiaries in the EC. Part of these jobs consist of relatively simple warehousing and administrative tasks, but qualified service functions and staff functions in marketing and planning are relatively important as well. This will apply even more to the recently established European headquarters of Japanese electronics firms.

A positive effect of Japanese DFI stems from the location of Japanese firms' plant establishments. Encouraged by financial and other incentives, Japanese electronics firms have shown an inclination to locate manufacturing plants in areas in the UK and France that are characterised by high structural unemployment. With labour relatively immobile, such investments are likely to help reduce regional mismatches on the labour market.

1.5.2 The Electronics Trade Balance

Since a substantial share of DFI has been of the 'tariff-jumping' type, it is likely to have been substituting for exports. Evidence is provided in Chapter 7, where a clear relationship is found between Japanese plant establishments in the EC, declining exports from Japan, and increased EC production for a number of products. In addition, a comparison with exports to, and investment in, the US suggests that trade policy measures have led to export substituting DFI. An econometrical analysis of exports to the EC by individual Japanese electronics firms confirms that Japanese manufacturing investment in the late 1980s has been substituting for exports.

On the other hand, the evidence in Chapter 7 points to a partially offsetting growth in components exports from Japan. The information on procurement behaviour in Table 1.19 also showed a reliance on components imports from Japan: roughly half the procurement by Japanese electronics firms' subsidiaries in the EC in 1993 originated here. However, the share of imports from Japan has come down in the late 1980s, while the data are suggestive of a continuously increasing emphasis on in-house production of components in existing subsidiaries.

The evidence thus suggests that the effect of Japanese manufacturing investments on the electronics trade balance of the EC *vis-à-vis* Japan has been positive.[102] An indication for this is also given by developments in the consumer electronics trade balance of the EC *vis-à-vis* Japan in the late 1980s. In 1989, the trade deficit of the EC *vis-à-vis* Japan showed a year-on-year decline for the first time, be it only marginally, from 5.5 to 5.3 billion ECUs, and the deficit remained roughly stable until 1993.[103]

1.5.3 Value Added and Local Content

The growth in Japanese components manufacturing in the EC, both through investments by independent component producers and through increased in-house production by final goods producers, signifies the shift from mere assembly activities to integrated production. The most illustrative example is the integration of Japanese DRAM plants into wafer etching. The trend towards integration is an important one, since the manufacture of components tends to be more technology intensive than product assembly and requires more skilled labour and training of employees.

In Chapter 8 the response of Japanese firms to local content requirements in the EC is analysed in more detail. It is estimated there that the local content of Japanese consumer electronics subsidiaries in the EC reached 66 per cent of sales value in 1990, of which roughly half was generated by in-house value added. For the whole electronics industry, the MITI survey in 1990 reported an average local content ratio of 65 per cent. Two thirds of Japanese affiliates reached local content levels of 45 per cent, the threshold level implied by rules of origin for products such as CTVs and VCRs. These figures suggest that Japanese firms had reached relatively high local content levels by 1990.

However, the available information on developments in the 1990s would suggest that local content has not increased substantially in recent years. Procurement figures for 1993 presented in Table 1.19 indicated no further reduction in the share of Japan in procurements, although in-house value added may have increased. The MITI survey in 1993 reports an average local content ratio of 65, unchanged from 1990.[104]

Local content requirements appear to have been the driving force behind the increase in local content of Japanese manufacturing. High local content levels as a response to policy measures are also likely to have some less positive effects on the EC economy. In the 1990 MITI survey, almost half of Japanese electronics subsidiaries reported that the reason they raised or were planning to raise local content levels was the existence of local content regulations. In contrast, only 29 per cent of the subsidiaries increased local content because this was more cost effective.[105] Hence, it is likely that increases in local content have led to increases in production costs.

A second point to note is that, although local content is high, components supplied by independent local manufacturers are few. Independent components supplies made up only 12 per cent of the sales value of Japanese firms' consumer electronics production in the EC in 1990 (Chapter 8). Most of the local content was generated in-house or by affiliated subsidiaries in the EC, as is also suggested by the figures on intra-group procurements in Table 1.14. If the growing production by independent Japanese components manufacturers in the EC is taken into account as well, the conclusion must be that Japanese firms tend to avoid procuring components from EC firms.

The reliance on Japanese components reflects the importance of component design and quality for the competitiveness of consumer electronics goods. Key components are designed and produced in-house. Other component production is traditionally taken care of by suppliers and subcontractors that have a long-term relationship with the larger core firms. Relationships with subcontractors and long-standing suppliers are part of an organisation of production characterised by 'lean production' methods, just-in-time deliveries of components, and joint development of components for new products. As described in Section 1.1, this type of production management constitutes a competitive advantage of Japanese electronics firms, and the firms pursue a strategy to transfer the system abroad (Dunning and Gittelman 1992, Caves 1993). It is well known that Japanese automobile manufacturers' investments in the US were followed by a large number of Japanese components suppliers, usually members of the vertical *keiretsu* of the manufacturers, setting up manufacturing plants. This led to the creation of geographically concentrated networks of inter-related Japanese manufacturing plants (e.g. Kimura and Pugel 1995, Head, Ries, and Swenson 1995). In the EC, a development towards the creation of Japanese manufacturing networks is evident in the electronics industry.

Japanese firms regularly complain about insufficient quality and reliability and high prices of components supplied by EC firms, and point out that only through in-house components manufacturing or procurements from Japanese suppliers can they remain competitive.[106] On the other hand, long term supplier–client relationships between Japanese firms are inherently difficult to break, even for efficient EC components producers. An increasing dominance of Japanese firms in final product markets will almost automatically lead to falling demand for EC components producers, in the absence of efforts to integrate EC suppliers in the supply chain of Japanese firms. As for the latter, the information available is not too encouraging. Very few Japanese firms report that they provide EC suppliers with technological assistance to help them meet quality and design requirements (Nihon Boueki Shinkoukai 1990c–1992c), and in 1990 only 5 per cent of Japanese electronics subsidiaries reported that they had been able to increase local content by providing some form of assistance to local suppliers (Nihon Tsuushou Sangyoushou 1991).

Paradoxically, it can be argued that the EC's local content requirements actually reduced the prospects for EC components suppliers (see Chapter 8). Considering that involving new suppliers in procurement schemes tends to be a time-consuming process, the necessity to increase local content as quickly as possible may have led Japanese firms to transfer components production to the EC or to buy components from long-term suppliers, rather than to develop new procurement links. Once in-house production is in place or Japanese suppliers have started to supply components from European plants, it becomes less likely that Japanese firms shift to European suppliers in future.

In addition to the value added of EC production and the value of EC procurements, the technological sophistication of what is produced matters in an assessment of Japanese manufacturing investment. Here Japanese electronics firms do not score that well. Generally, Japanese firms tend to transfer only the manufacture of more mature product generations. For instance, Japanese IC producers manufacture the more mature generations of DRAMs in the EC, while production of the newest generation is concentrated in Japan and, more recently, in the US (Furlotti 1991).[107] Similarly, the latest generation of VCRs with improved recording technology and features is imported from Japan, and so are camcorders, a technologically complex and relatively novel product. A survey by the Export–Import Bank of Japan in 1991 revealed that the transfer of production of high value-added products to the EC had a very low priority for Japanese electronics firms (Takaoka and Satake 1991). The innovative base of Japanese firms is Japan, where they develop new products, test the reactions of Japanese consumers, who tend to demand high quality standards, and try to reach satisfactory efficiency levels through 'learning by doing' and expanding the scale of manufacturing operations. The internationalisation strategies of Japanese firms generally have not gone as far as to reduce this kind of reliance on the home country.

1.5.4 Diffusion of Know-how and Technology

Unambiguously favourable effects of Japanese manufacturing DFI on the EC economy arise where DFI contributes to the development of local labour skills, the introduction and diffusion of superior technologies and management and engineering practices, and an improvement in manufacturing productivity. There is no doubt that Japanese firms' competitiveness relates to an important extent to the use of 'Japanese style' production practices, such as just-in-time delivery systems and the development of suppliers, a focus on quality control through statistical control methods and work team quality control (quality circles), an emphasis on worker participation and responsibility, the assignment of functional flexible tasks at the shop floor, and flexibility in adapting assembly lines for the manufacture of a range of products. Introduction of these practices may improve the local skill base and productivity directly, i.e. through successful implementation in Japanese plants, or indirectly, i.e. through emulation by local EC assembly firms and EC components suppliers. The degree of diffusion of management and engineering practices and the development of local skills in manufacturing and engineering will be greater in the case of joint ventures and other forms of cooperation with local partners, in cases where manufacturing activities are extended to design and development, and where there is a greater delegation of responsibilities to local workers and managers. The available evidence is reviewed below.

There are strong indications that emulation of Japanese style working and production practices by EC firms has been an important phenomenon. Oliver and Wilkinson (1992) surveyed UK firms in 1992 and found that one half to two thirds of them had introduced practices such as just-in-time manufacturing, quality circles, and flexible manufacturing (reduced setup times). Moreover, the large majority of the firms implementing such practices rated their introduction successful to very successful. Oliver and Wilkinson did not investigate what role the existence of local Japanese manufacturing plants has had in facilitating such emulation, but it is clear that the relative success of a large number of Japanese firms' manufacturing plants established in the second half of the 1980s gave strong encouragement to UK firms. The median date of introduction of Japanese style practices in the UK firms, 1988–1989, is suggestive of adoption after Japanese investors had shown that these practices can be successful in the UK. In contrast, as noted above, the information available suggests much fewer beneficial effects in terms of technology transfer to EC components suppliers. Although it is reported that some Japanese firms have actively worked to develop the local supply infrastructure (Morris, Munday, and Wilkinson 1994: 48), the scale of procurements of complex components in particular is limited, and Japanese firms rely on supplies from related or independent Japanese components producers.

Diffusion of technology and emulation of best production and engineering practices are most likely to take place through the establishment of Japanese–EC joint ventures. In Section 1.4.2 it was reported that joint ventures are a factor of importance in Japanese manufacturing activities in the EC. While the first experience with EC–Japanese joint ventures in CTV production was clearly discouraging for EC firms, recent joint ventures appear better matched and may enable EC firms to regain some competitiveness in the manufacture of products such as copiers, facsimiles, laser printers, VCRs, and CD players in which Japanese firms are leading in design and efficiency.[108]

In addition to joint ventures, other forms of cooperation and business tie-ups are important in some areas, but are much less well documented. For example, Grundig (controlled by Philips) in Germany has a tie-up with

Matsushita in VCRs: with technological assistance from Matsushita, Grundig manufactures key components such as magnetic heads, which Matsushita uses at its German VCR assembly plant. EC–Japanese alliances are most important in semiconductors, but here the prevailing pattern is one of production consignment to EC firms in the absence of Japanese investment. Siemens regained a position as DRAM manufacturer through a tie-up with Toshiba in 1M DRAMs and produces DRAMs and other integrated circuits on consignment from Toshiba (Kimura 1994). Toshiba also consigns DRAM production to SGS-Thomson while relying less strongly on EC investment: it was the only major Japanese semiconductor firm not to have established integrated DRAM production by 1994. Kimura (1994) also reports that other 'second tier' semiconductor firms, such as Matsushita, Oki, and Sanyo, have no production bases in the EC but are involved in marketing agreements and product consignments with the major EC semiconductor firms Siemens, SGS-Thomson, and Philips.

The extension of manufacturing operations to applied research, development, and design activities is likely to increase the benefits of DFI substantially. R&D and design activities provide highly skilled employment opportunities and give local engineers opportunities to learn about Japanese-style product development and engineering techniques. Benefits are also derived from the redesign and adaptation of products and production processes to allow the incorporation of local components, from technical support to manufacturing plants leading to increased productivity, and from product designs better suited to local consumers. Basic research, as opposed to applied R&D and design, has clear positive spillover effects through its contribution to the science base, particularly if results are published. On the other hand, it has been argued that such research tends to be closely linked to laboratories in Japan rather than local manufacturing activities and therefore lacks positive interaction with the local economy (Casson 1991).

Until the late 1980s, overseas R&D activities by Japanese MNEs were very limited. Studies analysing overseas R&D of large MNEs using information on the location of laboratories in US patent data invariably show that Japanese firms lag behind US and European firms in the internationalisation of R&D (Cantwell 1989, Patel and Pavitt 1991, Patel 1995). Patel (1995) finds that during 1985–1990 a mere 1 per cent of US patenting by the 139 largest Japanese MNEs was based on research conducted outside Japan. This compared to 8 per cent for US MNEs.

It is harder to gather evidence on Japanese firms' overseas R&D expenditure and R&D personnel. The only source on Japanese firms' overseas R&D are the yearly MITI surveys. Elsewhere it has been pointed out that the published R&D figures are likely to underestimate overseas R&D because the R&D related questions suffer from pervasive non-responses (see Belderbos 1995a and Chapter 9). Bearing this in mind, the 1989 MITI survey counted a total of 2,732 personnel engaged in R&D in foreign subsidiaries of Japanese electronics firms, of whom 461 were employed in EC subsidiaries (Nihon Tsuushou Sangyoushou 1991). The ratio of overseas R&D personnel to all overseas employees was a mere 0.8 per cent but was higher for the EC, at almost 2 per cent. In contrast, the ratio of R&D to manufacturing employees reached 9.8 per cent for the electronics industry in Japan (Nihon Soumuka Tokeikyoku 1990: 87). These figures show a concentration of R&D in the home country which is, to a lesser extent, also observed for US MNEs. For example, US MNEs in the consumer electronics and electrical appliances industry had 6.9 per cent of US personnel dedicated to R&D, while this ratio was only 2.5 per cent abroad. R&D personnel in US firms in 1982 was relatively more concentrated in the EC, however, where the share of R&D to total personnel reached 5.4 per cent (Nihon Kaihatsu Ginkou 1988). Economies of scale in R&D in high technology industries and the need for close communication between the research department and decision centres generally favour centralisation of R&D in the home country, in particular when the home country has a substantial and diversified science base (e.g. Patel and Pavitt 1991, Pearce 1989).

The question whether the small scale of overseas R&D abroad is a particular trait of Japanese firms is addressed in Chapter 9, which presents evidence on the determinants of overseas R&D for a sample of Japanese electronics firms. The results indicate that overseas R&D increases significantly with both the degree of internationalisation of sales and manufacturing and the experience in operating foreign plants. This suggests that the lack of overseas R&D can to an important extent be attributed to Japanese firms' still relatively low international production ratios and their relatively late internationalisation.

The evidence on Japanese electronics firms' R&D and design activities in the EC shows a rapid increase in such activities, though from a small base. A non-comprehensive list of R&D and design centres established up to 1991 is presented in Table 1.24. The list includes R&D facilities that were set up as a separate subsidiary but omits R&D centres attached to manufacturing subsidiaries, since the information on establishment dates and employment tends to be most reliable for separate facilities. Nor are R&D centres attached to two Euro-Japanese manufacturing joint ventures included: Siemens-Matsushita Components develops passive components, and Canon-Olivetti develops laser printers (Nihon Kaihatsu Ginkou 1988).

What stands out from Table 1.24 is the marked increase in the number of establishments in the early 1990s. At least eight separate R&D centres were set up during 1990–1991, which is probably more than the total number up to 1990.[109] The take-off in R&D investments in the 1990s is even more

Table 1.24 R&D affiliates of Japanese electronics firms in the EC, 1991

Company	Ctry	Subsidiary name	Estbl	Empl	(J)	Activity
Sony	UK	Sony Broadcast	1978	30	(na)	Digital VCRs, software
Fujitsu	UK	Fujitsu Microelectronics	1983	8	(0)	ASIC design
Ricoh	G	Ricoh Deutschland	1986	8	(3)	Fax design
Canon	UK	Canon Research Centre	1988	15	(1)	Software development
Sony	G	European Technology Centre	1988	41	(na)	Satellite CTV and communication R&D
Matsushita Electric Works	G	Euro Matsushita Electric Works	1989	5	(1)	Factory automation R&D
Sharp	UK	Sharp Laboratories of Europe	1990	30	(3)	Software development, basic R&D, language systems
Fujitsu	UK	Fujitsu Europe Telecom R&D Centre	1990	30	(3)	Telecommunications software, product development
Matsushita	UK	D2B Systems[a]	1990	15	(0)	Software development
NEC	G	European Technology Centre (Düsseldorf)	1990	35	(0)	Semiconductor design
Canon	Fr	Canon Information Systems	1990	21	(3)	Software development, image processing research
Toshiba	UK	Toshiba Cambridge Research Centre	1991	8	(1)	Basic semiconductor research
Matsushita	G	Panasonic European R&D Centre	1991	20	(5)	CTV, VCR design

Notes: Ctr = country; Estbl = time of establishment; na = not available; G = Germany; De = Denmark; Fr = France; Empl (J) = number of research employees in 1991–1992 (no. of Japanese employees in parentheses).

[a] Joint venture of Philips (75%) and Matsushita (25%).

Sources: Nihon Boeki Shinkoukai (1990c), Nihon Denshi Kikai Kougyoukai (1992a), Touyou Keizai (1992a), Nihon Kaihatsu Ginkou (1988), *Electronics Business*, 17 September 1990, Furlotti (1991), JETRO (1993b).

pronounced if we take into account the R&D centres for which further information was not available. Hitachi reportedly started R&D activities at three different locations in the EC in 1991: ASIC design in Maidenhead, UK, basic research in submicron production technology in Cambridge, UK, and product design in Munich, Germany (see *Electronics Business*, 17 September 1990). Fujitsu established a design facility for large scale ICs near Heathrow Airport in the UK in June 1990, and NEC began audio and video design activities in its Telford plant in the UK in 1990. The yearly JETRO surveys among Japanese manufacturers show that he growth in EC R&D and design activities has continued through 1994 (Nihon Boueki Shinkoukai 1995c). At the end of 1994, 85 R&D and design centres in the electronics field could be counted, of which 64 were incorporated in existing manufacturing subsidiaries. These figures compare with a total number of 174 Japanese manufacturing subsidiaries classified by JETRO in the electronics industry.

It is clear from Table 1.24 that the R&D centres are small in scale and generally employ 10–40 personnel. The two most important R&D activities are product design and software development. Product design and development activities focus on the adaptation of products to suit European technical requirements and characteristics of demand, and in some cases on the adaptation of production processes to allow for the incorporation of EC-produced components. A prime example is the design of application-specific ICs (ASICs), which have to be customised according to the demands of each client. The location of this type of development and design activity overseas is part of Japanese firms' internationalisation strategies and has gained much in importance in the 1990s. Takaoka and Satake (1991) reported that 57 per cent of Japanese electronics firms surveyed by the Export–Import Bank of Japan in 1990 regarded the localisation of product development in the EC as one of the priorities in their strategy for the EC market.

Most of the R&D and design facilities function as a 'listening post' as well, feeding back information on technological and market developments to Japanese R&D centres. More specific technology sourcing appears to be the main purpose of the establishment of software engineering centres. Software development is a field in which Japanese firms are often said to be lacking skills and experience, while there is a scarcity of software engineers in Japan (Genther and Dalton 1992). European expertise in software development also has played a role in the acquisitions of ICL by Fujitsu and Office Workstations by Matsushita (see Table 1.17).

A further characteristic of Japanese R&D is the concentration of centres in the UK and Germany. Product design needs feedback from manufacturing and marketing, and the UK and Germany are the two largest markets for Japanese electronics and the countries where most of Japanese firms' manufacturing plants are located. The facility in Rennes set up by Canon appears the only R&D affiliate located in France by 1991, although Ricoh is also reported to undertake R&D activities, i.e. components development for office automation equipment, in its Wettolsheim plant (Nihon Kaihatsu Ginkou 1988).

A last issue is the appointment of EC personnel to management positions in Japanese electronics subsidiaries. While focusing on the training of shop floor workers, Japanese MNEs have often been alleged to fail to train and promote local managerial personnel at overseas subsidiaries (e.g. Senker 1991). The figures presented in Table 1.25 show that these allegations do have substance. The percentage of Japanese electronics firms' subsidiaries in the EC where Japanese expatriates were appointed to management positions is shown for 1990 and 1993. In 1990, Japanese nationals were

Table 1.25 Japanese expatriates in management positions at EC electronics subsidiaries in 1990 and 1993 (%)

Position	1990	1993
President	79	77
Vice-president	71	44
Finance	64	48
Sales	46	30
Procurement	42	18
Planning	40	23
R&D	27	14
Personnel affairs	22	19
Total management	53	37
All employees	3.0	1.9

Source: Nihon Tsuushou Sangyoushou (1991, 1994).

appointed as presidents of Japanese subsidiaries in the EC in 79 per cent of all cases; in addition, 71 per cent of vice-presidents were Japanese as well. A majority of appointments for Japanese nationals was also recorded for heads of the finance division, which stems from the need to keep control over activities such as investment and financing, and to facilitate close relationships with the parent firm and the main bank. In total, local managers were appointed to less than half the management positions available in 1990. This compared with an expatriate ratio of only 3 per cent for all employees. However, the situation for local managers appears to have improved considerably by 1993. The share of Japanese appointments decreased for all functions and fell to 37 per cent for all managers. The number of Japanese vice-presidents dropped to less than half, and Japanese nationals as head of the finance division became a minority as well. The only function with a high and stable share of Japanese appointments was that of president.

It is necessary to interpret these figures with some caution. About 60 per cent of the electronics subsidiaries tend to respond to this part of the survey, and there may well be a self selection process present: firms that cannot report appointments of local managers choose not to respond. Self selection may have increased as this issue has become more sensitive. Nevertheless, it would be safe to conclude that Japanese firms have recently made progress in appointing local managers. It is likely that several years of experience in operating manufacturing activities in the EC has allowed Japanese firms to do so.

1.5.5 Efficiency, Competition, and Consumer Prices

A specific characteristic of Japanese electronics firms' DFI in the EC is its strong relationship with EC trade policy. It was argued that in the absence of trade policy measures, and in particular antidumping actions, in many cases Japanese firms would likely have preferred to concentrate manufacturing in Japan or in their 'regional core networks' in South-East Asia, and to export to the EC. Similarly, local content requirements have forced Japanese producers to increase the value added of EC production activities and have prompted components firms to manufacture in the EC. In both cases, manufacturing in the EC is a 'second best' option and is likely to lead to higher production costs.

In the literature on strategic trade policy, trade policy measures are regarded as a means to put domestic firms at an advantage against foreign rivals to ensure that 'home' firms capture a larger share of profits in international oligopolistic markets.[110] In Section 1.3.5 it was suggested that EC antidumping measures indeed reflect elements of industrial policy designed to shield EC firms from Japanese competition. Chapters 3 and 4 formally consider how antidumping measures and local content requirements, by directly or indirectly increasing the costs of Japanese producers, may have helped to increase the market share and profits of EC producers. However, to the extent that this is achieved, it will be associated with inefficiencies in resource allocation, increases in the average production costs for sales in the EC, and increases in consumer prices. This in turn is likely to be associated with EC-produced electronics goods which are not able to compete on world markets, but only on an EC market protected from import competition. Circumstantial evidence was provided by Table 1.18, which showed that only 4 per cent of the electronics output by Japanese plants in the EC was sold outside the EC. Likewise, while the EC electrical and electronics industry as a whole saw 5 per cent annual growth in the second half of the 1980s, the share of extra-EC exports in sales continued to decline (CEC 1993: 9–12).

On the other hand, the investment response to antidumping and local content measures allowed Japanese firms to avoid paying duties. This has played an important role in the inability of antidumping measures to protect EC firms' production in the EC, as witnessed in several antidumping cases discussed in this chapter (e.g. CD players and typewriters). The relocation of EC firms' production to Asia also indicates that price competition has continued to be severe and that cost and price increases associated with Japanese DFI in connection with antidumping have probably not been that important. There is some evidence that Japanese firms' recently gained experience in transferring production abroad has enabled them to manufacture in the EC without substantial cost increases.[111] In this regard, Ozawa

(1991) argues that Japanese DFI in the US and the EC is developing from a 'second best' to a 'first best' strategy. To what extent this holds true cannot be judged on the basis of the present analysis. As a partial test, it would be interesting to monitor if the Japanese manufacture of products for which the prospect of further trade barriers are now minimal, such as CD players and typewriters, will remain in the EC.

1.6 Conclusions

The investments by Japanese electronics firms in the EC are part of an internationalisation strategy adopted in the mid-1980s spurred by the rise in global protectionism, the appreciation of the yen, and emerging trends in the electronics industry at large. DFI was facilitated by unusually low capital costs in the late 1980s and a positive stance of host governments towards Japanese DFI, while membership of vertical and horizontal *keiretsu* have lowered barriers to DFI in several ways.

The EC attracted increasing shares of both exports and DFI by Japanese electronics firms during the second half of the 1980s, reflecting the renewed interest in the EC market stemming from the unification programme and the relative neglect of the EC by Japanese firms in the past. Manufacturing investment in the EC was strongly induced by a range of trade policy measures against Japanese electronic imports and EC assembly plants taken by the EC since the beginning of the 1980s. These included tariff increases, a voluntary export restraint (for VCRs), antidumping actions, local content requirements, and stricter rules of origin. These measures had essentially made the threat of a 'Fortress Europe' materialise for Japanese electronics firms as early as 1990. A clear relationship can be observed between the timing of trade policy measures and the establishments of Japanese plants in the EC. This and evidence presented in detail in Chapter 6 suggests that Japanese manufacturing in the EC would have been substantially less in the absence of EC trade policy measures.

On the one hand, the major EC electronics firms such as Philips, Thomson, and Olivetti have actively used the antidumping instrument to gain protection from Japanese competition. The EC appears to have used the discretion allowed under EC and GATT antidumping rules to address the 'Japan problem': the advance of Japanese firms in high technology markets of the EC, the relative weakness of EC firms, and the increasing bilateral trade deficit. On the other hand, 'tariff jumping' DFI by Japanese firms has made antidumping a less effective weapon. Antidumping in several electronics industries, such as CD players and typewriters, has not been able to ensure sustained production by EC firms in the Community, as EC firms have eventually relocated production to Asia. In these cases antidumping has led to a predominantly Japanese owned EC industry. The evidence suggests that the EC has used the antidumping instrument and rules of origin opportunistically to attract Japanese manufacturing investment and to strengthen the electronics industry with Japanese manufacturing skills and technology. An examination of recent trends in antidumping policy shows that the target of EC antidumping actions in electronics increasingly shifted to South Korean and other South East Asian firms in the early 1990s. Although Japanese firms with manufacturing operations in the EC have benefited from such antidumping protection, they have not yet joined formally in an antidumping complaint.

During 1986–1991, employment in manufacturing subsidiaries in the EC rose fourfold to reach almost 80,000 people in 1991. At the same time, Japanese electronics firms expanded their distribution networks in the EC, increasing the number of distribution subsidiaries to 416 by 1990, employing at least 27,000 people. While manufacturing investments in the early 1980s were still oriented towards individual countries, Japanese firms have increasingly adopted pan-European investment strategies, characterised by specialisation of production in different manufacturing plants and intra-EC flows of components and final goods. Whereas most investment until 1989 was in greenfield plants, the years 1989–1991 showed a wave of Japanese acquisitions, among which Kyocera's take-over of AVX and Fujitsu's take-over of ICL. Japanese firms clearly attempted to build up market positions ahead of the completion of the Internal Market.

Japanese electronics firms' DFI in the EC has to some extent helped to stem the decline in manufacturing employment in the EC electronics industry and has had a positive effect on the industry's trade balance with Japan. Further favourable effects on the EC economy are arguably following from a shift from assembly activities to technology intensive components production, emulation of best production and management practices by EC firms, and diffusion of Japanese technological and managerial know-how, in particular through joint ventures. On some counts, however, Japanese DFI scores less well. Japanese firms show a strong preference for procurement of components in the EC from their own EC plants and from the plants of other Japanese suppliers, and are reluctant to include EC components manufacturers in their supplier networks. Japanese firms also show a reluctance to transfer production of high value added products abroad, have limited R&D and design facilities in the EC, and are not inclined to appoint local personnel to management positions.

At least in overseas R&D and the appointment of local managers, Japanese firms appear to have been making steady progress in the early 1990s. A great number of R&D and design centres have been established from 1989 onwards, and there is evidence of increased involvement of local personnel in management. On the other hand, the pace of new manufacturing investment has clearly slowed down. Divestments from manufacturing operations became a significant phenomenon after 1991, when the completion of the Internal Market failed to produce the expected growth in EC electronics sales. At the same time, new investments reflect more of a longer term commitment to the EC market than a direct response to trade policy measures. Japanese firms, though, still have some way to go to attain the status of EC 'insiders' comparable to that of US electronics firms.

APPENDIX 1.1

Japanese Electronics Firms and Industrial Groups

Table A1.1 presents some indicators of the importance of membership of vertical and horizontal business groups to major Japanese electronics firms. It lists all Japanese electronics firms with consolidated sales exceeding 250 billion yen. There are two types of industrial groups in Japan (see also Dodwell 1988):

1. *Horizontal business groups*. These cover a wide spectrum of industries and are centred around major banks and trading companies. There are six major horizontal business groups in Japan: Mitsui, Sumitomo, Mitsubishi, Fuyo, Dai Ichi Kangyo (DKB), and Sanwa. Together, these own more than 30 per cent of the private sector's assets in Japan (Dodwell 1988).
2. *Vertical business groups*. These cover vertically connected firms gathered around a parent or core company. There are about 40 large vertical business groups in Japan.

The largest electronics firms are parent firms in vertical business groups. These groups mostly comprise vertically related firms (subcontractors, trading firms), but also include firms active in specialised activities in the electronics sector (satellite firms) and firms active in other sectors (machinery, chemicals, construction, finance). The largest vertical business group in the electronics industry is the Hitachi group. It comprised 733 affiliated firms in Japan alone in 1992. Only some of these firms (590) enter the consolidated accounts of Hitachi, so that the consolidated sales of the Hitachi group (almost 8 trillion yen) still underestimates the size of the group.[112] Other large vertical business groups are headed by Matsushita, Toshiba, and Fujitsu. Matsushita has two satellite firms, Matsushita Electric Works and Matsushita Communication, which are among the largest electronics firms in Japan. These satellite firms themselves have a considerable number of affiliated firms. For the major producers of consumer electronics goods and household appliances, the last column of the table gives the number of affiliated retailers in Japan. Here Matsushita is by far the largest group, followed by Toshiba and Hitachi.

Almost two thirds of the major electronics companies are members of horizontal business groups (while some of them are at the same time members of a vertical business group). For only one third of the major firms, however, are the ties to the horizontal group judged to be strong.

Table A1.1 Horizontal and vertical group linkages of the largest Japanese electronics firms, 1992

Company	Sales	Business group	Affiliated firms Japan	Cons. firms Japan	Affiliated retailers Japan
Integrated					
Hitachi	7,766	—	733	(590)	11,000
Toshiba	4,722	(Mitsui)	537	(87)	13,000
Mitsubishi Electric	3,343	Mitsubishi	256	(70)	5,000
Computers, telecommunications					
NEC	3,774	Sumitomo	209	(66)	3,000
Fujitsu	3,442	DKB	209	(121)	
Oki	681	Fuyo	93	(6)	
Matsushita Communication	546	(Sumitomo), Matsushita	25	(13)	
Control and industrial equipment					
Matsushita Electric Works	1,078	(Sumitomo), Matsushita	133	(13)	
Fuji Electric	909	DKB, Furukawa Electric	129	(23)	
Omron	483	(Mitsubishi)	51	(42)	
Tokyo Electric	278	(Mitsui), Toshiba	35	(5)	
Yokogawa Electric	266	Fuyo	67	(17)	
Consumer/audio/video					
Matsushita	7,450	(Sumitomo)	na	(87)	25,000
Sony	3,915	(Mitsui)	99	(69)	3,000
Sanyo	1,616	Sumitomo	136	(29)	6,000
Sharp	1,555	(Fuyo)	30	(8)	3,500
JVC	839	(Sumitomo), Matsushita	81	(9)	2,000
Pioneer	613	—	47	(17)	

Office machines, cameras, watches				
Canon	1,869	Fuyo	na	(na)
Ricoh	1,017	—	132	(66)
Citizin	412	(DKB)	85	(23)
Casio	383	—	41	(34)
Minolta	356	—	36	(13)
Nikon	272	Mitsubishi	44	(4)
Olympus	260	Sumitomo	27	(9)
Components				
Nippon Denso	1,481	(Mitsui), Toyota	56	(6)
TDK	535	—	39	(29)
Alps	461	Mitsui	28	(3)
Kyocera	453	(Sanwa)	18	(11)
Murata	280	—	25	(21)
Nitto Denko	260	—	34	(9)

Notes: The table includes all listed electronics firm with over 250 billion yen consolidated turnover. Sales are consolidated sales in Fiscal Year 1991 (year ending March 1992). Industrial group between brackets indicates weaker links to horizontal business groups. Cons. = consolidated, DKB = Dai Ichi Kangyo.

Sources: Nihon Keizai Shimbunsha (1993); Dodwell (1989); Keizai Chousa Kyoukai (1990); Flath and Nairu (1989), Mackintosh-BIS (1991).

APPENDIX 1.2

Subsidiaries and Employment of Japanese Electronics Firms in the EC

A list of subsidiaries of Japanese electronics firms in the European Community in 1990 and numbers of employees in these subsidiaries is provided in Table A1.2.

Table A1.2 Subsidiaries and employment of Japanese electronics firms in the EC in 1990, by company

Company (group)	Products (see Notes)	No. of subsidiaries		No. of employees			
		All	Manf.	All	Manf.	Sales	Increase 1986–90 (%)
Matsushita group							
Matsushita[a]	consumer, ofm	17	10	6,097	4,255	1,842	87
JVC	audio, video	17	5	na	2,413	na	na
Mats. Components	component	2	2	528	528	0	456
Kyushu Matsushita	tel, prn	1	1	500	500	0	est
Mats. Elec. Works	electr. relays	3	1	318	238	80	47
Mats. Communication	car-audio, tel	2	2	198	198	0	est
Matsushita Denso	fax	1	1	65	65	0	est
Mats. Denshi Oyo Kiki	magnetrons	1	1	16	16	0	est
Total		44	23	+10,135	8,231	+1,922	184
Sony group							
Sony	audio, video	13	5	na	6,240	na	na
Aiwa	audio	3	1	587	516	71	94
Sony Magnescale	scales	1	0	6	0	6	est
Total		17	6	na	6,765	na	na
Canon group							
Canon	ofm, cameras	17	3	7,848	1,861	5,987	110
Copyer	copiers	2	0	24	0	24	200
Total		19	3	7,872	1,861	6,011	110

Table A1.2 (*Continued*)

Company (group)	Products (see Notes)	No. of subsidiaries		No. of employees			
		All	Manf.	All	Manf.	Sales	Increase 1986–90 (%)
Toshiba group							
Toshiba	cons, indu	20	5	3,954	2,122	1,832	93
Tokyo Electric	scales, prn	7	3	571	320	251	18
Topkon	medical eq	4	0	80	0	80	63
Onkyo	audio	3	0	55	0	55	129
Toshiba Litec	halogen lamps	1	1	49	49	0	est
Total		35	9	4,709	2,491	2,218	84
Hitachi group							
Hitachi	cons, indu	4	3	1,950	1,520	430	na
Hitachi Sales	cons, indu	9	0	625	0	625	15
Hitachi Maxell	tapes	2	1	na	530	na	na
Nissei Sangyo	compo	2	0	80	0	80	23
Hitachi Denshi	meas eq	2	0	49	0	49	0
Hitachi Koki	power tools	4	0	0	0	na	na
Hitachi Medico	medical eq	1	0	5	0	5	est
Kokusai Electric	wireless eq	1	0	18	0	18	100
Total		25	4	+3,259	2,050	+1,207	na
Fujitsu group							
Fujitsu[b]	indu, ICs	11	4	2,757	2,515	242	372
Fujitsu Isotec	prn	1	1	200	200	0	est
Advantest	IC testers	3	1	80	40	40	900

Fujitsu General	consumer	3	0	50	0	50	22
Fujitsu Ten	car-audio	1	0	7	0	7	133
Total		19	6	3,094	2,755	339	392
NEC group							
NEC	cons, indu	13	3	2,998	1,608	1,390	135
Anritsu Electric	meas eq	3	0	71	0	71	87
Ando	IC testers	1	0	11	0	11	10
Total		17	3	3,080	1,608	1,472	140
Sanyo group							
Sanyo Electric	consumer	9	4	1,669	1,249	420	–18
Sanyo Denki Boeki	consumer	4	2	1,199	913	286	est
Total		13	6	2,868	2,162	706	41
Kyocera	components	15	3	2,842	2,313	529	9,700
Sharp	cons, copiers	6	4	2,818	2,152	666	116
Konica	copiers, cameras	6	1	2,342	138	2,204	130
Ricoh	ofm, cameras	8	2	na	931	0	na
Mitsubishi group							
Mitsubishi Electric	cons, indu	8	5	1,525	984	541	na
Akai	audio	4	1	657	457	200	46
Total		12	6	2,182	1,441	741	na
Brother group							
Brother	cons, prn	3	3	990	990	0	560
Brother International	cons, prn	11	0	869	0	869	18
Total		14	3	1,859	990	869	109
Seiko group							
Seiko Epson	printers, PCs	9	3	1,041	674	367	178
Seiko Denshi Kogyo	compo, LCDs	3	2	22	8	14	100

Table A1.2 (*Continued*)

Company (group)	Products (see Notes)	No. of subsidiaries		No. of employees			
		All	Manf.	All	Manf.	Sales	Increase 1986–90 (%)
Hattori Seiko	watches	3	0	400	0	400	176
Seikosha	printers	1	1	107	107	0	est
Total		16	6	1,570	789	781	189
Pioneer	audio	10	2	1,372	471	901	28
Alps group							
Alps	components	4	3	1,246	1,006	240	299
Alpine	car-audio	3	0	71	0	71	est
Total		7	3	1,317	1,006	311	322
Yuasa Battery	batteries	4	2	1,165	1,133	32	442
Omron	indu, PCBs	16	2	1,059	185	874	91
Oki	indu, compo	10	1	964	499	465	1,653
Murata	components	7	2	640	360	280	na
TDK	tapes	3	1	539	350	189	205
Tabuchi Denki	power sources	1	1	520	520	0	174
Minolta	ofm, cameras	10	2	na	500	na	na
Shimadzu	meas eq	2	2	468	468	0	1,571
Tamura	transformers	1	1	457	457	0	est
Star Micronics	meas eq, prn	4	1	449	306	143	580
Hosiden	tel parts	2	1	440	434	6	11,000

Clarion	car audio	3	2	416	395	21	179
Orion	VTRs	1	1	400	400	0	est
Citizin group							
Citizin Trading	watches	3	1	214	54	160	–4
Citizen	watches, prn	4	2	162	116	46	853
Total		7	3	376	170	206	57
Nitto Denko	components	4	1	385	334	51	41
Olympus	cameras, copiers	3	1	+366	na	366	est
Janome	sewing eq	2	1	351	217	134	–6
Terumo	medical	1	1	350	350	0	1
Kenwood	audio	6	1	348	49	299	47
Funai Denki	consumer	3	2	340	330	10	11,000
Dainippon Screen	optoelectric eq	4	0	315	0	315	111
Makita Electric	power tools	7	0	313	0	313	52
Mita	copiers	7	0	304	0	304	111
Casio	consumer	3	0	286	0	286	30
Mitsutoyo	meas eq	4	1	237	59	178	est
Mitsumi	components	3	2	234	224	10	4,580
King Kogyo	cash registers	1	0	230	0	230	0
Nippon Columbia	audio	2	1	177	141	36	est
Aisin Seiki	control eq. cars	3	0	173	0	173	82
Terasaki Denki	power switches	1	1	160	160	0	est
Dainippon Printing	projection screens	1	1	160	160	0	est
Daikin Kogyo	airconditioners	1	1	149	149	0	60
Nippon Denso	car parts	4	0	148	0	148	est
SMK	components	2	1	141	124	17	985
Rohm	semiconductors	2	0	132	0	132	136

Table A1.2 (*Continued*)

Company (group)	Products (see Notes)	No. of subsidiaries		No. of employees			
		All	Manf.	All	Manf.	Sales	Increase 1986–90 (%)
Nihon CMK	PCBs	1	1	130	130	0	est
Horiba	meas eq	3	3	126	126	0	62
JEOL	medical	4	0	120	0	120	21
Nihon Seiki	meas eq for cars	1	1	114	114	0	est
Amano	time recorders	1	1	109	109	0	est
JST	connectors	5	5	104	104	0	est
Yamauchi Electric	rubber compo	1	1	100	100	0	est
Showa Plastics	audio cabinets	1	1	100	100	0	est

Notes: Manf = subsidiaries with manufacturing function; Sales = subsidiaries with only sales function; est = subsidiaries newly established in the period 1986–1990: no employees in the EC in 1986; + = actual number of employees is higher.

Product abbreviations: indu = industrial electronics, cons = consumer electronics, eq = equipment, comm = communication equipment (including tel = telephones, fax = facsimiles), electr. relays = electronic relays, ofm = office machines (including copiers, scales = electronic scales, meas eq = measuring equipment, prn = printers, PCs = personal computers, compo = components, ICs = integrated circuits, PCBs = printed circuit boards, LCDs = liquid crystal displays. Product list refers to products manufactured in EC plants where the firm has EC manufacturing operations, and to main product lines of the parent company otherwise.

[a] Does not include Siemens-Matsushita components.

[b] Does not include the acquistion of ICL.

Sources: Touyou Keizai (1987a, 1991a), Nihon Boueki Shinkoukai (1987c, 1990c), Nihon Denshi Kikai Kougyoukai (1990a), EACEM (1990).

APPENDIX 1.3

The Increasing Japanese Presence in the EC Electronics Industry

Table A1.3 illustrates the increasing Japanese presence in the EC electronics industry over the period 1982–1990.

Table A1.3 The increasing Japanese presence in the EC electronics industry, 1982–1990

	1982	1985	1986	1987	1988	1989	1990
EC consumer electronics market							
(million ECUs)							
Production	8,671	8,895	12,111	12,526	12,906	12,243	13,020
Apparent consumption	13,487	14,304	18,550	19,201	21,055	20,968	22,020
Net imports	3,637	5,409	6,439	6,675	8,149	8,725	9,000
of which: Japan					5,500	5,374	
(thousand persons)							
EC employment	147	134	131	127	123	126	
of which:							
Japanese firms[b]					16	19	
(%)					(13)	(15)	
Number of plants				224	165	174	
of which:							
Japanese plants[b]					43	58	
(%)					(19)	(33)	
CTV market							
(million units)							
Sales	11.3	12.9	15.0	16.1	18.4	18.0[h]	18.8[h]
EC production	8.2	11.0	12.3	11.9	13.2	13.0	
of which:							
Japanese firms	0.8[g]		1.9[f]	2.2[f]	3.5[c]	4.0[c]	
Japanese imports	0.7	0.8	0.8	0.5	0.4	0.4	
(% sales)							
EC production	80	85	82	74	72	72	

of which:							
Japanese firms	7		13	14	19	22	
Imports	20	15	18	26	28	28	
of which:							
Japan	6	6	5	3	2	2	
Korea		7	3	7	9	4	
VCR market							
(million units)							
Sales	5.0	5.4	6.5	8.2	10.1[h]	11.1[h]	12.1[h]
EC production	0.9	2.2	2.9	4.2	5.0	6.2	
of which:							
Japanese firms	0.7[d]	1.7[d]	2.3[f]	3.0[f]	4.6[c]	5.6[c]	
Japanese imports	4.0	3.1	3.3	3.5	3.2	3.6	
(% sales)							
EC production	17	40	45	51	52	56	
of which:							
Japanese firms	14	31	35	37	46	51	
Imports	83	60	55	49	48	44	
of which:							
Japan	80	58	51	43	33	32	
Korea		2	6	16	13	5	
Microwave oven market							
(million units)							
EC sales[h]		2.1	3.1	4.9	7.1	6.5	6.2
EC production		0.7	0.9	1.6	2.9	4.0[c]	
of which:							
Japanese firms					0.9[c]	1.3[c]	
Japanese imports[l]	0.3[d]	1.5	1.5	1.5	1.1	0.8	0.5
Japanese imports magnetrons[l]		0.7	1.1	1.8	3.1	3.2	1.4

Table A1.3 (*Continued*)

	1982	1985	1986	1987	1988	1989	1990
Copier market							
(thousand units)							
EC production						980[c]	
Production Japanese firms			80[f]	150[f]	524[c]	650[c]	
Japanese imports	641[d]	827[d]		442[l]	391[l]	335[l]	
Electric typerwriter market							
(thousand units)							
EC production[c]						2,750	
Production Japanese firms[c]					400	620	
Japanese imports		420[d]	350[d]			129[l]	165[l]
CD player market							
(thousand units)							
EC sales		655	2,095	3,951	6,203	7,766	
Production capacity Japanese firms[j]					>1,000		
Japanese imports[l]		523	1,545	2,289	3,198	2,514	2,001

Sources: CEC (1990, 1992), if not stated otherwise.

[b] source: EACEM (1990).
[c] source: Dempa (1990a); 1989 figures concern forecasted/planned production.
[d] source: Watanabe (1988).
[e] source: Nihon Yushutsunyuu Ginkou (1989).
[f] source: Nihon Kaihatsu Ginkou (1989).
[g] source: Mackintosh International (1985: 77).
[h] source: Euromonitor (1992).
[j] source: calculations based on EACEM (1990) and Yano Keizai Kenkyuujo (1989b).

APPENDIX 1.4

Data Sources on Japanese DFI

There are various sources of information on Japanese firms' overseas activities, all of which have their respective advantages and disadvantages. The most important sources of information on Japanese (electronics) firms' overseas activities are discussed below.[113]

A1.4.1 MOF's Data on Japanese DFI

The most commonly used data on Japanese DFI are data on notifications of overseas investments originally published by the Ministry of Finance (MOF) in the *Zaisei Kinyuu Toukei Geppou* (*Financial Investment Statistics Monthly*). However, using these data is fraught with problems (see also Komiya 1987). First, DFI flows measure only the share in overseas investments financed from Japan, a share that is not necessarily large. For example, in the MITI survey among Japanese MNEs in 1989, Japanese electronics firms' subsidiaries in the EC reported that only 9 per cent of investment outlays was financed by loans from the parent firm.

Second, although MOF data are disaggregated by country, these figures may not reflect the relative importance of countries as hosts to Japanese subsidiaries. This is because the country invested in often is not the country where the funds are used to increase manufacturing or sales capacity. For instance, Japanese firms' DFI to countries such as France or Germany often flows through finance subsidiaries located in the Netherlands, a route that is preferred because of tax advantages. This makes the Netherlands an important recipient of DFI in the MOF data, while the actual level of investment is rather small. Data gathered at the level of the overseas affiliates (Sections A1.4.2–A1.4.5 below) do not face these problems and generally provide a more accurate picture of investment patterns by industry and country.

A1.4.2 MITI's Surveys of Japanese MNEs

Japan's Ministry of International Trade and Industry (MITI) conducts a yearly survey among Japanese multinational enterprises which is published as *Wagakuni Kigyou no Kaigai Jigyou Katsudou* (*Report on the Foreign Activities of Japanese Firms*). Every three years, this survey is conducted in a more extensive form and published as *Kaigai Toushi Toukei Souran* (*Directory of Direct Foreign Investment*). The survey is loosely based on the US Department of Commerce's *Benchmark Survey* among US MNEs, but has as its major drawback that it is not mandatory and therefore suffers from low response ratios. For instance, the response ratio for the extensive survey over fiscal year 1989 (published in 1991) was only 46 per cent in terms of the number of parent firms; if one describes the response ratio in terms of the number of overseas subsidiaries, the ratio rises to 72 per cent (which suggests that non-responding firms were mainly small in size). Response ratios also differ over time and across sections of the survey, necessitating caution in drawing conclusions from the aggregate industry data and developments over time.

Another disadvantage of the surveys is the rather broad industry classification which it shares with MOF's DFI data, grouping electronic components, consumer electronics, computers, and industrial electronics all in the sector 'electrical machinery', while copiers are grouped together with the optical and clock industries in the sector 'precision machinery'.

Because of these disadvantages, Chapter 1 has used other, more detailed, data sources to describe Japanese electronics firms' investments in the EC. However, the compelling advantage of the MITI survey is the information provided on employment and sales by Japanese manufacturing subsidiaries worldwide, and the detailed information on the activities of manufacturing subsidiaries, such as sales and procurement patterns and the role of local managers. The survey data are used in this chapter to provide insight into global investment patterns, procurement and sales behaviour, and the role of local managers.

In some of the other chapters in this book, the disadvantages of the MITI survey data could be overcome by using more disaggregated data or the original responses. Access to these unpublished data was obtained through the Institute of International Trade and Investment, the MITI related institution which prepares MITI's publications on Japanese firms' DFI. In Chapter 8, local procurement by Japanese firms is analysed for the consumer electronics and components sub-sectors using figures that are based on a sample of firms with reliable responses. In Chapter 9, overseas R&D expenditures by Japanese electronics firms are analysed by studying the original firm-level data for responding firms.

A1.4.3 Touyou Keizai

An extensive source of data on Japanese firms' investments abroad is *Kaigai Shinshutsu Kigyou Souran* (*Directory of Multinational Enterprises*), published by Touyou Keizai. This source provides a near complete listing of Japanese MNEs' manufacturing and distribution subsidiaries abroad, and provides information on the number of employees, paid-in capital, and line of business, among others. The data on Japanese electronics firms' manufacturing and distribution subsidiaries in the EC in this chapter were constructed from the original subsidiary lists (obtained on tape from the publisher), for the years 1986 and 1990. Touyou Keizai itself does not publish tables of employment by country and industry.

However, Touyou Keizai does not provide employment information for several major Japanese electronics firms. For such firms, information on manufacturing employment in 1990 was based on other sources (described under Sections A1.4.4 and A1.4.5), so that the figures for manufacturing employment in 1990 in the tables give a fairly accurate presentation of the state of Japanese electronics firms' investment in the EC in that year. Employment in sales subsidiaries is still underestimated by around 20 per cent.

There are three major causes of discrepancies in employment figures according to Touyou Keizai and MITI. First, the data based on Touyou Keizai in this chapter provide an almost complete coverage of manufacturing subsidiaries, while the response ratio of MITI's survey is around 70–80 per cent. Second, the definition of the electronics industry is broader in the Touyou Keizai figures. Third, MITI's survey includes all foreign affiliates in which Japanese firms have a capital stake of more than 10 per cent, while the tables based on Touyou Keizai as a rule include only affiliates with a capital stake of at least 40 per cent. While the former two factors lead to lower MITI figures, the latter factor tends to push the MITI figures up: for example, MITI's Fiscal 1990 employment figures for the EC will include the 1,430 employees of German CTV manufacturer Loewe Opta, in which Matsushita acquired a 25 per cent stake.

A1.4.4 JETRO Surveys on Japanese Affiliates Abroad

JETRO (Japan External Trade Organisation) offices abroad regularly carry out surveys among Japanese manufacturing subsidiaries. The results for Europe are published (yearly since 1989) as *The Current Management Situation of Japanese Manufacturing Enterprises in Europe* in English (the Japanese version is Nihon Boueki Shinkoukai (1985c–1995c)). The JETRO publications list Japanese manufacturing subsidiaries and employment provided by these subsidiaries. Over time, the coverage of the surveys has improved. The results of the JETRO surveys were used to add to the employment figures provided by Touyou Keizai.

A1.4.5 Lists Of Overseas Affiliates of Japanese Electronics Firms

There are several other sources of information on Japanese manufacturing investment focusing on the electronics industry. The Electronics Industries Association of Japan (EIAJ, or Nihon Denshi Kikai Kougyoukai) publishes an annual list of overseas subsidiaries reported by its member firms: *Kaigai Houjin Risuto* (*List of Overseas Affiliates*). The coverage of this list is far from comprehensive, mainly because the survey is limited to member firms of the Association. The EIAJ list was used to enhance Touyou Keizai's data. In addition, there are several databooks providing information on individual Japanese electronics firms which list information on overseas manufacturing activities: Dodwell's *Structure of the Japanese Electronics Industry* (1988), Dempa's *Electronics Buyers Guide* (1990b–1992b), and various databooks published by Denshi Keizai Kenkyuujo.

NOTES

1. Six of the world's ten largest electronics firms had their home base in Japan, and Japanese electronics firms were responsible for one third of worldwide

electronics sales of the 100 largest electronics firms at the end of 1989 (*Electronic Business*, 12 November 1990).

2. Nihon Tsuushou Sangyoushou (1995). The foreign production ratios are estimated to be 32 and 37 per cent for the US and European electronics industry, respectively, in 1983 (Dunning and Pierce 1985).
3. The main limitation is the absence of copiers and optical instruments classified under precision machinery.
4. For instance, Dunning (1986) found that Japanese CTV plants in the UK in 1984 could operate within 5–10 per cent of the productivity level of Japanese plants.
5. See Urata (1991) for a discussion of Japanese DFI in Asia. Such investment is found to be significantly higher in Japanese industries with both high export and import intensities, suggesting that DFI in Asia promotes intra-industry trade.
6. In the years of ever increasing Japanese share prices, Japanese firms were able to borrow billions of dollars in the Euro-currency market at low interest rates by attaching warrants (giving creditors the right to buy shares at fixed prices in future) to issues of corporate bonds.
7. Electronics exports in Figure 1.1 include exports of electrical machinery, precision machinery, and office machines in the Japanese classification. DFI data are not available for the latter two industries, hence DFI figures in Figure 1.1 are limited to electrical machinery.
8. In terms of cumulative DFI, the EC still lags behind the US substantially, with DFI reaching only a quarter of DFI in the US.
9. Note that the DFI figures in Figure 1.1 exclude the acquisitions of record and film companies MCA by Matsushita and CBS and Columbia Pictures by Sony. These acquisitions are classified under the service industry.
10. See Nihon Tsuushou Sangyoushou (1995). DFI in the US even showed a rebound in 1993 to 1.3 billion dollars.
11. This assumes that all foreign production is to serve foreign markets, ignoring foreign production for 'reverse imports' to Japan. Such imports were of limited importance for overseas production until the early 1990s. In the case of CTVs, where reverse imports have progressed most rapidly, *total* Japanese imports of CTVs in 1990 amounted to 1 million units (see e.g. Dempa 1992a). This implies that reverse imports did not surpass 5 per cent of foreign production. Reverse imports of VCRs by the largest eight Japanese manufacturers was still limited to 815,000 units in 1995 (see *Nikkei Weekly*, 31 July 1995).
12. Note that the definition of the 'foreign production share' differs from the definition of the 'foreign production ratio' in Table 1.1. In the latter, the denominator is the value of production in Japan only.
13. In France the distinctive SECAM system is used instead of the PAL system.
14. See also Cawson *et al.* (1990) for a detailed discussion of the political economy of CTV protection in the EC.
15. See Van Bael and Bellis (1990) and Bellis (1990) for a description and analysis of EC antidumping law and practice. See also Chapter 6 for a more detailed account of EC antidumping practice and a comparison with the US antidumping system. An undertaking is an agreement between the filing party (EC firms) and the antidumping authority (the EC Commission) on the one

hand, and the exporter under investigation on the other, by which the authority ends the antidumping investigation without levying duties, while the exporter agrees on specific conduct.

16. See Ishikawa (1990) for a discussion of the events.
17. The agreement also included price floors for Japanese VCRs. In addition, Japan agreed to 'monitor' exports of CTVs, CRTs, and hi-fi products. The EC simultaneously started retrospective statistical surveillance of these imports from Japan (Strange 1993: 461).
18. Although the VER formally expired in 1986, surveillance of VCR imports continued and allegedly there was an understanding that Japanese exports should not surpass 1.7 million units (Tyson 1992).
19. After negotiations at the GATT, the EC in exchange eliminated tariffs for portable radios, cassette players, and clock radios, and reduced the tariff for integrated circuits from 17 to 14 per cent.
20. Funai had earlier (in 1989) reached agreement on an export price undertaking with the EC Commission as well on an undertaking concerning Funai's assembly of VCRs in the EC. The export price undertaking in exchange for the 18 per cent provisional duty must have made export a more attractive option again and may have played a role in the reduced EC operations in the early 1990s. In contrast, Orion, which did not co-operate with the EC Commission and continued to pay a 13 per cent duty, expanded its EC manufacturing operations.
21. The EC Commission does not publish information on antidumping petitions that do not lead to the opening of an investigation, but news on antidumping petitions may reach Japanese firms in particular if they have OEM links with EC firms (in case of Shintom). See also Section 1.4.5 on Japanese divestments in the EC.
22. In exchange for the increase in this tariff, the tariff for reel-to-reel tape recorders was eliminated.
23. The Commission takes two to six months to decide whether to open an investigation after receiving a complaint from an EC industry (in the microwave oven case the complaint was filed in July 1986), but complaints are made public only after the Commission decides to investigate (Bellis 1990: 48). In addition, it may take several months to prepare a dumping complaint before it can be filed. Japanese firms may have knowledge of such dumping petitions and preparations through their membership of European trade and manufacturers associations, although EC producers usually avoided having to deal with Japanese producers by filing dumping complaints through several *ad hoc* organisations which are specifically set up to file antidumping complaints.
24. The Commission's official notices on the microwave oven investigation do not provide any information about which firms petitioned and exactly why the petition was withdrawn. Watanabe (1988) mentions Moulinex, Bosch, and Philips as petitioners.
25. On the other hand, the fact that a substantial share of EC output is accounted for by Japanese firms while imports from Japan decreased, had not prevented the Commission from levying antidumping duties on Japanese firms' imports, as will be seen below in the cases of audio tapes and microdisks.
26. Although Motorola incurred a loss in 1986, the firm had actually been increasing market shares from 1986 to 1988. The Commission apparently terminated

the investigation based on this finding and did not assess whether dumping had occurred (see Decision 651 published in the *Official Journal of the European Communities*, 30 December 1988). It also happens that the car telephone case is the only one in which the sole complainant was an EC subsidiary of a US firm, but it is not certain whether this had a bearing on the Commission's decision. On a previous occasion, Motorola had been successful when it joined the antidumping complaint of SGS Thomson and Siemens concerning imports of DRAMs from Japan.

27. The start of audio tape manufacturing operations of the German plant of Fuji Photo Film could not be established exactly, but was estimated as 1989.
28. Calculations are based on information provided in Commission Regulation No. 3262 as published in the *Official Journal of the European Communities*, 13 November 1990.
29. Japan asked a GATT panel to review the Commission's decision in October 1992. The Panel report, issued in April 1994, generally found in favour of the Commission. On one issue concerning the calculation of dumping margins, the report urged the EC to adapt its methods. The EC has however postponed adoption of the report.
30. Formally, the Commission dropped the reel investigation because it considered reels and cassettes not to be the same products ('like products' in the antidumping terminology). See Regulation No. L 313, *Official Journal of the European Communities*, 13 November 1990. Oddly, in an almost exactly similar antidumping case concerning videocassette tapes and video tape reels from South Korea and Hong Kong, tape reels and cassettes *were* considered 'like products'. See Regulation No. L 356, *Official Journal of the European Communities*, 24 December 1988.
31. Calculations are based on information contained in the EC Commission's Regulation No. 920 imposing provisional duties on microdisks from Japan, China, and Taiwan, published in the *Official Journal of the European Communities*, 21 April 1993.
32. The complainant was, ironically, Verbatim. Duties were levied but this apparently was not sufficient to ensure the survival of Verbatim as an independent microdisk producer. Two large US producers which also manufacture in Japan, 3M and Memorex Telex, were not involved in the US antidumping case.
33. See Imports of Videocassettes and Video Tape Reels Originating in the Republic of Korea and Hong Kong, Regulation L 356, published in the *Official Journal of the European Communities*, 24 December 1988, and Imports of Video Tapes in Cassettes Originating in the People's Republic of China, Regulation L 106, *Official Journal of the European Communities*, 26 April 1991.
34. In addition, Ricoh in 1990 announced the establishment of an Austrian joint venture with Philips to produce fax machines (Burger and Green 1991). However, it could not be confirmed whether fax production was in operation in the early 1990s.
35. In addition, NEC announced the establishment of a laptop PC plant in Germany in 1991 but apparently changed plans later and chose to increase production in the US.
36. EC legislation Council Regulation No. 1761, published in the *Official Journal*

of the European Communities, 26 June 1987. See Ishikawa (1990) for a discussion.

37. Apart from the five electronics products listed in Table 1.4, investigations were initiated into Japanese plants assembling ball-bearings and numerically controlled machine tools. No final measure has been published in the VCR case. The investigation here had not been concluced when the GATT panel (see below) ruled against the new amendment.
38. On the other hand, in one case local content rules have let to the withdrawal from manufacturing in the EC: Silver Seiko had assigned assembly of electric typewriters to the UK firm Astec, but withdrew from this arrangement in 1988, when the EC commission levied a duty because the plant did not reach the 40 per cent non-Japanese content.
39. See also ‘A Little Local Difficulty’ and ‘A Spark of Life’, *Far Eastern Economic Review*, 18 May 1989, for discussions of the EC’s ‘disguised local content policies’.
40. See GATT Document L/6676, 26 May 1990. In fact, in one case it has been reported that an EC producer did not reach the 40 per cent local content its Japanese rivals had to reach. This concerned the UK copier plant of Rank Xerox (Vermulst and Waer 1990).
41. Failure to reach consensus on the anti-circumvention issue finally led to the absence of such a clause in the new GATT code. This left the EC free to adopt its own legislation, and in the new EU antidumping regulation adopted by the Council on 22 December 1994, a broadly similar anti-circumvention clause was included. To ensure GATT conformity, duties are now to be collected on the parts imported by the assembly plant when these cross external EC borders. The measures can also be applied to assembly plants in third countries. See *Official Journal of the European Communities*, L 349/1, 31 December 1994, and Van Bael (1995).
42. In a comparable case in 1986, exports of electronic typewriters by the Japanese firm Brother from its Taiwan plant were considered of Japanese origin because the Taiwan plant did not add enough value to the products (Vermulst and Waer 1990: 73). Here the decision was based on the 45 per cent value added test.
43. In addition, antidumping actions against imports from Japanese affiliates in South East Asian countries became more prevalent in the late 1980s and early 1990s; see Section 1.3.4.
44. See CEC (1991b: 12–15), Furlotti (1991) and *Electronics Business*, 17 September 1990: 79. US firms that had no wafer etching facilities in the EC followed a similar investment strategy. Kimura (1994) reports that by 1993 Toshiba had not yet finalised integrated production at its German site.
45. For instance, Strange (1993: 330) reports that Alps was asked by its Japanese clients to invest in the EC. Alps produces electronic subassemblies in the EC but not in the US, which is a direct result of the EC antidumping actions mentioned.
46. In addition, Yamato Scale planned to start assembly operations in France in 1989 (Touyou Keizai 1995a: 806), but it could not be confirmed whether operations have actually begun, Tokyo Electric, in contrast, apparently stopped the assembly of scales in the EC in the early 1990s and pulled out of EC manufacturing activities altogether in 1994 (see Section 1.4.5).

47. In addition, two small Japanese CD player exporters had asked for a review of their case (Strange 1993: 444).
48. See Commission Decision 376/93 published in the *Official Journal of the European Communities*, 29 June 1993. See Appendix 1.3 below for some figures on the presence of Japanese firms in the typewriter industry and other EC industries.
49. See Notice C 307 published in the *Official Journal of the European Communities*, 25 November 1992. According to a report in the *Japan Times* in November 1992, an 'EC source' also added that the fact that Japanese producers now had extensive EC manufacturing operations played a role in this decision.
50. Exports from Japanese plants in Asia to the EC amounted to 1 million units annually, with Sharp responsible for 200,000 and Sanyo responsible for 250,000 units (see *Nikkei Weekly*, 25 March 1993). Exports from plants of Hitachi and Sanyo in China had already been subject to antidumping duties by virtue of the 1988 antidumping case against small screen television imports from Hong Kong, South Korea, and China.
51. Commission Decision 710/95 published in the *Official Journal of the European Communities*, 27 March 1995.
52. Commission Decision 1645/95 published in the *Official Journal of the European Communities*, 7 July 1995.
53. Notice 95/C 104/03 published in the *Official Journal of the European Communities*, 25 April 1995.
54. See *Official Journal of the European Communities* L 349/1, 31 December 1994 and Van Bael (1995).
55. South Korean firms could of course respond by starting up their own production of heads and scanners in the EC.
56. See also the *Financial Times*, 19 October 1995, 'Pressure Grows for EU to Overhaul Dumping Policy'.
57. Antidumping action is not likely to please the French government, which owns part of the Thomson group. Considering that France usually is the staunchest supporter of antidumping action against Asian firms and that member states ultimately have to approve antidumping measures, the likelihood of antidumping action in this case may not be high.
58. As noted above, the Council's voting rules had been changed before the enlargement of the EC, in 1994. Previously a qualified majority had been necessary to endorse antidumping actions, but a simple majority is sufficient under current law.
59. Although the extension of duties to high speed copiers gave protection to EC producers in a new market segment.
60. *Official Journal of the European Communities*, 7 July 1995: 26.
61. *Official Journal of the European Communities*, 7 July 1995: 26.
62. Decision 3029/93 published in the *Official Journal of the European Communities*, 30 October 1993.
63. It has been reported that Japanese firms manufacturing in the EC have informally asked the EC Commission to take action; see *Financial Times*, 19 October 1995, 'Pressure Grows for EU to Overhaul Dumping Policy'.
64. See e.g. van Marion (1992). See also Willy de Clerk, former chairman of the

EC Commission, for a defence of antidumping policy along these lines in the *Financial Times*, 21 November 1988.

65. See Yamamura (1986), Blair *et al.* (1991), Belderbos and Holmes (1995). Appendix 1.1 provides some figures concerning the number of affiliated retailers in Japan for major electronics firms.
66. See e.g. *Financial Times*, 22 March 1992.
67. See *Nikkei Weekly*, 1 January 1994. Moreover, virtually all private branch exchanges bought by core member firms of the Sumitomo Group were supplied by group firm NEC.
68. See for instance Horlick (1990) for a discussion related to US antidumping practice; see also Chapter 2.
69. See Nicolaides (1992), Finger (1992), and Horlick (1990), among others, for further discussion of this issue.
70. To simplify the issue: overhead and administrative costs incurred by wholesalers and retailers are deducted from export prices but are not deductible from home market prices. See Section 6.2.2 for further discussion. It is illustrative that Japanese firms with large distribution arms in Europe and Japan are often found to have the highest dumping margins (Bell 1987, van Marion 1992).
71. Although it should be noted that in some of these cases the degree of product differentiation and complexity make undertakings harder to enforce, providing some justification for the preference for duties over undertakings.
72. See Council Regulation No. 2112/90 published in the *Official Journal of the European Communities*, No. L 193/4, 25 July 1990.
73. See Council Regulation No. 535/87 published in the *Official Journal of the European Communities*, No. L 65/12, 24 February 1987.
74. See CEC, *Tenth Annual Report from the Commission to the European Parliament on the Community's Anti-Dumping and Anti-Subsidy Activities*, Document SEC (92) 716, Brussels, as quoted in GATT (1993).
75. EC Commission's Regulation No. 920/93 imposing provisional duties on microdisks from Japan, China, and Taiwan, published in the *Official Journal of the European Communities*, 21 April 1993.
76. The political circumstances for protection in the electronics industry may have been especially favourable. Considering that a qualified majority of member states until 1994 had to approve each definitive antidumping action, it is significant that two countries that are usually considered proponents of liberal trade may have had their reasons for supporting antidumping actions. The Netherlands is the home country of Philips, which still has substantial R&D and manufacturing operations there, while the UK government, since the early 1980s eager to attract Japanese investment, must have noticed that it was the main beneficiary of antidumping-induced Japanese manufacturing investment in the EC. Moreover, two other liberal trade oriented countries may have had an interest in antidumping actions because of the presence of Philips- or Thomson-affiliated manufacturers: Bang and Olufson (Philips) in Denmark, and Grundig (Philips) and Telefunken (Thomson) in Germany.
77. See also *The Economist*, 18 February 1989, 'Set Up or Stay Out'.
78. See *Financial Times*, 19 October 1995, 'Pressure Grows for EU to Overhaul Dumping Policy'.

79. Besides the 1995 copier case review, the Council of Ministers only narrowly approved antidumping action by eight to seven votes in the 1995 microwave oven case. In two other recent cases in other industries, antidumping measures proposed by the EC Commission were actually rejected. In the case of Gum Rosin from China the Commission decided to terminate the investigation without imposing measures, because there was no qualified majority of member states to approve antidumping measures (see *Official Journal of the European Communities*, 12 February 1994). In the recent case of powdered activated carbon from China, a majority of member states apparently indicated a willingnes to vote against definitive measures, so duties lapsed with the expiry of the provisional measures (see Tim Jones, 'Antidumping "Sea Change" as Carbon Duties are Lifted', *European Voice*, 15 February 1996).
80. Subsidiaries that combine manufacturing functions with some sales activities are classified as manufacturing subsidiaries.
81. See Appendix 1.4 for a discussion of data sources on Japanese direct foreign investment.
82. This view was supported by a Matsushita manager in an interview in 1990. Other Japanese companies have expressed similar views (Kume and Totsuka 1991).
83. In 1990 Matsushita still had only a 35 per cent stake in the venture; in 1991 it increased its stake to 50 per cent. See also Section 1.4.2.
84. Note that numbers of employees in 1986 and 1990 are underestimated because no employment data were available for a number of firms.
85. Only the vertical *keiretsu*, in which there is a clear hierarchical relationship between parent and subsidiaries, are considered in Appendix 1.2.
86. The subsidiary was renamed JVC Video Manufacturing and employment was reduced to 280 by 1995 (Nihon Boueki Shinkoukai 1995b). See also Section 1.3.4.
87. Sazanami (1992) reaches similar conclusions for the manufacturing industry as a whole.
88. Morris, Munday, and Wilkinson (1994: 22) corroborate this finding of negligible exports outside Europe for Japanese (electronics) plants in Wales.
89. The definition of company group refers to vertical *keiretsu*. Some caution should be exercised in interpreting the figures on intra-group deliveries. It could be that procurements from other countries include procurements from a central European components distribution centre operated by the Japanese firm, which would obscure the actual origin of procurements.
90. More reliable data on in-house value added are presented in Chapter 8 where a more detailed analysis of MITI data on Japanese procurement behaviour is presented. The problem is circumvented by restricting the analysis to subsidiaries with sufficient information for all relevant variables.
91. Electronics sales data are taken from CEC (1992), which uses a narrow definition of the electronics sector. Sales figures tend to be smaller than total consolidated sales of the firms.
92. This is not true for the EC semiconductor market as a whole. Toshiba and NEC reached only seventh (4.9 per cent) and eighth (4.1 per cent) places, respectively, in terms of EC market share here (CEC 1991b: 12–11).
93. The definition of consumer electronics used by the EACEM is stricter than the

definition used in this chapter (e.g. microwave ovens are not included), which makes the figures incomparable with those in Tables 1.12 and 1.13.

94. The number of European plants operated by EC firms decreased rapidly in the late 1980s: form 181 in 1987 to 106 in 1989 (CEC 1991b).
95. The figure for total employment is taken from CEC (1990) as the sum of employment in the electrical and electronic engineering industry (NACE 34) and the computer and office machinery industry (NACE 33).
96. Note that the figures are limited strictly to factory employment, measured at the plant level. US factory employment reached just over 1 million in 1990, while total employment in the electronics sector was over 2.5 million.
97. See JETRO (1990b, 1993b, 1995b). JETRO uses a different industry classification from the one used in this chapter and includes all subsidiaries in which Japanese firms' capital stake is greater than 10 per cent.
98. For instance, the figures presented in Section 1.4.1 showed a much greater increase in employment than in the number of subsidiaries during 1986–1990. Similar observations were made for Japanese manufacturing plants in Wales. Japanese firms were found to have substantially increased employment in Wales, but mainly through expansion projects for existing plants (see Morris, Munday, and Wilkinson 1994: 36).
99. Sony is also producing printed circuit boards for CTVs and CRT yokes at the Bridgend factory. Employment was expected to eventually reach 4,000 personnel in the two plants.
100. See, for instance, Graham and Krugman (1990) for a discussion of the effects of DFI on host economies. Micossi and Viesti (1991) and Thomsen and Nicolaides (1991) provide assessments of Japanese DFI in Europe.
101. See CEC (1994). But note that CEC (1994) apparently uses different employment definitions compared with earlier publications, which complicates the analysis of trends.
102. Strange (1993) calculates substantial positive effects of Japanese DFI on the UK trade balance. Given that the UK has attracted most Japanese investments and that UK plants often supply the continental markets in addition to the UK market, the effects on the trade balance of the EC as a whole are likely to be less pronounced.
103. See CEC (1994) and Appendix 1.3. It should be noted, on the other hand, that the 1993 trade deficit of 5.2 billion ECUs was recorded while EC consumer electronics sales had declined by almost 15 per cent.
104. Nihon Tsuushou Sangyoushou (1994). The average local content figures should be interpreted with caution, since MITI does not correct for non-response and uses unweighted averages. Furthermore, the sample of subsidiaries responding to the survey changes every year (owing to different response patterns, new investments, and divestments), which complicates the identification of trends.
105. See Chapter 8. In contrast, these percentages were 4 and 48, respectively, for Japanese electronics subsidiaries in the US.
106. See for instance, Nihon Boueki Shinkoukai (1990c) and Oliver and Wilkinson (1992: 274).
107. There is some evidence of a narrowing lead time here: both NEC and Fujitsu announced the start of manufacturing of 16M DRAMs in their UK plants.

108. In addition, there are joint ventures between EC and Japanese firms elsewhere. For instance, Thomson operates a VCR plant with Toshiba in Singapore and Philips manufactures VCRs in a joint venture with JVC in Malaysia.
109. A parallel trend in R&D activities by Japanese firms can be observed in the US, where Japanese firms increased the number of greenfield R&D subsidiaries to 70 by 1991, mostly in product design and software engineering. Japanese firms spent an estimated 770 million dollars on R&D in the US in 1989 and 1,215 million dollars in 1990, up from 307 million dollars in 1987 (Genther and Dalton 1992, US Department Of Commerce 1993).
110. See e.g. Krugman (1986a). The introduction to Part II of this book gives an overview of the main arguments in the strategic trade policy literature.
111. For instance, Abo (1994) reports that Sanyo's CTV plant in the UK has reached a productivity level comparable to that of its Japanese plant.
112. Affiliated subsidiaries include consolidated firms (*renketsu gaisha*), related firms (*kankei gaisha*), and subsidiary firms (*kogaisha*). Related firms are not consolidated because they have weaker links with the parent, while subsidiary firms usually are too small to be consolidated (see Nihon Keizai Shinbunsha 1993).
113. Additional information concerning data sources on Japanese overseas manufacturing can be found in Appendix 6.1.

PART II

Strategic Trade Policy and Japanese Electronics Firms: *Theoretical Essays*

Introduction: Strategic Trade Policies and Multinational Firms

The first influential studies of strategic trade policy were written by Brander and Spencer (1983, 1984) and Krugman (1984). The novelty of their analysis was a focus on the effects of trade and industrial policies in *oligopolistic* industries. One feature of oligopolistic industries is that entry barriers, such as economies of scale or the need to possess technological or marketing skills, keep the number of (potential) competitors small. Entry barriers allow incumbent firms to reap excess returns ('oligopoly rents') persistently, in the form of profits or premium wages paid out to workers. In other words, the industry is characterised by imperfect competition: prices are higher than marginal cost and rents are not dissipated through competition, as in the perfect competition model.

Another consequence of the small number of firms active in the industry is that each firm will be aware of the actions of the other firms and will take into account that any of its own actions may induce its rivals to change theirs. Firms' actions have a *strategic* nature to the extent that they reflect expected reactions of rivals. This raises the possibility that a firm engages in strategic behaviour which in itself may not be optimal, but becomes so because of the responses it induces by rival firms. The most illustrative example of such strategic behaviour is excess capacity creation: this is in itself a costly strategy, but it may increase profits if rival firms are deterred from entry or capacity expansion because of it (e.g. Dixit 1980). Another way to increase profits is through actions that raise rival's costs, for instance by lobbying the government to set product standards which rival firms have to adhere to, or by petitioning for antidumping actions against imports by foreign firms.[1]

What Brander and Spencer (1984) showed is that governments can assist domestic firms to strategically commit to actions that increase their share of industry profits *vis-à-vis* foreign rivals. They illustrated this for the most simple case of tariff protection. Tariffs levied on imports by foreign oligopolists raise export costs and allow domestic firms to increase their market share and profits at the cost of foreign rivals. In this way, trade policies are used as an instrument for profit or rent shifting. The increase in domestic firms' profits plus the tariff revenues can, under certain circumstances, be greater than any decrease in consumer surplus[2] brought about by the higher market price that is likely to result. Trade policies, in other words, can increase domestic welfare (with 'welfare' defined as the sum of profits, tariff revenues, and consumer surplus). This result differed markedly from traditional results obtained under perfect competition, where free trade is invariably the best policy from the viewpoint of domestic welfare. The only argument for the imposition of a tariff as a first best policy discussed previously in the literature is the case of a large country importing from a foreign monopolist. Such a country is able to increase domestic welfare by setting an 'optimal' tariff on imports, inducing the monopolist to lower its ex-tariff price (Corden 1974).

Krugman (1984) focused on the role of increasing returns to scale. If unit costs are decreasing in production levels, the free trade outcome is one of market prices above marginal cost, and by definition this is not optimal. In the case of dynamic scale economies or *learning by doing* (where marginal costs are a decreasing function of cumulative production), an initial cost advantage of firms may have long lasting effects on competitive positions. Again, the marginal cost pricing rule, characterising perfect competition, does not hold and market equilibria are not necessarily optimal. An equally important feature of increasing returns is that strategic trade policies are more likely to be powerful instruments. If the trade protection granted to domestic firms allows them to increase their production and move down the cost or learning curve faster, protection results in lower costs to the domestic firm, which increases its competitiveness on world markets. Competitive advantages of firms and comparative advantages of countries can be 'created' by government policies, rather than being solely dependent on factor endowments as posited in traditional trade theories. Krugman (1984) in this vein illustrated with a simple model how import protection under increasing returns can promote export competitiveness.

There is also an argument for policy intervention if an industry's growth is associated with economies of scale that are *external* to the firms. In this case there is a divergence between private and social rates of return. R&D activities by private firms, for instance, are likely to contribute to the development of the domestic science base and skills of researchers, which may in turn benefit firms in other industries. Government support in the form of R&D subsidies brings private returns on R&D closer to returns to the economy at large and will induce firms to invest more in R&D.[3] The potential of such external effects is highest in high technology industries, particularly in industries producing inputs that may help other industries to increase productivity, such as microelectronics or information technology industries. Since high technology industries also tend to be oligopolistic and to be characterised by entry barriers and increasing returns, the discussion on strategic trade policies has often focused on support for domestic high technology firms.

The seminal works of Brander, Spencer, and Krugman and the ensuing literature fuelled the debate on the merits of trade and industrial policies (such as tariffs, VERs, export subsidies, and R&D subsidies), which in the context of imperfect competition were usually termed *strategic trade policies*. Since a substantial share of international trade took place in oligopolistic industries, the potential for welfare increasing policies appeared great. Moreover, it was clear that, in a number of high technology industries such as semiconductors, industry rivalry was affected by increasing returns such as learning by doing. The debate took place against the background of rapid advance by Japanese firms in a number of industries such as semiconductors, consumer electronics, and cars, and of persistently high trade surpluses of Japan with Europe and the United States. It was perceived that at least part of Japanese firms' increased presence in world markets was a result of successful protective and industrial policies in Japan. Laura Tyson, currently chairperson of the Council of Economic Advisors to the Clinton administration, is probably the best known exponent of this position (Borrus, Tyson, and Zysman 1986, Tyson 1990, 1992). Krugman's (1984) study had the advance of Japanese firms in the DRAM industry in mind, an industry in which tariffs and non-tariff barriers had kept US firms' Japanese market shares low. In a later study, Baldwin and Krugman (1988) applied a similar model to the 16K DRAM industry to show that protection granted to Japanese firms on the domestic market could explain the rise of Japanese firms as DRAM producers. Japanese firms' preferential access to the Japanese market allowed them overcome an initial cost disadvantage *via-à-vis* US firms and become market leaders in the US market as well.

While much of the debate centred on potential positive effects of unilateral strategic policies, a central message of the Brander and Spencer (1983, 1984) and Krugman (1984) studies received less attention: if all countries chose to intervene to assist domestic firms, they all would be considerably worse off than in the free trade situation. Moreover, since unilateral strategic trade policies in most cases make other countries worse off (they are 'beggar thy neighbour' policies), they are likely to induce retaliation by other countries. Brander and Spencer (1984) saw their work as essentially making a strong case for multilateral tariff reductions. Their results illustrated the importance of multilateral negotiations where individual countries are not likely to have the incentives to reduce tariffs unilaterally. It was an attempt to explain the presence of tariffs and protectionistic policies, which traditional analysis of trade under perfect competition could not do. Similarly, Krugman's analysis implied an even greater need for free trade than in traditional trade theory: with economies of scale, an enlargement of markets though international trade is necessary to bring costs down.

Subsequent work on strategic trade policies unveiled a variety of other qualifications to the positive effect of strategic trade policies on domestic welfare. Results are sensitive to the kind of strategic interaction between oligopolists (Cheng 1988, Eaton and Grossman 1986, Bulow, Geanakoplos, and Klemperer 1985). Trade and industrial policies focusing on one industry elicit greater costs if the industry competes with other sectors for scarce resources, such as skilled engineers (Dixit and Grossman 1986). And the potential of rent shifting policies is likely to be smaller if increased rents attract (inefficient) entry (Horstman and Markusen 1986). It appears that the case for intervention is not the rule but rather the exception.

Serious doubts have also been raised about whether theoretical opportunities for welfare improving policies can be implemented in practice. Effective policies require that the government has access to an elaborate set of information on a variety of industry characteristics such as demand elasticities, costs, learning curves, foreign firms' strategies, and profits. Such information is typically not available. Since the rationale for intervention as well as the specific mode of intervention are so much dependent on industry characteristics, strategic trade policies cannot be based on general rules for intervention but are necessarily industry-specific and discretionary. This will create strong incentives for firms to engage in costly rent-seeking (lobbying) activities to convince the government that their industry needs protection or other forms of government assistance. Under these conditions, it is unlikely that governments are able to implement welfare improving policies correctly, and free trade is still generally the best rule of thumb to improve economic welfare (Helpman and Krugman 1989).

If strategic trade policies are difficult to implement, the question arises how successful they have been in practice. Several attempts have been made to derive empirically the welfare effects of strategic trade policies in specific cases, such as voluntary export restraints (VERs) for Japanese cars. Most of the studies have found that unilateral trade policies can improve on free trade, but that the magnitude of the effects is rather small.[4]

Strategic Trade Policy and Multinational Firms

The theory of strategic trade policy has not given much attention to the role of multinational firms. The literature usually assumes that it is in the interest of a country to assist domestically based firms to increase their market share and profits. But what if part of the domestic industry is controlled by foreign firms? If foreign firms repatriate profits to their home country, rent-shifting strategic trade policies are necessarily less effective in raising domestic economic welfare. Dick (1993a) shows for the US that, precisely in those industries where excess returns are important, the presence of foreign firms tends to be substantial. The practical potential of strategic trade policies is shown to be importantly reduced.

Strategic trade policies and direct foreign investment are moreover directly linked, if trade barriers for foreign firms induce tariff jumping DFI. Standard trade policy instruments such as quotas or tariffs become less effective if firms can avoid them by substituting foreign production for exports. For instance, Levinsohn (1989) has shown that, if the DFI option is introduced for a foreign exporting monopolist, subjecting the monopolist's exports to quotas or tariffs fails to ensure that the host country extracts all monopoly rents as in the 'optimal tariff' case.

Apart from Levinsohn (1989), there are remarkably few theoretical studies which explicitly take DFI decisions into account in relationship to strategic trade policies. Brander and Spencer (1987) show that a country facing structural unemployment may be able to commit itself to a policy of high tariffs and low taxes, altering foreign firms' trade-offs between exports and DFI in favour of the latter. Dei (1985) studies the joint effects of VERs and DFI but does not take a causal relationship between the two into account. Flam (1994) applies a model of DFI and strategic trade policy to the case of the EC's VER for Japanese cars, and shows how the country receiving Japanese DFI as a response to the VER (the United Kingdom) may benefit, while other countries in the EC are likely to be worse off. There is also related work on multinational firms' strategic DFI in a host country to deter entry by the host country's domestic firms (Motta 1992, Horstman and Markusen 1987, Smith 1987). While DFI is studied in the presence of tariff barriers, these studies are less concerned with the welfare effects of trade policies.

Analysis of Strategic Trade Policies in Chapters 2, 3, and 4

The analysis in Part II (Chapters 2, 3, and 4) extends and applies the literature on strategic trade policies with a focus on the role of multinational firms. The models are all adapted to resemble the conditions of rivalry between Japanese firms *vis-à-vis* European and US firms in the electronics industry. Since the analysis is applied to the electronics industry, the models adopt a partial equilibrium approach; i.e., they focus on industry effects and treat macroeconomic repercussions, such as exchange rate changes, as second order effects.

The analysis is in the spirit of Brander and Spencer (1983): unilateral strategic policies for imperfectly competitive industries are examined to gain understanding of the rationale for such policies and their potential merits. The focus is on rent shifting policies. The standard criterion of improvement in domestic welfare (the sum of consumer surplus, domestic firms' profits, and tariff revenues) is used to judge the effects of intervention. Profits accruing to foreign multinational firms in a host country are assumed to be repatriated and do not enter the host country's welfare function. Throughout, the strategic interaction in the oligopolistic industry is described by Nash–Cournot equilibrium: firms follow a capacity setting strategy, and in equilibrium no firm has an incentive unilaterally to change its capacity.[5] The models used are simple; for instance, the analysis is limited to the case of linear demand functions. As with previous models of strategic trade policy with imperfect competition, caution should be exercised in interpreting the results, since they may be sensitive to the specification chosen, such as the demand function and the mode of strategic interaction. Nevertheless, the insights obtained do have broader applicability and implications.

The analysis in Chapter 3 connects with Levinsohn (1989) as well as the literature on strategic DFI. It looks at the welfare effects of a tariff on a foreign duopolist's exports to a host country, in cases where the foreign firm has the option of avoiding the tariff by investing in local assembly facilities. The conditions under which DFI occurs are established. Rent shifting will still occur with tariff jumping DFI if production in the host country increases marginal costs, but the effects are necessarily smaller than in the absence of DFI. The optimal policy is to set the tariff just low enough to avoid it being 'jumped'.

High tariffs are a characteristic of EC trade policy in the electronics sector, and in Chapter 6 they are found to have a significant impact on DFI by Japanese firms. The EC antidumping duties that have frequently been levied on Japanese imports are much akin to tariffs.[6] On the one hand, antidumping petitions are filed by the domestic industry, which gives antidumping to some extent the character of a private instrument for raising rivals' costs. On the other hand, the predominant role of the antidumping administration in deciding on antidumping actions suggests that antidumping, particularly as administered in the EC, should rather be seen as an instrument of public policy. In case of EC antidumping decisions, the European Commission has considerable discretion in determining what specific antidumping measures are to be taken. In addition, EC antidumping law requires that the Commission investigates whether antidumping measures are in the general interest of the EC ('Community interest'), although it has been suggested that in practice 'Community interest' tends to be equated with the interest of the complaining producers.[7]

Once foreign firms have 'jumped' trade barriers, conventional trade policies lose their effectiveness. Domestic firms can be further assisted only if policies can discriminate against foreign-owned firms. Here local content requirements play an important role. Local content requirements stipulate that a certain proportion of inputs has to be procured domestically. Though not strictly trade policy measures, local content rules can have important effects on trade flows.[8] In the context of oligopolistic rivalry between domestic and foreign firms, they can be used as strategic trade policy instruments, shifting rents to domestic firms by increasing the procurements cost of foreign firms.[9] The effects of local content requirements are analysed in Chapter 4.

If DFI by foreign firms is a second best option induced by trade barriers, foreign firms are likely to rely on imported components for their local assembly. Even if a local content rule is formulated in general terms (applicable to all firms in the industry), the rule will *de facto* discriminate against foreign firms and work in favour of domestic firms since the latter are likely to have reached sufficient local sourcing levels. The most consequential EC local content rules affecting Japanese electronics firms—those administrated under the EC's 'screwdriver plant' amendment—were also *de jure* discriminatory, since they extended earlier antidumping actions against Japanese firms' exports.

The analysis in Chapter 4 takes into account the role of vertical linkages between the domestic components industry and foreign and domestic duopolists in the final goods industry. It focuses on the case where the domestic components industry is oligopolistic and possesses market power *vis-à-vis* the final goods industry, a situation that has not received sufficient attention in the literature. Local content rules, even if they are binding only for the foreign firm, may paradoxically reduce the market share and profits of the domestic final goods duopolist. Welfare effects are predominantly negative. These effects change if the domestic components industry is more competitive.

Before the analysis in Chapters 3 and 4 dealing with the case of EC trade policies targeting Japanese firms, Chapter 2 examines one of the landmark cases of perceived Japanese strategic policies: the rivalry between Japanese and US CTV manufacturers in the 1960s and early 1970s. The evidence suggests that Japanese CTV producers effectively formed a cartel in their home market. The firms' control over the domestic distribution network, combined with legal barriers to entry in the retailing industry, virtually precluded market access for foreign manufacturers and potential Japanese entrants alike. Japanese firms were found to be dumping, selling televisions in the US at prices substantially below prices in Japan and below total average costs. In an influential US antitrust case, *Matsushita* v. *Zenith*, US producers argued that the Japanese firms were conspiring to drive the US industry out of business. US producers eventually lost the case before the Supreme Court. Partly as a response to the failure of antitrust policy in the *Matsushita* v. *Zenith* case, US antidumping law was strengthened to deal with cases such as this.

In Chapter 2 a simple model is developed based on the stylised facts of the case. Given static economies of scale, the cartelisation of the Japanese market, and free entry into the US market, dumping could have followed from a profit maximising strategy of Japanese firms. Japanese firms' behaviour is shown eventually to have harmful effects for producers as well as consumers in the US. It is the anti-competitive conduct in the Japanese market that causes a negative 'spillover' to competition in the US. National antitrust practices are not designed to deal with this kind of situation, and the analysis suggests the need for co-ordination of competition rules and enforcement.

NOTES

1. See Salop and Scheffman (1983) on the concept of 'raising rivals' cost'.
2. Consumer surplus is calculated as the difference between what individual consumers would be willing to pay for a product and the actual price of the product.
3. This rationale for R&D subsidies is separate from the strategic R&D subsidies analysed in Brander and Spencer (1983).
4. See Krugman and Smith (1994) for recent contributions in this field. Other empirical work on strategic trade policies can be found in Baldwin (1991), Feenstra (1989), Baldwin (1988), and Krugman (1986b). Overviews of the strategic trade policy literature and discussions of its practical applicability are provided in Lawrence and Schultze (1990) Richardson (1990), Stegemann (1989), and Pugel (1987), among others. Holmes, Belderbos, and Smith (1992) discuss the potential for strategic policies in the information technology and electronics industries.
5. See e.g. Tirole (1989). Cournot rivalry is generally thought to represent oligopolistic industries where capital investments are important and production capacity is relatively fixed (such as in semiconductors or CRT production). Karp and Perloff (1989) find evidence that Nash–Cournot equilibrium is not too remote from actual conditions in the Japanese CTV industry. Kreps and Scheinkman (1983) have shown that Nash–Cournot equilibrium may be seen as a more general equilibrium concept than price strategy (Bertrand) equilibrium: price strategy equilibrium with capacity constraints and efficient rationing generates Cournot outcomes. (See also Vives (1989) for a discussion of the Cournot oligopoly concept.) Bulow, Geanakoplos, and Klemperer (1985) showed that the difference between Bertrand and Cournot interactions is not so much related to the strategic variable (capacity versus price) but stems from the fact that with Cournot rivalry firms' capacities are strategic substitutes (aggressive behaviour of one firm induces less aggressive behaviour by others), whereas with Bertrand competition, prices are strategic complements (firms have incentives to match other firms' aggressive price reductions).
6. As discussed at some length in Chapter 6, dumping duties have the character of customs duties in the EC antidumping system, but not in the US antidumping system.
7. The concept is not well defined in EC antidumping law, but it appears that the clause requires that the effects of antidumping actions on the profitability of the petitioning industry are confronted with the costs of antidumping protection to consumers and user-industries. A 'general interest' clause is not contained in US antidumping law, nor is there discretion in setting the level of duties.

8. Local content requirements fall under the heading of 'trade related investment measures' in GATT terminology.
9. An early treatment of local content requirements as a cost increasing and rent shifting instrument is Davidson, Matusz, and Kreinin (1987).

2

Dumping, Antitrust, and International Oligopoly: The Rise of the Japanese Colour Television Industry

2.1 Introduction

The US Supreme Court's decision in the case of *Matsushita* v. *Zenith*[1] continues to incite debate among economists and lawyers. The case involved an allegation by the US colour television (CTV) manufacturers Zenith and NUE that a group of Japanese firms, including Matsushita, had engaged in predatory below-cost pricing as part of a collusive plan to drive US firms out of the market. The case goes back at least to 1968, when Zenith filed an antidumping complaint against the Japanese firms. Despite a positive finding of dumping by the Treasury, the US administration was slow to impose antidumping duties. Accordingly, Zenith decided in 1974 to bring a private suit under US antitrust law (invoking also the little used 1916 antidumping act, based on antitrust principles). The case against Matsushita *et al.* went before the US District Court in 1974, and in 1986, after almost 20 years of litigation and procedural wrangling, the US Supreme Court finally dismissed the case on summary judgment without full examination of the evidence. Meanwhile. US trade laws had been tightened to allow redress in cases such as this.[2]

The Supreme Court's decision was ostensibly based on economic reasoning: the judges said, after a brief review of the evidence, that the allegations implied such economic irrationality on the part of the Japanese firms that predation was inherently unlikely. The evidence brought forward, however, did demonstrate concerted action by Japanese firms on both the US and the Japanese markets. Several observers have voiced the opinion that these irregularities should have warranted a full examination of the evidence, while others agree with the Supreme Court that there was no antitrust case to answer.[3]

The analysis in this chapter agrees with the former. An explanation is offered for the behaviour of Japanese firms in the industry which is based on economic theory of oligopolistic competition. In this explanation, the behaviour of Japanese firms had anti-competitive effects and harmed US producers, while providing no corresponding gains to US consumers. This is due not to a conspiracy to monopolise the market but rather to a spillover of collusive conduct and entry barriers on the Japanese market. Weak antitrust enforcement in Japan can be seen as an unconventional form of strategic trade policy allowing Japanese firms to increase market share and profits in the US, by facilitating the recoupment of fixed costs on the domestic market.

The findings highlight the difficulties in applying antitrust laws in the international market place. Although the announcement of the US Department of Justice in April 1992 that anti-competitive conduct abroad harming US producers will also be subject of litigation in US Courts may be seen as an attempt to counter these difficulties, the inevitable overlap with jurisdictions of other countries is likely to make enforcement unattainable. There are compelling arguments for the establishment of an international antitrust authority, or at least for a harmonisation of antitrust laws and enforcement policies, which would be welfare improving.

In the next section, the key facts pertaining to the Japanese and US CTV industries in the 1960s and 1970s are reviewed, followed by an overview of the litigation in the case in Section 2.3. After discussing explanations put forward in the literature on the case, including those provided by Blair *et al.* (1991) in Section 2.4, Section 2.5 provides an alternative explanation of *Matsushita* v. *Zenith*. The chapter concludes with a discussion of the implications of the findings.

2.2 Stylised Facts

From 1969 to 1977, the US market share of the seven Japanese CTV producers rose dramatically from 12 to 44 per cent.[4] Several sources indicate that during this period CTV prices in the US were significantly lower than those in Japan (see e.g. Blair *et al.* 1991, Yamamura 1986). There was no direct evidence, however, that Japanese export prices were below marginal costs. One of Zenith's expert witnesses, Horace DePodwin, produced calculations that supported this view, but he had to rely on aggregated constructed data which were rejected by the Supreme Court as of no evidential value.[5]

The seven Japanese CTV producers were engaged in two schemes which apparently were intended to *limit* competition between them on the US market. First, under the auspices of the Japanese Machinery Export Association, they agreed to each limit the number of US distributors to a maximum of five (the so-called 'five company rule'). Second, they agreed on minimum export prices to the US market; these so-called 'check prices' were administered through the Japanese Ministry of International Trade and Industry (MITI). While the minimum prices were adhered to at US customs, the Japanese firms secretly sought to give substantial rebates to their US distributors by transfers to Swiss bank accounts.

In addition, and crucial to understanding *Matsushita* v. *Zenith*, as will become clear, there was powerful evidence of the existence of a cartel agreement by the seven CTV producers in the Japanese market. Anti-competitive behaviour in the Japanese market was facilitated by weak enforcement of the Japanese Anti-Monopoly Law and a lack of credible entry threats related to the firms' control over retailing. In order to understand Japanese firms' behaviour, it is useful to describe the structure of the Japanese CTV industry in some detail.

In the 1950s, Japanese consumer electronics firms established vast networks of wholesalers and retailers in Japan (the so-called 'distribution *keiretsu*') which were to deal exclusively in the firms' own brands. The largest Japanese manufacturer, Matsushita, pioneered this strategy and came to control some 25,000 retail outlets all over Japan; Toshiba built up a network of 14,000 stores, Hitachi 10,000, Sanyo 6,000, Mitsubishi 5,000, Sharp 3,500, and Sony 3,000.[6] The cost of setting up the huge distribution network could be paid out of the surplus profits earned on the Japanese market which was protected until the end of the 1960s by quotas and high tariffs. During the 1960s and 1970s, almost all electric appliances in Japan were sold through manufacturer-controlled wholesalers and retailers. Entry in the retailing sector by volume retailers competing on price was extremely difficult because of government restrictions on the opening of large stores.[7]

Forward integration in distribution in the Japanese electronics industry had two major consequences for competition in the industry. First, it constituted a major barrier to entry for foreign firms and potential Japanese entrants. It is argued that the retail networks were set up exactly for this purpose (van Wolferen 1989), although retailers' lack of financial means in the 1950s and the manufacturers' strategy in controlling the quality of promotion and after-sales service were also important. In any case, during the 1960s and 1970s, the seven major manufacturers mentioned above dominated the Japanese CTV market, and no entry or exit occurred (Yamamura 1986).

Second, control over a vast network of retail outlets led to tight vertical restrictions which directly facilitated horizontal anti-competitive behaviour. The CTV producers used their control over retailers to fix retail prices, retail market shares, and margins, and to prevent retailers from selling competitors' products. These practices almost certainly inhibited forms of downstream pro-competitive behaviour that could have destabilised the manufacturers' horizontal cartel arrangements. The Japanese Fair Trade Commission (FTC), the body that is given the task of enforcing Japan's Antimonopoly Law, several times found evidence of vertical price fixing and other restrictions in breach of this law. For instance, in 1971 it found that Matsushita assigned geographic territories to wholesalers and fixed minimum prices for retailers.[8] However, the FTC refrained from using formal sanctions and instead relied on administrative guidance in this and other cases, in which firms were asked to change their behaviour. Since it was highly unlikely that sanctions would follow in case of non-compliance, firms were very often found repeatedly to breach the law.[9] Moreover, Japanese courts have been very reluctant to accept FTC findings as definitive proof of wrongdoing (Sanekata 1992a).

The possibility of engaging in vertical restrictions and vertical price fixing, the absence of credible threats of entry, and weak enforcement of the Anti-Monopoly Law all contributed to horizontal anti-competitive behaviour by the CTV manufacturers. There is powerful evidence that the CTV producers were effectively cartelising the market, collusively setting prices and producer market shares until well into the 1970s.[10] The FTC investigated the industry in 1956 and 1966, and these investigations produced unambiguous evidence that a cartel existed. In 1956 Japanese producers were found to have set up a 'market stabilisation council' which in effect established fixed prices for CTVs; disobedient retailers were boycotted. In 1966, a draft decision of the FTC stated that six producers held regular meetings under the auspices of the Electronic Industries Association of Japan (EIAJ), exchanged detailed information on prices, margins, production, and inventory, and co-ordinated price setting and sales volumes.[11] Although the Japanese firms pleaded 'no lo contendere'—they did not deny the charges—the case never came to a final decision. In 1977, eleven years later, it was dropped. In the same year, greater awareness of the harmful effects of cartels finally led to the introduction of a surcharge system which enabled the FTC to fine firms engaged in cartelisation. The Japanese firms had never faced a formal financial sanction until then.[12]

2.3 The Matsushita Litigation

The US firms began their action by seeking complaints under the US antidumping laws in 1968.[13] Faced with what appeared to be a reluctance by the administration to act decisively, Zenith and NUE in 1974 filed a case against Matsushita and the six other Japanese CTV producers under the Sherman and Robinson Patman Antitrust Laws and the 1916 (Wilson) Antidumping Act (see Blair *et al.* 1992: 356). They claimed that these firms had been engaged in a conspiracy since 1953 designed to keep prices high in Japan and low in the US, in order to drive US firms out of the market. They alleged that the check price system and the five company rule provided circumstantial evidence of a wider co-operation between Japanese firms to monopolise the US market through predatory pricing.

This line of argument had several weaknesses. First, the agreement on price setting and distribution in the US aiming at *reducing* the intensity of competition was incompatible with a conspiratory scheme of predatory pricing. Second, whereas the existence of some form of concerted action was indisputable, it was extremely hard to show that the aim was to secure a joint monopoly to raise prices, since the Japanese firms (1) never gained more than 45 percent market share and (2) were not found to have raised prices over a period of years.

In the first round, the US District Court accepted a request by Matsushita and the other defendants to have the charges thrown out on summary judgment on the grounds that there was no case to answer. The Court judged that most of Zenith's evidence was inadmissible, and that what was admissible could not reasonably sustain a conspiracy charge even if accepted. This judgment was reversed by the Appellate Court, which proposed sending the case to trial and accepting most of the excluded evidence. Finally the Supreme Court, by a 5 to 4 majority, overturned the Appeals Court judgment, and re-instated the dismissal on summary judgment. The justices cited the work of McGee, Easterbrook, and Bork to argue that predation was a very rare phenomenon and went on to suggest that it was particularly unlikely to have been possible in this case. The Majority said:

> If the factual context renders respondents' [i.e. Zenith's] claim implausible—if the claim is one that makes no economic sense—respondents must come forward with more persuasive evidence to support their claim than would otherwise be necessary. . . . Finally, if predatory pricing conspiracies are generally unlikely to occur, they are especially so where, as here, the prospect of attaining monopoly power seems slight. . . . Two decades after their conspiracy is alleged to have commenced, petitioners appear to be far from achieving this goal: the two largest shares of the retail market are held by RCA and the respondent Zenith. . . . The alleged conspiracy's failure to achieve its ends in the two decades of its asserted operation is strong evidence that the conspiracy does not in fact exist. . . . As presumably rational businesses, petitioners had every incentive not to engage in the conduct with which they are charged, for its likely effect would be to generate losses for the petitioners with no corresponding gains. . . . In sum, in the light of the absence of any rational motive to conspire, neither petitioners' pricing practices, nor their conduct in the Japanese market, nor their agreements respecting prices and distribution in the American market, suffice to create a 'genuine issue for trial'.[14]

The Majority concluded that Zenith's accusations—that Japanese CTV industry was attempting to drive the US industry out of business in order to monopolise the US CTV market—not only were untrue but could not possibly have been true. In the next section it will be argued that this conclusion is based on too many *a priori* assumptions. Although it cannot be argued that a reasonable fact-finder would necessarily have found predation, it is suggested that a reasonable fact finder might well have concluded that it did occur. There is room for dispute about what the appropriate definition of predation is, and there is room for dispute about whether or not the Japanese firms' conduct could fall within such a meaning.

The US definition of predation has evolved with circumstances, as the debate over the adoption of the Areeda–Turner criterion shows.[15] The Supreme Court Majority chose one specific definition of predation, which involves actually losing money in order to drive rivals out of business. But the Appellate Court and the Supreme Court Minority would probably have chosen a broader definition within which anti-competitive behaviour could have been identified. On the Supreme Court's definition of predation, it is highly unlikely that predation was occurring. However, if a broader definition of predation had been admitted, then the *prima facie* evidence, in the words of the Appellate Court, would have created 'a genuine issue of fact as to whether defendants conspired to dump color televisions in the United States with the specific intent to injure or destroy the industry in the United States'.

Although the Supreme Court's definition of monopolisation is not unreasonable, Scherer and Ross (1990) highlighted the multiple meanings of the term 'monopolise' that can be invoked under the US Sherman Act. The Japanese firms between them could be said to have obtained a dominant position in the world market. It did indeed happen that all but one US-owned producer of CTVs went out of business, though CTV production continues by foreign-owned firms.[16]

It can be argued that the Supreme Court pre-judged the outcome of a full investigation by looking only at a certain class of economic models. It is indeed likely that, if a like-minded court had subsequently examined the case in full, it would also have found no predation, so the Majority decision was internally consistent. But the recorded opinions of the Appellate Court and the Supreme Court Minority indicate that other interpretations were admissible on the basis of an initial reading of the facts. Because the Minority opinion argued that the facts did lend themselves to an interpretation of predation, it seems that there were reasonable people who might have found for Zenith on a more detailed inspection of the evidence.[17]

2.4 Explanations

The Court's decision provoked considerable dispute as to its wisdom and many lawyers and economists have given differing opinions on the case. The leading economic hypotheses that have been offered to explain what undoubtedly was unconventional conduct are reviewed in turn below. It is argued that there are a number of explanations of the facts that are consistent with modern industrial economic theory, construing Japanese firms' behaviour as rational conduct likely to drive US firms out of business in a way that was facilitated by the collusive exercise of market power in Japan.

2.4.1 *Sales* v. *Profit Maximisation*

First of all, the Supreme Court Minority, in the dissenting opinion, accused the Majority of simply imposing their own view of rationality and ignoring alternatives, thus trespassing on the territory of the 'fact finder'. First, Justice White, for the Minority, attacked the assumption of profit maximisation inherent to the traditional analysis of predatory pricing:

> Discussing the improbability of a predatory conspiracy assumes that petitioners valued profit maximisation over growth. In light of the evidence that petitioners sold their goods in this country at substantial losses over a long period of time, I believe that this is an assumption that should be argued to the fact finder, not decided by the Court.[18]

In fact, recent work by economists on the governance of Japanese firms suggests that the relative power of 'stakeholders' (managers, employees, firms, and banks within the same business grouping) versus stockholders leads to a stronger pursuit of market share at the cost of profits (see e.g. Odagiri 1992 and Aoki 1988). This suggests that a restriction of the economic analysis to models of profit maximisation may not explain the behaviour of Japanese firms in full.

2.4.2 *Strategic Investment Behaviour*

The Minority also argued that, without the concerted action on the Japanese and US markets, CTV production by US firms would have been higher. They cite with approval expert witness Horace DePodwin's opinion:

> As it was, however, the influx of sets at depressed prices cut the rates of return on television receiver production facilities in the US to so low a level as to make such investment uneconomic.[19]

In other words, Japanese firms might have been engaged in strategic behaviour to deter investments by US firms. Such behaviour can be profitable even if no full monopolisation of the market occurs. Dixit (1980) has shown that, by being the first to build capacity ahead of demand, firms may be able to deter entry by their rivals. Once the capacity is in place, the firm is pre-committed to incurring only marginal costs from extra production. A similar argument applies if incumbent firms have to decide about investment in new product lines or cost-reducing manufacturing processes and investments in additional capacity in growing markets. In general, structures that transform variable costs into fixed costs can provide a strategic advantage.[20] Such structures may not even be the result of a conscious strategic decision by firms, but rather the result of institutions, such as long term employment systems which make labour into a fixed cost for the firm. Modern game theoretic analysis of strategic behaviour by firms in imperfectly competitive markets has also shown that there are more kinds of predation than those leading to full monopolisation.[21] Firms may invest in excess capacity or set low prices in order to deter entry or to persuade rivals to accept lower market shares. This may succeed without prices being lower than average variable costs, in which case predation will not be identified by the Areeda–Turner rule. In sum, there exists a rich menu of strategic behaviour, and the possibility of behaviour to deter investments by US firms cannot be dismissed *ex ante*.

2.4.3 Learning and Scale Economies

Scherer and Ross argue that the definition of predation was set too narrowly by the Majority. They agree with the Minority that there was a case to be examined, but they base their argument on dynamic scale economies, arguing:

> if there were enduring economies associated with learning by doing (which seems likely) a high-domestic-price, low-export-price strategy would have been profitable even when continued for more than a decade as capacity was expanded. It would not have been necessary for the Japanese producers eventually to raise US prices to realise the pot of gold at the end of the predatory-pricing rainbow.[22]

Thus, the main argument here is that, in the presence of learning effects, predation losses could have been recouped without raising prices.[23] This was not raised by the claimants Zenith and NUE and hence was not taken into consideration by the Supreme Court.

2.4.4 Reputation Effects

Blair *et al.* (1991) offer one of the most recent and comprehensive explanations for the behaviour of Japanese firms. Like the Supreme Court Majority and also Elzinga (1989), they dismiss a predatory pricing conspiracy on the grounds that predation losses could never have been recouped. They also dismiss the possibility that the cartel in Japan was implicitly allowed by MITI as an instrument of strategic trade policy through which profits generated in Japan could subsidise sales in the US. They argue that, given the alleged loss-making pricing below marginal costs, such a policy would allow the exploitation of Japanese consumers without providing corresponding benefits (profits) to producers.

Instead, they offer an alternative explanation, suggesting that the primary motive for the lower prices in the US was to take advantage of a 'reputational externality'. With Japan-made products suffering from a low-quality image in the US, every high-quality Japanese CTV sold would make demand conditions for Japanese CTVs, and also for other Japan-made products, more favourable. MITI, representing the interest of Japanese industry in general, accordingly had a (legitimate) interest in subsidising sales in the US with profits generated in Japan, to benefit from a positive externality for other industries. Blair *et al.* Suggest that a simple scheme set up by MITI to encourage sales in the US could have generated the observed behaviour: MITI could have allowed the individual Japanese firms a share of the profits in Japan proportional to their market share in the US. Firms accordingly would have had an incentive to lower prices in the US even below marginal costs in order to increase sales, since the marginal losses on the US market would be automatically compensated by greater profits in Japan. Since under this scheme price competition in the US by Japanese firms would ultimately lead to destabilisation of the cartel, MITI needed to establish the minimum price system. This in turn gave individual firms an incentive to increase US market shares by secretly giving rebates to US buyers. Blair *et al.* conclude that, since MITI had a legitimate interest in pursuing positive externalities and there was no predatory intent, there was no breaching of antitrust laws, although US producers were clearly, and perhaps 'unfairly', harmed.

While at first glance the above explanation seems to incorporate all the stylised facts of *Matsushita* v. *Zenith*, it is unconvincing. First, it is not likely that there were many US consumers in the 1970s who still had a negative image of Japanese products, since US consumers already had experience with the reliability of Japanese calculators and black and white televisions.[24] It is implausible that the extra reputation effect through subsidised sales of CTVs was so large as to warrant a costly encompassing interventionist scheme set up by MITI as implied by the analysis of Blair *et al.*

Second, Blair *et al.* also stretch their explanation too far by arguing that the check price system was part of a grander scheme by MITI to balance concerted action, implying that firms giving secret rebates were trying to cheat MITI. This implies that the cheating firms expected that they would not be detected: if they were able to increase market share by giving secret rebates, MITI would reward them with greater profits in Japan. However, given the degree of concerted action and the intensity of information exchange, it is highly unlikely that a firm could post sudden sales increases in this way and be rewarded for it without other firms or MITI noticing it.[25] The existence of the check price system can be explained easily without resorting to conspiracy schemes. MITI has always seen its role as a protector of Japanese industry by aiming to minimise conflicts with major trading partners and so preserving a free flow of Japanese exports. In case of Japanese CTV exports, it feared that unbridled exports of cheaply priced

CTVs to the US would eventually lead to actions under antidumping law or trade acts. By establishing minimum prices, the existence of which was in fact public knowledge (see also Gregory 1986), it reduced the chance of dumping findings and showed its good will to the US administration.[26]

Third, the rejection by Blair *et al.* of the cartel as an instrument for strategic profit shifting hinges on the assumption that Japanese firms were making losses on sales below marginal costs. However, precisely in the case of important reputation effects, as analysed by Blair *et al.*, pricing below marginal costs, or 'forward pricing', is rational for profit maximising firms. If reputation effects are important, setting low prices in early periods helps to secure brand loyalty of more consumers and will lead to higher market shares and to profits in later periods more than offsetting the initial losses. Such reputation effects naturally will be much greater at the level of the individual brand that at the country level. Furthermore, as discussed above, pricing below marginal costs is compatible with rational profit maximising behaviour if there are cumulative learning effects on the production side. Thus, even if it is assumed that the available evidence substantiates below marginal cost pricing (which is disputable), this does not necessarily imply that profit maximising Japanese firms' could be found behaving like this only under the MITI administered scheme suggested by Blair *et al.*

2.4.5 An Explanation Based on Asymmetric Market Conditions

The above considerations suggest that the Supreme Court based its decision to dismiss the case on summary judgment on a narrow class of economic models. Below it is argued that probably the most important omission was failure to take into account the possibility that anti-competitive behaviour in the Japanese market might affect Japanese firms' behaviour in the US market. In the next section, an alternative explanation is offered, based on such spillovers of anti-competitive conduct from Japan to the US, which is compatible with the stylised facts of *Matsushita* v. *Zenith*. The results are obtained while maintaining the assumption of profit maximising firms and without including learning and reputational effects. It is shown that what may have mattered most for Japanese firms' behaviour is the asymmetry in market conditions: intense competition in the US market compared with a cartel and insurmountable entry barriers on the Japanese market. The fact that the Japanese firms could cartelise their home market and reap surplus profits there eventually could have driven out US firms and moreover might have eventually harmed US consumers.

The analysis has much wider implications for antitrust policy than those concerning the Supreme Court's handling of this case alone. The most important lesson to be learned from *Matsushita* v. *Zenith* is that in international markets competitive conditions in one country, which are ultimately

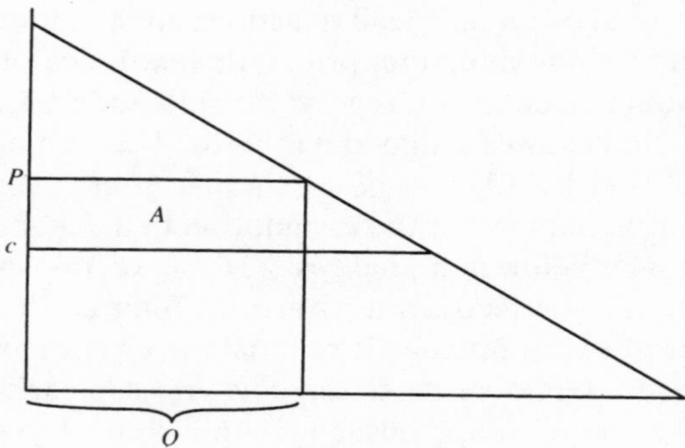

Figure 2.1 The US market before Japanese entry

the result of antitrust rules and their enforcement, can have a major impact on competition abroad. Antitrust policy itself can be used to give home firms a strategic advantage over foreign firms in the international market place.

2.5 A Model of International Rivalry in the CTV Industry

The evidence from the *Matsushita* v. *Zenith* case does not prove that Japanese CTV producers were engaged in predatory pricing in order to monopolise the US market. However, Japanese firms were undoubtedly price discriminating, selling CTVs in the US at prices substantially below prices charged in Japan, and thus reducing US firms' market shares. This entails dumping by modern antidumping law and raises issues of 'fair competition', but the absence of a proven monopolistic intent makes an antitrust case hard to mount unless international price discrimination *per se* is banned.

The idea that is incorporated in the analysis of the CTV industry in this section is that the behaviour of Japanese firms could have been the result of differences in the structure of the Japanese and US CTV industries, rather than the result of a monopolisation strategy with eventual increases of US prices to Japanese levels in mind. The assumptions of cartelisation of the Japanese market and effective control over the distribution system, blocking access to US firms and potential Japanese entrants alike, are sufficient to explain dumping and the exit of US firms.[27] Under these conditions, profit maximising Japanese firms will be found exporting at prices below Japanese prices and below full production costs, but export prices will still be above marginal costs.[28] Below the model and its analytical results are described. The full mathematical description of the model is given in Appendix 2.1.

Consider two markets for CTVs, one in the US and one in Japan, characterised by linear demand functions $P = a - bQ$ and $P^* = a^* - b^*Q^*$, respectively. (Asterisks refer throughout to variables related to Japan.) There are N identical firms producing in the US and N^* identical firms producing in Japan. Production costs involve a fixed cost F of acquiring the technology to produce and setting up production facilities, which is assumed to be the same for US and Japanese firms. Unit variable costs (c and c^*) are invariant with respect to output (hence marginal costs are equal to variable costs). Variable costs may differ between US and Japanese firms, which allows for a possible efficiency advantage of Japanese firms. In addition, there are fixed per unit transport costs t associated with exports.

The US CTV industry is oligopolistic such that prices exceed variable costs of production in the short term and firms may earn excess profits. It is assumed that equilibrium is of the Nash–Cournot form: firms simultaneously set production capacity and prices adjust to clear the market.

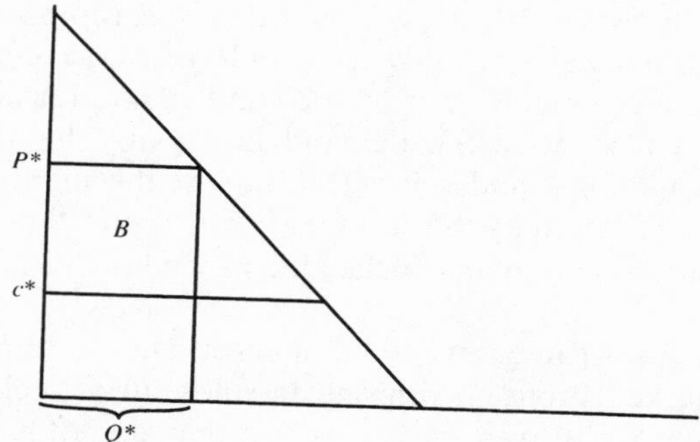

Figure 2.2 The Japanese market under a cartel

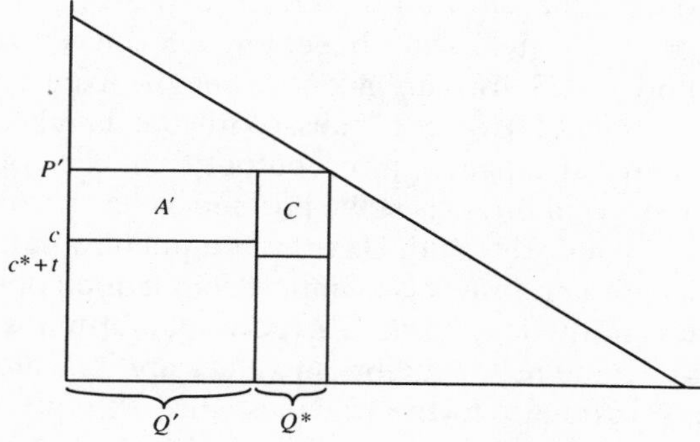

Figure 2.3 The US market after Japanese entry

However, in the long term excess profits eventually attract new entrants, which will bid profits to zero. In long term equilibrium in the US industry, firms earn just enough of a surplus over variable costs to cover the fixed cost. If prices rise above this level there will be entry, and if prices fall below it, exit. Price is above variable costs, but in equilibrium no other firm can afford the fixed cost of entry to take advantage of this.

This long term equilibrium situation on the US market before the entry of Japanese firms is represented by Figure 2.1. The US firms between them sell Q CTVs at a price P which is strictly higher than variable costs c. However, the variable profits earned by the industry, indicated by the surface A, are equal to the fixed cost incurred by the firms: $A = NF$, such that net profits in the industry are zero.

In contrast to the US industry characterised by free entry and exit, a fixed number of established firms, N^*, is active in Japan, while entry is prohibited. To highlight the effects of differential market structure in our analysis, it is assumed that co-operative behaviour by Japanese firms takes the extreme form of a production cartel designed to reap monopoly profits, which are shared equally by the N^* firms. This situation is represented by Figure 2.2. Since the US market is roughly twice as large as the Japanese market, it is assumed for convenience that $b^* = 2b$ and $a^* = a$: for any given price, demand in the US is twice the demand in Japan. The Japanese cartel behaves as a monopolist and sells Q^* CTVs at the monopoly price P^*. Variable profits, indicated by the surface B, are greater than the fixed cost: $B > N^*F$. This situation remains unchanged in the long term since no entry occurs.

The Japanese firms can enter the US market, but US firms cannot enter the Japanese market. Profit maximising Japanese firms seek to cover variable costs in the US plus transport costs, but they do not have to incur the fixed cost a second time. Selling in the US does not affect variable costs (abstracting from learning effects), but spreading the fixed cost over more units lowers average costs. Entry by the Japanese firms in the US market can be shown to have the short term effect of depressing prices in the US and increasing market volume, thus benefiting US consumers.

At depressed prices US firms are not covering the fixed cost; some must exit, and joint output of US firms falls. With the number of US firms adapting to the entry of Japanese firms, output from each of the surviving US firms in the new equilibrium is at the pre-import level, which guarantees that they can stay in business. With US firms' output now reduced, the price comes back to its pre-import level, so import competition does not actually benefit consumers in the long term. The new equilibrium is illustrated by Figure 2.3, in which the new equilibrium values are indicated by a prime. The new price, P', is equal to the previous price P. Japanese firms reap variable profits on the US market amounting to $Q^*(P' - c^* - t)$, indicated by the surface C. It is assumed in this figure that Japanese firms have an efficiency advantage which is greater than transport costs, $c^* + t < c$, though this is not crucial to the analysis. US firms are not able to capture the same output and variable profits as before with $Q' < Q$ and $A' < A$. This means that the fixed cost of fewer US firms can be supported and $N' < N$.

It can be shown that the ability of the Japanese firms to cartelise their home market and to charge monopoly prices means that it is likely that dumping will be observed in the sense of export prices being lower than both home prices and total average costs. The Japanese firms can afford to sell below their average costs since they can recoup the fixed cost through their profits on sales on the Japanese market only: $B > N^*F$. There is no traditional price predation here, in the sense of aiming to monopolise the market and raising prices to consumers. Japanese firms will not sell at US prices below variable costs. They aim at maximisation of profits, and entry in the US market strictly increases profits by C. In any case, there is no prospect of monopolisation of the US market because there is assumed to be free entry in the US.

The above analysis thus shows that the assumptions of free entry on the US market and a cartel barring any entry in Japan are sufficient to explain dumping by Japanese firms associated with the exit of US firms. Admittedly, these are restrictive assumptions. Free entry on the US market probably implies a more competitive market than is the case in reality. In the model, this assumption assures that profits and prices are kept low and are unaffected by Japanese imports. Likewise, the assumption of a cartelised Japanese market will exaggerate the extent of collusive practices on the Japanese market. Nevertheless, as long as competitive conditions in the US and Japan are anywhere near these stylised concepts, the results will hold and only the magnitude of the effects will differ.

It is worthwhile also to consider the assumptions concerning fixed and variable costs, which are important to the kind of analysis presented here. It was assumed that the fixed cost has to be incurred only once. This enables firms to exploit scale economies abroad. To the extent that CTV producers are involved in continuous rounds of R&D spending to introduce new and better models, this assumption is justified: the fruits of R&D can be transferred abroad to export markets at near zero marginal costs.[29] Following this logic, the analysis is also applicable if it is taken into account that since 1973 several Japanese CTV producers have been investing in manufacturing facilities in the US. This is because Japanese firms retain the advantage of covering the fixed R&D cost in the Japanese market.[30]

Finally, variable costs could also be a decreasing function of cumulative production if firms 'learn by doing' (Sherer and Ross 1990). In this case, the effects of asymmetric industry structure will only be strengthened: exclusive access to the Japanese market will give Japanese firms greater leverage over US firms and will enable them to further increase their US market share (Krugman 1984).

2.5.1 Policy Options for the US

The implications of the differences in industry structure and market access between the US and Japan can be seen more clearly by considering what would happen under a liberalisation of the Japanese market, leading to some form of reciprocal access. There are three possible cases:

1. under US pressure, entry of US firms into the Japanese market as members of the cartel is allowed, while the cartel remains in existence;
2. US firms are allowed to enter the Japanese market, but not potential Japanese entrants; US entry causes the cartel to collapse;
3. any Japanese and US firm is allowed to freely enter the market.

The results of the second case will be discussed. Suppose US firms are granted privileged access to the Japanese market, presumably by the promotion of US CTVs through the Japanese distribution network.[31] Japanese

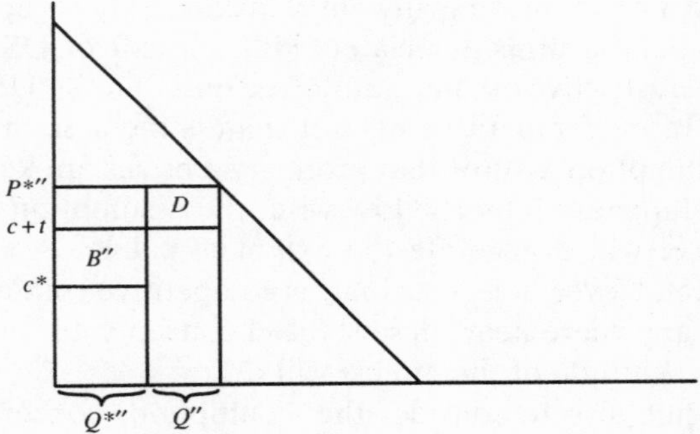

Figure 2.4 The Japanese market under reciprocity

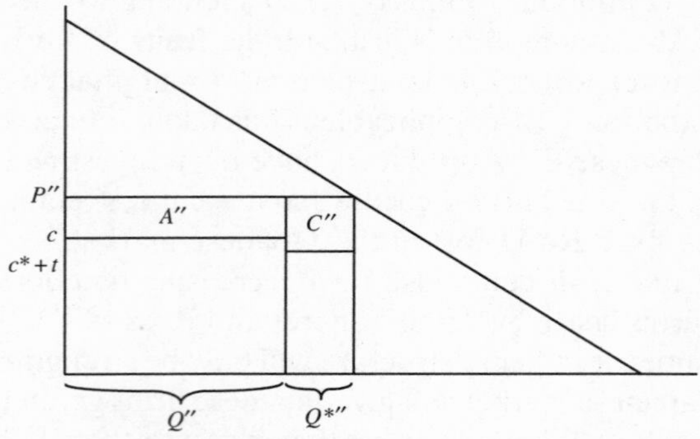

Figure 2.5 The US market under reciprocity

firms are not able to operate the cartel under these conditions and competition on the Japanese market becomes characterised by oligopolistic rivalry just as in the US market.

The new equilibrium on the Japanese market is illustrated by Figure 2.4. (Equilibrium variables are now indicated by a double prime.) The entry of US firms brings prices in Japan down to $P^{*''}$. Variable profits of Japanese firms decrease to C'', but for convenience it is assumed that these are still sufficient not to force existing Japanese firms out of business. US firms are now able to earn variable profits on the Japanese market indicated by the area D.

The entry of US firms into the Japanese market has positive consequences for competition in the US market, as is illustrated by Figure 2.5. Since US firms now earn variable profits on the Japanese market as well, more US firms are able to earn sufficient profits to cover the fixed cost of entry. Profits in Japan and the US are bid down by new US entrants until $N''F = A'' + D$, with $N'' > N'$. The intensified competition by a greater number of US firms will cause the price of CTVs in the US to fall: $P'' < P'$. Because US firms are now able to sell in Japan, they have higher total production than before, spread the fixed cost over more sales, and are able to tolerate the lower home price.

Reciprocity would thus bring gains to consumers compared with the *status quo*. In this sense the sum of Japanese behaviour in both markets is harmful to US consumers as well as producers. Given that this harm arises from anti-competitive behaviour by Japanese firms, albeit in the Japanese market, Japanese behaviour could be said to fall within a broad notion of 'predation', which would be termed 'market share predation without monopolisation'.

The results are quite robust to the choice of reciprocity. If reciprocity takes the form of US producers joining the Japanese cartel (case 1), results would be even more favourable for US firms and US consumers, as long as US entrants (attracted by high profits) are also allowed to join. If reciprocity takes the form of entirely free entry for Japanese and US firms alike (case 3), US firms will still benefit, but less than in the other two cases, since Japanese entrants will take a share of the world market. The price in the US market will still come down, while the price in Japan evidently will decline even more.

2.6 Conclusions and Implications

Conclusions that follow directly from the analysis of the international CTV industry will be discussed first, after which the broader implications of *Matsushita* v. *Zenith* for antitrust policy are highlighted.

2.6.1 The Implications of the Model

In Section 2.5, a highly simplified model was presented which suggests that asymmetric market access caused by diverging competition policies can induce profit maximising firms to export at prices below average costs and below domestic prices. In this model, exports by Japanese firms to the US market force some US firms to exit, driving down prices in the short term, while the equilibrium price in the long term is unchanged. Reciprocal access for US firms on the Japanese market would given US firms the opportunity to reap export revenues. This would not only enable more US firms to survive, but would also lead to increased competition on the US market and lower US prices. US consumers would thus benefit from the opening of the Japanese market.

The latter result contrasts with the conventional view that dumping, as long as there is no eventual monopolisation, while harming US producers, at least benefits US consumers. The analysis shows that depressed prices may just be a short term phenomenon. This is a direct consequence of the exit of US firms in the long term, and not the result of a deliberate monopoly pricing plan. The analysis suggests that an assessment of dumping and price discrimination should take long term effects on entry and exit into account. Japanese firms' behaviour, while harming US producers, may ultimately harm US consumers as well, compared with a situation of full reciprocal market access. Thus, anti-competitive behaviour abroad can create negative 'spillovers' to other countries' industries in global markets, and US antitrust authorities may have a legitimate interest in prohibiting such anti-competitive behaviour.

If the model approximates reality, a major message evolving from the analysis here is that differences in competition policy can have effects similar to strategic trade policies, giving asymmetric advantages to firms competing on international markets. MITI may have had the motive to allow Japanese firms to cartelise their home market to reap economies of scale while prohibiting entry by foreign firms. In fact, these effects are quite similar to modern analysis of strategic trade policy under increasing returns to scale (e.g. Krugman 1984). Non-enforcement of antitrust laws, by allowing firms to collude and restrict entry, may function as a tool of strategic policy.[32]

By taking a few salient characteristics (cartelisation and prohibited entry in Japan, free entry and exit in the US, and some kind of economies of scale), results consistent with the stylised facts of *Matsushita* v. *Zenith* can be obtained. In this view, anti-competitive behaviour in the US takes the form of 'market share predation without monopolisation'. This means that Japanese market shares are being increased in the US and injury is being inflicted on US firms (with no gain to consumers) as a result of the incentive structure created by anti-competitive behaviour in the Japanese market.

The behaviour follows from cartelisation of the Japanese market, even if independent profit maximising behaviour applies in the US market. Although no predatory intent or collusion needs to be assumed in the US market, the consequences of Japanese firms' pricing below average total cost can be anti-competitive and harmful to US interests. This departs from the orthodox view of predatory pricing that predation should be seen as harmful only if there is an intent to monopolise.

Although it is not claimed that this is the only explanation for the observed behaviour and stylised facts, it is a distinct possibility. If the explanation is correct, it is hard to predict whether a full examination of the evidence would have led to a finding of predation. This is because it seems unlikely that the behaviour of Japanese firms would lead to a finding of price predation under the Areeda–Turner criterion. On the other hand, one can argue that the cartel in Japan was set up willingly to provide Japanese firms with surplus profits which could finance long term below-average cost pricing to increase market share at the cost of US producers. The resulting price discrimination could have been found to be violating the Robinson Patman Act if the courts had been willing to give that Act an international dimension. While the analysis suggests that a full investigation of the evidence would have been warranted, it is argued in the following section that the broader implications of *Matsushita* v. *Zenith* are of much greater importance.

2.6.2 Broader Implications of the **Matsushita *v.* Zenith** *case*

The review of alternative explanations for *Matsushita* v. *Zenith* including the explanation provided in Section 2.5 would lead one to doubt the economic reasoning behind the Supreme Court's decision to dismiss the case on summary judgment. But at the same time, one could still argue that litigation of this kind is bound to fall at some point in the judicial process, just because there is an inherent ambiguity in the evidence. A predation case is almost always speculative and ultimately unprovable, so why open the way for potentially competition-deterring litigation even if it means allowing a few scoundrels to flourish? Where competing economic models each offer a different alternative counterfactual scenario, any antitrust court is going to have to take a position on the basis of inherently unobservable data on what would have happened if the alleged offender had acted otherwise. The difficulty of doing this had led courts to be very doubtful about making predation decisions. This scepticism is even shared by some economists who do believe in the possibility of predation. Milgrom and Roberts (1990) have argued that, while predation is more likely than McGee (1985) supposed, it is nevertheless almost always unprovable.

The *Matsushita* v. *Zenith* case may seem all the more difficult to solve since it was argued that the case was basically one of 'market share predation without monopolisation', which is likely to pass traditional predation tests such as the Areeda–Turner criterion.[33] However, anti-competitive effects on US industry ultimately stemmed from weak antitrust laws and enforcement in Japan. This implies that this class of anti-competitive behaviour can be prevented by applying uniform antitrust standards to globalised industries.[34]

Indeed, the announcement by the US Department of Justice in April 1992 that anti-competitive behaviour abroad affecting US producers (exporters) would be the subject of US antitrust litigation shows a growing awareness of the possible spillover effects of anti-competitive behaviour abroad. However, this type of extra-territorial application of US antitrust law will almost necessarily conflict with antitrust policies of foreign countries.[35] It is clear that international codes governing alleged transnational anti-competitive or predatory behaviour are called for. Presumably, such rules would in first instance affect national policies, in that they would require certain degrees of harmonisation of antitrust law, or at least the removal of incompatibilities. They would specify rules under which countries, users, or alleged victims of predation could act against firms whose behaviour in one market was affecting outcomes in another.

The need for international antitrust enforcement is all the more apparent if one considers another reality of global competition: the fact that firms all to often take recourse to trade protection laws such as antidumping and countervailing duties. The same evidence pertaining to *Matsushita* v. *Zenith* led to a finding of dumping under the 1921 Antidumping Act in 1971, but the US Treasury Department delayed levying duties. In 1974 domestic producers also applied for import relief under the 1974 Trade Act, and in 1976 they petitioned for higher import tariffs under the 1930 Tariff Act. In 1977 all these pending cases finally were closed after the signing of an 'orderly market arrangement' in which Japanese firms through MITI promised to limit CTV exports and maintain minimum prices.

These developments suggest that, by refusing to apply antitrust law to the *Matsushita v. Zenith* case, the judges left no recourse other than trade law or outright protectionism to aggrieved domestic firms. This is important, because trade policy measures such as antidumping fail to address the origin of the problem: anti-competitive conduct in the foreign (in this case Japanese) market. Trade policy measures are retaliatory in character, restricting competition at home in response to restrictive policies or conduct abroad. The literature on strategic trade policy has shown that retaliation by one country in response to another country's trade and industrial policies almost invariably results in a decline in economic welfare in both countries.[36]

Moreover, the application of trade laws often harms consumers and may even have serious anti-competitive effects. Antidumping law, for instance, is ostensibly based on the same economic notions of predation for monopolisation and one might suppose that the same criteria would apply. But in practice the system is very different (Nicolaides 1992, Finger 1992: Chapter 2). Antidumping law does not accord symmetrical rights to all producers and neglects interests of consumers and user industries.[37] The nature of the procedures and burden of proof are quite different. Many observers of antidumping practices in the US and the EC argue that procedures are biased towards a finding of dumping. Although dumping duties may be levied only if they are causing 'material injury' (such as a decline in profits) to the petitioning industry, a genuine proof of causality between such 'injury' and the alleged dumping is usually not required. Antidumping practices are thus found to discriminate against foreign firms and to be open to protectionist abuse.[38]

Furthermore, Prusa (1992a) has shown that US producers may make strategic use of antidumping actions to induce foreign importers to agree on undertakings restricting price setting and sales. Such private undertakings are allowed as settlements of antidumping cases and the firms involved are exempted from antitrust persecution. Stegemann (1991a) argues that undertakings that frequently settle EC antidumping cases provide opportunities for illegal price fixing beyond the purposes of antidumping law. Messerlin (1990) and Stegemann (1991b) show that EC industries with a history of collusive conduct tend to petition more for antidumping protection, while antidumping cases involving these industries are relatively often settled through undertakings. Thus, trade laws, rather than acting against predatory or anti-competitive behaviour, may facilitate anti-competitive behaviour.

It is rather ironical that, while economists and lawyers are going through sophisticated debates on the economic logic of antitrust policy, the reality has rapidly surpassed them and has led to recourse to trade instruments with much more harmful effects to consumers, whose interests competition policy is supposed to protect. At least one class of problems, those stemming from differences in antitrust enforcement, can be dealt with through the harmonisation of antitrust laws and their enforcement. This is likely to provide welfare and efficiency gains worldwide while at the same time reducing the possibility of excusing disguised protectionism and anti-competitive conduct by alleging 'unfair' behaviour by foreign firms.

APPENDIX 2.1

A Model of International Rivalry in the CTV Industry

Consider two markets for CTVs, one in the US and one in Japan, characterised by linear demand functions $P = a - bQ$ and $P^* = a^* - b^*Q^*$, respectively. (Asterisks refer throughout to variables related to Japan.) There are N identical firms producing in the US and N^* identical firms producing in Japan. Production costs involve a fixed cost F of acquiring the technology to produce and set up production facilities, which is assumed to be the same for US and Japanese firms. This fixed cost has to be incurred only once: it facilitates production for the domestic market as well as exports. Unit variable costs (c and c^*) are invariant with respect to output. Variable costs may differ between US and Japanese firms, which allows for a possible efficiency advantage of Japanese firms. In addition, there are fixed per-unit transport costs t associated with exports.

In order to highlight the effects of differential market structure, it is assumed that the US industry is characterised by free entry in the long term, while co-operative behaviour by Japanese firms takes the extreme form of a production cartel. Any profits earned by US firms are in the long term bid down by new entrants. In contrast, the colluding Japanese firms share positive monopoly profits, even in the long term, since entry is impeded by the incumbent firms' control over distribution. Furthermore, Japanese firms export to the US market and are able to spread the fixed cost F over two markets, whereas US firms do not have the possibility of exporting to Japan.

A.2.1.1 The US Market before Japanese Entry

In order to examine the effects of Japanese exports on the US market, the equilibrium on the US market before the entry of Japanese firms is first described. It is assumed that Nash–Cournot equilibrium prevails. The standard expressions for production quantities and profits of individual firms i and for the equilibrium market price are:

(1) $$q_i = \frac{a-c}{b(N+1)}$$

(2) $$\Pi_i = \frac{(a-c)^2}{b(N+1)^2} - F$$

(3) $$P = \frac{a+Nc}{N+1}$$

The above equations can be considered as representing short term equilibrium on the US market. In the long term, any surplus profits in (2) will attract entry by new firms until profits earned by each firm are reduced to zero. Solving $\Pi_i = 0$ for the long term equilibrium number of firms,

$$(4) \quad N = \frac{a-c}{\sqrt{Fb}} - 1$$

The number of firms that can profitably operate is greater the larger the market (indicated by the inverse of the slope of the demand function b), the smaller the fixed cost, and the higher the price the product can demand on the market relatively to variable production costs ($a - c$). Substituting (5) into equation (1) gives long term equilibrium output for the representative firm:

$$(5) \quad q_i = \sqrt{\frac{F}{b}}$$

Equilibrium output increases with the fixed cost and market size. Total output by US firms is N times individual firm output:

$$(6) \quad Nq_i = \frac{a-c-\sqrt{Fb}}{b}$$

Finally, market price becomes:

$$(7) \quad P = c + \sqrt{Fb}$$

There is a markup on variable costs which is dependent on the ratio of the fixed cost to market size.

A.2.1.2 The Japanese Market

The N^* Japanese firms sell CTVs in both the Japanese and the US markets. Assuming constant variable costs and perfectly segmented markets, Japanese firms' production decisions for both markets can be treated separately. Output and profits for a Japanese firm in the cartelised home market are equal to monopoly output and profits divided by the number of incumbent Japanese producers, N^*. Hence, output and profits of the representative firm are:

$$(8) \quad q^*_{i,D} = \frac{a^* - c^*}{2N^*b^*}$$

$$(9) \quad \Pi^*_{i,D} = \frac{\left(a^* - c^*\right)^2}{4N^*b} - F$$

A suffix D denotes output or profits on the domestic Japanese market. The monopoly price is the standard:

$$(10) \quad P^* = \frac{1}{2}\left(a^* + c^*\right)$$

A.2.1.3 Entry of Japanese Firms into the US Market

Short term Nash–Cournot equilibrium on the US market after Japanese entry implies the following exports of Japanese firms:

$$(11)\quad q^*_{i,E} = \frac{a-\left(c^*+t\right)+N\left(c-c^*-t\right)}{b\left(N+N^*+1\right)}$$

A suffix E denotes Japanese firms' export sales. Export quantities depend on Japanese firms' variable export costs relatively to variable costs of US firms and the total number of firms supplying the market.

US firms now face competition by Japanese firms. Short term Nash–Cournot production quantities and profits and the equilibrium price become:

$$(12)\quad q_i = \frac{a-c+N^*\left(c^*+t-c\right)}{b\left(N+N^*+1\right)}$$

$$(13)\quad \Pi_i = \frac{\left[a-c+N^*\left(c^*+t-c\right)\right]^2}{b\left(N+N^*+1\right)^2} - F$$

$$(14)\quad P = \frac{a+Nc+N^*\left(c^*+t\right)}{N+N^*+1}$$

Comparing (12)–(14) with equations (1)–(3), it can be seen that the immediate effect of Japanese imports is to drive production and profits of US firms down while depressing prices.[39]

In the long term, the smaller profits in (13) do not allow all US firms previously in the market to recoup the fixed cost F. The number of firms surviving in the industry, derived from the condition that US firms' profits in the long term are equal to zero, is:

$$(15)\quad N = \frac{a-c-N^*\left(c+\sqrt{Fb}-c^*-t\right)}{\sqrt{Fb}} - 1$$

This equilibrium number of firms is smaller than the equilibrium number before the entry of Japanese firms in equation (4), with the extent of the decline depending on the profitability of export sales of Japanese firms (the difference between the long term US price and export costs). Thus, in the long term the entry of Japanese firms on the US market has to force some US firms to exit. After Japanese imports are accommodated by the exit of some firms, output of the remaining US firms returns to the level that will just allow coverage of the fixed cost, while the price on the US market returns to the long term equilibrium:

$$(16)\quad q_i = \frac{F}{\sqrt{b}}$$

(17) $P = c + \sqrt{Fb}$

Thus, apart from the short term price decline, US consumers do not gain from Japanese import competition. This result relates to the assumption of free entry and exit on the US market, which supposes that competitive conditions prevail in the long term, with or without Japanese competition. Total production by US firms declines to:

(18) $Nq_i = \left[a - c - \sqrt{Fb} - N^*\left(c + \sqrt{Fb} - c^* - t\right)\right] / b$

The magnitude of the decline in total output of US firms again depends on the difference between the long term equilibrium market price and Japanese firms' variable costs.

A.2.1.4 Price Discrimination and Pricing below Average Costs

Collusion and entry barriers on the Japanese market contrast with free entry on the US market. This may lead to dumping according to two established definitions:

1. the US price is below the price in Japan plus transport costs;
2. the US price is below average costs of Japanese firms.

The condition that the short term US price is lower than the Japanese price plus transport costs implies:

(19) $\frac{1}{2}\left(a^* + c^*\right) + t > \frac{a + Nc + N^*\left(c^* + t\right)}{N + N^* + 1}$

It can be shown that, except for the case of extremely low variable costs of Japanese firms, inequality (19) will hold.[40] Dumping is sustained in the long term if the following condition holds:

(20) $\frac{1}{2}\left(a^* + c^*\right) + t > c + \sqrt{Fb}$

Generally, it is highly likely that the monopoly price in the Japanese market is above the free entry competitive price in the US market. This is particularly so if transport costs are non-negligible (as is the case for CTVs). The only exception is the case of a large cost advantage of Japanese firms, leading to relatively low prices in Japan even under monopolistic pricing. A sufficient condition for (20) to hold is that Japanese firms do not have a cost advantage: $c^* \geqslant c$.[41]

Dumping in terms of the US price below Japanese firms' average costs occurs in long term equilibrium if:

(21) $c^* + t + \frac{F}{q^*_{i,D} + q^*_{i,E}} < \sqrt{Fb} + c$

After some calculations, this leads to:

(21′) $2N^*b^*\left[Fb - \left(\sqrt{Fb} + c - c^* - t\right)^2\right] - \left[b\left(a^* - c^*\right)\left(\sqrt{Fb} + c - c^* - t\right)\right] < 0$

Since the second term between brackets is positive, a sufficient condition is that the first term is negative. This gives:

(21″) $c^* + t < c$

If Japanese firms have a cost advantage over US firms which is greater than transport costs, the long term US price is always lower than Japanese firms' average costs. If this is not the case, then dumping in terms of below-average cost pricing is more likely to occur the smaller the number of Japanese firms (N^*), the larger the Japanese market (the higher b^*), and the greater the value Japanese consumers attach to CTVs (a^*).

The necessary and sufficient conditions (20) and (21″) imply that long term price discrimination and pricing below total average cost can occur simultaneously. Comparing the sufficient conditions under which price discrimination takes place with those under which below-average cost pricing occurs, it appears that the conditions are opposed: Japanese firms will always be found dumping by one of the two definitions. If Japanese variable costs are low compared with variable costs of US firms, Japanese firms will certainly be found pricing below average costs. If variable costs of Japanese firms are equal to or higher than variable costs of US firms, the long term US price will always end up lower than the price in Japan and Japanese firms will be found persistently to price-discriminate.

A.2.1.5 Reciprocity

The asymmetric market access case is compared with the case of reciprocal market access. In modelling reciprocity, it is assumed that US firms are sufficiently competitive to export to the Japanese market once entry barriers disappear. There are three hypothetical ways in which the opening of the Japanese market could take place. First, US producers could be invited to join the Japanese cartel. Second, US firms could be granted privileged access to the Japanese distribution network only, while competition by US firms in Japan would lead to a breakdown of the cartel. However, Japanese entrants still would not gain access to the distribution network (N^* remains fixed). Third, the Japanese government could dissolve the distribution network entirely, giving both US firms and potential Japanese entrants every chance to enter the market. This last situation essentially gives the 'reciprocal dumping' case analysed in Brander and Krugman (1983) and Venables (1985). Here he second case is analysed.

The focus is on the consequences of reciprocity for US firms and equilibrium on the US market. US firms are now able to sell in both the US and the Japanese markets. They earn variable profits on exports to Japan as long as variable costs plus transport costs are lower than the equilibrium price on the Japanese market. It is assumed that after the breakdown of the cartel, Nash–Cournot equilibrium prevails on the Japanese market. Profits of US firms in the short term are:

$$(22)\quad \Pi_i = \frac{\left[a - c + N^*\left(c^* + t - c\right)\right]^2}{b\left[N + N^* + 1\right]^2} + \frac{\left[a^* - c - t + N^*\left(c^* - c - t\right)\right]^2}{b^*\left[N + N^* + 1\right]^2} - F$$

The second term represents the gain in profits arising from exports to Japan. This gain in profits will eventually enable more US firms to recoup the fixed cost and survive. In order to derive the equilibrium number of US firms under reciprocity, it is convenient to establish a relationship between the parameters of demand in the US and Japan. Since the US CTV market is roughly twice as large as the Japanese market, assume that $b = 2b$ and $a^* = a$: for every given price, demand in the US is twice the demand in Japan. The equilibrium number of US firms can be calculated as:

$$(23) \quad N = \frac{\sqrt{\frac{3}{2}}\sqrt{\left[a - c - N^*\left(c - c^* - t\right) + \frac{1}{3}t\left(2N^* - 1\right)\right]^2 + \frac{2}{9}t^2\left(2N^* - 1\right)} - N^*\sqrt{\frac{2}{3}Fb}}{\sqrt{Fb}} - 1$$

The number of US firms surviving under reciprocity is always greater than in the asymmetric market access case in (15). This can be seen more easily by setting transport costs to zero:

$$(24) \quad N\big|_{t=0} = \frac{\sqrt{\frac{3}{2}}\left[a - c - N^*\left(c + \sqrt{\frac{2}{3}Fb} - c^*\right)\right]}{\sqrt{Fb}}$$

Clearly, in (24), N is always larger than in (15) with transport costs set to zero.[42] The greater number of US firms competing with Japanese firms on the US market implies that competition intensifies, which results in a US price that is strictly lower than under asymmetric market access:

$$(25) \quad P = c + \sqrt{\frac{2}{3}Fb}$$

Thus, by increasing competition, the opening of the *Japanese* market benefits *US* consumers. Furthermore, total sales by US firms in the US market grow. To see this, set transport costs to zero, in which case total sales become:

$$(26) \quad Nq_{i,D}\big|_{t=0} = \left[a - c - N^*\left(c + \sqrt{\frac{2}{3}Fb} - c^*\right) - \sqrt{\frac{2}{3}Fb}\right] \Big/ b$$

Comparing (26) with (18) shows that total sales volume of US firms on the US market increases.

NOTES

1. *Matsushita Electric Industrial Co., Ltd.* v. *Zenith Radio Corporation*, 106 S. Ct. 1348 (1986).

2. Parallel trade policy complaints continued in the meantime. The 1974 Trade Act was passed with this industry largely in mind, and the alleged loopholes in this act prompted further moves in Congress.
3. See Schwartzman (1993), Milgrom and Roberts (1990), Sherer and Ross (1990), and Ordover, Sykes, and Willig (1983) for examples of the former, and Blair *et al.* (1991), Elzinga (1989), and Elzinga and Mills (1989) for examples of the latter.
4. A similar increase in market share was recorded for black and white televisions.
5. Blair *et al.* (1991: 362) regard the DePodwin estimates as 'reason for suspicion' for below marginal cost pricing. Schwartzman (1993: Chapter 6) regards the DePodwin data as evidence that US prices were below average total costs.
6. See Appendix 1.1, Flath (1988), and Flath and Nairu (1989).
7. The Large Scale Retail Store Law virtually prohibited entry of large stores in popular retail areas; see e.g. Potjes (1993), Batzer and Laumer (1989), and USITC (1990).
8. See *JFTC Decision Reporter (Kousei Torihiki Iinkai Shinketsu Shuu)*, 1971: 187–208.
9. Schwartzman (1993), Sanekata (1992a), and Flath (1988). See Dick (1993b) and Flath and Nairu (1989) on the economic effects of current vertical restraints in Japanese retailing.
10. See Yamamura (1986) and Schwartzman (1993: Chapter 5) for detailed descriptions of the evidence.
11. The six firms were Sanyo, Toshiba, Sharp, Hitachi, Matsushita, and Mitsubishi; Sony was not implicated. See *JFTC Decision Reporter (Kousei Torihiki Iinkai Shinketsu Shuu)*, 1978: 37–44.
12. It has also been reported that the regular meetings by the Japanese manufacturers were finally abolished in 1977, which must have been related to these developments (Schwartzman 1993: 87).
13. For fuller details of the litigation including the antidumping aspects, see Schwartzman (1993).
14. 106 S. Ct., 1356–1361.
15. The Areeda–Turner criterion is considered the basis for US antitrust decisions in predation cases. The criterion implies that firms accused of predatory pricing have a case to answer if prices are below marginal costs. If prices are above this level but below average total costs, a predation case can be established only if complainants can prove predatory intent on the part of the accused firms.
16. In a recent development, Zenith, the last independent US CTV producer, was acquired by Lucky Goldstar Electronics of South Korea in late 1995.
17. Jorde and Lemley (1991) argue that the Court chose to apply a particularly strict criterion of proof at summary judgment because the allegations were of a predatory conspiracy which is *per se* illegal, whereas if only one firm had been involved a rule of reason would have left further discretion in a full trial. This issue does not concern the economic analysis but highlights the potential economic significance of different criteria of proof applied by courts.
18. US Supreme Court Minority Opinion in Matsushita. 106. Ct., 1365.
19. Horace DePodwin cited by US Court of Appeals in Matsushita. 106. Ct., 1364.
20. See for instance Smith (1987) for the case of entry deterring foreign investment.

21. See Milgrom and Roberts (1990) for an overview of the literature.
22. Scherer and Ross (1990: 470).
23. This is true even without any predation strategy: in the presence of learning effects, firms have an incentive to sell below marginal costs to increase sales early on, learn by doing, and profit later from lower marginal costs; see e.g. Gruenspecht (1988).
24. See also Ordover, Sykes, and Willig (1983) on this argument.
25. Another point of critique is that the scheme suggested by Blair *et al.* implies that firms with the largest sales in the US would get most profits in Japan, while in reality this was rather the reverse: large sellers in the US such as Sony and Sharp reaped relatively lower profits in Japan.
26. Although the avoidance of trade friction was in the collective interest of Japanese firms, individual firms had an incentive to cheat, at least as long as the check prices were above marginal costs. Since the arrangement was informal, MITI did not have a direct way to punish firms if it found evidence of cheating. Moreover, it is conceivable that MITI was not too preoccupied with punishing cheating firms as long as US Customs did not discover the discounts and so was not able to substantiate dumping.
27. The model presented here takes as the starting point the analyses in Brander and Krugman (1983) and Venables (1985). Brander and Krugman show that in oligopolistic industries dumping can be in accordance with normal profit maximising behaviour if exporting firms have a smaller market share abroad than at home and so perceive a greater demand elasticity on export markets. In a symmetric two-country model a situation of 'reciprocal dumping' can arise, with firms in both countries dumping their products in export markets. Such dumping may be welfare enhancing by increasing competition if transport costs are not too high. Venables extends the analysis to long term equilibrium by allowing profits to attract entry. These models are adapted by introducing anti-competitive behaviour and entry barriers in the Japanese market. In this case dumping becomes unilateral, while its pro-competitive effects are limited.
28. This implies that Japanese firms were not making strategic losses on exports. While price discrimination was indisputable, there has been no direct evidence of pricing below marginal costs. The fact that the institutional traits of Japanese firms such as lifetime employment systems tend to transfer variable costs into fixed costs may have caused estimates of Japanese marginal costs to be systematically too high. Furthermore, any pricing below marginal costs that did occur may have been 'forward pricing' behaviour which is consistent with profit maximisation.
29. The fixed cost can also be taken as constant at the manufacturing level as long as there is excess capacity on the home market, such that exports can be accommodated by an existing manufacturing plant. In the long term, the notion of a fixed outlay necessary for production implies that there have to be economies of scale in production with average costs declining as output increases. Since CTV manufacturing is characterised by economies of scale with a minimum efficient plant size of 500,000 units, Japanese firms can profit from economies of scale in manufacturing by exporting to the US only as long as their sales in Japan are lower than this minimum plant size. This, however, probably only applied to the early exporting experience of smaller firms such as Mitsubishi and

Sharp. The assumption of a fixed cost in this case is more representative of economies of scale in R&D.

30. See also Dei (1990) for an extension of the Brander–Krugman model of reciprocal dumping to direct foreign investment.
31. There are at least two recorded efforts by US CTV manufacturers to sell CTVs in Japan through Japanese firms. In Detrouzos, Lester, and Solow (1989) it is reported that Zenith tried to sell CTVs in Japan through C. Itoh, one of the general trading companies, in 1962. MITI, however, refused to grant C. Itoh the right to use dollars to import the sets. In 1973, Motorola tried to sell its Quasar CTVs through Aiwa, a subsidiary of Sony, at prices a third lower than Japanese sets. The following year Matsushita bought Motorola's CTV operations and imports apparently stopped. See also Schwartzman (1993: Chapter 2) for a discussion of barriers to entry on the Japanese market which US firms have been facing.
32. While this increased the profits of Japanese producers, Japanese consumers obviously lost and the effects on total Japanese welfare are not necessarily positive. The Japanese government may have had a stronger motive to relax antitrust rules if it values the positive effects for Japanese industry more highly than the losses to consumers. To some extent, this could be related to positive external effects of growth in CTV production (not incorporated in the model), for instance through R&D activities and manufacturing experience which can be used for other products.
33. It was not assumed that Japanese firms were making losses by pricing below marginal costs.
34. Schwartzman (1993: Chapter 4) argues that the Areeda–Turner principle and most analyses of predation pay inadequate attention to the international dimension. However, his conclusion that all export prices below home prices should be considered predatory goes much further than the argument in this chapter.
35. In fact, in case of Japan, which is still judged to be a country with very weak antitrust enforcement, the US government has followed another route by urging it to toughen antitrust laws and enforcement. Sanekata (1992b) speaks of an antitrust 'renaissance' in Japan starting in the early 1990s. In 1991, the FTC increased penalties on cartels from 1.5 per cent of sales made during the period of cartelization to 6 per cent. In the same year, for the first time in 17 years, the FTC brought charges against the conspirers of a cartel under criminal law.
36. See the brief overview of the strategic trade policy literature in the Introduction to Part II.
37. Consumers and user industries have no voice in antidumping procedures in the US (Finger 1992). The EC Commission is obliged to consider the 'Community interest' in deciding to levy duties but in practice has more or less equated the interests of the Community with the interests of the petitioning industries (Van Bael and Bellis 1990, Bell 1987). See also Chapter 1.
38. Bell (1987), van Bael and Bellis (1990), Boltuck, François, and Kaplan (1991), Hindley (1988), and Finger (1992). See also the discussion in paragraph 1.3.5.
39. The condition for these effects to occur is that the export costs of Japanese firms are less than the short term US market price: $c^* + t < (a + Nc)/(N + 1)$. This will always hold, because otherwise Japanese firms would not have entered the US market in the first place.

40. Inequality (19) always holds if the variable costs of US and Japanese firms are equal ($c = c^*$). Allowing for cost differences, substituting $N = 2$ and $N^* = 2$ gives the non-trivial case in which dumping is *least* likely to occur. If, for convenience, $a = a^*$ is assumed (as below), then $4c - c^* - 3a < 6t$ is obtained. Since a is greater than c, a sufficient condition for dumping to occur is that the cost advantage of Japanese firms is limited to 6 times transport costs.
41. If $a^* = a$ is assumed (as below), then taking the case of $c^* = c$ and substituting (4) leads to the condition $N > 1 - 2t/\sqrt{Fb}$, which must hold.
42. Allowing for positive transport costs in (23) shows that the equilibrium number of US firms will actually be greater, the higher transport costs: US firms gain more on their home market from this natural barrier to trade than they lose on the Japanese market. This effect occurs because the US market is larger than the Japanese market and because of the asymmetry in competitive conditions, by which part of the cost increase can be earned back in Japan through higher prices, but none of it can be earned back in the US where free entry ensures an unchanged price.

3

Strategic Trade Policy and Tariff Jumping DFI

3.1 Introduction

The literature on direct foreign investment (DFI) recently has been supplemented by several formal studies of DFI emphasising its possible strategic character in oligopolistic industries (Motta 1992, Davies and Lyons 1988, Smith 1987, Horstman and Markusen 1987). A major result of these studies is that the sunk cost character of DFI makes it instrumental as an irreversible commitment to increased sales in the host country, which may deter entry by host country firms. Central to entry-deterring DFI is the notion that DFI leads to lower variable costs as opposed to exports, by saving transport costs and reducing variable marketing expenditures.[1] It is this reduction in variable costs that allows the multinational firm to increase sales. The strategic character of DFI results in a rich menu of implications for tariff policy of the host country. While a tariff may induce the firm to set up local production to substitute for exports (tariff jumping DFI), this investment at the same time may render the entry of domestic firms unprofitable, with negative welfare consequences. In contrast, if a domestic firm is assumed to be able to move first, a tariff may provide the extra incentive necessary to make entry by the domestic firm profitable, while the entry decisions by the domestic firm may induce the foreign firm not to invest in the host country or not to enter the market at all (Motta 1992: 1567).

Although the literature on strategic DFI provides important new insights, the models are arguably not readily applicable to the occurrence of tariff jumping DFI by Japanese electronics firms in the countries of the European Community. As seen in Chapter 1, a range of Japanese electronics exports, including VCRs, printers for personal computers, plain paper copiers, and CD players, have been subject to EC antidumping actions during the 1980s. The EC in most cases imposed substantial antidumping duties, which in EC antidumping practice are much akin to conventional tariffs. Japanese firms more often than not opted to avoid paying duties by setting up assembly plants in the EC. By the time of the final determination in the antidumping cases, they usually had already established manufacturing operations.[2]

While a substantial part of Japanese investment in the EC can be characterised as tariff jumping,[3] Japanese DFI has several characteristics which differentiate it from strategic DFI. First, the electronics sectors concerned tend to be dominated by established firms, both Japanese and European, and it is not apparent that the possibility of new entry played an important role. In most cases it was EC industry, not the Japanese producers, which 'moved first' by petitioning for antidumping duties, to which the Japanese firms then responded. Second, Japanese firms also appeared reluctant to invest in the EC in the absence of any duties, which appears due to the fact that production in Japan or South-East Asia was more cost-effective. Hence, the variable cost reducing effect of DFI is not likely to have played a role.[4] This suggests that, rather than focusing on the entry-deterring potential of DFI, tariff jumping DFI by Japanese firms should be seen as a response to trade policy measures which threatened to increase costs *vis-à-vis* European rivals. Tariffs and antidumping duties in this view are policy instruments to 'raise rivals' costs' and shift rents from foreign to domestic producers, as emphasised in strategic trade policy literature (e.g. Brander and Spencer 1984). However, as Levinsohn (1989) has shown, the possibility of DFI restricts the effectiveness of such strategic trade policies. The question rises whether trade policy measures that induce DFI can be welfare improving for the host country.

This chapter presents an analysis of tariff policy which may induce tariff jumping DFI. DFI is associated with increased variable production costs as compared with production for export. Adopting a simple Cournot duopoly framework, the conditions under which the foreign firm will invest are examined and the welfare effects of tariff jumping DFI are compared with those of conventional tariff policy without DFI.[5] It is shown that tariffs which induce DFI may still be welfare improving, provided that the domestic firm is not a high cost producer. However, from the viewpoint of domestic welfare, it would be preferable to restrict the tariff to a level that does not induce tariff jumping DFI.

The remainder of this chapter is organised as follows. The next section introduces the duopoly model. In Section 3.3 the choice between DFI and export is analysed. Section 3.4 examines the welfare effects of tariff jumping DFI compared with conventional tariff policy and Section 3.5 concludes.

3.2 Cournot Duopoly

This section describes a Cournot duopoly model which is used to analyse tariff jumping DFI and its welfare effects. The model is kept as simple as possible in order to highlight the central mechanisms and effects. The setup follows previous work by Motta (1992), Sleuwaegen and Yamawaki (1992), and Davies and Lyons (1988).

Consider a host country with an incumbent domestic producer (firm D). Firm D supplies the host country market but faces import competition from a foreign producer (firm M) based in a foreign country. For simplicity, assume that firm D does not export and that firm M's sales consist only of exports to the host country.[6] Both firms set production capacities simultaneously and equilibrium in the industry is of the Nash–Cournot type. Firm M exports at constant marginal costs c_E^* and firm D produces at constant marginal costs c. (A suffix E denotes export costs and an asterisk indicates variables related to firm M.) Without loss of generality, transport costs are assumed to be negligible. Demand in the host country is described by the linear inverse demand function $P = a - bQ$, with $Q = q + q^*$ and the inverse of b a measure of market size.[7]

Firm M faces the choice between exporting to the host country and investing in a local manufacturing plant. If it sets up production in the host country it has to incur a fixed cost F, which includes the costs of setting up the plant and other costs associated with starting up manufacturing operations in an unknown environment with different cultural, social, legal, and business practices. After incurring F, firm M can produce at constant marginal costs c_F^*. (A suffix F indicates costs under foreign production.)[8] These marginal costs, however, are higher than the marginal costs associated with exporting: $c_F^* > c_E^*$. Hence, firm M will not invest in the absence of a tariff, t, on its exports. The assumptions of the model are illustrated in Figure 3.1.

Firm M is exporting to the host country market as the tariff is levied. Profits of firm M and D in the presence of a tariff are given by (1) and (2), respectively:

$$(1)\quad \Pi^* = q^*\left[a - b\left(q^* + q\right) - c_E^* - t\right]$$

$$(2)\quad \Pi = q\left[a - b\left(q^* + q\right) - c\right]$$

Firms maximise profits with respect to output, which leads to the Nash–Cournot production quantities:

$$(3)\quad q^* = \left[a - 2\left(c_E^* + t\right) + c\right] / 3b$$

$$(4)\quad q = \left[a - 2c + c_E^* + t\right] / 3b$$

Production of both firms is dependent on relative marginal costs and is greater the larger the market (the higher $1/b$). The tariff increases marginal costs of firm M and reduces its equilibrium output, while increasing output of firm D. The former effect is stronger than the latter, resulting in a reduction in total industry output. This leads to an increase in the equilibrium price:

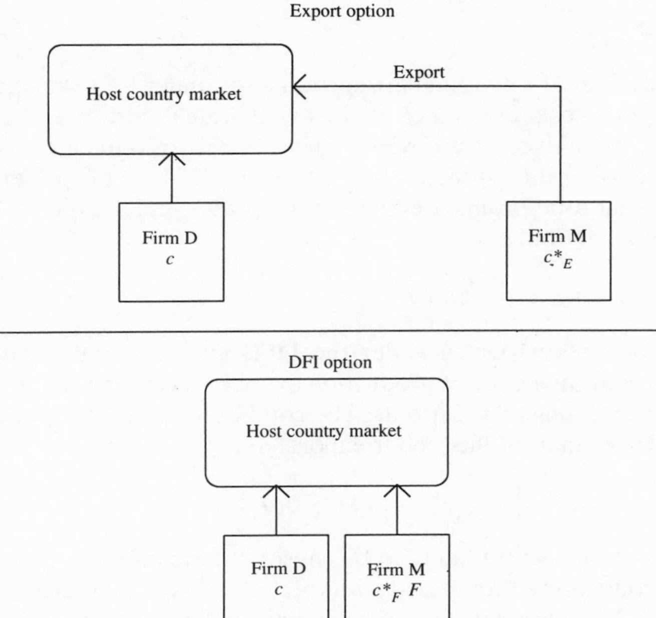

Figure 3.1 Exports v. DFI in the duopoly model

(5) $P = \left[a + c + c_E^* + t\right]/3$

Profits of firm M and firm D are obtained by substituting the equilibrium price and production quantities in (1) and (2):

(6) $\Pi^* = \left[a - 2\left(c_E^* + t\right) + c\right]^2 / 9b$

(7) $\Pi = \left[a - 2c + c_E^* + t\right]^2 / 9b$

As with production, profits increase with lower relative marginal costs.[9] A tariff increases profits of firm D and decreases profits of firm M

3.3 Export versus DFI

At a certain level of the tariff, firm M will find tariff jumping DFI more profitable than exporting. A *necessary* condition for DFI to occur can be immediately established: the tariff must be higher than the difference in marginal production costs in the host and home country:

(8) $t > c_F^* - c_E^*$

If (8) holds, firm M's marginal production costs under DFI are smaller than total marginal costs under export. Lower marginal costs are necessary to recoup the extra fixed cost F which has to be incurred in case of DFI.

The necessary and sufficient condition for DFI to be preferred over exports is that total profits are higher than profits under exports. Profits of firm M under DFI are:

(9) $\Pi^{*\prime} = \left[a - 2c_F^* + c\right]^2 / 9b - F$

A prime denotes variables under the DFI option. Variable profits now depend on marginal costs of production in the host country c_F^*, the fixed cost F is subtracted to get total profits. The condition that profits under DFI in (9) are greater than profits under exports in (6) is:

(10) $\left[a - 2c_F^* + c\right]^2 - \left[a - 2\left(c_E^* + t\right) + c\right]^2 > 9bF$

The DFI option is more likely to be chosen the smaller are marginal costs of local production c_F^* compared with total marginal export costs $c_E^* + t$, the higher firm D's marginal costs, the smaller the fixed cost F, and the larger the market.[10]

Since tariff jumping DFI occurs only if firm M can reduce marginal costs, it must follow that DFI limits the effectiveness of tariff policy designed to 'raise rivals' costs'. In the next section the welfare effects of tariff jumping DFI are examined and compared with those of tariff policy without DFI.

3.4 Welfare Effects

It is assumed that the host country uses the tariff to maximise domestic welfare. In the case where firm M chooses to export, a tariff increases profits of firm D and wins tariff revenue, but will increase price and cause a decline in consumer surplus. Figure 3.2 illustrates the welfare effects of tariff policy under export.

Figure 3.2 is drawn such that $c > c_E^*$ (firm M has a production cost advantage), but this is not crucial to the analysis. Host country welfare is the sum of consumer surplus (the area *CS*), tariff revenue (the area *TR*), and profits of firm D (the area *DPS*) or:

(11) $\left(a - P\right)Q/2 + tq_E^* + \left(p - c\right)q$

The welfare maximising tariff can be calculated by maximising (11) with respect to t. Solving for t results in:

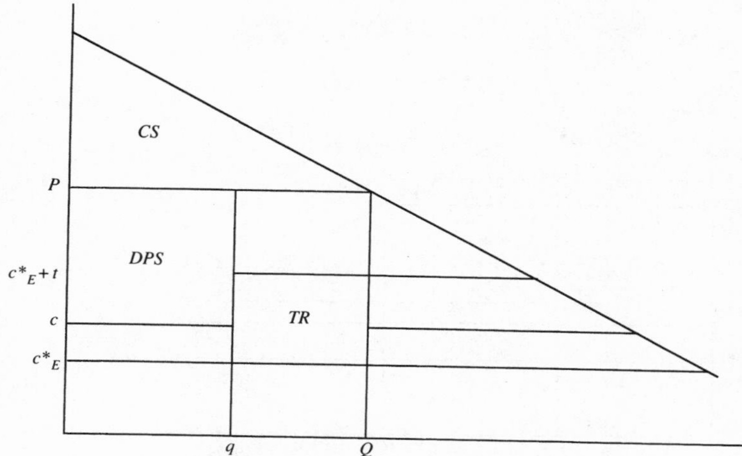

Figure 3.2 Welfare effects of a tariff under export

(12) $t = \left(a - c_E^*\right)/3$

The welfare maximising tariff only depends on the difference between the demand curve intercept and marginal costs of firm M. The tariff is higher the greater the 'intensity of demand': the higher the price the good can demand on the host country market relatively to the marginal costs of producing the good. Put differently, the optimal tariff is higher the greater the potential profits of firm M. This result obtained in the duopoly model is exactly the same as the 'optimal' tariff in the case of a host country facing a foreign monopolist (compare Levinsohn 1989). Marginal costs of firm D only affect the distribution of domestic welfare between consumer surplus and firm D's profits, and do not enter the equation.

Now suppose that the welfare maximising tariff is higher than the tariff jumping level which can be derived from (10).[11] The tariff will be jumped and the DFI equilibrium will result. Does the DFI equilibrium leave the host country better off than the free trade equilibrium? Figure 3.3 illustrates the effects on consumer surplus and profits.

If the imposition of a tariff induces DFI, marginal production costs of firm M rise from c_E^* to c_F^*. Compared with the free trade equilibrium, production and profits of firm M decrease, while output of firm D increases from q to q'. Total output in the industry decreases to Q' while price increases to P'.

Domestic welfare under free trade is equal to consumer surplus (the areas A, B, C, and D) and profits of firm D (the area E). Under DFI consumer surplus shrinks to A, while profits of firm D increase with areas F

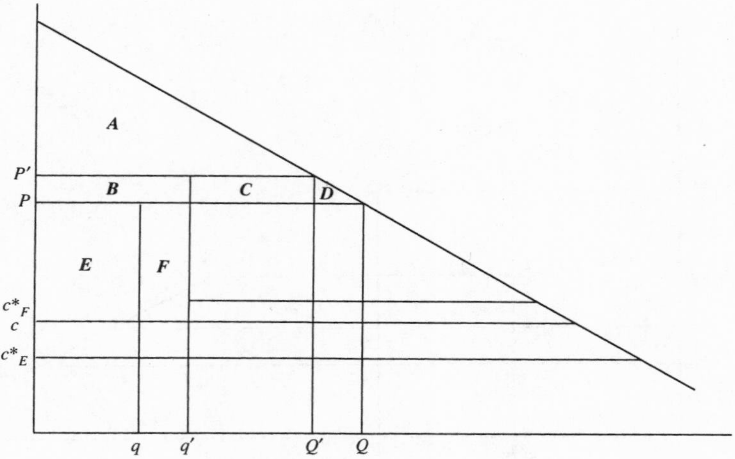

Figure 3.3 Welfare effects of tariff jumping DFI

and *B*. The net welfare effect of DFI is positive if the area *F* is greater than areas *C* and *D*. Area *F* represents the net shift in profits from firm M to firm D, area *C* is the gain in profits for firm M resulting from the price increase, and area *D* is the deadweight loss to consumers resulting from the rise in price. The condition for welfare to increase, $F > C + D$, translates to:

$$(13)\quad (q'-q)(P-c) > q^{*\prime}(P'-P) + (Q-Q')(P'-P)/2$$

Substitution and rearranging gives:

$$(14)\quad (c_F^* - c_E^*)\left[(c_E^* + c_F^*)/2 - c\right]/3b > 0$$

Since the first part on the left hand side of the equation is positive, domestic welfare increases if marginal costs of firm D are lower than the average marginal costs of firm M under exporting and DFI. Domestic welfare will increase as long as firm D has a cost advantage *vis-à-vis* firm M. Where firm M has a cost advantage over firm D in case of export, tariff jumping DFI can be welfare improving only if this advantage is turned into a *disadvantage* when firm M manufactures in the host country (this situation is illustrated in Figure 3.3). If firm M has a clear cost advantage based on superior manufacturing techniques and this cost advantage is maintained when manufacturing abroad, then tariff jumping DFI reduces the host country's welfare.

The relative marginal costs in (14) determine the market shares of firms M and D in case of free trade and tariff jumping DFI. Condition (14) can also be rephrased: domestic welfare increases if the average market share of firm D before and after tariff jumping DFI is greater than the average market share of firm M. This condition does not rest on the duopoly assumption but can be generalised to 'raising rivals' cost' policies in Cournot oligopoly, as is shown in the appendix to this chapter. Generally, raising foreign firms' costs increases domestic welfare unambiguously if the domestic industry is market leader. If the foreign industry has the larger market share, raising rivals' costs increases domestic welfare only if it results in a reduction of the foreign industry's share below that of the domestic industry. If foreign firms are market leaders, only policies that increase foreign firms' costs by a large margin can increase welfare while less stringent policies have negative results.

If the DFI inducing tariff is welfare increasing, is it the optimal policy for the host government? It is easy to show that it is not. The optimal policy would be to set the welfare maximising tariff as in (12) and to block DFI. Assuming that this is not a feasible policy option, it can be shown that a second best policy is to set the tariff just under the tariff jumping level. For explanatory convenience, assume that F is equal to zero. The DFI inducing tariff then follows from (8). If the tariff is equal to $c_F^* - c_E^*$, firm M will be indifferent between DFI and exporting. However, the host country is not. If DFI is chosen, marginal costs, output levels, consumer surplus, and profits are the same as under export, but no tariff revenue will be gained. Hence, the host country's welfare is always greater under export. The introduction of a fixed cost F does not alter this result. It follows that, if there is a DFI inducing tariff lower than the welfare maximising tariff, a second best policy is to set the tariff marginally under the DFI inducing level.

The analysis so far has been limited to welfare effects in the host country. A last issue concerns the effect on world welfare. The analysis assumed that the host country can freely engage in 'beggar thy neighbour' policies, in this case tariff policy which raises the costs of foreign firms and lets domestic firms capture part of foreign firms' profits. In case firm M has a cost advantage, a tariff leads to a rise in price, a fall in total output, and a shift in market share from the more efficient producer M to firm D. While world welfare, measured by the sum of profits of firms M and D, consumer surplus, and tariff revenue, is likely to decrease, this is even more so when the tariff induces DFI. With tariff jumping DFI, the shift in market share from firm M to firm D is accomplished by forcing firm M to produce in the host country at higher marginal costs. Whereas the tariff redistributes welfare to the host country, DFI leads to a pure welfare loss in terms of a reduced efficiency of production. The efficiency loss is even larger if it is taken into account that firm M in addition has to incur the fixed cost F.

3.5 Concluding Remarks

This chapter examined the conditions under which tariff jumping DFI occurs in the context of a Cournot duopoly model. Effects on market prices, quantities, and welfare of conventional tariff policy were analysed and compared with the effects of tariff jumping DFI. The model was couched in terms of the experience of Japanese electronics firms' investments in the EC during the 1980s. A major feature incorporated in the model is that DFI is cost increasing for the investing firm.

Setting a tariff which induces cost increasing DFI can increase the host country's welfare provided that the domestic firm does not have a cost disadvantage *vis-à-vis* the foreign firm. Precisely, welfare increases if the average market share of the domestic firm under export and DFI is larger than the average market share of the foreign firm, a result that can be generalised to Cournot oligopoly settings. However, possible welfare gains are always smaller than the gains of a welfare maximising tariff in the absence of DFI. If the welfare maximising tariff exceeds the tariff level at which DFI occurs, setting the tariff marginally below the DFI inducing level will be preferable. World welfare is more negatively affected by tariff jumping DFI than by conventional tariff policy.

It follows from the analysis that, in the case where exporting foreign firms have a cost advantage over domestic firms, DFI inducing tariffs are welfare improving only if this cost advantage is turned into a disadvantage when producing in the host country. If it can be assumed that it was Japanese electronics firms' export cost advantage which resulted in their often dominant market positions in the EC, then it would appear that DFI inducing antidumping duties resulted in welfare losses. Although the transfer of assembly operations to the EC is likely to have been cost increasing, there is no evidence that this has given EC firms a cost advantage. Japanese firms have by and large been able to maintain their EC market shares after antidumping actions, and they appear to have been successful in transferring management and engineering capabilities to EC plants.[12] The introduction of the 1987 'screwdriver plant' amendment to EC antidumping law, effectively administered as a local content requirement for Japanese plants in the EC, can be seen as a further cost raising measure to enhance the effectiveness of antidumping action in protecting EC firms. The welfare effects of such local content rules are considered in Chapter 4.

The analysis also suggests that a first best 'raising rivals' cost' policy is to set a welfare maximising tariff and to prohibit DFI. Local content rules or, more generally, anti-circumvention measures can to an extent be regarded as policy measures aimed at discouraging DFI in case of antidumping actions.[13] Yet it is also clear that 'raising rivals' cost' is not the only rationale for antidumping actions inducing DFI. Certainly, DFI has more positive welfare effects than those captured by the standard economic welfare criterion used in the analysis in this chapter. For instance, positive effects may arise from an increase in employment. Brander and Spencer (1987) have shown that, once the presence of structural unemployment is assumed, it is in the interest of a host country to commit to high tariffs and relatively low corporate taxes in order to *encourage* inward investment. As discussed in Section 1.5, positive effects of Japanese DFI may also stem from diffusion of technology and management practices. If these effects can be taken into account, Japanese DFI, even if cost increasing, may be found to have positive effects on the EC economy.

APPENDIX 3.1

Welfare Effects of Raising Rivals' Costs under Cournot Oligopoly

The welfare effects of policies that raise the costs of foreign firms selling on a host country market are described by equation (13) in the main text. Consider a host country market which is supplied by N domestic firms with marginal costs c and N^* foreign firms with marginal costs $c^{*\prime}$. The host government's policy increases foreign firms' marginal costs to c^*. If equilibrium in the industry is of the Nash–Cournot form, output of an individual domestic firm i is:

$$(1)\quad q_i = \frac{a - c + N^*\left(c^* - c\right)}{b\left(N + N^* + 1\right)}$$

Similarly, output of individual foreign firms is:

$$(2)\quad q_i^* = \frac{a - c^* + N\left(c - c^*\right)}{b\left(N + N^* + 1\right)}$$

Output after the cost raising measure follows (1) and (2) with $c^{*\prime}$ substituted. Applying the above expressions to (13) after multiplying individual firms' output by the number of firms leads to the condition:

$$(3)\quad \frac{N^*\left(c^{*\prime} - c^*\right)}{b\left(N^* + N + 1\right)^2}\left[\left(N - N^*\right)a - Nc\left(1 + 2N^*\right) + N^*\bar{c}^*\left(1 + 2N\right)\right] > 0$$

where $\bar{c}^* = (c^{*\prime} + c^*)/2$ are average marginal costs of foreign producers before and after the cost raising measure. Welfare is more likely to increase the more numerous are the domestic producers in comparison with foreign firms and the lower the marginal costs of domestic firms compared with the average marginal costs of foreign firms. This generalises the duopoly case: substituting $N = N^* = 1$ gives equation (14) in the main text. It can be seen that condition (3) is equal to the condition that the average market share of domestic firms before and after the cost raising measure is greater than the average market share of foreign firms. This condition can be written as:

$$(4)\quad N\left(q_i' + q_i\right)/2 - N^*\left(q_i^{*\prime} + q_i^*\right)/2 > 0$$

where a prime indicates output after the cost raising measure. Substituting (1) and (2) and the relevant marginal costs gives:

(5) $$\frac{1}{b\left(N^*+N+1\right)}\left[\left(N-N^*\right)a-Nc\left(1+2N^*\right)+N^*\bar{c}^*\left(1+2N\right)\right]>0$$

Given the positive nominator in (3), (5) implies exactly the same condition as (3).

NOTES

1. This argument goes back to Hirsch (1976).
2. In the US, Japanese DFI in the electronics industry occurred following antidumping actions in pagers, cellular mobile telephones, and private branch exchanges (PBXs), among others. See Chapter 6 and Dalton and Genther (1991).
3. Chapter 6 provides evidence. Japanese DFI is also found to be related to comparatively high EC import tariffs for (consumer) electronics products.
4. In addition, the fixed cost of setting up an electronics assembly plant is generally small compared with, for instance, automobile assembly. This weakens the value of DFI as a 'commitment' and therewith the strategic character of DFI.
5. In this, the analysis follows Levinsohn (1989). The latter study focuses on the equivalence of tariff and quota policy if foreign firms are able to respond by investing in the host country.
6. Alternatively, it can be assumed that firm M treats the host and home country's markets as 'segmented': production and marketing decisions for the home and host market are taken separately. See also Brander and Krugman (1983).
7. If individual inverse demand q_i can be represented by $P = a - \beta q_j$ and if $\Sigma_{j=1}^{N} q_j = Q$ with N the number of consumers, then the parameter b equals β/N, and is inversely related to the number of consumers. See Davies and Lyons (1988).
8. Implicitly it is assumed that firms M and D have both incurred a firm specific outlay necessary to acquire the technology to produce. This technology can be considered a firm-specific asset which can be transferred abroad at near zero marginal costs to facilitate DFI. See Horstman and Markusen (1989).
9. A standard result of the Cournot model with linear demand is: $\Pi = (q)^2 b$: an individual firm's profits are equal to squared output times the slope of the demand function.
10. In Section 6.3 the conditions for tariff jumping DFI are generalised to the oligopoly case.
11. If the fixed cost F is assumed negligible, from (8) it is derived that the welfare maximising tariff will be jumped if $a + 2c_E^* - 3c_F^* > 0$. With the intercept greater than marginal costs, this implies that the tariff will not be jumped only if production costs in the host country are considerably higher than production costs in the home country. Tariff jumping DFI in response to the tariff is of course less likely if the fixed cost is important.
12. See the data in Appendix 1.3 and the discussion of antidumping cases in Sections 1.3.3. and 1.3.4.

13. Thomsen and Nicolaides (1991), for instance, stress that local content requirements are likely to discourage DFI, but there is no evidence that this has actually occurred in the context of EC measures against Japanese firms. See also Chapter 8.

4

Local Content Requirements and Successive Market Power

4.1 Introduction

The growing use of local content requirements (LCRs) by developing as well as industrialised countries has led to a substantial body of literature analysing their effects. A LCR stipulates that firms producing a good in a country are to procure a certain proportion of intermediate inputs domestically. Traditionally, LCRs have been imposed on subsidiaries of foreign multinationals in less developed countries, with the purpose of developing the domestic intermediate goods industry. LCRs have been increasingly popular in industrialised countries as well, but appear different in application and objectives from LCRs in developing countries. In industrialised countries. LCRs are often imposed on foreign-owned firms' manufacturing operations with the purpose of creating a 'level playing field' for domestic final goods producers by forcing similar procurement conditions on to foreign firms. LCRs in these cases typically follow up on import restrictions which induced the foreign firms to set up manufacturing activities in the host country.

One example of a LCR in such a setting is the rule of origin for automobiles contained in the North American Free Trade Agreement (NAFTA). Automobiles can be traded duty-free between NAFTA countries only if a minimum of 62.5 per cent of value added is generated in the region. The rule of origin *de facto* affected the North American assembly activities of Japanese firms which relied on imports from Japan for key components (Lopes-de-Silanes, Markusen, and Rutherford 1993). A voluntary export restraint (VER) on Japanese automobile exports had been instrumental in attracting the Japanese car manufacturing investments.

Another example of the increasing popularity of LCRs is provided by recent experience in the European Community. Although there are no formal LCRs in effect in the EC and the Commission of the European Communities denies that LCRs exist, in practice LCRs have appeared in several guises.[1] A characteristic of LCRs in the EC is that most of them target the manufacturing activities of a specific group of firms: Japanese automobile and electronics manufacturers. LCRs typically follow trade policy measures restricting Japanese firms' exports (voluntary export restraints for cars and VCRs, and antidumping measures for a broad range of electronics goods), which induced the establishment of Japanese plants in the EC. Japanese firms' preference for the use of components manufactured in their own factories or by long-standing suppliers in Japan made them a target of a variety of LCRs (see Section 1.3.3 for details). For instance, a LCR for VCRs was negotiated in the context of a VER in 1983. A new anti-circumvention clause in antidumping law in 1987 was essentially administered as a LCR for Japanese plants assembling seven different (mostly electronics) products. A new rule of origin for semiconductors in 1989 *de facto* forced further integration of Japanese DRAM manufacturing activities in the EC. LCRs are in some cases negotiated in the context of incentive packages for inward investment. For instance, Nissan promised authorities in the United Kingdom that its Sunderland automobile plant would eventually reach 80 per cent local content as part of a broader agreement involving substantial subsidies.

Most existing theoretical studies of LCRs are not well equipped to analyse the effects of LCRs under the circumstances described above. A number of studies focus on the effects of LCRs on output and value added in the intermediate goods market, while assuming that the final goods market is import competing and perfectly competitive (Grossman 1981, Vousden 1987, Krishna and Itoh 1988). This ignores repercussions on the final goods market, which can be considerable if this market is imperfectly competitive and protected from import competition. Both are characteristics of rivalry between EC and Japanese electronics firms on the EC market. *De facto* discriminatory LCRs will raise the procurement cost of foreign producers and can be used as an instrument to shift rents to domestic firms. Thus, LCRs can be used as a tool of strategic trade policy, 'raising rival's costs' in imperfectly competitive markets in the spirit of Salop and Scheffman (1983) and Brander and Spencer (1984).

In a number of other studies LCRs are analysed in the context of imperfect competition on the final goods market. Hollander (1987) studies the effects of LCRs on a vertically integrated multinational which can shift production stages to the country imposing the LCR, but abstracts from rival firms on the final goods market. Richardson (1991) analyses the effects of a LCR in the context of duopolistic rivalry between a foreign and domestic final goods producer, but treats the duopolists as price takers on the final goods market, while endowing them with market power on a perfectly competitive intermediate goods market. The issue of 'raising rivals' costs' is specifically addressed in Davidson, Matusz, and Kreinin (1987) and Lopes-de-Silanes, Markusen, and Rutherford (1993). The former study does not model the effects of LCRs on the intermediate goods industry and treats the LCR as a simple cost parameter for foreign firms. The latter study examines the effects of a LCR if imposed in conjunction with a VER restricting imports in a general equilibrium framework, while treating the components industry as a price taker.

What the literature on rent shifting LCRs has ignored is the possibility of imperfect competition on the components market. The analysis in this chapter contributes by considering the effects of LCRs under successive market power on the components and final goods markets. A model of final goods duopoly with a domestic and foreign-owned firm is developed. The final goods industry is protected from import competition and the domestic components industry is imperfectly competitive. The setup is chosen with the circumstances under which LCRs were imposed on Japanese firms in the EC in mind. Where only a small number of firms exist in the components industry, a LCR increases market power of components producers and also shift rents from downstream to upstream firms (see also Grossman 1981: 598). The welfare effects of LCRs are found to be crucially dependent on competition in the components industry.

The remainder of this chapter is organised as follows. In Section 4.2 the model of successive market power is described and the effects of LCRs on quantities, prices, and profits are derived. Section 4.3 examines the welfare effects of LCRs. A number of extensions and consequences of LCRs under alternative industry conditions, including free entry in the domestic components industry, are considered in Section 4.4. Section 5.5 concludes.

4.2 LCRs under Successive Market Power

Consider two firms, a domestic firm D and a foreign multinational M, supplying final goods to a domestic market which is protected from import competition.[2] Nash–Cournot equilibrium prevails on the final goods market and demand is described by the linear inverse demand function $P^F = a - bQ^F$, with $Q^F = q_D + q_M$ and the inverse of b a measure of market size. The firms produce the final good with the same technology from two complementary inputs, the intermediate good and labour, at constant returns to scale. Production of one unit of the final goods requires exactly one unit of the intermediate good and one unit of labour.

Marginal costs of firm D are equal to the unit wage, w, and the price, P^Z of the intermediate good z on the domestic components market. The domestic components industry is imperfectly competitive: it consists of N symmetric firms, and Nash–Cournot equilibrium is assumed to prevail. The domestic components producers are assumed to be endowed with market power on the components market, while the final goods producers take the price of the component as given.[3] The market price for components is a markup μ higher than constant marginal production costs of the intermediate good: $P^Z = c + \mu$. Firm M imports all components from its captive plants abroad. In order to simplify the analysis, transport costs and tariffs on imported components are abstracted from, and it is assumed that marginal costs of components production are equal domestically and abroad. Firm M thus derives an advantage from its vertical integration, which allows it to import components at marginal costs c.[4]

The host country imposes a LCR in volume terms: a fraction ε_D ($0 \leqslant \varepsilon_D \leqslant 1$) of total components input has to be procured domestically. Since firm D buys all its components domestically, the LCR is binding only for firm M.[5] Foreign and domestically produced components are assumed to be perfect substitutes.

With the LCR imposed, profits of firms M and D are given by (1) and (2), respectively:

$$(1) \quad \Pi_M = q_M\left[a - b(q_M + q_D) - w - \varepsilon_M c - \varepsilon_D P^Z\right]$$

$$(2) \quad \Pi_D = q_D\left[a - b(q_M + q_D) - w - P^Z\right]$$

where $\varepsilon_M = 1 - \varepsilon_D$ is the share of imported components used by firm M. Solving for the first order conditions and substituting $P^z = c + \mu$ leads to the following duopoly quantities:

$$(3) \quad q_M = \left[a - w - c + \mu(1 - 2\varepsilon_D)\right]/3b$$

$$(4) \quad q_D = \left[a - w - c - \mu(2 - \varepsilon_D)\right]/3b$$

Production for both firms is higher the larger the final goods market (the smaller b) and the greater the 'intensity of demand' (the greater the difference $a - w - c$). As long as the markup on marginal costs of the components μ is positive and the LCR is less than unity, firm M has a cost advantage which results in a higher production volume. Although it may appear that production of firm D increases in the LCR, the crucial repercussions on the components market have yet to be taken into account: the LCR affects demand for components and therewith the markup.

Components producers maximise profits given demand for components, with the latter dependent on the LCR and rivalry between the duopolists. Domestic components producers derive demand for components as $q_D + \varepsilon_D q_M$, which gives the following inverse demand function:

$$(5) \quad P^Z = c + \frac{1 + \varepsilon_D}{1 - \varepsilon_D \varepsilon_M}\frac{a - w - c}{2} - \frac{1}{1 - \varepsilon_D \varepsilon_M}\frac{3}{2}bQ^Z$$

The intercept of the inverse demand function is separated into two terms: marginal costs and a term dependent on the LCR. A small LCR shifts the demand curve out, but the reverse occurs if the LCR nears unity. The slope coefficient is also dependent on the LCR in a non-linear way. Non-linearity occurs because two opposing effects are at work. On the one hand, the LCR has a positive effect on demand by forcing firm M to shift procurements to the domestic components industry. On the other hand, this shift increases marginal costs of firm M and thereby average marginal costs in the industry, which results in a reduction in final goods output, depressing demand for components.

Given the derived demand curve, the domestic components producers maximise profits:

$$(6)\quad \Pi_i^Z = q_i^Z\left[P^Z\left(Q^Z\right) - c\right]$$

where $Q^Z = Nq_i^Z$ since the firms are symmetric. Nash–Cournot equilibrium output for each firms becomes:

$$(7)\quad q_i^Z = \frac{1+\varepsilon_D}{N+1}\,\frac{a-w-c}{3b}$$

Profit maximising output is a linear, increasing function of the LCR. If the LCR is raised from zero to unity, output volume doubles. Given the demand contracting effects of a high LCR in (5), it follows that the market price of components has to fall over some range of the LCR. The equilibrium markup on the components market can be calculated as:

$$(8)\quad \mu = \frac{1+\varepsilon_D}{1-\varepsilon_D\varepsilon_M}\,\frac{1}{2(N+1)}(a-w-c)$$

A LCR leads to a higher equilibrium markup but only up to a point,[6] at which the markup starts to decline if the LCR is raised further. Given the market power the components producers are endowed with, the markup is adjusted to reflect changes in demand conditions resulting from the LCR reflected in (5). The markup is higher the greater the intensity of demand $(a - w - c)$ and the more concentrated the components industry (the smaller N).

Profits of components producers are production volume times the markup, which gives:

$$(9)\quad \Pi_i^Z = \frac{(1+\varepsilon_D)^2}{1-\varepsilon_D\varepsilon_M}\,\frac{1}{(N+1)^2}\,\frac{(a-w-c)^2}{6b}$$

Profits are an increasing function of the LCR: they quadruple if the LCR is raised from zero to unity.

The markup for the components crucially affects rivalry between firm M and firm D on the final goods market. Substituting (8) in (3) and (4) gives equilibrium output of the firms:

$$(10)\quad q_M = \left[1 - \left(2 - \frac{3\varepsilon_M}{1-\varepsilon_D\varepsilon_M}\right)\frac{1}{2(N+1)}\right]\frac{a-w-c}{3b}$$

$$(11)\quad q_D = \left[1 + \left(1 - \frac{3}{1 - \varepsilon_D \varepsilon_M}\right)\frac{1}{2(N+1)}\right]\frac{a - w - c}{3b}$$

Output of firm M is decreasing in the LCR. Output by firm D declines as well if the LCR is raised from zero to 0.5. For higher LCRs, output starts to increase, and in the extreme case of a LCR equal to unity it reaches exactly the level without a LCR. The intuition behind these effects is that an increase in the markup on the components market, induced by greater demand for components from firm M if a LCR is imposed, initially hurts firm D harder than firm M. This is because firm D has to pay the increase in the markup over all its inputs, while firm M procures only as much as the LCR, ε_D, on the domestic components market. Of course, the increase in marginal costs for the extra input that has to be procured domestically by firm M, μ, is greater than the increase in μ brought about by the extra demand, but firm D has to pay the latter increase over all its inputs. It is easy to show that up to a LCR of 0.5, not only does firm D's output decline, but this decline is stronger than the decline in output of firm M. Thus, small LCRs result in a loss of market *share* for firm D. All these effects are reversed for LCRs higher than 0.5, when firm M is more dependent on the domestic components market. High LCRs eventually increase procurement costs of firm M more than those of firm D, thus 'raising rivals' costs' and market share of firm D. In the extreme case of a LCR equal to unity, cost conditions for firms D and M are equalised and both firms supply half of the final goods market. All these effects are mitigated, but not altered qualitatively, if the components industry is more competitive (N large).

It is easily seen that total output is a declining function of the LCR. Profits of firms M and D, given Cournot conjectures and linear demand, are equal to squared production volume times the market size parameter b: they follow the same pattern as production volume. Total profits of domestic firms (profits of firms D plus profits of components producers) are increasing in the LCR. While the LCR does 'raise rivals' costs' and shifts rents from firm M to domestically owned firms, market power in the components industry allows components firms to appropriate such rents, and the domestic final goods producer D sees its profits decline. By increasing market power of the imperfectly competitive components industry, the LCR magnifies the inefficiency in the industry, and rent shifting comes at great cost in terms of output reduction.[7]

It is useful to compare the results with those found in Richardson (1991) and Lopes-de-Silanes, Markusen, and Rutherford (1993). Richardson analyses LCRs in the case where the two final goods producers are duopsonists on the components market and the components industry is perfectly competitive but characterised by increasing marginal costs. In

Richardson's analysis, it is the latter condition which establishes that a LCR, by increasing output of components, pushes up the price on the market and leads to a decline in profits of the domestic firm. This result is similar to the findings in the present analysis, except that in Richardson's model the increase in price results from a cost increase, while here it stems from increased market power of components producers. Richardson (1991) also finds that, for a small LCR, output and profits of the foreign firm may increase. This is because the LCR serves to firm M as a credible commitment to purchase a certain amount of components on the domestic market (it does not have to take into account the effect of this purchase on the price of the components), pushing back the output of the domestic firm.

In the general equilibrium model of Lopes-de-Silanes, Markusen, and Rutherford (1993), a LCR with simultaneous introduction of a VER has only a small positive effect on domestic final goods producers' profits and output.[8] Here domestic firms are hurt by an increase in prices of production factors and intermediate goods brought about by the extra demand for components by foreign firms. The results of the present analysis suggest that, apart from factor market repercussions, price increases for intermediate goods and harmful effects for domestic downstream producers are likely if the intermediate goods industry has market power.

4.3 Welfare Effects

In the context of strategic rent shifting, the common way to judge the effectiveness of policy measures is by their effects on domestic welfare.[9] Assuming that profits of firm M are repatriated, domestic welfare is the sum of components firms' profits, profits of firm D, and consumer surplus. Profits of the components industry are N times individual firms' profits as given in (9). Profits of firm D are equal to $b(q_D)^2$ with q_D given in (11). Consumer surplus is $b(Q^F)^2/2$, which leads to:

$$\text{(12)} \quad \left[2-\left(1+\frac{3\varepsilon_D}{1-\varepsilon_D\varepsilon_M}\right)\frac{1}{2(N+1)}\right]^2 \frac{(a-w-c)^2}{18b}$$

Consumer surplus is a declining function of the LCR.

The net effect of the LCR depends on the relative magnitude of the decline in consumer surplus, the increase in profits of domestic components producers, and the decline in profits of firm D. It can easily be seen that demand and cost characteristics do not affect this trade-off, while competition on the components market (the number of producers, N) does. Figure 4.1 shows the effect of a LCR on domestic welfare, under various assumptions concerning the number of components producers.[10]

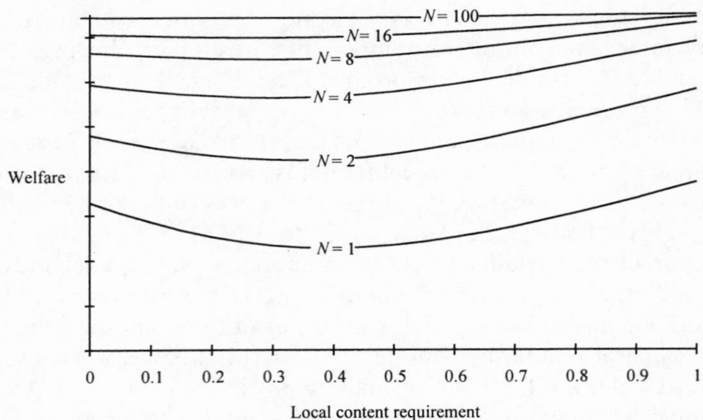

Figure 4.1 Welfare effects of a local content requirement

In both concentrated and relatively competitive domestic components industries, a LCR up to a point above 0.5 reduces welfare compared with a situation of free trade. Only if the LCR is raised further will welfare increase to reach levels higher than in the free trade case. The initial decline in welfare is greater, and the level at which welfare may eventually increase higher, the more concentrated the components industry.

The result that small LCRs reduce welfare contrasts with the findings in Richardson (1991) and Davidson, Matusz, and Kreinin (1987) where positive welfare effects are possible for small LCRs. The latter analysis does not take the repercussions of a LCR on the price of components into account and therefore only measures the effects of (in this case effective) 'raising rivals' costs'. Richardson (1991), on the other hand, assumes that the final good is an importable with its price fixed in the world market and so does not consider declines in consumer surplus arising from cost increases in the domestic final goods industry.

4.4 Extensions

The predominantly negative effects of LCRs depend crucially on the assumption of successive market power. In this section the likely consequences of LCRs under alternative vertical market structures are discussed: final goods oligopoly, free entry in the components industry, co-operative vertical bargaining and vertical integration, and direct foreign investment (DFI) in components manufacturing.

4.4.1 *Final Goods Oligopoly*

Belderbos and Sleuwaegen (1995) extend the model to successive oligopoly and find that the qualitative results of the duopoly model generally hold in this setting: domestic final goods producers are not able to increase profits while welfare declines for small LCRs. The welfare effects of LCRs are particularly negative if the final goods industry is relatively competitive, because rent shifting to the components industry in this case comes at greater cost in terms of reductions in output and consumer surplus.

4.4.2 *Free Entry on the Components Market*

The effects of LCRs alter significantly if the assumption of imperfect competition on the components market is relaxed. In order to highlight the importance of competition in the components industry, the model is adapted to allow any increase in profits brought about by the LCR to attract entry by new firms. By increasing competition, entry brings down components prices and is likely to lead to more beneficial effects of the LCR.[11]

Entry in the components market requires that a firm incurs a fixed cost, F, of setting up a manufacturing plant. In long term equilibrium, firms enter and bid down profits in the industry until variable profits are equal to the fixed cost F and entry becomes unprofitable. The markup on marginal production costs is still positive, but a demand shock such as the imposition of a LCR, which increases the markup and profits, will attract entry. This puts a check on the increase in the components price.

The model is adapted to allow for N, the number of firms in the components industry, to be endogenous and by adding the zero profit condition: $\Pi_i^Z - F = 0$. Using the profit equation in (9) gives the equilibrium number of firms:

$$(13) \quad N = \frac{1+\varepsilon_D}{\sqrt{1-\varepsilon_D\varepsilon_M}} \frac{1}{\sqrt{6bF}}(a-w-c)-1$$

The equilibrium number of firms is an increasing function of the LCR. In addition, the number of firms is higher the smaller the fixed setup cost (F), the larger the market (the smaller b), and the greater $(a - w - c)$. The long term equilibrium markup of components can be derived by substituting (13) in (8):

$$(14) \quad \mu = \sqrt{\frac{3bF}{2(1-\varepsilon_D\varepsilon_M)}}$$

The markup rises but only modestly (15 per cent at most) if the LCR is raised from zero to 0.5, only to fall if the LCR is raised further to unity. The increase in the price of components resulting from the LCR is less strong than in the no-entry case. Output and profits of firm D must then be more favourably affected:

$$(15)\quad q_D = \frac{a-w-c}{3b} - \frac{2-\varepsilon_D}{\sqrt{1-\varepsilon_D \varepsilon_M}}\sqrt{9F/6b}$$

Output by firm D and profits are now an increasing function of the LCR. Since the increase in the markup is checked by entry of components producers, the adverse effect on profits and output of firm D is mitigated. At the same time, the LCR still leads to a considerable increase in procurement costs of firm M, since each unit procured at the domestic components market implies an extra cost μ. This 'raising rivals' costs' effect is now dominating rent shifting in the final goods industry.

Other effects of the LCR in the model with entry are a decline in total final goods production and a decline in consumer surplus (since average marginal costs in the industry still increase). It can also be shown that a small LCR increases domestic welfare. If the LCR is increased further, welfare can increase or decrease depending on market size (positive) and the fixed setup cost (negative).[12]

4.4.3 Co-operative Bargaining and Vertical Integration

In the case of successive market power, final goods and components producers will generally be able to improve industry profits by cooperation. The outcome of cooperation would be to set monopoly output and maximise joint profits. If firms could agree on a profit sharing rule, each firm would be able to increase profits. The effects of LCRs in such a co-operative bargaining framework are analysed in Beghin and Sumner (1992) in the case of a bilateral monopoly of domestic firms. The authors conclude that LCRs in this setting, while they may increase the use of domestic components, do not alter output and price, which remain at the profit maximising monopoly level. LCRs do increase the share of industry profits allocated to the components producer.[13] Hence, LCRs allow rent shifting to the components industry without generating price and output distortions.

Co-operative bargaining in the context of rivalry between domestic and foreign firms on the final goods market conceivably takes the form of bargaining between domestic final goods and components producers (Belderbos and Sleuwaegen 1995). Consider the case of a components monopoly and final goods duopoly. Efficient bargaining between firm D and the components producer implies that both firms jointly will behave as a vertically integrated firm: the industry resembles a vertically integrated duopoly. If a LCR is introduced, firm M is forced to procure components from the domestic producer. The optimal response of the domestic components producer is to utilise this market power and set the components price for firm M high enough to make sales unprofitable, in order to reap monopoly profits jointly with firm D. However, firm M is already committed to the market through its local assembly plant, which makes exit costly. Confronted with the threat of vertical foreclosure, firm M will have strong incentives to establish its own components manufacturing plant, which would leave the LCR ineffective in shifting rents to domestic firms. The optimal response by the components producer will then be to set the price of components procured by firm M just below the investment-inducing level.[14]

Generally, in the case of bargaining between domestic final goods and components producers, LCRs are more effective in shifting rents from foreign firms to the domestically owned industry as a whole. Co-operation or vertical integration implies that the markup set by components producers does not affect the competitive position of firm D, and the firms avoid the inefficiency associated with the exercise of successive market power in the uncooperative context.

4.4.4 Direct Foreign Investment in Components Manufacturing

Effects of LCRs are also likely to alter substantially where the possibility of direct foreign investment in components manufacturing is taken into account. In general, if the domestic components industry has market power, the possibility of DFI by foreign final goods producers faced with a LCR will change optimal pricing policy of the components producer and put a check on the components price increase (Jie a Joen, Sleuwaegen, and Belderbos 1995). Negative effects on domestic final goods producers and industry output will be mitigated. Profit increases in the domestic components industry resulting from LCRs may also attract DFI by independent firms. Such investment will again reduce the power of domestic components producers to increase price in response to LCRs, which mitigates the negative effects of LCRs. On the other hand, foreign investors will also be able to reap a share of increased rents in the industry.

There are two examples of analysis of LCRs in the presence of DFI; both study rather special cases and find that LCRs can have positive welfare effects. Hollander (1987) considers welfare effects of a vertically integrated foreign multinational responding to a LCR by shifting more production stages to the host country, and finds that small LCRs can increase welfare. Richardson (1993) extends the analysis of LCRs to include international capital flows in the intermediate goods sector. In a general equilibrium framework, and assuming perfect competition and constant returns to scale, the extreme result is obtained that LCRs have no effect at all on domestic prices of intermediate goods.

4.5 Conclusions

This chapter has analysed the effects of local content requirements (LCRs) when the final goods industry is a duopoly of a foreign firm (called M) and a domestic firm (called D) supplying a protected domestic market, and the domestic components industry is imperfectly competitive. The structure of the model was chosen to resemble some of the circumstances under which LCRs were imposed on Japanese electronics producers in the EC. Firm D procures components from the domestic industry, while firm M procures components from related overseas producers. Although in this setting a LCR *de facto* affects only firm M directly and thus 'raises rivals' costs', it also raises the market price of components, which increases procurement costs of firm D. Horizontal rent shifting from firm M to firm D is dominated by rent shifting from the final goods to the components industry, and the LCR causes a drop in profits and market share of firm D. Industry output and consumer surplus decline and small LCRs cause a reduction in domestic welfare. The conclusion is that, as long as the components industry has market power, LCRs are likely to have adverse effects on the domestically owned final goods industry as well as on domestic welfare.

The results can be generalised to final goods oligopoly but alter substantially if the components industry is characterised by free entry. If profits attract entry in the industry, a LCR increases profits of firm D and a small LCR may increase domestic welfare. Likewise, the effects of LCRs change positively in the case where domestic final goods producers and components producers can engage in co-perative bargaining or can vertically integrate, and if LCRs induce a response in the form of direct foreign investment in components manufacturing by foreign firms.

In practice, LCRs in the EC have increased the use of a variety of EC-manufactured electronics components, each produced under particular industry conditions. Where the production of components is capital and scale intensive and industries are oligopolistic (e.g. capacitors, integrated circuits, and CRTs), the successive market power model may apply and LCRs are likely to have allowed components producers to increase prices. Other components tend to be produced by a large number of small firms lacking market power (e.g. plastic components and metal parts). In some cases (e.g. CRTs), vertically integrated EC final goods producers are important sellers on EC components markets and LCRs may have benefited them directly.[15] In other cases, Japanese firms are important EC components producers, and LCRs increasing demand for EC-produced components also benefited Japanese firms.[16] Furthermore, the empirical evidence presented in Chapter 1 suggests that Japanese firms reacted in much more diverse ways to the LCRs than by buying more components from local producers.[17] Firms set up their own integrated manufacturing plants or invited related subcontractors to set up plants, while a number of independent Japanese components manufacturers set up EC manufacturing activities to supply Japanese plants in the EC. While these dynamic responses to the imposition of LCRs do not benefit EC components producers, they are likely to have favourable effects by expanding the domestic components industry and avoiding component price increases. In order to gain a better understanding of the effects of LCRs, future theoretical work should focus on heterogeneous industry structures and the dynamic effects of LCRs, in particular the relationship with DFI.

APPENDIX 4.1

Domestic Welfare

Full expressions for domestic welfare in the case of components oligopoly, and free entry in the components industry, respectively, are given below.

A4.1.1 Domestic Welfare under Components Oligopoly

Total domestic welfare consists of consumer surplus, profits of domestic components producers, and profits of the domestic final goods producer:

$$(1)\quad \frac{(a-w-c)^2}{9b}\left\{\frac{1}{2}\left[2-\left(1+\frac{3\varepsilon_D}{1-\varepsilon_D\varepsilon_M}\right)\frac{1}{2(N+1)}\right]^2+\frac{3}{2}\left[\frac{(1+\varepsilon_D)^2}{1-\varepsilon_D\varepsilon_M}\frac{N}{(N+1)^2}\right]^2 +\left[1+\left(1-\frac{3}{1-\varepsilon_D\varepsilon_M}\right)\frac{1}{2(N+1)}\right]^2\right\}$$

It can be shown that, if the number of components producers N goes to infinity, welfare reaches a maximum of $(a - w - c)^2 / 3b$. See also Figure 4.1.

A4.1.2 Domestic Welfare under Free Entry in the Components Industry

Domestic welfare under free entry in the components industry consists of consumer surplus and profits of the domestic final goods producer, $b(Q^F)^2/2 + b(q_D)^2$, or:

$$(2)\quad \frac{1}{2}b\left[\frac{2(a-w-c)}{3b}-\sqrt{F/6b}\,\frac{\varepsilon_D+1}{\sqrt{1-\varepsilon_D\varepsilon_M}}\right]^2 +b\left[\frac{a-w-c}{3b}-\frac{2-\varepsilon_D}{\sqrt{1-\varepsilon_D\varepsilon_M}}\sqrt{F/6b}\right]^2$$

This can be rewritten as:

$$(3)\quad \frac{1}{3}\left[\frac{(a-w-c)^2}{b}+\frac{3}{4}F\left(1+\frac{2-\varepsilon_D}{1-\varepsilon_D\varepsilon_M}\right)-\frac{(a-w-c)\sqrt{6F/b}}{\sqrt{1-\varepsilon_D\varepsilon_M}}\right]$$

The LCR only weakly affects the third term in (3). Welfare may increase as long as the second term is increasing in the LCR. This term reaches a maximum in the LCR at $\varepsilon_D = 0.27$.

NOTES

1. See also *Far Eastern Economic Review*, 18 May 1989.
2. Hence (residual) demand is assumed not to be affected by imports. Although this is a restrictive assumption, import barriers for final goods, in particular antidumping measures, are an important feature of the industries affected by LCRs. In many cases (such as small copiers) Japanese firms are world market leaders and Japanese DFI has substantially reduced imports into the EC. In cases where imports from third countries (e.g. South Korea) are important, such imports have often subsequently been targeted by antidumping actions. See Section 1.3 for details.
3. Generally, leadership assumes pre-committed investments by the components producers in the technology and capacity to produce the component. Capital intensive production with high fixed costs is a feature of a number of electronic component industries such a as CRTs, capacitors, and integrated circuits. The assumption of price leadership by the components industry follows earlier work on successive oligopoly (e.g. Greenhut and Ohta 1976, Salinger 1988, Krishna and Itoh 1988).
4. This is assumed to explain the observed reluctance of Japanese firms to procure intermediate goods in the EC. If it is allowed that transport costs and co-ordination costs of vertical integration result in costs of intermediate goods imports that are strictly higher than c, firm M may procure part of its inputs on the domestic market without the LCR, as in Richardson (1991). This, however, would complicate the analysis, while it does not affect the qualitative results of the model.
5. It is assumed that the local content requirement is binding; that is, the punishment of non-compliance is severe enough to induce firm M to comply. Japanese firms have in almost all cases under the 'screwdriver plant' amendment chosen to comply with LCRs rather than pay antidumping duties on EC-assembled products (see Chapter 1).
6. This level can be calculated at $\sqrt{3} - 1 \approx 0.73$.
7. For instance, in the case of a components monopoly, it can be shown that even a small LCR reduces final goods output below the level that would have been set by a final goods monopolist (Belderbos and Sleuwaegen 1995).
8. Comparison with the results of Lopes de Silanes, Markusen, and Rutherford is not straightforward because they do not calculate effects of a LCR *given* the presence of a VER, but rather the effects of a VER-cum-LCR.
9. In contrast, in the traditional literature on LCRs the objective of the government is usually taken to be an increase in value added of domestic activities (see e.g. Grossman 1981).

10. See the appendix to this chapter for the full expression for domestic welfare.
11. Of course, once entry is free in the components industry, nothing stands in the way of firms D or F vertically integrating by setting up a components manufacturing subsidiary. To highlight the effects of competition on the components market, vertical integration and direct foreign investment in components manufacturing are ignored in this section but are discussed below.
12. See the appendix to this chapter for the derivation of domestic welfare as a function of the LCR.
13. Beghin and Knox Lovell (1993) find these results confirmed by an empirical analysis of the Australian tobacco leaf and tobacco markets, an example of government sanctioned co-operative bargaining between vertically related industries where LCRs have been in place.
14. Analogue results will be obtained if firm D is vertically integrated. See Jie a Joen, Sleuwaegen, and Belderbos (1995) for an analysis of LCRs with co-operative bargaining and direct foreign investment. A contrasting analysis of vertical foreclosure is provided in Spencer and Jones (1992). Here a foreign vertically integrated (Japanese electronics) firm exports both final goods to a host country market and intermediate goods to a host country rival firm. Vertical foreclosure by the foreign firm is checked by the possibility of host country investment in intermediate goods production.
15. Philips has been supplying the EC CTV plants of Matsushita, Sanyo, and Hitachi with CRTs since the plants were established. The fact that imports of CRTs from Japan have been restricted by an informal VER and were a less attractive option because of origin rules (see Chapter 1) must have played a role in Japanese firms' procurement decisions. Investment by Japanese firms in their own CRT plants was less likely to be profitable because of the high investment cost and the importance of scale economies in CRT production. Until Matsushita's 1995 acquisition of Nokia's German CRT plants, Japanese CRT manufacturing in the EC was limited to a UK plant operated by Sony.
16. For example, Murata and Kyocera are important producers of capacitors, Fujitsu, NEC, and Hitachi produce DRAMs, and Alps produces CTV tuners.
17. See Chapter 8 for evidence and further discussion of the effects of EC local content requirements.

PART III

The Internationalisation of Japanese Electronics Firms: *Empirical Essays*

5

The Decision to Invest Abroad: Business Groups and Regional Core Networks

5.1 Introduction

The sharp increase in Japanese direct foreign investment in North America and Europe over the last decade has provoked a substantial amount of research into the determinants of Japanese DFI. There is now an extensive body of literature suggesting that Japanese manufacturing investments in industrial countries are explained by similar factors (mainly firm-specific advantages) to those that explain foreign investments by US or European firms.[1] Across industries, Japanese DFI is positively related to industry traits such as R&D and advertising intensity (as proxies for firm-specific intangible assets owned by firms in the industry), while import barriers also have induced investments. Recent studies by Hennart and Park (1994) and Kogut and Chang (1996) found that previous experience in operating manufacturing plants abroad induces more subsequent investments, results that are again similar to those found for US firms (Yu 1990).

While the importance of firm-specific advantages in explaining Japanese DFI is thus well established, there are at least two issues that have been left basically untouched in the literature (see Caves 1993). First, there are indications that there is a role for inter-firm linkages within Japanese business groups, or *keiretsu*. For instance, Hoshi, Kashyap, and Sharfstein (1992) found that firms that are members of one of the six bank-centred (horizontal) *keiretsu* are significantly less liquidity constrained in their investment decisions than non-member firms. This could imply that membership of horizontal business groups also helps to facilitate the financing of risky foreign ventures. In another recent study, Head, Ries, and Swenson (1995) showed that the choice of the location of US manufacturing plants established by Japanese firms can be explained partly by the presence of plants of member firms of the same manufacturer-centred (vertical) *keiretsu* in the area. This raises the question whether the presence of group activities also gives a separate inducement to DFI by other group firms.[2]

A second shortcoming of the existing empirical literature is the almost complete limitation of analysis to DFI in the US. At the same time of the surge in Japanese DFI in Western industrialised countries, however, Japanese firms also established themselves as dominant investors in South-East Asia (Gold, Eonomou, and Tolentino 1991). The larger Japanese multinational enterprises (MNEs) are the main forces behind this trend, establishing 'regional core networks' of complementary manufacturing plants in different countries in South-East Asia, making use of comparative locational advantages in labour costs and skills (Nakakita and Urata 1991). However, a distinctive characteristic of Japanese DFI in this region is the equally important role of small and medium-sized Japanese companies, which in many cases are lacking strong firm-specific advantages (MITI 1990: 45).[3] Gold *et al.* argue that historical, political, and in particular cumulative economic ties between Sough-East Asian countries have now given rise to the formation of a trade and investment bloc, in which the economic distance between participating countries, and hence the barriers that firms face in establishing production subsidiaries abroad, are greatly reduced. This would imply that firm-specific advantages are much less important in explaining Japanese DFI in this region.

This chapter addresses the above two issues. Using micro-data on 204 Japanese firms in the broad electronics and precision machinery sector, it examines whether the determinants of Japanese DFI in Asia are different from the determinants of DFI in North America and Europe, and tests for the influence of inter-firm relationships in both bank-centred horizontal business groups and manufacturer-centred vertical business groups. while the majority of previous studies has substituted the industry for the firm as the level of analysis, the focus of the present study is on characteristics of the firm and the probability that firms choose to become an MNE.

The setup of the chapter is as follows. The next section develops the arguments concerning the determinants of Japanese DFI, based on mainstream internalisation theory and including the effects of inter-firm relationships within business groups. Section 5.3 describes the empirical model and the data used. Results are presented in Section 5.4, and Section 5.5 concludes.

5.2 Determinants of Japanese DFI

Hypotheses concerning the determinants of the decision to invest abroad in North America and Europe on the one hand, and in South-East Asia on the other, are to be developed in relation to mainstream internalisation theory, theories of corporate finance, and particular traits of inter-firm links within Japanese business groups.

5.2.1 Internalisation Theory

Mainstream theory of the MNE considers a firm's possession of intangible assets such as special technological, management, or marketing skills as the central determinant of DFI (e.g. Caves 1982, Dunning 1981).[4] Firms need to possess some kind of competitive advantage over foreign rivals to overcome the inherent disadvantages of operating abroad in an unfamiliar environment. Firms have a strong incentive to exploit intangible assets themselves, since these are by their nature hard to capitalise in arm's length markets. The decision to set up a foreign plant and not to export from the home country is explained by locational factors such as high transportation costs, relative production costs, and, increasingly important, various tariff and other barriers impeding exports to foreign markets.

Empirical studies have shown that Japanese DFI in the US follows this logic. In addition, it is conceivable that Japanese firms also possess a more specific type of intangible asset which is based on an efficient organisation of manufacturing processes. Efficient use of human resources, just-in-time delivery of components, and strict quality control are all elements of these organisational skills. Experience has shown that these skills can be transferred abroad to foreign manufacturing ventures (Caves 1993).

In contrast to Japanese DFI in Western industrialised countries, it can be argued that firm-specific advantages play a much lesser role in the decision to invest in South-East Asia. The argument that the geographical and cultural proximity of South-East Asian countries, and their historical, political, and economic ties with Japan, have greatly reduced economic distance in the region implies that Japanese firms face significantly smaller disadvantages when operating in this region compared with Western industrialised countries. Traditionally, active government support and the assistance of Japanese trading houses (*sougou sousha*) have reduced costs, risks, and informational requirements of investing in South-East Asia.[5] With the increasing economic integration between Japan and South-East Asia, in which the regional core networks of established MNEs play a major role, and with the active policy of South-East Asian countries to attract Japanese DFI, the barriers to foreign investment are further reduced. This, coupled with the relative absence of strong local competing firms in South-East Asian markets, suggests that Japanese firms may be stimulated to invest in this region even if they lack the firm-specific advantages accruing from substantial investments in R&D and marketing that are often necessary to compete in Western industrial markets.

5.2.2 Corporate Finance

In early theories of DFI based on capital market imperfections, the MNE is seen primarily as engaging in capital cost arbitrage in a world with imperfect capital markets (e.g. Aliber 1970). The hypothesis that firms invest abroad because they have capital cost advantages over foreign firms has appeal in explaining Japanese DFI, since Japanese firms are often seen as having access to low cost capital.[6] In the late 1980s, these capital cost advantages stemmed mainly from high levels of liquidity in Japanese firms.[7] Since, in a world of imperfect capital markets, internally generated funds are available at lower costs to the firm than external funds, liquidity is often found to influence investment decisions (Hoshi, Kashyap, and Scharfstein 1992; Belderbos 1992). This will apply in particular to decisions to invest abroad, about which the costs and benefits are more uncertain (Caves 1993). The hypothesis follows that firms which possess a large enough pool of internally generated funds have a capital cost advantage which can be transferred abroad.[8]

5.2.3 Horizontal Business Groups

Horizontal business groups are large bank-centred diversified groups of basically independent firms. The advantages of group relationships are seen as derived from stable supply and demand through long term business relationships, a relaxation of capital constraints for risky investments through the monitoring function of the main bank, and information exchange on new markets and technologies (Flath 1993, Odagiri 1992, Nakatani 1984, Goto 1982).

As argued by Hoshi, Kashyap, and Sharfstein (1992) and Flath (1993), the monitoring function of the main bank of a horizontal business group can solve part of the agency problems of debt, by allowing for a better assessment of investment projects than the market could have made. Member firms can rely on the main bank of the group to finance investment projects which would otherwise have been hard to finance through arm's length markets. It follows that members of horizontal groups are less likely to be hindered by a lack of funds to finance risky foreign ventures than non-member firms. The relationship between liquidity and DFI is expected to be weak or absent.

It is conceivable that members of a horizontal business group may also benefit from the experience of other member firms and the group trading firms in operating manufacturing plants and doing business abroad. Informational requirements (with respect to market trends, location, recruiting employees, etc.) and lack of experience are important barriers to foreign investment for small and medium sized firms, and they can be overcome by information sharing within a horizontal *keiretsu*. Moreover, firms might find it easy to sell their foreign produce to member firms in the region with which they have a long-term business relationship, or to let marketing be handled by one of the trading firms belonging to the group. There is some evidence pointing in this direction. A study by Yamamura and Wassman (1989) found that investment in the US by members of horizontal business groups tends to be clustered in specific areas, which suggests that networks are important at least in choosing the location of DFI. The present study will examine whether manufacturing activities of member firms have an impact on the decision to invest abroad.

5.2.4 Vertical Business Groups

Vertical business groups are groups of subcontractors, satellite firms, and trading firms around major large-scale assembly type manufacturers such as Toyota and Hitachi. Here the leading or 'core' firm usually exerts control over the management of the other firms in the group, enforced by shareholding, financial ties, and the dispatch of managers.

Aoki (1988) has argued that this mode of inter-firm relationships constitutes an advantage over foreign firms in particular in industries where a large number of production steps have to be co-ordinated. However, such advantages need to be transferred abroad, where it could be difficult to replicate inter-firm networks to include foreign firms.[9] Indeed, the difficulty that large Japanese automobile and electronics firms had in replicating subcontracting networks abroad by forging ties with local components suppliers may help to explain why these firms internationalised their production relatively late. In contrast, inter-firm linkages will be less difficult to repeat abroad if they involve ties between foreign subsidiaries of Japanese firms.

In the present study, the focus is on these inter-firm linkages between Japanese firms at home and abroad, and how these are expected to facilitate member firms to grow multinational. DFI by firms in vertical business groups is likely to be even more strongly affected by information exchange and supplier links than DFI by members of horizontal groups. In North America and Europe, formal and informal pressure on Japanese firms to increase the local purchases of components used in their manufacturing operations has given Japanese subcontractors an important incentive to establish production plants abroad as well, to supply their core firms with locally produced components. DFI is facilitated by the core company which provides assistance and an exclusive market for the subcontractors' components. These patterns of leading Japanese firms being followed by related components suppliers have been especially apparent in the car industry in the US but are also observed in the electronics industry in Europe (see

Chapter 1). In Asia the regional core networks of major automobile and electronics firms provide markets and facilitate investment for subcontractor firms. The hypothesis follows that the presence of overseas networks of a vertical business group exerts a positive influence on subcontractor firms' decision to invest abroad.

5.3 The Empirical Model

The hypothesis that the determinants of the decision taken to invest in South-East Asia differ from those taken to invest in Western industrial countries is tested at the firm level, against statistical data on Japanese firms listed at Japanese stock exchanges in 1989 and active in the broad electronics and precision machinery sector (which includes heavy electrical equipment, white goods, communications equipment, consumer electronics, office machines, cameras, and measuring equipment). In this sector, the number of firms is relatively large, DFI in both Western countries and South-East Asia is prominent, and there is a large variety in firm size.

In order to analyse the determinants of the decision to invest abroad in different regions, all foreign investments up to June 1989 are taken into account and firms are classified as belonging to one of three firm types:

1. domestic firms without any foreign production;
2. firms with at least one manufacturing subsidiary in South-East Asia but without manufacturing investments in North America or Europe (hereafter referred to as 'Asia-bound MNEs');
3. firms with at least one manufacturing subsidiary in Europe or North America (referred to as 'West-bound MNEs'); they may or may not operate manufacturing subsidiaries in South-East Asia as well.[10]

The sample includes 204 firms classified by firm type as shown in Table 5.1. The firms are more ore less evenly distributed over firm types. Most West-bound MNEs (66 firms) also operate manufacturing plants in South-East Asia, with a small number of West-bound MNEs operating plants in North America and Europe only (13 firms).

A multinominal logit model is used to relate the probabilities that a firm belongs to one of these three types (or states) to a set of features of the firm:

$$(1)\quad P_i^s = \frac{\exp\left[\alpha^s + \beta^s X_i + \gamma^s X_i^s\right]}{\sum_{q=1}^{3} \exp\left[\alpha^q + \beta^q X_i + \gamma^q X_i^q\right]}$$

where P_i^s is the probability that firm i belongs to state s, α^s are constants, X_i are firm-specific variables with coefficients β^s, and X_i^s are variables that are

Table 5.1 Classification of the 204 Japanese electronics firms

Manufacturing subsidiary in:	No. of firms	Label
Japan only	65	Domestic firm
Japan and South-East Asia	60	Asia-bound MNE
Japan, South-East Asia and North America/ Europe	66	West-bound MNE
Japan and North America/Europe	13	West-bound MNE
Total	204	

firm- and state-specific with coefficients γ^s. To identify the model, the coefficients α, β, and γ have to be normalised to zero for one state.

In line with the hypotheses put forward in Section 5.2.1, the explanatory factors include the following firm characteristics related to the possession of firm-specific intangible assets: R&D intensity (*RDINT*, measured as the ratio of R&D expenditures over value added), sales cost intensity (*MARKINT*, direct and indirect sales costs as a percentage of sales), and human resource intensity (*HUMRES*, the labour cost of white-collar employees over total labour cost).[11] The inclusion of sales force expenditures in addition to advertising outlays in *MARKINT* arguably makes the variable a better proxy for reputation and marketing expertise in the industrial electronics sector, where direct sales costs tend to be high. *HUMRES* is a proxy for the availability and quality of managerial and staff workers who could be expatriated to transfer organisational skills to foreign plants.

In addition, a high capital intensity of production indicated by a high capital to labour ratio (*CAPLAB*, the value of fixed, depreciable capital over total labour cost) may indicate possession of intangible assets. The rise of Japanese electronics firms as global competitors is often claimed to be related to the adoption of highly efficient, productivity raising mass production techniques (Franko 1983). Also, the most capital intensive firms are in a better position to benefit from comparative advantages of Western industrial countries where capital is a relatively abundant factor. *RDINT*, *MARKINT*, *HUMRES*, and *CAPLAB* are all expected to have a strong impact on the decision to become a West-bound MNE but a weaker impact on the decision to become an Asia-bound MNE.

In addition to the above mentioned structural characteristics of the firm, it is useful to control for firm size (*EMPL*, measured by the logarithm of employment[12]). The main effect this is expected to pick up is that a certain firm size is usually required for carrying the overhead cost associated with setting up a foreign organisation and international communication network.[13]

From the perspective of corporate finance, firms that possess capital cost advantages in the form of a large pool of internally generated funds are expected to show a higher probability to invest abroad. As best proxy for the availability of internally generated funds, *INTFUNDS*, pre-tax profits[14] divided by the capital outlays taken over the last three years was calculated.

In order to establish the effects of inter-firm links in horizontal business groups, the firms in the sample were classified as to whether they belonged to one of the six large horizontal *keiretsu*. There are several ways to classify firms as members of a horizontal business group or as independent firms. In the present study, the classification available from Dodwell Marketing Consultants' *Industrial Groupings in Japan* was used (Dodwell 1989). This source bases its classification on the shareholding structure of firms, adapted to take account of historical ties, bank loans, dispatch of managers, and ties to other groups. The Dodwell classification was preferred over other available sources because it applies the strictest standards to group ties and therefore provides the best test of whether systematic differences between members and non-members in foreign investment decisions exist.[15] Table 5.2 shows the results of this classification applied to the Japanese firms in the sample. Out of the 204 firms in the dataset, 72 are classified as members of horizontal business groups. The group that is most represented among the listed electronics firms is Dai-Ichi Kangyo, followed by Sumitomo and Fuyo, while the Mitsui and Sanwa groups are poorly represented.

Membership of a horizontal business group is expected to influence the decision to invest abroad in several ways. First of all, there are the possible general benefits of belonging to horizontal business groups through information exchange and risk reduction. A dummy variable, *HORGROUP*, is

Table 5.2 Membership of horizontal business groups and number of manufacturing subsidiaries of group firms in South-East Asia and Europe/North America

Horizontal business group	Number of member firms in the sample	Group manufacturing subsidiaries: South-East Asia	Group manufacturing subsidiaries: Europe/North America
Mitsui	4	14	11
Mitsubishi	11	17	15
Sumitomo	17	46	25
Fuyo	17	24	10
Dai-Ichi Kangyo	20	23	11
Sanwa	3	2	1
Total	72		

included which takes the value 1 if a firm is considered a member of one of the six large bank-centred *keiretsu*. *HORGROUP* is expected to have a positive effect on the propensity to invest abroad. In addition, since member firms may be less liquidity constrained in their foreign investment decisions, liquidity is expected to have a weaker effect on DFI decisions. To capture this effect, an interactive term combining *INTFUNDS* with *HORGROUP* is included in the model. The coefficient is expected to be negative.

Member firms of horizontal business groups may also find it more easy to invest abroad if other member firms have already established distribution and manufacturing networks there. To account for this factor, the number of manufacturing subsidiaries established by all other member firms of the group in the electronics industry in South-East Asia (*HORASIA*) and North America/Europe (*HORWEST*), respectively, are included as explanatory variables measuring experience effects.[16] Table 5.2 shows that the number of manufacturing subsidiaries of member firms varies from 2 to 46 in South-East Asia and from 1 to 25 in North America and Europe. *HORASIA* is expected to have a positive effect on the probability that a firm is an Asia-bound MNE, while *HORWEST* is expected to have a positive effect on DFI in Europe and North America. Since *HORASIA* and *HORWEST* are state-specific variables which are expected to influence only the decision to invest in, respectively, South-East Asia and Europe/North America, the coefficients of these variables for other states are restricted to zero in the estimating model.[17]

Firms are considered to be affiliated subcontractors (*SUBCON* dummy = 1) if they belong to a vertical business group; i.e. if they are partially or wholly controlled via equity ownership or dispatch of personnel by the core firm with which they have a subcontracting or original equipment manufacturing (OEM) relationship. Since subcontracting firms' manufacturing operations are integrated in the core firms' domestic network, and their dependence on the core firm may make them unable to define an overseas investment strategy independently, *SUBCON* is expected to have a negative sign. Out of the 204 firms in the analysis, 49 were classified as subcontractors in a vertical business group. Table 5.3 shows the number of subcontractors in the dataset by major core firm. Fujitsu appears as the largest vertical business group in terms of number of listed subcontractors, followed by Hitachi, NEC, and Matsushita.

Where the core firm has established a manufacturing network abroad, the same link with the core firm will lower barriers to foreign investment. To capture this effect, two variables are included, *VERASIA* and *VERWEST*, which count the number of manufacturing subsidiaries of the core firm in South-East Asia and North America/Europe, respectively. Table 5.3 illustrates the size of the manufacturing networks established in

Table 5.3 Subcontractors by major vertical business group and number of manufacturing subsidiaries of the core firm in South-East Asia and Europe/North America

Core firm	Number of subcontractors in the sample	Core firm's manufacturing subsidiaries: South-East Asia	Core firm's manufacturing subsidiaries: Europe/North America
Fujitsu	9	5	4
Hitachi	7	10	5
NEC	7	4	7
Matsushita	6	28	17
Toshiba	4	7	6
Other	16		
Total	49		

South-East Asia and North America/Europe by the major core firms. Matsushita has set up the largest network of manufacturing plants and operates 28 manufacturing subsidiaries in South-East Asia. Fujitsu, on the other hand, provides its subcontractors with a relatively small manufacturing network abroad.

Besides the firm-specific and group-specific variables mentioned above, a set of industry dummies is used to capture the effect of differences in industry environment and industry-wide locational factors, including various kinds of barriers to trade. Seven industries corresponding to broad product groups are distinguished: consumer electronics (*CONSUM*), office equipment and computers (*OFFCOMP*), telecommunications equipment (*TELCOM*), parts and components (*COMPO*), automation and control equipment (*AUTOM*), medical and scientific equipment (*MEDICAL*), and heavy electrical equipment (*HEAVY*).

5.4 Empirical Results

The multinomial logit model of equation (1) is used to analyse which firm features determine the probabilities that a firm belongs to one of the three categories (domestic firm, West-bound MNE, Asia-bound MNE). Tables 5.4 and 5.5 present the estimation results. The first two columns present the estimated coefficients and t-ratios for the probability that a firm is a West-bound or Asia-bound MNE, respectively, with domestic firm taken as reference state. The third column contains the differences between the coefficients for West-bound and Asia-bound MNEs and corresponding t-ratios.

5.4.1 *Internalisation and Corporate Finance*

Table 5.4 presents the results of the model with the explanatory variables limited to firm-specific factors. The results for the probability that a firm is a West-bound MNE broadly confirm the hypotheses based on internalisation theory: the coefficients of *RDINT*, *MARKINT*, *HUMRES*, and *CAPLAB* all have a positive sign and are significantly different from zero. Japanese DFI in Western industrialised countries thus has driving forces similar to DFI by Western firms, a finding that is in accordance with recent empirical work on Japanese DFI in the US.

In addition, firm size is important for the decision to become a West-bound MNE, which is likely to be related to the high fixed setup costs of establishing overseas manufacturing subsidiaries and communication networks. The significantly positive effect of *INTFUNDS* supports the view that the availability of internally generated funds is often necessary to finance risky foreign investment projects. Among the industry dummies, the coefficients of *CONSUM* and *COMPO* are significantly positive, relative to the omitted industry dummy *HEAVY*. Firms in the consumer electronics and electronic components industries are more likely to have invested in Europe and North America than can be explained by firm characteristics only. This can be related to trade restricting measures taken in the US and the EC against Japanese imports (e.g. colour televisions and semiconductors). It is also likely to reflect the relatively strong competitive advantages of Japanese firms *vis-à-vis* North American and European firms, which allow Japanese firm to compete with Western firms on their home ground.

The second column of Table 5.4 shows the effects of firm characteristics on the probability of a firm becoming an Asia-bound MNE. In sharp contrast to the results for the decision to become a West-bound MNE, none of the firm characteristics except *HUMRES* and *EMPL* have a significant influence on the probability of a firm becoming an Asia-bound MNE. The possession of intangible assets, apart from the availability of human resources, evidently is not a prerequisite for setting up manufacturing plants in South-East Asia. This is in accordance with the view that both the relative absence of strong competing firms and cumulative economic ties between Japan and South-East Asia have resulted in strongly reduced barriers for DFI in the region. The positive effect of *HUMRES* indicates that DFI in South-East Asia is facilitated if the firm can draw on human resources and transfer organisational skills to foreign plants. Firm size exerts a positive influence, indicating that a certain threshold size of the firm is often required to be able to draw on the managerial and financial resources necessary to invest abroad. However, the coefficient of firm size is significantly smaller than the coefficient estimated for the decision to become a West-bound MNE.

Table 5.4 Multinomial logit model of the probability that Japanese electronics firms are domestic firms, west-bound MNEs, or Asia-bound MNEs: internalisation factors and corporate finance

Reference state	West-bound MNE Domestic firm	Asia-bound MNE Domestic firm	West-bound MNE Asia-bound MNE
log *EMPL*	2.07***	1.02***	1.05***
	(2.60)	(3.04)	(3.62)
RDINT	7.29***	2.49	4.80**
	(2.60)	(1.00)	(2.09)
MARKINT	0.28**	0.09	0.18*
	(2.06)	(0.77)	(1.86)
CAPLAB	0.92**	0.08	0.84**
	(2.00)	(0.20)	(2.14)
HUMRES	4.81**	4.70***	0.11
	(2.31)	(2.80)	(0.06)
INTFUNDS	0.50**	0.18	0.32*
	(2.45)	(1.11)	(1.88)
Constant and industry dummies			
Constant	–21.91***	–10.52***	–11.39***
	(–6.36)	(–3.88)	(–4.30)
CONSUM	4.40***	3.60***	0.79
	(2.70)	(2.61)	(0.76)
OFFCOMP	1.63	0.30	1.25
	(1.45)	(0.33)	(0.42)
TELCOM	–1.15	–0.85	–0.30
	(–0.87)	(–0.90)	(–0.23)
COMPO	3.42***	2.20***	1.22
	(3.73)	(3.25)	(1.51)
AUTOM	1.20	0.42	0.701
	(1.02)	(0.49)	(0.71)
MEDICAL	1.64*	0.49	0.77
	(1.81)	(1.30)	(0.92)
Observations	204		
McFadden's R^2	0.35	χ^2	36.4

Notes: Asymptotic *t*-ratios between brackets, *= significant at 10% level, **= significant at the 5% level, ***= significant at the 1% level. Coefficients in the third column are differences between the coefficients in the first and second columns. The omitted industry dummy is *HEAVY*.

The coefficient of *INTFUNDS* has the expected positive sign but is insignificant. Liquidity plays a lesser role in the decision to invest in Asia, which can be explained by smaller risk factors attached to investments in Asia. Among the industry dummies, again the coefficients of *COMPO* and *CONSUM* are significantly positive, though somewhat smaller than for the decision to become a West-bound MNE. Higher than average DFI in South-East Asia in these industries is likely to reflect that in the consumer electronics industry and related components industries, as well as in the semiconductor industry, the production process can be separated into stages which make substantially different use of capital, skilled labour, and unskilled labour (Nakakita and Urata 1991). This has driven the development of regional core networks in South-East Asia which in turn act as catalysts for investment by other firms.

The coefficients in the third column of Table 5.4 are the differences in the coefficients of the first and second column with corresponding *t*-ratios. They show the effects of firm characteristics on the probability that a firm is a West-bound MNE and not an Asia-bound MNE. The coefficients of *EMPL*, *RDINT*, and *CAPLAB* are positive and significantly different from zero at the 5 or 1 per cent (*EMPL*) level, while the coefficients of *MARKINT* and *INTFUNDS* are significant at the 10 per cent level. *HUMRES*, as measure of human resources and organisational skills within the firm, is the only variable that does not differentiate West-bound MNEs from Asia-bound MNEs.

5.4.2 Inter-Firm Linkages within Business Groups

Table 5.5 shows the results of the extended multinomial logit model including the variables related to business groups. The estimated effects of *EMPL*, *RDINT*, *MARKINT*, *CAPLAB*, *HUMRES*, and *INTFUNDS* on the probability that a firm is a West-bound MNE differ only marginally from those estimated in the model without business group factors.

The variables related to horizontal business groups do not contribute to the explanation of investment decisions in Western industrialised countries. The coefficient for *HORGROUP* has a negative sign but is insignificant.[18] Nor does membership of a horizontal *keiretsu* seem to play an important role through relaxation of liquidity constraints: the coefficient of the interactive term *HORGROUP***INTFUNDS* has the wrong (positive) sign, but is not significantly different from zero. The coefficient of *HORWEST* has the expected positive sign but is not significant either. While horizontal *keiretsu* networks may influence the *location* of manufacturing plants, the results do not indicate that they play a major role in the *decision* to invest in Western industrialised countries.

Membership of a vertical business group does have a significant effect on the probability that a firm will become a West-bound MNE. The coefficient for *SUBCON* is negative and significant: all things equal, subcontractors in a vertical business group are less likely to take the decision to become a West-bound MNE. On the other hand, the results also indicate that this general effect may be offset if the core firm has invested extensively in manufacturing operations in Europe and North America.[19] The coefficient of *VERWEST* has a positive sign and is significant at the 10 per cent level. This lends support to the hypothesis that subcontractors are assisted by their core firms in setting up manufacturing plants in Europe and North

Table 5.5 Multinomial logit model of the probability that Japanese electronics firms are domestic firms, West-bound MNEs, or Asia-bound MNEs: internalisation factors, corporate finance, and business groups

Reference state	West-bound MNE	Asia-bound MNE	West-bound MNE
	Domestic firm	Domestic firm	Asia-bound MNE
log *EMPL*	2.24***	0.96**	1.28***
	(5.07)	(2.58)	(3.80)
RDINT	8.09***	0.92	7.16***
	(2.66)	(0.36)	(2.66)
MARKINT	0.27*	0.08	0.25**
	(1.84)	(0.03)	(2.43)
CAPLAB	1.09**	0.06	1.06**
	(2.11)	(0.07)	(2.28)
HUMRES	4.17*	5.63***	–1.47
	(1.84)	(2.99)	(–0.78)
INTFUNDS	0.56**	0.28	0.29
	(2.55)	(1.60)	(1.62)
*HORGROUP*INTFUNDS*	0.57	–1.35**	1.92***
	(0.88)	(–2.56)	(3.00)
HORGROUP	–0.43	0.10	–0.53
	(–0.36)	(0.10)	(–0.48)
*HORGROUP*HORASIA*		0.07**	
		(2.23)	
*HORGROUP*HORWEST*	0.02		
	(0.27)		
SUBCON	–4.62***	–4.72***	0.09
	(–2.58)	(–3.29)	(0.08)
*SUBCON*VERASIA*		0.43***	
		(2.64)	
*SUBCON*VERWEST*	0.54*		
	(1.88)		

Table 5.5 (*Continued*)

Reference state	West-bound MNE	Asia-bound MNE	West-bound MNE
	Domestic firm	Domestic firm	Asia-bound MNE
Constant and industry dummies			
Constant	−23.14***	−10.25***	−12.89***
	(−5.95)	(−3.39)	(−4.21)
CONSUM	4.66***	3.40**	1.26
	(2.90)	(2.46)	(1.14)
OFFCOMP	1.81	0.68	1.13
	(1.44)	(0.66)	(0.97)
TELCOM	−1.57	−1.24	−0.30
	(−1.11)	(−1.19)	(−0.23)
COMPO	3.72***	2.69***	1.02
	(3.64)	(3.38)	(1.14)
AUTOM	2.03	1.78	0.26
	(1.50)	(1.49)	(0.22)
MEDICAL	1.44	1.14	0.30
	(1.44)	(1.49)	(0.32)
Observations	204		
McFadden's R^2	0.43	χ^2	55.8

Notes: see Table 5.4.

America, often in response to formal and informal local content requirements.

The results for the variables related to horizontal and vertical business groups strongly confirm the importance of inter-firm linkages in explaining the decision to invest in South-East Asia. While membership of a horizontal business group as such does not exert an influence on the decision to become an Asia-bound MNE (the coefficient for *HORGROUP* is insignificant), the significantly negative coefficient for the interactive term between *INTFUNDS* and *HORGROUP* suggests that members of horizontal business groups are not liquidity constrained in their decision to invest in Asia. This conforms with the view that member firms can borrow at relatively low cost from their main bank and group-related financial institutions to expand in Asia. The significantly positive effect of *HORASIA* confirms that the presence of group firms in South-East Asia may reduce informational constraints for potential investors, and facilitate the marketing of the products through long-term supplier linkages with other member firms and the trading firm active in the region.

The negative coefficient for *SUBCON* again suggests that subcontractor firms that are dependent on their core firm are generally less likely to invest abroad. On the other hand, the size of the regional network of the core firm in South-East Asia, *VERASIA*, has the expected positive effect with the coefficient significant at the 1 per cent level. This result demonstrates the importance of regional core networks established by the major electronics firms in South-East Asia in reducing the barriers for related subcontractor firms to set up manufacturing plants there.

In conclusion, the results strongly confirm the importance of horizontal and vertical business groups in explaining the probability that Japanese electronics firms start manufacturing operations in South-East Asia.[20] While the possession of firm-specific intangible assets is in general a prerequisite for investment in Western industrialised countries, inter-firm linkages are major determinants of the decision to invest in South-East Asia.

It was also investigated whether internalisation factors affect the decision to invest abroad differently for members of both horizontal and vertical business groups compared with independent firms, by adding interactive terms with the group dummies. No robust effects were found except for the interactive term between *RDINT* and *SUBCON*, which reached positive significance in some specifications for the decision to become both Asia-bound and West-bound MNEs. This result is suggestive of a complementary relationship between R&D activity of subcontractors and that of the core firms. Such complementarity is also suggested by Suzuki (1993), where evidence is found of substantial spillovers of core firms' R&D activities to subcontractors in the Japanese electronics industry.

Finally, the extent to which the results are sensitive to the timing of investment was investigated, by splitting up the sample for firms that invested abroad before 1986 and those that invested more recently. The statistical results did not indicate a significant change in the regime of the model for early versus late investors.[21]

5.5 Conclusions

This chapter has analysed the determinants of the probability that Japanese electronics firms set up manufacturing operations in South-East Asia (Asia-bound MNEs) on the one hand, and in Europe and North America (West-bound MNEs) on the other. Among the factors tested for their effects on investment probabilities were both *firm-specific* factors related to the possession of intangible assets and *inter-firm* ties within horizontal and vertical business groups.

The results for West-bound MNEs confirm the hypothesis of the internalisation theory that firms need to possess intangible assets to be able to expand abroad through the establishment of overseas manufacturing plants. R&D intensity, marketing intensity, and human resource intensity all have significantly positive effects on the probability that Japanese electronics firms are West-bound MNEs. In addition, capital intensive firms are more likely to become West-bound MNEs. The determinants of Japanese investment in Europe and North America are thus similar to those found for MNEs based in other industrialised countries. In addition, evidence is found that firms that are less liquidity constrained are more likely to invest in Europe and North America. Inter-firm linkages are relatively unimportant in explaining the probability to invest in Europe and North America. The exception is that subcontractor firms have an incentive to follow their core firm abroad to supply the core firm's plants with locally produced components. This finding could also be related to formal and informal pressure on Japanese firms to increase local purchases of components used in their manufacturing operations.

In sharp contrast, the probability of setting up a manufacturing plant in South-East Asia is found to be related only to the size of the firm and the availability of human resources which allow for the transfer of organisational skills abroad. The possession of intangible assets based on investments in R&D and marketing is not a prerequisite for DFI in South-East Asia. This suggests that cumulative economic ties between Japan and South-East Asia, coupled with the absence of strong local competitors, greatly reduce the barriers Japanese firms face in expanding in this region. Convincing evidence is found that barriers are further reduced for members of horizontal and vertical business groups. First, the probability of investing in South-East Asia for members of a horizontal business group is positively related to the number of manufacturing plants operated by other electronics firms in the horizontal business group there. The presence of member firms in South-East Asia is likely to reduce informational constraints for potential investors, and facilitate marketing of the products through long-term supplier links with other member firms and the trading firm active in the region. Second, the evidence suggests that members of horizontal business groups are not liquidity constrained in their decisions to start manufacturing in South-East Asia. Third, while subcontractor firms in a vertical business group in general tend to be tied to the domestic manufacturing network of the group, the size of the core firm's regional core network in South-East Asia exerts a significantly positive influence on the probability of subcontractors becoming Asia-bound MNEs. This result demonstrates the importance of regional core networks established by the major electronics firms in South-East Asia in reducing the barriers to related firms setting up manufacturing plants there. Thus, a striking finding is that, while the possession of *firm-specific* intangible assets is in general a prerequisite for investment in Western industrialised countries, it is *inter-firm* linkages that are the major determinants of the decision to invest in South-East Asia.

The results point to the importance of inter-firm links in lowering barriers to DFI for Japanese firms. This has an interesting parallel with previous empirical results with respect to the experience effect in the process of DFI (Hennart and Park 1994, Kogut and Chang 1996, Yu 1990). The results here suggest that at least part of this experience is not necessarily tied to the firm but is also transferable to other firms through inter-firm links within horizontal and vertical business groups.

It is difficult to assess the extent to which the findings are specific to Japanese firms. Regional differences are likely to exist also in the determinants of DFI by American and European firms within their respective trade blocs (NAFTA and EU) versus DFI outside these blocs. While the organisation of firms in horizontal and vertical *keiretsu* may be specific to Japanese industry, the importance of inter-firm linkages such as long-term supplier links in general is not. Neither of these issues has received due attention in the empirical literature on Western multinational firms, and both offer ample scope for further research.

APPENDIX 5.1

Variable Definitions, Means, and Standard Deviations

Table A5.1 lists the variable definitions, means, and standard deviations of the independent variables in the models of Tables 5.4 and 5.5.

Table A5.1 Variable definitions, means, and standard deviations

Symbol	Variable definition	Mean (standard deviation)
EMPL	Number of employees, fiscal years 1986–1988	4,063 (9,799)
RDINT	R&D intensity: R&D expenditures/value added, fiscal years 1986–1988	0.171 (0.134)
MARKINT	Marketing intensity: (Direct and indirect sales costs)* 100/sales, fiscal years 1986–1988	4.001 (3.301)
CAPLAB	Capital labour cost ratio: Gross fixed depreciable capital/total labour costs, fiscal years 1986–1988	1.051 (0.670)
HUMRES	Human resource intensity: Non-manufacturing labour cost/total labour cost, fiscal years 1986–1988	0.346 (0.156)
INTFUNDS	Internally generated funds: Operating + non-operating profits/gross fixed capital investments, fiscal years 1986–1988	1.141 (1.492)
HORGROUP	Dummy variable, =1 if the firm belongs to one of the 6 large horizontal *keiretsu*; Dodwell definition, 1988	0.353 (0.479)
HORASIA	Number of electronics manufacturing subsidiaries of the horizontal *keiretsu* to which the firm belongs in South-East Asia minus the manufacturing subsidiaries of the firm there, June 1989. Applies if *HORGROUP* = 1.	24.597 (11.812)

Table A5.1 (*Continued*)

Symbol	Variable definition	Mean (standard deviation)
HORWEST	Number of electronics manufacturing subsidiaries of the horizontal *keiretsu* to which the firm belongs in North America/ Europe minus the manufacturing subsidiaries of the firm there, June 1989. Applies if *HORGROUP* = 1.	13.264 (6.606)
SUBCON	Subcontractor: dummy variable, =1 if the firm is a member of a vertical *keiretsu*: the firm is controlled by a core firm and the core firm is a major client, 1989	0.240 (0.428)
VERASIA	Number of manufacturing subsidiaries of the core firm in South-East Asia, June 1989. Applies if *SUBCON* = 1.	8.837 (8.042)
VERWEST	Number of manufacturing subsidiaries of the core firm in North America/Europe, June 1989. Applies if *SUBCON*= 1.	0.061 (4.634)
CONSUM	Dummy variable, =1 if the firm's major line of business is consumer electronics	0.098 (0.298)
OFFCOMP	Dummy variable, =1 if the firm's major line of business is office machines and computers	0.108 (0.311)
TELCOM	Dummy variable, =1 if the firm's major line of business is telecommunications	0.078 (0.270)
COMPO	Dummy variable, =1 if the firm's major line of business is electric or electronic components	0.361 (0.463)
AUTOM	Dummy variable, =1 if the firm's major line of business is factory automation and control equipment	0.069 (0.253)
MEDICAL	Dummy variable, =1 if the firm's major line of business is medical and scientific equipment	0.162 (0.369)
HEAVY	Dummy variable, =1 if the firm's major line of business is heavy electrical equipment	0.177 (0.382)

APPENDIX 5.2

Data Sources

Information on overseas manufacturing subsidiaries of Japanese firms was extracted from Touyou Keizai (1985a–1992a). This source provides the most complete listing of foreign subsidiaries of Japanese firms. Data were cross-checked with information available in Dodwell (1988), Nihon Denshi Kikai Kougyoukai (1989a–1992a), and Dempa (1986b–1992b). Establishments up to June 1989 were counted. Foreign subsidiaries in which Japanese firms had an equity stake of less than 25 per cent were not counted as investments. The information was used to classify firms as domestic firms, Asia-bound MNEs or West-bound MNEs, and to calculate the number of manufacturing subsidiaries of core firms in vertical business groups and those of electronics firms in horizontal business groups. The number of overseas manufacturing subsidiaries of horizontal business groups include electronics manufacturing subsidiaries of the trading firm.

Employment, sales, sales costs, wage costs, value added, fixed capital, and pre-tax profits were all taken or calculated from Nihon Kaihatsu Ginkou Setsubi Toushi Kenkyuujo (1986–1989). The information in this database is derived from unconsolidated financial reports of listed firms; consolidated financial figures are not available in detail in Japan. Data on R&D expenditures and gross fixed capital investment were taken from Touyou Keizai (1986d–1990d). Firms were classified into seven industries based on information on sales by product group from these two sources.

Information on membership of horizontal business groups was taken from Dodwell (1989). Information on membership of vertical business groups was taken from Touyou Keizai (1990c). The latter information was combined with information on the most important client firms available from Touyou Keizai (1991b) to create the variable *SUBCON*.

APPENDIX 5.3

Predictive Power and Magnitude of Effects

A5.3.1 Predictive Power

Table A5.2 shows the percentage of firms classified correctly as belonging to their firm type in the models of Tables 5.4 and 5.5. The 'predicted' firm type in this case

Table A5.2 Percentage of firms with correctly predicted firm type

	Domestic firm	Asia-bound MNE	West-bound MNE
Internalisation factors model (Table 5.4)	72	47	78
Internalisation and business groups model (Table 5.5)	74	62	78

Table A5.3 Percentage point changes in the probability that a firm is a domestic firm, Asia-bound MNE, or West-bound MNE, caused by a 1 per cent increase in explanatory variables

	Domestic firm	Asia-bound MNE	West-bound MNE
EMPL	–0.37	–0.06	0.42
RDINT	–0.19	–0.12	0.31
MARKINT	–0.14	–0.11	0.25
CAPLAB	–0.14	–0.12	0.27
HUMRES	–0.36	0.24	0.12
INTFUNDS	–0.11	–0.01	0.12
*HORGROUP*INTFUNDS*	0.02	–0.10	0.08
HORASIA	–0.06	0.13	–0.07
HORWEST	–0.01	–0.01	0.02
VERASIA	–0.09	0.19	–0.10
VERWEST	–0.10	–0.09	0.19
Sample frequencies	31.9	29.4	38.7

Notes: calculated on the basis of coefficients in Table 5.5 in the sample frequencies and with the regressors in the sample mean. Since the sum of the probabilities necessarily has to be one, the pseudo-elasticities add up to zero.

is the type with an estimated probability greater than 0.33, following the 'maximum probability' rule (see e.g. Cramer 1991). The table shows that the improved predictive power in the business groups model stems largely from a better classification of Asia-bound MNEs: the percentage of Asia-bound MNEs correctly classified as such increases from 47 to 62 per cent.

A5.3.2 Magnitude of Effects

The coefficients of the multinominal logit model can not be directly interpreted as effects on probabilites. Table A5.3 shows pseudo-elasticities: the absolute (percentage-point) increase in the probabilities with respect to a 1 per cent increase in the explanatory variables other than dummy variables. The pseudo-elasticities are calculated with the independent variables taken in the sample mean. To give an example, if a firm increases its employment by 1 per cent, the probability that the firm is a West-bound MNE increases by 0.42 percentage point, while the probability that the firm operates only domestically decreases by 0.37 per cent point and the probability that the firm is an Asia-bound MNE decreases by 0.06 per cent point.

APPENDIX 5.4

Test Results: Early versus Late Investors

This section presents the results of multinominal logit analysis of the probability of becoming MNE for investors before or in 1985 ('early' investors) and for investors after 1985 ('late' investors.) Since the exogenous variables in the model are measured in 1986–1989 or 1989, it is possible that these variables are less representative for the 'early' investors (although most variables tend to be relatively stable over time, at least in relative terms). Also, the environment in which Japanese firms take investment decisions changed over time, which may have a bearing on the importance of various determinants of DFI. There may thus be a structural shift in the model depending on the timing of DFI.

To analyse a possible regime shift, data were collected on the establishment time of the first manufacturing plants of Japanese firms in South-East Asia and North America/Europe. The establishment dates of subsidiaries given in Touyou Keizai's (1990a–1991a) directory (our main source of information on Japanese investment) were not used. They would not give a reliable picture, because a large number of Japanese subsidiaries were established initially to deal with distribution and sales support, with manufacturing activity following at a much later date. Instead, Touyou Keizai's (1985a) directory was examined to determine whether the Japanese firms were listed there as operating a manufacturing plant in the two regions. This exercise could not be wholly accurate because the coverage of Touyou Keizai's survey

Table A5.4 Classification of firms: early versus late investors

	No. of early investors	No. of late investors
Asia-bound MNEs	39	21
West-bound MNEs	45	34

in 1985 was less than complete (for our 1989 classification it was possible to use several other sources to verify Touyou Keizai's investment information), but it provided a rough classification of 'early' and 'late' investors. Of the 60 Asia-bound MNEs, 39 invested before or in 1985 and 21 after 1985. Of the 79 West-bound MNEs, 45 invested before or in 1985 and 34 after 1985. The shares of 'early' and 'late' investors are similar for both types of MNE, at roughly 60 and 40 per cent, respectively.

In order to test for a regime shift, the multinominal logit model was estimated for two sub-samples of the 204 firms: (1) domestic firms and 'late' Asia- and West-bound MNEs, and domestic firms and (2) 'early' Asia- and West-bound MNEs. The results are presented in the Tables A5.5 and A5.6. The qualitative results of the full

Table A5.5 Multinomial logit model of the probability that Japanese electronics firms are domestic firms, West-bound MNEs, or Asia-bound MNEs: only investors before 1986

Reference state	West-bound MNE	Asia-bound MNE	West-bound MNE
	Domestic firm	Domestic firm	Asia-bound MNE
log *EMPL*	2.43***	1.10**	1.34***
	(4.28)	(2.39)	(2.86)
RDINT	10.45**	−2.39	12.83***
	(2.54)	(−0.62)	(2.81)
MARKINT	0.30	0.03	0.26
	(1.38)	(0.19)	(1.42)
CAPLAB	1.11**	−0.22	1.33**
	(2.09)	(−0.37)	(2.02)
HUMRES	4.46	4.68**	−0.22
	(1.53)	(2.00)	(−0.08)
INTFUNDS	0.81**	0.42*	0.39*
	(2.99)	(1.96)	(1.78)
*HORGROUP*INTFUNDS*	−0.32	−2.59**	2.27*
	(−0.28)	(−2.41)	(1.69)
HORGROUP	−1.70	−0.66	−1.04
	(−0.88)	(−0.42)	(−0.56)
*HORGROUP*HORASIA*		0.12**	
		(2.04)	
*HORGROUP*HORWEST*	0.10		
	(0.79)		
SUBCON	−2.78	−6.13***	3.34
	(−1.11)	(−2.81)	(1.64)
*SUBCON*VERASIA*		0.43*	
		(1.81)	
*SUBCON*VERWEST*	0.23		
	(0.56)		

Table A5.5 (*Continued*)

Reference state	West-bound MNE	Asia-bound MNE	West-bound MNE
	Domestic firm	Domestic firm	Asia-bound MNE
Constant and industry dummies			
Constant	–26.27***	–11.79***	–14.47***
	(–4.95)	(–3.12)	(–3.26)
CONSUM	4.86**	3.80**	1.06
	(2.17)	(2.06)	(0.65)
OFFCOMP	2.45	1.03	1.43
	(1.40)	(0.613)	(0.74)
TELCOM	–0.71	0.79	–1.51
	(–0.36)	(0.63)	(–0.73)
COMPO	4.17***	4.23***	–0.06
	(2.89)	(3.52)	(–0.04)
AUTOM	1.31	3.50**	–2.19
	(0.67)	(2.29)	(–1.20)
MEDICAL	0.84	1.82*	–0.99
	(0.58)	(1.74)	(–0.66)
Observations	145		
McFadden's R^2	0.52		

Notes: see Table 5.4.

Table A5.6 Multinomial logit model of the probability that Japanese electronics firms are domestic firms, West-bound MNEs, or Asia-bound MNEs: only investors in or after 1986

Reference state	West-bound MNE	Asia-bound MNE	West-bound MNE
	Domestic firm	Domestic firm	Asia-bound MNE
log *EMPL*	3.69***	1.19**	2.49***
	(3.90)	(2.21)	(2.64)
RDINT	9.67*	4.65	5.02
	(1.84)	(1.33)	(0.95)
MARKINT	0.35	–0.15	0.50**
	(1.65)	(–0.75)	(2.13)
CAPLAB	1.70**	–0.06	1.77**
	(2.23)	(–0.10)	(2.20)
HUMRES	5.34	6.61***	–1.27
	(1.55)	(2.65)	(–0.38)

Table A5.6 (*Continued*)

Reference state	West-bound MNE	Asia-bound MNE	West-bound MNE
	Domestic firm	Domestic firm	Asia-bound MNE
INTFUNDS	0.79	0.31	0.48
	(1.53)	(1.29)	(0.92)
*HORGROUP*INTFUNDS*	1.96	–0.80	2.76**
	(1.61)	(–1.34)	(2.25)
HORGROUP	0.38	0.28	0.10
	(0.21)	(0.22)	(0.05)
*HORGROUP*HORASIA*		0.07*	
		(1.97)	
*HORGROUP*HORWEST*	–0.10		
	(–1.05)		
SUBCON	–9.24**	–3.10	–6.14
	(–2.31)	(–1.65)	(–1.56)
*SUBCON*VERASIA*		0.30	
		(1.36)	
*SUBCON*VERWEST*	1.17**		
	(2.00)		
Constant and industry dummies			
Constant	–37.55***	–12.97***	–24.58***
	(–4.30)	(–2.84)	(–2.83)
CONSUM	8.25***	3.95**	4.30*
	(3.06)	(2.26)	(1.72)
OFFCOMP	3.57*	1.11	2.46
	(1.78)	(0.89)	(1.18)
TELCOM	–2.73	–2.53*	–0.20
	(–1.15)	(–1.70)	(–0.08)
COMPO	5.62***	1.88*	3.74**
	(3.14)	(1.83)	(2.09)
AUTOM	4.87**	0.43	4.44*
	(2.17)	(0.25)	(1.89)
MEDICAL	2.85*	0.54	2.31
	(1.73)	(0.54)	(1.38)
Observations	124		
McFadden's R^2	0.48		

Notes: see Table 5.4.

sample model generally hold for the two sub-samples: all the signs of the coefficients are the same and both sub-sample models show the important differences between West-bound MNEs and Asia-bound MNEs. Although in a few cases the explanatory variables that were significant in the full sample fail to reach significance in one of the sub-sample models, this can be attributed mainly to the fact that the models are estimated with much smaller samples.

One difference can be discerned which may be related to the modern development of Japanese industry. In the 'early' investor model, *INTFUNDS* is significant for the decisions to become both Asia-bound and West-bound MNEs, while *HORGROUP*INTFUNDS* is significantly negative for the decision to invest in South-East Asia. In the 'late' investor model, on the other hand, none of the variables related to internal finance reach significance (although the coefficients have similar signs). The results suggest a diminished importance of internal funds and bank finance within horizontal business groups by 'late' investors. This is likely to be related to deregulation and development of the Japanese financial sector, which has allowed Japanese firms to increase the use of external sources of finance.

NOTES

1. An incomplete listing is: Pugel, Kragas, and Kimura (1996), Kogut and Chang (1996), Kimura and Pugel (1995), Fukao *et al.* (1994), Hennart and Park (1994), Chang and Kogut (1992), Drake and Caves (1992), Sleuwaegen and Yamawaki (1992), Kogut and Chang (1991), Mann (1990), and Kimura (1989). See also Caves (1993) for an extensive survey of the literature.
2. Hennart and Park (1994) found a positive effect of parent firms' investments in the US in 1984 on investment by second tier *keiretsu* members in 1986. The effect was not significant, though, which they attribute to the relative paucity of Japanese investments at the time. In a recent study, Kimura and Pugel (1995) confirm that member firms of vertical *keiretsu* are responsible for a relatively large share of US production in industries that supply automobile and electronics producers.
3. This pattern has been observed since the 1960s and has given rise to a literature describing Japanese DFI as induced by changes in comparative advantage instead of by firm-specific advantages (Kojima 1978).
4. DFI may also occur through internalisation of the market for intermediate inputs other than intangibles, if it involves vertical integration to reduce transaction costs (Hennart 1982).
5. Kojima (1978) and Ozawa (1979) argued that the Japanese government saw the relocation to South-East Asia of manufacturing activities for which Japan had lost its comparative advantage as an indispensable part of industrial (restructuring) policy in the 1960s and 1970s. DFI was actively promoted by the government via tax breaks and through institutions as the Export–Import Bank of Japan, which provided assistance and low interest loans. The foreign plant was often set up as a joint venture with one of the major Japanese trading houses (*sougou sousha*) which could boast decades of experience in dealing with Asian countries. The Japanese government also used targeted official development aid to create an environment in which Japanese ventures could flourish. Presently,

Japan is the largest provider of aid to Indonesia, Malaysia, South Korea, and Thailand (Gold, Eonomou, and Tolentino 1991).

6. See Hodder (1991) for a discussion of capital cost advantages of Japanese firms.
7. This coincided with a wave of Japanese acquisitions of US firms (Kester 1991).
8. Liquidity may also lead to over-investment, which is stressed in the free cash flow theory put forward in Jensen (1986). If a firm generates a cash flow that is greater than the cash flow required to finance all projects in the firm's core business, managers can use the surplus—the free cash flow—at their discretion. Managers will choose not to pay this surplus out to shareholders, but will use it for diversified investment projects and acquisitions. This theory also predicts a positive relationship between (foreign) investment and liquidity.
9. See Caves (1993). See Sako (1992) for a case study analysis of supplier networks of Japanese firms in Japan and in the UK.
10. North America includes the US and Canada. Europe includes EFTA, EC, and Eastern European countries. South-East Asia includes South Korea, Taiwan, Hong Kong, the ASEAN countries (the Philippines, Indonesia, Malaysia, Thailand, Brunei, and Singapore), and China.
11. All these variables are calculated on the basis of the average data over fiscal years 1986–1988. See Appendix 5.1 for a description of the variables; Appendix 5.2 gives the data sources.
12. Rather than sales, employment is used as a measure of firm size. Since Japanese electronics firms differ in the extent to which they rely on upstream vertical integration, subcontracting, or independent parts suppliers, sales is not a straightforward measure. Use of total assets as the measure of size is also fraught with problems stemming from diverging valuation of land assets. See Aoki (1988) for discussions of the interpretation of Japanese firms' financial reports. For similar reasons value added was used as the factor to scale R&D expenditures.
13. Firm size itself may also generate benefits for the firm, i.e. better access to capital markets, which can be transferred abroad (see Dunning 1981).
14. Pre-tax profits include non-operating revenues, which have been high and often have surpassed profits from normal activities in the second half of the 1980s because of growing financial activities (*zaiteku*) (see also Kester 1991). Note that capital outlays are the outlays for fixed capital in Japan: high ratios will be associated with opportunities to use funds generated in Japan to finance ventures abroad.
15. While another source that is widely used, Keizai Chousa Kyoukai's *Keiretsu no Kenkyuu*, classifies Sony (Mitsui), Toshiba (Mitsui), Matsushita (Sumitomo), and Sharp (Fuyo) as members of horizontal business groups, the group ties are judged too weak for such a classification by Dodwell. The empirical model was estimated once more using the *Keiretsu no Kenkyuu* definition (Keizai Chousa Kyoukai 1990). Similarly signed, though less statistically significant, effects were found.
16. Although the restriction to manufacturing activities of electronics firms carries the limitation that it measures only part of the business groups' activities abroad, manufacturing experience in electronics is most likely to provide benefits to potential foreign investors.

17. The estimated coefficients for *HORASIA* and *HORWEST* are of the form γ^s in equation (1).
18. Compare Fukao *et al.* (1994). Using a dummy variable for horizontal *keiretsu* membership, no empirical support was found for the hypothesis that *keiretsu* members have higher overseas production ratios.
19. From the coefficients for *SUBCON* and *SUBCON***VERWEST* in Table 5.5 and the number of group subsidiaries in Table 5.3, it can be seen that subcontractors of the parent firm Matsushita are, all things equal, *more* likely to become West-bound MNEs.
20. This is also shown by the improved fit of the model of Table 5.5 compared with the model of Table 5.4. McFadden's R^2 increases from 0.35 to 0.42 and the predictive power of the model (see Appendix 5.3) also improves substantially for the decision to become an Asia-bound MNE.
21. Appendix 5.4 presents the test results. The minor differences that could be discerned appear related to the modern development of Japanese industry; i.e., a diminished importance of internal funds and bank finance within horizontal business groups for late investors is likely to be related to deregulation and development of the Japanese financial sector. See also Odagiri (1992) on the declining importance of loans from the main bank and the increasing importance of equity finance in Japan since the 1980s.

6

Testing the Tariff Jumping Hypothesis

6.1 Introduction

The determinants and effects of antidumping actions have been subject of analysis in an increasing number of theoretical and empirical studies. The effects of antidumping laws on welfare and domestic and foreign firms' prices and quantities are analysed under various market structures in theoretical work (e.g. Reitzes 1993, Leidy and Hoekman 1990, Webb 1992, and Staiger and Wolack 1992), while Messerlin (1989) documents the trade restricting effects of antidumping actions in the European Community. Another line of research has examined industries' incentives to petition for antidumping measures in vertically related industries (Hoekman and Leidy 1992 and Belderbos, Jie a Joen, and Sleuwaegen 1995). Leipziger and Shin (1991) and Feinberg and Hirsch (1989) examine empirically which factors govern domestic industries' propensity to petition for antidumping measures, and Feinberg and Kaplan (1990) present empirical evidence that antidumping protection may 'cascade downwards' from upstream to downstream industries. Possible anti-competitive effects of antidumping laws have been addressed: Stegemann (1991a and 1991b) discusses the relationship between EC antidumping actions and collusive practices, while Prusa (1992a) shows how firms may have used the antidumping instrument in the United States to facilitate collusive price arrangements with exporters. Last but not least, there is a substantial and growing number of empirical studies analysing whether economic or political-economic factors influence US and EC antidumping decisions (e.g. Tharakan and Waelbroeck 1994, Baldwin and Steagall 1993, DeVault 1993a, Moore 1992, Eymann and Schuknecht 1992, Prusa 1992b, Tharakan 1991a).

Surprisingly, the empirical and theoretical literature on antidumping has ignored the relationship between antidumping and direct foreign investment (DFI). Since antidumping laws both in the EC and the US have been adapted in the late 1980s in an attempt to deflect 'circumvention' of antidumping orders by foreign firms through the establishment of local assembly plants (Van Bael and Bellis 1990, Horlick 1990), one would expect the phenomenon to be of considerable significance. Yet no systematic effort has been undertaken to establish the extent to which antidumping actions have affected foreign investment decisions, nor have the implications of such tariff jumping DFI been considered in theoretical models.

In Chapter 1 it was shown that the timing of Japanese manufacturing DFI in the EC has often been closely related to the initiation of antidumping actions against Japanese exporters. Although a number of empirical studies of Japanese DFI have confirmed the importance of other trade barriers such as voluntary export restraints (VERs) as a factor promoting Japanese DFI in Europe and the United States (Sleuwaegen and Yamawaki 1992, Kogut and Chang 1991, Heitger and Stehn 1990, Pugel, Kragas, and Kimura 1996, Drake and Caves 1992), the role of antidumping measures has not been investigated.

In this chapter, an empirical model is developed to establish the extent to which antidumping and other trade restricting measures taken by the United States and the European Community have been independent determinants of manufacturing DFI by Japanese electronics firms. The analysis uses detailed data at the firm level on market shares and plant establishments in the US and EC for each of 35 products in the electronics and precision machinery industries. The use of market shares allows for direct measurement of firms' competitiveness at the product level where trade policy measures and investment decisions are taken. Comparison of DFI decisions in the EC and the US provides interesting insights into the role of trade policies, since there are important differences in the pattern of antidumping actions across products in the two regions. The analysis in this chapter also highlights the consequences of differences in antidumping law and practice between the EC and the US for the occurrence of tariff jumping DFI. It will be seen that EC antidumping provides much greater incentives for such DFI than US antidumping actions.

The issue of tariff jumping DFI is important in the present discussion about antidumping measures in general and EC trade policies more specifically. Although it is undisputed that theoretically antidumping actions may induce 'tariff jumping' DFI, it has been suggested that the actual importance of EC trade policies for Japanese DFI has been limited, or at best unsubstantiated (Thomsen 1993, Thomsen and Nicolaides 1991). The argument is that Japanese firms' DFI, rather than a mere response to trade policies, reflects the diminished attractiveness of Japan as a production location for mature products. The results presented in this chapter go some way to settle this empirical issue: antidumping measures, in addition to customs tariffs and quantitative restrictions, are found to have a significant and substantial effect on Japanese firms' DFI. In contrast, there is no indication that the maturity of products exerts an important influence on DFI in the EC and the US.

The remainder of this chapter is organised as follows. The next section discusses US and EC antidumping and other trade policies targeting Japanese electronics firms. Differences between the US and EC antidumping systems are highlighted to derive hypotheses concerning the relationship between antidumping actions and DFI. Descriptive statistics on Japanese electronics firms' manufacturing investment in the US and the EC for the 35 products are provided. Section 6.3 develops a simple oligopoly model based on the analysis in Chapter 3 to relate DFI decisions to trade policy measures and firm and industry characteristics. Section 6.4 describes the data and empirical model, and Section 6.5 presents the empirical results. Section 6.6 concludes and discusses implications of the findings.

6.2 Antidumping and Other Trade Restrictions in the US and the EC

Although antidumping law and practice in the US and the EC are both based on the GATT antidumping code, there are substantial differences between the two systems. It is important to discuss such differences at some length where they may lead to different responses by Japanese firms to US and EU antidumping actions. Before the antidumping systems of the EC and the US are discussed in Section 6.2.2, an overview of antidumping actions against Japanese electronics firms is provided in the next section. Other EC and US trade barriers for Japanese electronics exporters such as tariffs are considered in Section 6.2.3. Lastly, in Section 6.2.4 trade restrictions are compared with the pattern of Japanese manufacturing investment for the 35 electronics goods to view the possible linkages between trade policy and DFI.

6.2.1 EC and US Antidumping Actions against Japanese Electronics Firms

The EC Commission has taken antidumping measures against a range of Japanese electronics exports since the early 1980s. Since antidumping measures in the EC targeting Japanese electronics firms were discussed in detail in Chapter 1 and a list of trade policy measures was provided in Table 1.3, no further comments are necessary here.

A list of US antidumping actions and other trade policy measures targeting Japanese electronics exports is provided in Table 6.1. US antidumping actions against Japanese electronics firms have a longer history than EC antidumping actions and go back to the well documented 1968 CTV case (see Schwartzman 1993, Gregory 1986, and Chapter 2). Substantial dumping margins were found for most firms; these were published in 1971. Sony was the first Japanese firm to set up US assembly activities in 1972, followed by Matsushita in 1974.[1] Because of procedural problems, duties were not levied until March 1978. The Orderly Market Agreement concluded in 1978 relieved the Japanese firms of paying further retroactive duties, but did not

Table 6.1 US trade policy targeting Japanese electronics exports

Orderly Market Agreement (OMA)			
Period	*Products*		
1978–1981	CTVs		
1986–	Semiconductors		
Punitive tariff			
Period	*Products*	*Tariff (%)*	
1987–1991	PCs, CTVs	100	
Antidumping			
Start investigation	*Product*	*Decision*	*Cancellation*
1968	CTVs	duties	—
1969	Large power transformers	duties	—
1969	Tuners for consumer electronics	duties	1994
1972	Microwave ovens	no dumping	1972
1975	Tantalum capacitors	no injury	1976
1979	Microwave ovens	duties	1980
1979	Electric motors	duties, undertakings	—
1979	Electric typewriters	duties	1994
1981	Satellite broadcasting equipment	duties	—
1982	Pagers	duties	—
1983	Cell site transceivers	duties	1989
1984	Mobile cellular phones	duties	—
1985	64KB DRAMs	duties, undertakings*	—
1985	EPROMs	duties, undertakings*	—
1985	256KB DRAMs	duties, undertakings*	—
1986	Cathode ray tubes	duties	—
1988	3.5 microdisks	duties	—
1988	Digital readout systems	no injury	1989
1988	Thermostats for heaters	no injury	1989
1988	Power transmission tools	no dumping	1989
1989	Business telephone systems (PBX)	duties	—
1989	Laser scattering instruments	duties	—
1990	Flat panel displays	duties	1993
1990	Word processors	duties	1994
1991	Commercial microwave ovens	no dumping	1991
1992	Power tools	duties	—

* US–Japan Semiconductor Trade Agreement: antidumping actions have been suspended since its conclusion in 1986.

** Retaliatory tariff under Section 301 of the US Trade Act imposed on certain CTVs and 16-bit computers after non-compliance of Japan with the Semiconductor Trade Agreement.

Sources: See Appendix 6.1.

lead to the cancellation of the antidumping action.[2] During 1977–1979, all remaining major exporters set up manufacturing plants in the US: Sanyo in 1977, Mitsubishi and Toshiba in 1978, Sharp and Hitachi in 1979. Two firms followed several years later: Japan Victor Company (JVC) in 1982 and Orion in 1986. The antidumping measures for CTVs were still in place in 1994 and have been extended to cover projection CTVs and liquid crystal display (LCD) CTVs in the late 1980s. In addition, CTVs were hit by retaliatory tariffs under Section 301 of the US Trade Act in 1987, when US authorities concluded that Japan had not complied with the US–Japan Semiconductor Trade Agreement.

Compared with EC antidumping cases listed in Table 1.3, US antidumping actions include fewer consumer electronics and office machinery products and more (heavy) electrical equipment (power transformers, electric motors, power tools) and telecommunications equipment (satellite broadcasting equipment, pagers, cell site transceivers, mobile cellular phones, business telephone systems). Microwave ovens, electric typewriters, semiconductors, mobile phones, and computer microdisks have been subject to antidumping actions in both the EC and the US. Three separate cases were initiated against microwave oven imports from Japan. The first investigation in 1972 did not find evidence of dumping. The second in 1979 found significant dumping margins only for Toshiba. Before the outcome of this investigation was published, export leader Sharp had already established a manufacturing plant in the US (Gregory 1986). The petition was withdrawn in 1980.[3] The third case, covering only commercial microwave ovens, was cancelled after a finding of no injury.

6.2.2 Antidumping Law and Practice in the US and the EC: Implications for Tariff Jumping DFI

Antidumping law and practices in the US and EC have been described and discussed in detail in the economic and legal literature (e.g. Van Bael and Bellis 1990, Jackson and Vermulst 1990, Finger 1992, Destler 1992, Boltuck and Litan 1991, Tharakan 1991b). Given that both the US and EC antidumping systems are based on the GATT code, the number and substance of differences in law and practice between the two jurisdictions is remarkable. In this section those characteristics of US and EC antidumping systems are discussed that are likely to have an impact on the decision by Japanese exporters to invest in the EC or the US. It will be argued that an antidumping action in the EC provides a greater inducement for tariff jumping DFI than a comparable antidumping action in the US.

The US and EC antidumping systems have gained popularity with domestic industries since 1979, when both jurisdictions changed the antidumping law to incorporate the provisions of the GATT antidumping code negotiated in the Tokyo Round. Under the Tokyo Round antidumping code, a domestic industry may petition for and get relief from imports if two conditions are met. First, the imports must be sold at a price that is less than the 'normal value',[4] where 'normal value' can be defined as either the price in the exporter's home market or the fully allocated production cost. Second, the dumped imports must be found to cause 'material injury' to the domestic industry, where 'material injury' is defined as 'harm which is not immaterial or inconsequential' (Destler 1992: 149). It is the injury criterion that was importantly relaxed in the 1979 US and EC antidumping law revisions. Prior to 1979, it was required that dumped imports must be the 'principal cause' of injury to the industry (Van Bael and Bellis 1990: 204). In practice, injury findings became much more common after 1979 both in US and EC antidumping investigations while the number of yearly petitions under antidumping law increased sharply.[5]

Since 1979, both the EC and the US have on several occasions changed antidumping practice or made amendments to their antidumping laws, usually to the benefit of petitioners. The discussion here will focus on antidumping practice during the 1980s, since most antidumping cases against Japanese electronics firms were field after 1979.[6]

Institutions Before discussing substantive and practical differences between the US and EC antidumping systems, it is useful to consider the differences in the institutions administering the antidumping system. In the EC a single institution, the Commission of the European Communities, has a predominant role in the antidumping process. The Commission receives a complaint, decides whether to proceed with it, carries out the investigation into whether dumping and injury have occurred, and has the power to set provisional duties. On the other hand, the Commission has to hear comments of the Council of Advisors, representing EC member states, during the investigation, and final antidumping duties ultimately have to be approved by the European Council of Ministers. Although it has been argued that the Council effectively rubber-stamps the Commission's proposals (Bellis 1990: 45–46), it would appear that the Commission formulates proposals to take the political and economic interests of the EC member states (and hence their voting behaviour) into account.[7]

In the US, the responsibility for the investigative process is split between the US Department of Commerce (DOC) and an independent agency, the International Trade Commission (ITC). The DOC receives the complaint and calculates dumping margins, while the ITC is solely responsible for the determination of whether 'material' injury occurred. In the case of a positive dumping finding by the DOC and a positive injury finding by the ITC, the DOC issues the antidumping order.

It has been argued that, since under the EC system dumping and injury are examined in tandem, it is conceivable that a positive finding for one may bias the investigation towards a positive finding for the other (Bellis 1990: 84). In practice, cases where dumping but no injury is found are very few in the EC, while in the United States the ITC has given a negative determination of injury in more than 40 per cent of dumping cases (Destler 1992: 241).[8]

Prospective v. *retrospective duties* Probably the most important difference between the EC and US antidumping systems is the way antidumping duties are levied. In the US antidumping system, duties are levied retrospectively (see Horlick 1990). After the Department of Commerce finds dumping and the International Trade Commission finds injury, no duties as such are levied but exporters are required to make cash deposits. These deposits are an estimate of the duties the exporters would have to pay based on the calculated dumping margin and past export volume. Actual payable duties, however, are calculated in a review one year later, based on the actual shipping volume in that year and a calculation of the actual dumping margin for such shipments. If no dumping is found in the review, the exporter will get a full refund, including interest, of the cash deposit. Hence, the US operates a *duty avoidance* antidumping system, providing incentives to exporters to raise prices and avoid paying duties.[9] Antidumping actions are directed at avoiding future harm to the US industry. This is possible because the DOC and ITC complete the first investigation within several months, limiting harm to the industry by dumped imports prior to the antidumping order.

In the EC antidumping system, on the other hand, duties are levied on a prospective basis (Vermulst 1990). If the EC Commission finds dumping and injury in its investigation, duties are set which apply to all future exports until the antidumping order expires. Although in theory exporters are able to apply for a review after one year and exporters are able to claim refunds if they can show they are not dumping, in practice neither the refund nor the review system functions effectively.[10] Hence, the EC system is best characterised as a *duty payment* system: antidumping duties punish exporters for past dumping and are in effect very similar to conventional tariffs (Bellis 1990: 61). Give that the EC Commission usually takes more than 18 months to reach a provisional antidumping decision, this is understandable, since most harm to the EC industry will already have been done once the order is issued.

The prospective character of the duties does have important consequences for exporters' responses, because such duties do not provide much disincentive for future dumping. On the contrary, if an exporter raises its price, it will have to pay higher duties given that duties are set as a percentage of price (Van Bael 1990: 406). This situation may have led the EC to adapt the antidumping law in 1988 to include the 'anti-absorption clause', which specifies that exporters are required to increase prices to the extent of the duty and are not allowed to 'absorb' the duty. If exporters do not increase prices, the domestic industry can petition for an investigation in which the duty will be treated as a cost for the exporter in calculating dumping margins. If the exporter is found to have 'absorbed' the duty, further (retroactive) duties can be levied. The anti-absorption clause has been invoked only twice in case of Japanese electronics firms: CD players in 1991 and electronics scales in 1994. The former petition was withdrawn and results in the latter case are not yet known, so it is too early to determine the effects of the clause. Given that the initial antidumping order works against price adjustment, it is certainly conceivable that the prospect of further duties under the clause will only be perceived as an increased 'tariff barrier'.

Co-operation and legal fees If a Japanese firm is the target of an antidumping investigation, it will be required to submit detailed information on exports, domestic sales, costs, and prices. Preparing this information is costly, and under the US system most of the, possibly strategic, data will be passed on to US petitioners. In order to increase the chances of a favourable decision, firms in practice need to seek legal advice and representation. Hence, firms have to incur a non-trivial (mostly fixed) cost in their attempt to limit the damage of antidumping actions by co-operating with antidumping authorities.[11]

If an exporter provides insufficient information or fails to co-operate, both the EC Commission and the US Department of Commerce assign a duty which corresponds to the highest antidumping margin calculated for any of the responding firms. Although this generally gives exporters strong incentives to co-operate, there may be cases in which firms choose not to do so in order to avoid the cost of co-operation and legal representation. For small exporters, the cost of co-operation may well be too high compared with export revenues. They may opt not to co-operate and, if high duties are imposed, may stop exporting.[12] Large exporters may choose to avoid paying duties by investing in local manufacturing at an early stage, in which case there is not much to gain from co-operation.[13]

The implication for empirical research is that the level of duties assigned to individual exporters cannot be taken as an exogenous trade barrier to which the firms respond. In the case of US antidumping actions, actual duty levels depend on the price adaptation strategy of the firm. In addition, in both the EC and US systems, dumping duties depend on the decision whether to co-operate fully with the antidumping authorities or not.

Duration of antidumping measures Since 1984, the EC applies a 'sunset' provision to its antidumping measures. Barring any reviews, the duties decided upon in the final determination apply throughout a period of five years. After the five year period, the antidumping measures expire unless the EC industry petitions for a 'sunset review' of the case, and dumping and injury are again established. Under US antidumping law, there is no sunset clause.[14] Antidumping actions can last almost indefinitely, as long as the domestic industry resists revocation.[15] Antidumping measures in the case of CTVs and large power transformers, for instance, have been in force for more than 25 years. In the CTV case, the antidumping action has over the years been extended to cover projection televisions and liquid crystal display (LCD) televisions, which were considered to fall within the scope of the existing antidumping ruling. Duties, however, may vary considerably over the years under the retrospective duty system with annual reviews.[16]

Determination of dumping duties Before duties are determined, the antidumping authorities calculate the dumping margin, i.e. the difference between the 'normal value' and the export price. The 'normal' value is the price charged in the home market of the exporter if representative price data are available. The GATT code proscribes that comparison between export price and 'normal value' has to be made at the ex-factory level. Since reliable ex-factory price data are not available, these have to be calculated from other price data. This is done by taking the price charged to the first independent buyer (both for exports and for domestic sales) and subtracting taxes and costs ('netting back'). The dumping margin is then calculated as the amount to which the 'normal' value (the home market price) exceeds the export price. Most observers of antidumping practice argue that margin calculations in both the US and the EC are 'tilted' towards a finding of dumping (e.g. Van Bael and Bellis 1990, Hindley 1988, Boltuck and Litan 1991, Finger 1992). However, there is at least one reason to suggest that such 'tilts' are stronger in the case of EC antidumping practice, in particular where antidumping actions concern Japanese electronics exporters.

Since the large Japanese electronics firms are integrated firms, selling through related wholesalers and retailers in Japan and through related importers and wholesalers in the EC, the first sales to independent parties is often to consumers (in Japan) or retailers (in the EC). In theory this is no problem, since the cost incurred by the related wholesalers and retailers can be deducted to get the ex-factory price. However, in the first important antidumping case involving Japanese electronics firms (the 1985 electric typewriter case), the Commission changed its calculation method for the home market price. Since 1985, the Commission has not allowed any deduction for overheads, general administrative and indirect selling expenses of related wholesalers and retailers in the home market (Van Bael and Bellis 1990, Bellis 1990: 70–75, Bell 1987, Didier 1990). Since all such costs are deducted in case of exports, this introduces a bias towards higher dumping margins.[17] The US has also restricted such indirect expenditure deductions in the case of related distribution firms in the home country, arguing that deductions are easily manipulated by the exporters. However, such restrictions have been much less drastic: the Department of Commerce can put a 'cap' on such deductions if they exceed the deductions made for the export price (Horlick 1990: 145).

In many antidumping cases in both the US and the EC, 'normal value' is not calculated based on sales prices in the home market. The GATT code allows 'normal value' to be calculated on the basis of fully allocated costs if home market sales are judged not to be 'in the ordinary course of trade', which often implies that home market prices are judged to be below cost.[18] The problem here is that the calculation of 'normal value' based on fully allocated cost requires numerous assumptions concerning 'reasonable' amounts of general administrative expenses and profits (Van Bael and Bellis 1990: 302), which gives antidumping authorities substantial discretion in determining dumping margins. Horlick (1990: 124) argues that the DOC however tends to follow rather rigid guidelines. In contrast, it has been argued that the EC Commission has used its discretion to introduce calculation methods which have raised antidumping margins.[19]

Another difference between the US and the EC antidumping systems concerns the determination of dumping duties. In the US case, dumping duties are simply equal to the calculated dumping margins. In the EC, on the other hand, the dumping duty set may be lower than the calculated dumping margin if a lower duty is sufficient to take away the injury caused to the domestic industry. The EC Commission appears to have an important degree of discretion in calculating this injury-based dumping duty. In some cases, it appears that the practice has partly offset the bias introduced in the margin calculated for integrated Japanese firms, but on the whole, dumping duties based on the 'injury' criterion have been substantial (Bellis 1990).

Anti-circumvention There are two major ways in which firms may try to avoid paying antidumping duties: by establishing a manufacturing plant in a third country and exporting from there, or by establishing a manufacturing plant in the country that imposed the antidumping duties (tariff jumping DFI). Both the US and the EC have taken measures against such circumvention of antidumping measures.

Third country anti-circumvention actions follow two routes. First, the EC Commission as well as the DOC have authority to include exports from third countries in the scope of an antidumping measure. The GATT code suggests that, if the product is not altered in a major way by the operations in the third country, third country exports can be considered 'like products', i.e. to fall within the scope of the existing antidumping order. Prior to 1988, the DOC has included third country exports in the investigation on an *ad hoc* basis.[20] Since the 1988 US Omnibus Trade and Competitiveness Act, third country exports can automatically be included if the value added in third countries is 'small'. The EC Commission has mostly used *rules of origin* to determine if exports from a third country fall within the scope of the antidumping ruling.[21] The GATT-conform rule of origin is not specific, stating that a product should be considered to originate in a country if the 'last substantial process' is performed in that country. The EC Commission has in the past adopted several product-specific rules of origin to clarify the general rule. For example, in case of televisions, the EC rule requires a value added of 45 per cent to confer origin. In at least one case (copyers from Japan), the EC Commission decided to introduce a new product-specific rule of origin, tailor-made to bring exports by Japanese firms from a third country (the US in this case) into the scope of the antidumping duty.[22]

It is important to note that the extension of dumping measures to imports from third countries through the application of rules of origin or the 'small operations' criteria is automatic to the extent that no evidence has to be submitted that third country imports are dumped and causing injury. The extension of antidumping duties to third country imports is not automatic in case of a second anti-circumvention measure: the opening of a new investigation concerning the imports from third countries. In this case a petition has to be filed by the domestic industry, and dumping and injury have to be established again. In US antidumping practice, a specific anti-circumvention investigation is opened focusing on third country manufacturing plants of firms found dumping from their home country in the original investigation. In EC antidumping practice there is no such specific third country circumvention investigation, but, if petitioned for, a new investigation into dumping from those third countries is opened (which may also include exporting firms based in those third countries only). In substance, the US and EC actions do not differ. The US Department of Commerce has investigated four cases of alleged circumvention of antidumping orders by Japanese electronics firms (colour televisions in 1980, colour cathode ray tubes in 1990, typewriters in 1991, and word processors in 1992), but none of these led to affirmative action. The EC Commission initiated antidumping investigations with reference to possible circumvention by Japanese firms only once (CD players in 1991), and here the petition was eventually withdrawn. Antidumping cases against exporters from South-East Asian countries including Japanese affiliates were initiated at least three times (small screen colour televisions (1988), electronic weighing scales (1992), and colour televisions (1992)). Here all cases led to the imposition of duties.

While there appear no substantial differences between the US and the EC in the treatment of third country circumvention, a major disparity occurs in the handling of circumvention through tariff jumping DFI. Prior to 1987, the reliance by the EC Commission on rules of origin effectively meant that it had no provision to stop this kind of circumvention.[23] To remedy this situation it introduced the 'screwdriver plant' amendment in June 1987 (see also Chapter 1). Broadly speaking, the amendment states that the domestic industry can petition for an anti-circumvention investigation, and duties can be extended to products assembled in the EC plants, if more than 40 per cent of components are imported from the investing firm's home country. Seven petitions, all targeting Japanese firms, were filed under this amendment until a GATT Panel ruling against it led the Commission to suspend further actions. Since most Japanese firms had already committed themselves to EC manufacturing before the 1987 change in the law, and since withdrawal was costly, the anti-circumvention measures do not appear to have discouraged investments. The EC Commission in practice administered the 'screwdriver plant' amendment as a local content rule, in all cases accepting settlements without duties if the plants reduced their components imports (Bellis 1990: 59). Almost all Japanese firms chose to avoid paying duties by reducing their dependence on components imported from Japan and by increasing the value of components sourced in the EC.

In contrast with the EC Commission, the DOC has used a flexible definition of 'like' product to include subassemblies and major components in the scope of antidumping orders. Prior to 1988, this was done on an *ad hoc* basis (as with third country imports). There are at least two cases involving Japanese electronics firms in which the DOC extended the antidumping order to subassemblies: cell site transceivers (1984) and mobile cellular phones (1984). In these cases dumping duties were applied to imported subassemblies from Japan without investigating whether such subassemblies were dumped injuriously as well.[24] With the 1988 Omnibus Trade and Competitiveness Act, this practice was formalised, and antidumping orders can be extended to components and subassemblies if 'tariff jumping' circumvention is deemed likely.

In conclusion, US practice in the case of 'tariff jumping' circumvention will make the establishment of assembly operations in the US less attractive for Japanese firms, while anti-circumvention actions in the EC appear not to have effectively discouraged investment.

Discretion In terms of discretion allowed to antidumping authorities in the determination of dumping cases, the EC and the US antidumping systems are at opposing ends (Vermulst 1990: 441). The EC has considerable discretion in handling antidumping cases at various stages in the investigation and determination. The EC Commission decides whether to accept a petition, in a process that is undisclosed. It has, as shown above, interpreted the GATT code and its own antidumping laws liberally in the calculation of dumping margins. Even more room for discretion is available in the injury determination where neither the GATT code nor EC antidumping law provides for detailed cirteria. If injury is found, the

Commission may then use the injury calculations to set dumping duties lower than the dumping margins. In theory, the Commission can also decide not to levy duties where antidumping actions are not in the 'Community interest', a concept that is not further defined in EC antidumping law.[25] The Commission has been reluctant to disclose all its calculations; nor does it operate a system of disclosure of confidential information submitted by petitioners and exporters, such that antidumping decisions lack transparency. It is apparent that the discretionary character of antidumping investigations has allowed industrial policy considerations to influence antidumping decisions (see Chapter 1 and GATT 1993). In particular, the EC appears to have used the antidumping instrument to deal with the 'Japan problem': the advance of Japanese firms in high technology markets of the EC and the increasing bilateral trade deficit. Although the Commission has broad independent powers in conducting antidumping investigations, there is evidence that the political and economic interests of the different member states can have an important bearing on the final shape of antidumping measures.[26]

In contrast with EC antidumping practice, US antidumping decisions are generally reached by the application of detailed technical rules. Antidumping is often referred to as the 'technical track' of protection (Feinberg and Kaplan 1990). There is in practice no undisclosed preselection process as in the EC. The decisions on dumping and injury are made by separate institutions, the DOC and the ITC, respectively. The ITC is a bipartisan committee in which Commissioners serve for seven years. It appears to reach decisions relatively independently from political interests and the direct influence of Congress and government.[27] Although frequent disagreements between individual ITC Commissioners, and the fact that individual Commissioners show consistent biases against or for injury findings, suggest there is still considerable room for interpretation of the rules (Horlick 1990: 158), the injury determination is considered much more rule-based than in the EC, resulting in a greater number of negative decisions.[28] Also, the US decision process is relatively transparent, since relevant data on dumping decisions, including submissions of exporters, are provided to all parties.[29] The Department of Commerce is required to apply duties equal to the rate of the dumping margin and has no leeway to change antidumping decisions where these would harm other parties.[30]

The implication is that Japanese firms, confronted with an antidumping investigation, will find the US procedure relatively predictable, while greater uncertainty and the possibility of politically motivated outcomes surrounds EC investigations. This conceivably makes reliance on exports a more risky strategy in EC antidumping cases.

US and EC antidumping and tariff jumping DFI How do EC and US antidumping actions affect the decision by Japanese firms to invest in local manufacturing? The differences between the US and EC antidumping systems discussed above suggest that the EC system provides fewer incentives to continue exports, and greater incentives to jump antidumping duties by setting up local manufacturing plants, than the US antidumping system. The prospective duty system increases the cost of exports and works as a disincentive to raising prices, whereas in the US raising export prices reduces payable duties. The start of an antidumping investigation inflicts greater potential harm to Japanese exporters in the EC than in the US, given the likely greater 'tilts' towards positive dumping and injury findings in the EC. Moreover, the EC has shown that any discretion available to the EC Commission in antidumping investigations can be used to the detriment of Japanese exporters. Under both EC and US antidumping practices, exporting from third countries may not avoid paying duties, but restrictions on tariff jumping DFI have not been as effective in the EC. Although EC actions are limited to a period of five years, while revocation of antidumping measures in the US is difficult, duties cannot be reduced during the period as in the US. Likewise, the fact that the EC Commission may set duties lower than the calculated dumping margin will not bear much assurance, given the discretion the Commission has in determining the duties.

It follows that the start of an antidumping investigation in the EC constitutes a bigger threat to Japanese exporters and provides greater incentives for tariff jumping DFI than a comparable antidumping investigation in the US. In both cases the effect on DFI is expected to be greater in affirmative cases when the threat of antidumping duties has materialised. However, firms may choose to invest before the actual (and possibly negative) dumping determination if they estimate that the chance of affirmative action is high. Given that it may require time to arrange for local production, deciding on investment after the duties are imposed will mean that the firm will still be forced to pay duties during a transitory period while it relies on exports.

The level of duties may give an indication of the extent of the barrier to exports and the incentive for DFI, but duties are problematic indicators where firms choose not to co-operate. Moreover, in the US, the retrospective character of the antidumping duties makes any dumping duty determined in the investigation an unreliable measure of actual duties faced by exporters. The empirical analysis will therefore simply focus on the effect of (affirmative) antidumping actions on investment decisions.

Anticipatory DFI The mere existence of antidumping legislation will affect Japanese firms' behaviour and may induce anticipatory behaviour. The possibility of antidumping action will arise if exports serve a substantial part of the EC or US markets and if dumping margins are likely to be found. Given the continuous appreciation of the yen and possible biases in margin calculations and injury determinations, positive dumping and injury findings are not easily ruled out. Japanese firms increasing their presence in EC and US markets where local competitors are also vying for market share will in many cases anticipate antidumping actions.[31] Japanese firms may increase prices to reduce the likelihood of antidumping actions or dumping findings. However, the most certain way to avoid harmful consequences of antidumping actions is to reduce export volume drastically and replace exports by local production.[32]

Anticipatory investment can have important advantages over tariff jumping investment (which takes place after the antidumping action has been initiated). Waiting for antidumping actions to materialise may imply paying antidumping duties in a transitory period while preparing for local production. Moreover, after positive findings of dumping and injury, dumping duties may be extended to imported parts (in the US), or local manufacturing activities may be affected by local content requirements (in the EC during 1987–1990). Avoiding a positive finding of dumping and injury has the benefit of avoiding these cost increasing measures which target the firms' overseas manufacturing activities.[33]

Anticipatory DFI by Japanese electronics firms does not appear to have been important until the end of the 1980s. Most manufacturing investment in the EC and the US took place at the time of antidumping investigations (see Chapter 1). However, from the late 1980s, it appears that Japanese firms have been more actively anticipating antidumping measures and investing in manufacturing plants in the absence of trade policy measures. The most obvious example is the wave of investment in facsimile production in the EC and the US in 1989–1990. (See also Section 6.2.4 below.) To what extent the threat of antidumping actions played a role here is difficult to assess, but the rapid growth in exports from Japan in the late 1980s, coupled with the presence of EC and US firms (Philips, Olivetti, Alcatel, Xerox) eager to establish a presence in this growing market, certainly made it a likely candidate for antidumping actions.

Modelling empirically the effects of antidumping threats would require the collection of detailed data on developments in US and EC production, imports, consumption, and price. Such data are not typically available at the product level and the task of accurately measuring the threat of antidumping measures is beyond the scope of the analysis in this chapter.[34] The empirical analysis will be limited to the effects of actual antidumping actions. The effects of these actual measures on DFI can be considered a lower bound of the effects of trade policy (threats) on DFI. The analysis does take into account other trade policy measures, which are described in the next section.

6.2.3 Tariffs and Other Trade Policy Measures

Electronics exports from Japan are subject to common tariffs, which are expected to affect DFI and export behaviour. Table 6.2 lists the pre-

Table 6.2 EC and US pre-Uruguay tariffs for 35 electronics products (%)

Product	EC tariff	US tariff
Audio and video equipment		
CRT CTVs	14.0	5.0
LCD CTVs	14.0	5.0
Projection CTVs	14.0	5.0
VCRs	14.0*	3.9
Camcorders	4.9	4.2
Headphone stereos	0.0*	3.7
Radio cassette players	0.0*	4.9
Stereo sets	14.0	4.9
CD players	9.5**	3.9
Laser disk players	4.0	3.7
Car audio	14.0	3.7
Audio tapes	4.9	4.2
Video tapes	4.9	4.2
Home electrical and electronic equipment		
Microwave ovens	5.1	4.0
Refrigerators	3.0	2.9
Washing machines	5.1	2.8
Airconditioners	5.3	2.2
Vacuum cleaners	4.0	3.4
Communication equipment		
Mobile phones	6.5	6.0
Pagers	12.0	6.0
Facsimiles	7.5	4.7
Telephone switching systems (PBXs)	7.5	8.5
Computers and peripherals		
PCs	4.9	3.9
Workstations	4.9	3.9
FDDs	4.9	3.7
HDDs	4.9	3.7
Dot matrix printers	4.9	3.7
Laser printers	4.9	3.7
Inkjet printers	4.9	3.7
3.5 microdisks	4.9	4.2
Other office machines		
Calculators	12.0	3.7
Copiers	7.2	3.7
Typewriters	4.6	2.2
Precision machinery		
Watches	3.0***	3.9
Cameras	7.2	3.0

* From 1986.

** Increased to 16.5% in 1987 and gradually brought back to 9.5% again in 1989.

*** Estimated from tariff set in value terms.

Sources: see Appendix 6.1.

Uruguay Round tariffs for the 35 electronics products that are included in the empirical analysis. For almost all products, EC tariffs exceed US tariffs. For several audio and video products, pagers, and calculators, the EC maintains double digit tariffs and the difference between them and US tariffs is substantial. US tariffs are higher only for headphone stereos, radio cassette players, and telephone switching systems (PBXs). For the former two products, the EC tariff was abolished in 1986 to compensate for the increase in the tariff for VCRs from 8 to 14 percent, in accordance with GATT rules (Kostecki 1989). In May 1989, the EC Commission proposed to the Customs Co-operation Council that it classify camcorders as VCRs, which would have increased the tariff to from 4.9 to 14 per cent, but this suggestion was finally rejected in 1991.[35] Both the EC and the US have relatively low and uniform tariffs for computers and peripherals. The only sector that is protected by relatively high tariffs in the US is communications equipment.

It can be observed that the sectors with the highest tariffs (audio and video equipment in the EC and communications equipment in the US) are also the sectors where antidumping actions have most frequently been initiated. This is natural, since the same import-competing industries that are able to form lobbies against moves to reduce tariffs in tariff negotiations (or to press for tariff increases, in the EC VCR case) will be more likely to utilise the antidumping instrument to seek protection from import competition. Tariff levels, in some crude way, may therefore also be an indicator for the likelihood of trade policy measures such as antidumping. This feature will be discussed further in Section 6.5.

Other, mostly quantitative, import restrictions on Japanese imports in the electronics sector have been discussed in Section 6.2.1 for the US and in Chapter 1 for the EC. Here it suffices to summarise the main import barriers for the products covered in the analysis. In the US, CTV imports have been restricted during 1978–1981 through an OMA, and a retaliatory tariff was slapped on CTVs and PCs in 1987 (Table 6.1). In the EC, CTV exports have been restricted by PAL licenees during the 1970s, through import quota and other restrictions at the national level in France, Italy, and Spain, and by way of an industry-to-industry VER during 1973–1985 in the UK. VCR imports from Japan have been restricted by a VER in 1983–1986, have been subject to restrictive import licences in France (GATT 1993, Tyson 1992), have been restricted by Spain (Kostecki 1989), and have been subject to a tariff increase in 1986. CD players faced a temporary tariff increase during 1987–1989, and hi-fi equipment (stereo sets) have been subject to national import restrictions in France, Italy, and Spain (Kostecki 1989, GATT 1988).

Trade policy threats Besides antidumping measures, tariffs, and other import barriers mentioned, there have been cases where a clear threat of import restrictions has not resulted in specific action. One example in the US in the short-listing of copying machines from Japan as a candidate for retaliatory tariffs under the Section 301 case involving Motorola's access to the Japanese mobile telecommunications equipment market.[36] An example in the EC is the proposed tariff increase for camcorders by the EC Commission mentioned above. There have been other 'signals' to Japanese firms that EC industry and the Commission were contemplating trade policy measures. For instance, in June 1991 EC President Delors held talks with representatives of the European computer industry, which was reportedly seeking 'high tariffs' on imported PCs.[37]

A more formal signal of the EC Commission's apprehension concerning Japanese imports is the implementation of retrospective or prior surveillance of imports (see Strange 1993: 96, 461). The Commission introduced retrospective monitoring of imports of CTVs, VCRs, hi-fi equipment, and quartz watches from Japan in 1983. (Most of these measures lasted until 1992.) Prior surveillance of imports was introduced for a short period in 1987 for CTVs and PCs, in response to the retaliatory tariff imposed on these goods by the United States.[38] There are however no specific actions the EC Commission can take if the monitored imports are increasing and it is unclear to what extent the measures are inviting export restraint.[39] In the second half of the 1980s, the cumulation of antidumping measures and the hotly debated threat of the creation of a 'fortress Europe' with the completion of the Internal Market in 1992 generally made Japanese firms perceptive of future trade barriers. This provided the background for manufacturing investments in products such as PCs and facsimile machines, which were not subject to specific import restrictions. As mentioned before, since it is almost impossible to measure the effects of trade policy threats, the analysis will be limited to actual trade policy measures.

6.2.4 US and EC Trade Policy and Japanese DFI: 35 Electronics Products

A first indication of the relationship between trade policy and Japanese manufacturing investment is provided in Table 6.3, which lists the number of Japanese producers, the number of firms that operated manufacturing plants in the US or EC in 1992, and US and EC trade policy measures for each of the 35 products in the analysis. For instance, in the case of conventional colour televisions with a cathode ray tube (CRT CTVs), 9 out of 17 Japanese producers operated a plant in either the US or the EC. Of these, 8 operated plants in both regions, and one additional firm operated a plant only in the US.

The relationship between EC trade policy measures and investment patterns is best illustrated by the cases of VCRs, CD players, stereo sets, dot matrix printers, and copiers. In the case of VCRs, 15 out 20 Japanese firms invested abroad, but 11 of these operated plants only in the EC. The differences are even stronger for CD players, where there is only one plant in the US versus 10 in the EC.[40] In the case of dot matrix printers there are 8 Japanese firms with a plant in Europe only, and in case of copiers this number is 4. Although trade restrictions in case of stereo sets are imposed by only 3 member states of the EC, there appears to be a relationship with Japanese firms' investment: 7 firms were manufacturing only in the EC.[41]

The effects of US trade policy measures is best illustrated by the cases of projection CTVs, pagers, and private branch telephone systems (PBXs). Six firms are producing projection CTVs in the US, whereas only one (Sony in Spain) assembles such CTVs in Europe.[42] There are no pager plants in the EC, while 3 firms set up manufacturing operations in the US, at least one of which responded directly to the imposition of antidumping duties.[43] In the case of PBXs, 7 firms produce in the US, but only one in the EC. In the case of personal computers, the relationship between the US retaliatory tariff and investment patterns seems less apparent: 3 firms set up plants only in the US, but another 5 in both the EC and the US. The timing of investment in the US, however, shows a relationship with the imposition of the retaliatory tariff: 5 of the US plants were established in 1987.

Table 6.3 Number of Japanese electronics firms with manufacturing plants in the EC and the US in 1992

Product	Number of firms					Trade policy	
	All firms	DFI firms	Only US	Only EC	Both	USA	EC
Audio and video equipment							
CRT CTVs	17	9	1	0	8	OMA, AD	VER[a], quota[b]
LCD CTVs	14	0	0	0	0	AD	—
Projection CTVs	8	7	6	0	1	AD	—
VCRs	21	15	1	11	3	—	VER, AD[c]
Camcorders	10	1	0	1	0	—	—
Walkmans	8	0	0	0	0	—	—
Radio cassette players	17	1	1	0	0	—	—
Stereo sets	18	10	1	7	2	—	quota[b]
CD players	23	11	1	10	0	—	AD, tariff[d]
Laser disk palyers	14	0	0	0	0	—	—
Car audio	18	9	2	3	4	—	—
Audio tapes	9	4	0	1	3	—	AD
Video tapes	9	5	0	0	5	—	—

Table 6.3 (*Continued*)

Product	Number of firms					Trade policy	
	All firms	DFI firms	Only US	Only EC	Both	USA	EC
Home electrical appliances							
Microwave ovens	10	6	0	2	4	AD	AD
Refrigerators	11	1	1	0	0	—	—
Washing machines	8	0	0	0	0	—	—
Airconditioners	11	5	1	2	2	—	—
Vacuum cleaners	8	2	1	0	1	—	—
Communication equipment							
Mobile phones	20	8	5	0	3	AD	AD
Pagers	13	3	3	0	0	AD	—
Facsimiles	26	11	4	4	3	—	—
PBXs	19	8	7	1	0	AD	—
Computers and peripherals							
PCs	18	8	3	1	4	Tariff[e]	—
Workstations	10	5	4	1	0	—	—
FDDs	17	4	2	1	1	—	—
HDDs	20	5	2	1	2	—	—
Dot matrix printers	20	13	1	8	4	—	AD
Laser printers	25	5	2	2	1	—	—
Inkjet printers	6	1	0	1	0	—	—
3.5 microdisks	17	8	4	0	4	AD	AD
Other office machines							
Calculators	7	0	0	0	0	—	—
Copiers	18	7	0	4	3	—	AD
Typewriters	12	6	1	3	2	AD	AD
Precision machinery							
Watches	6	2	0	0	2	—	—
Cameras	10	0	0	0	0	—	—
All products	**499**	**180**	**54**	**64**	**62**		

Notes: Number of firms excludes foreign-affiliated companies; AD = antidumping investigation.

[a] UK only.

[b] National restrictions administered by France, Italy, and Spain.

[c] Funai and Orion only.

[d] Temporary tariff increase.

[e] Temporary retaliatory 100% tariff.

Sources: see Appendix 6.1.

For a number of products, the absence of trade policy measures coincides with the (near) absence of Japanese investments: walkmans, radio cassette players, laser disk players, washing machines, inkjet printers, calculators, and cameras. On the other hand, there are other examples where investments do not coincide with trade policy measures: car audio, video tapes, facsimiles, workstations, FDDs, HDDs, and laser printers. In addition, there is one case, LCD CTVs, where an antidumping measure did not lead to Japanese investment.[44] In Section 6.5 it will be seen to what extent trade policy measures affect individual firms' investment decisions for the 35 products, controlling for other factors such as market size. The next section first presents a simple model of tariff jumping DFI which relates DFI decisions more generally to tariff barriers and firm and industry characteristics.

6.3 Tariff Jumping DFI in a Simple Oligopoly Model

In order to gain insight in the firm and industry characteristics affecting DFI decisions, the basic model of tariff jumping DFI in the Cournot duopoly case of Chapter 3 is extended to the oligopoly case. The model highly simplifies the role of antidumping measures by incorporating trade barriers as a simple duty levied on exports. Price adaptation in response to, or in anticipation of, antidumping measures is not considered.[45] The tariff is taken as an exogenous factor to which Japanese firms can respond by tariff jumping DFI. While simplifying the response to trade barriers, the model helps to bring out the basic industry and firm characteristics affecting the decision of export versus DFI, on which the empirical model in Section 6.4 can be based.

6.3.1 DFI v. *Exports*

Consider an industry in which N^* Japanese firms are active. The firms export to the foreign (US or European) market where N local rival firms are incumbent. Total market volume is $Q = Nq_i + N^*q_i^*$. Firms differ in their level of constant marginal costs, denoted by c_i for foreign firms and c_i^* for Japanese firms. Firms with lower marginal costs may be considered to possess firm-specific technological or organisational advantages based, for instance, on previous investment in research and development (R&D) activities. The firm-specific advantages can be transferred abroad in case of DFI: firms with lower costs in Japan are assumed to be able to produce at lower costs in the foreign country as well. For simplicity, firm-specific advantages are confined to cost reducing R&D, while the analysis abstracts from other advantages in the market place such as quality of the firm's products (vertical product differentiation) or horizontal product differentiation.

Assuming linear demand in the foreign country, the expression for profits of an individual Japanese exporting firm in Nash–Cournot equilibrium is:

$$(1)\quad \Pi_i^* = \frac{\left[a-\left(c_{i,E}^*+t\right)+\sum_{j=1}^{N^*}\left(c_{j,E}^*-c_{i,E}^*\right)+\sum_{i=1}^{N}\left(c_i-c_{i,E}^*-t\right)\right]^2}{b\left(N^T+1\right)^2}$$

where a suffix E denotes exports. Profits decline in the firm's (tariff) costs $(c_{i,E}^* + t)$ but are increasing in rival Japanese and foreign firms' marginal costs. Denoting the average marginal costs of Japanese firms and foreign firms by $\bar{c}_E^*$ and $\bar{c}_i$, respectively, equation (1) can be more conveniently written as:

$$(2)\quad \Pi_i^* = \frac{\left[a-\left(c_{i,E}^*+t\right)+N^*\left(\bar{c}_E^*-c_{i,E}^*\right)+N\left(\bar{c}-c_{i,E}^*-t\right)\right]^2}{b\left(N^T+1\right)^2}$$

Profits of an individual Japanese firm are higher (lower) if marginal costs are lower (higher) than the industry average in Japan and abroad. The tariff reduces profits directly by affecting the marginal cost of exporting, and indirectly by improving the relative cost position of foreign firms. Profits are higher the more concentrated the industry, and the larger the market (taking the inverse of b as a measure of market size).

If a Japanese firm decides to manufacture in the foreign country, it avoids paying the tariff, but marginal costs of production may be higher. It is assumed that the difference between marginal costs under export and marginal costs under DFI is equal for all Japanese firms. A Japanese firm's marginal costs under export reflect the firm's underlying technological capability. The increase or decrease in marginal costs under DFI will be mainly related to the availability and costs of production factors and intermediate inputs, which affects all firms in a similar way. Marginal costs of production abroad then can be written as $c_{i,E}^* + l$, where l is the increase in marginal costs arising from foreign locational disadvantages; l may be negative, in which case there are foreign locational advantages.

In case of DFI, Japanese firms also incur a fixed cost F of preparing for and setting up the production plant abroad. A large part of this fixed cost will be similar for all firms, based on land acquisition, construction cost, and machinery procurement. To some extent F will depend on the experience a firm has in marketing and manufacturing abroad; for instance, the cost of gathering information on investment locations, and possibly land and construction costs (if the production line can be set up in an existing manufacturing facility), will be lower for experienced firms. In the analysis the fixed cost will be treated as firm-specific: F_i.

Consider a situation in which all Japanese firms are exporting. The foreign country now increases the tariff. In equilibrium, a number of Japanese firms, N_F^* (the suffix F denotes DFI), decides to invest while N_E^* firms continue to export. Japanese firm i, considering investment in the foreign country, would obtain the following profits under DFI:

$$(3)\quad \Pi_{i,F}^* = \frac{\begin{bmatrix} a-\left(c_{i,E}^*+l\right)+N_E^*\left(\bar{c}_E^*-c_{i,E}^*-l+t\right) \\ +N_F^*\left(\bar{c}_E^*-c_{i,E}^*\right)+N\left(\bar{c}-c_{i,E}^*-l\right) \end{bmatrix}^2}{b\left(N^T+1\right)^2} - F_i$$

Profits are higher the lower the firm's marginal costs, the greater its cost advantage, if there are locational advantages abroad (l negative), the higher the tariff (hurting the competitiveness of the remaining exporting Japanese firms), the more concentrated the industry, the larger the foreign market, and the lower the fixed cost.

The firm will invest abroad only if the fixed cost can be recouped by a sufficient increase in variable profits. Hence, a necessary condition for DFI is that variable profits increase. Comparing (2) and (3), it can be easily seen that the difference in the term in brackets in the numerator is $(N^T - N_F^* + 1)(t - l)$: unsurprisingly, the firm is more likely to invest the higher the tariff and the greater the locational advantages of production abroad. If the term $t - l$ is negative, variable profits under DFI are lower than profits under export and DFI is not profitable. A positive tariff or locational advantage, constituting a decrease in the marginal costs of servicing the foreign market, is a necessary condition for DFI. Generally, the condition for profits to increase can be written as:

$$(4)\quad (t-l)\left(N^T-N_F^*+1\right)\left[(t-l)\left(N^T-N_F^*+1\right)+2b\left(N^T+1\right)\sqrt{\Pi_{i,E}^*}\right] > F_i b\left(N^T+1\right)^2$$

Given a positive term $t - l$, the firm is more likely to invest the higher its profits under exports (the smaller its marginal costs and the greater its marginal cost advantage over Japanese and foreign rivals), the larger the market, the smaller the fixed cost associated with DFI, and the more concentrated the industry. The likelihood that (4) holds and the firm chooses to invest then can be expressed as:

$$(5)\quad \text{Prob}\left(\text{DFI}_i^*\right) = f\left(c_{i,E}^{*^-}, \bar{c}_E^{*^+}, \bar{c}^+, t^+, l^-, F_i^-, N^{T-}, (1/b)^+\right)$$

6.3.2 Market Share in Japan and DFI

Equations (4) and (5) describe the conditions under which DFI occurs in terms of relative marginal costs, among other factors. Direct cost measures for individual firms are not available, but data are available on individual Japanese firms' market shares in Japan for individual products. In this section it will be shown that Japanese market shares under certain conditions can be considered a revealed measure of firm-specific (cost) advantages. Assume that there is an international oligopoly of foreign and Japanese firms but that the Japanese and foreign market are segmented (compare Brander and Krugman 1983). Foreign firms may export to the Japanese market if they can earn variable profits. Exporters' market shares and profits, however, are reduced because of import barriers in Japan, which for simplicity are assumed to translate to an extra unit export cost of t^*. If Nash–Cournot equilibrium prevails on the Japanese market, a Japanese firm's sales on the Japanese market is expressed as:

$$(6)\quad q_{i,J}^* = \frac{\left[a^* - c_{i,E}^* + N^*\left(\bar{c}_E^* - c_{i,E}^*\right) + N\left(\bar{c} + t^* - c_{i,E}^*\right)\right]}{b\left(N^T + 1\right)}$$

Market share of the Japanese firm is:

$$(7)\quad s_{i,J}^* = \frac{a^* - c_{i,E}^* + N^*\left(\bar{c}_E^* - c_{i,E}^*\right) + N\left(\bar{c} + t^* - c_{i,E}^*\right)}{N^T a^* - N^* \bar{c}_E^* - N\left(\bar{c} + t^*\right)}$$

Market share is higher the smaller marginal costs, the greater the cost advantage of the firm relative to Japanese and foreign firms, the higher the import barrier t^*, and the smaller the total number of firms active in the market. Thus, a Japanese firm's market share in Japan can be taken as a revealed measure of the firm's cost advantage, adjusted for the number of rival firms active in the market and import barriers on the Japanese market. Expression (5) is rewritten as:

(8) $$\text{Prob}\left(\text{DFI}_i^*\right) = f\left(s_{i,J}^{*\,+}, t^+, l^-, F_i^-, (1/b)^+\right)$$

with:

$$s_{i,J}^* = F\left(c_{i,E}^{*\,-}, \bar{c}_E^{*\,+}, \bar{c}^+, N^{T^-}, t^{*+}\right)$$

The relationship between firm-specific cost advantages relevant for the DFI decision and Japanese market shares is not perfect. Japanese firms' market shares in Japan are higher the higher the import tariff t^*. If import barriers in Japan are high, market shares will overestimate Japanese firm's cost advantage over foreign firms. The possible consequences of this potential bias in Japanese market share data will be discussed below.

6.4 Empirical Model and Data

To examine the effect of antidumping and other trade policy measures on individual Japanese firms' investment decisions, a micro-level database was constructed of Japanese firms' market shares in Japan and plant establishments in the US and the EC. The scope of the analysis was widened to Europe (including countries of the European Free Trade Area or EFTA) and North America (including Canada and Mexico). EFTA markets are often serviced from plants in the EC such that the Western European market is most relevant for investment decisions. In Mexico, plants are often managed from across the border and set up to supply the US market. In practice, none of the 35 products in the analysis is produced in EFTA countries or Canada but not in the EC, or the US, respectively, while Mexican plants added only three investment observations.[46] Detailed notes on data sources and data construction are provided in Appendix 6.1.

The database covers the 35 electronics products listed in Table 6.3. Only final goods are included to focus on products with comparable marketing channels. Direct foreign investments by components suppliers are likely to be influenced by subcontractor relationships within vertical *keiretsu* and the presence of captive markets if parent firms have set up assembly plants abroad (see Chapter 5).[47] This would complicate the task of finding indicators of the relevant market size; the limitation to final goods allows for the use of more readily available consumer sales data. The 35 products also have in common that the manufacturing process is of the assembly type. Assembly operations can be relocated abroad at relatively low cost while the differences in setup costs are likely to be small across products. The product approach allows for precise measurement of the effects of antidumping actions which often target specific products or even product subclasses (such as dot matrix printers). Nearly one in two products have been targeted by trade policy measures in either the EC or the US (Table 6.3).

For each product, Japanese manufacturers were identified based on Japanese electronics industry data and Japanese market share data. Foreign-owned firms such as Japan IBM, Fuji Xerox, and Marantz (owned by Philips) were excluded from the list. This resulted in a comprehensive list of Japanese producers for each product, including smaller privately held firms. It was then determined whether the firms had set up manufacturing plants for the products in the US or the EC using product-level foreign investment data from several sources. Plants in operation in 1992 were counted. The result was a total of 499 firm–product combinations, with manufacturing investment in either the US or EC recorded 180 times (Table 6.3). The number of investments in the EC comes out as slightly higher than in the US: investments in both regions occurred 62 times, investment in only the EC 64 times, while investment in only the US occurred 54 times. The number of individual firms included in the database is 131 (out of which 29 are privately held), which implies that on average each firm is manufacturing 4 products. For each firm and product, data were collected on market shares held in Japan in 1990–1991.

6.4.1 Empirical Model and Explanatory Variables

The empirical model should explain the decision of Japanese firm i producing product j to set up manufacturing operations in region x, where $x \in (US, EC)$. A logit model is used to relate the probability that a firm has invested in a manufacturing plant to firm, product, and region characteristics.[48] Adding product and region indices to condition (8) gives:

$$\text{(9)} \quad \text{Prob}\left(\text{DFI}^{*}_{i,j,x}\right) = \frac{\exp(\alpha + \beta X)}{1 + \exp(\alpha + \beta X)}$$

$$\text{with} \quad X = \left(s^{*+}_{i,j}, t^{+}_{j,x}, l^{-}_{j,x}, F^{-}_{i,j,x}, (1/b)^{+}_{j,x} \right)$$

Market shares in Japan are firm- and product-specific. Fixed investment costs are firm- and region-specific, as argued above, and may vary across products as well. Trade barriers and market size are product- and region-specific but do not differ across individual firms. Locational (dis)advantages reflect mostly macroeconomic, region-specific, factors, yet these may affect investment decisions differently across products. It is assumed that investment decisions are reached in a comparable manner in each product sector, such that one coefficient can be estimated for each independent variable.

Two different market share variables (s^*_{ij}) are included in the analysis owing to the fact that precise market shares are not available for smaller players in the Japanese market. *SHARE5* is a dummy variable which takes the value 1 if the firm has more than 5 per cent of the Japanese market in 1990–1991 and 0 otherwise. *SHARE* measures the actual market share where it is greater than 5 percent. The advantage of using market shares is that direct measurement of firm-specific capabilities as they differ across products are considered, rather than using more 'generic' measures of firm-specific capabilities such as R&D and marketing intensity at the firm level. In the simple Cournot model presented in Section 6.3, market shares depend solely on individual firms' marginal cost advantage over rival firms. Although the theoretical model thus ignored that firms are also competing it terms of product quality and product differentiation based on investments and firm capabilities in marketing, service, and quality control, these dimensions should be reflected in market share data as well.

The use of Japanese market share data does introduce some potential biases in the analysis. Japanese market shares may not accurately measure Japanese firms' competitiveness *vis-à-vis* foreign firms if there are significant barriers to entry in the Japanese market, as discussed above.[49] This is not a problem in the empirical analysis as long as such barriers do not differ across products, but if they do, market shares will not be comparable across products. In practice, the number of cases where foreign firms hold substantial market shares in Japan is small. Products for which individual foreign firms hold a market share greater than 5 per cent are pagers and mobile phones (Motorola), personal computers (Apple and IBM), workstations (Hewlett Packard, Sun Microsystems), copiers (Xerox), and audio/video tapes and microdisks (3M). On the one hand, this will reflect the competitiveness of these (US) firms. On the other hand, the absence of foreign competitors in the consumer electronic and electrical appliance markets in Japan could be related to structural entry barriers in the Japanese market such as major firms' control over wholesaling and retailing.[50] More generally, individual Japanese firms' market shares in Japan also reflect investments in distribution and marketing which are specific to Japan. Matsushita's sales strength in a range of consumer electronics and electrical goods is partly related to its marketing strength which is due to its control over more than 25,000 retail outlets in Japan. Conversely, several latecomer firms in the Japanese consumer electronics industry such as Funai and Orion are only marginal players in the Japanese market but important suppliers in US and EC markets.

As a partial solution to these problems, regional export intensity is included in the analysis in addition to the market share variables. *EXPORT* expresses for each firm the 1992 value of exports to Europe and North America, respectively, as a percentage of total sales. Since *EXPORT* will be higher for those firms that direct more resources to US or EC markets relative to the home market, inclusion of this variable will correct for differences in region-specific marketing efforts. To the extent that *EXPORT* is lower for firms that rely solely on import barriers to maintain market share in Japan, the variable may also correct for the imperfection of market share indicators in this respect. Here however, the corrective power will be limited in the case where firms export a broad range of products.

Several indicators of trade policy measures are substituted for the tariff variable ($t_{j,x}$). First there is the conventional tariff barrier (*TARIFF*) as presented in Table 6.2. The effect of antidumping actions is measured by two variables. *AD* is a dummy variable which is assigned the value 1 if an antidumping investigation has been initiated in region *x* against Japanese imports of product *j*, and *AD_EUROPE* is a dummy variable which takes the value 1 if the antidumping investigation is initiated in the EC. Since EC antidumping measures, as hypothesised, provide greater incentives to tariff jumping DFI, *AD_EUROPE* is expected to have a positive sign. *AD* takes on the value 1 in all the antidumping cases mentioned in Table 6.3, except for CRT CTVs in the US and VCRs in the EC. In both the 1983 EC VCR case and the US CTV case, the antidumping action prepared the way for voluntary export restraints. Although it is impossible to disentangle the effects of the antidumping actions from the effects of the VERs, it is probably more adequate to assign the greatest magnitude to the VER.[51] In these cases, as well as the case of CRT CTVs in the EC,[52] the dummy variable *VER* is assigned the value 1. Two other region- and product-specific dummy variables are included. The variable *PCTARIFF* takes on the value 1 in case of personal computers in the US, to control for the 100 per cent tariff levied on Japanese imports in 1987. The variable *HIFIQUOTA* takes on the value 1 in case of stereo sets in the EC to correct for the effect of national quota in France, Italy, and Spain.

The variable *MARKET* is a measure of market size ($1/b$) in Europe and the US in 1991. In most cases, the most reliable data on market size were available in volume terms. To enable comparisons of market size across products, *MARKET* measures European or US market size as a percentage of the 'Triad' market (Europe, the US, and Japan).

Locational advantages ($l_{j,x}$) are expected to be largely related to macroeconomic factors and therefore region-specific. A simple dummy variable, *EUROPE*, is included, which is expected to be positive (negative) if the investment environment is more favourable in Europe (the US). One important reason why locational advantages may differ across products is that products differ in technological sophistication and in the extent to which manufacturing experience is accumulated. In accordance with Vernon's product cycle theory (Vernon 1979), production technologies are more easily transferred abroad and adapted to local conditions, and foreign locations are more likely to have cost advantages, if technologies and products are mature and relatively standardised. It has been argued that Japanese DFI in the US and Europe by and large follows this product cycle pattern (Thomsen 1993, Ozawa 1991). The variable *MATURE* is included to control for such effects. *MATURE* measures the number of years since the start of production in Japan for each product and is expected to be positively related to DFI.[53]

The fixed cost $F_{i,j,x}$ is not likely to differ much across products on the basis of plant setup costs since the products included in the analysis have in common that the assembly stage can be easily separated and transferred abroad.[54] To the extent that mature production techniques are more easily transferred and require less sophisticated machinery and schooling of local employees, *MATURE* should pick up part of this fixed cost effect. The firm-specific experience element in the fixed cost variable is expected to be picked up partly by the *EXPORT* variable. Firms that concentrate sales in a specific region will have acquired knowledge about the business environment which reduces the cost of preparing for manufacturing investment. *EXPORT* is thus expected to have a positive sign, both because of the fixed cost factor and as an indicator of overseas marketing intensity.

A additional explanatory variable is included to control for possible effects of membership of business groups on DFI decisions. Is has been shown that subcontractor firms within vertical business groups are, *ceteris paribus*, less likely to invest in the EC and the US. On the other hand, if the core firm has set up an extensive network of manufacturing plants abroad, subcontractor firms have an important incentive to establish plants abroad to supply the core firm.[55] In contrast, no evidence has been found that membership of a horizontal bank-centred business group affects Japanese DFI in developed countries. Since the present analysis is limited to final goods, the extra incentive to subcontractor firms to transfer production abroad to supply the core firm does not play a role. The sample does include manufacturers which sell part of their output directly to a core firm on an original equipment manufacturing (OEM) basis. It may be that such firms do not decide on their own internationalisation strategy: DFI decisions will be co-ordinated with the core firm in particular when the core firm is manufacturing the product as well. To control for this characteristic of firms, the variable *DEPENDENT* is included. *DEPENDENT* is a dummy variable which takes on the value 1 if firm *i* producing product *j* is member of a vertical business group under control by a core firm, if the core firm is a major customer, and if the core firm is producing product *j* as well. *DEPENDENT* is expected to have a negative effect on the DFI decision.

The dataset contains 499 product–firm combinations for two regions, which gives 998 observations for analysis. The number of observations had to be reduced, for two reasons. First, reliable data for the regional *EX-*

PORT variable were unavailable for some firms (48 observations). Second, in a relatively small number of DFI cases, the manufacturing plant was acquired by the Japanese firm through a take-over of a local manufacturer (21 observations). In the case of acquisitions, the DFI decision is expected to be fundamentally different from DFI in greenfield plants or joint ventures. Take-overs often take place precisely in order to acquire technological and marketing capabilities, rather than being based on existing capabilities of the firm.[56] This is by definition the case if it concerns foreign investment in businesses in which the firm has not previously been active, and it appears that quite a few acquisitions can be classified as such.[57] Acquisitions are thus expected to follow a different logic than described in the theoretical and empirical model. Since they are too few in number to allow for meaningful analysis of the determinants of acquisitions, the 21 observations were left out of the analysis.[58] The total number of observations was reduced to 929.

A last remark concerns the timing of investment and explanatory variables. Preferably a dynamic empirical model would have been specified, in which investment decisions in year t are related to trade barriers, market conditions, and market shares relevant in that year. Time series data on DFI are unfortunately not available at the product level.[59] The empirical model relates cumulative investment to the occurrence of trade barriers in the 1980s (and some in the 1970s), while it is assumed that market shares and regional export concentration have not changed in a major way during the 1980s. Some preliminary analysis of historical market share data showed market shares to be relatively stable over time. Individual top shares are relatively more susceptible to change than membership of the select group of market leaders: *SHARE5* is more stable than *SHARE*. Although *EXPORT*, as it measures regional export orientation, may also be a relatively stable characteristic of firms, the variable will also be partly endogenous when direct foreign investment leads to export substitution. This will introduce a negative relationship between DFI and export while the expected relationship is a positive one. These considerations suggest some caution in interpreting the results of the empirical analysis. Another potential bias is introduced in the case where firms had set up manufacturing plants in the US or the EC but had ceased production by 1992. Surprisingly, perhaps, no divestments from US and EC production are apparent and this does not constitute a problem.[60]

6.5 Empirical Results

Table 6.4 presents the estimation results of the logit model explaining the probability that Japanese firms have set up a manufacturing plant in the US

Table 6.4 Logit model explaining the probability that Japanese electronics firms have set up a manufacturing plant in Europe or the United States by 1992, 35 products

Constant	–5.52**
	(–9.26)
EUROPE	–0.27
	(–0.89)
SHARE5	2.48**
	(8.10)
SHARE	2.60*
	(2.34)
EXPORT	2.20*
	(2.50)
DEPENDENT	–0.14
	(–0.29)
MARKET	2.80**
	(3.08)
AD	1.27**
	(3.75)
AD_EUROPE	1.05*
	(2.34)
VER	2.14**
	(4.58)
PCTARIFF	2.55**
	(4.15)
HIFIQUOTA	2.28**
	(3.28)
TARIFF	12.1**
	(2.79)
MATURE	–0.23
	(–0.22)
Observations	929
Loglikelihood	–333.5**
McFadden's R^2	0.33

Notes: Asymptotic *t*-ratios between brackets, * = significant at the 5% level, ** = significant at the 1% level.

or the EC for each of the 35 electronics products.[61] The results strongly confirm the effects of trade policy measures on tariff jumping direct foreign investment. All of the trade policy variables (*VER*, *AD*, *PCTARIFF*, *HIFIQUOTA*, and *TARIFF*) have positive coefficients and are significant at the 1 per cent level. Firms are much more likely to set up manufacturing plants in the US or the EC for products that have been target of VERs or antidumping (*AD*) actions. In addition, the national quota for hi-fi equipment (*HIFIQUOTA*) in the EC and the retaliatory tariff for personal computers in the US (*PCTARIFF*) have a significantly positive effect on investment. Conventional tariff barriers (*TARIFF*) are also associated with significantly more manufacturing investment. The latter positive impact on investment will have taken place mostly in the EC, since the EC on the whole maintains considerably higher tariff levels for the 35 products than the US. As discussed in Section 6.2.3, it is conceivable that, apart from the export-cost effect of tariff barriers, high tariff levels are associated with higher perceived trade policy threats. Since trade policy threats as such are not included in the analysis, *TARIFF* may partly measure the response of Japanese firms to such potential trade restrictions.

The results also confirm the hypothesis, based on the analysis of the US and EC antidumping systems in Section 6.2.2, that EC antidumping actions pose a bigger threat to exports and give greater incentives for tariff jumping DFI than do US antidumping actions. The variable *AD_EUROPE* is positive and significant at the 5 per cent level. The fact that antidumping duties tend to work as conventional tariffs, the greater 'tilts' in the EC antidumping systems towards findings of dumping and injury, and the lack of effective measures against circumvention through tariff jumping DFI in local assembly operations are all likely to contribute to the stronger effect of EC antidumping actions on DFI. It was also tested whether the fact that EC or US antidumping actions did not lead to the imposition of duties gave rise to weaker responses in the form of DFI. An additional dummy variable, taking on the value 1 if an antidumping action was cancelled, was included. Its sign was negative, as expected, but the coefficient was insignificant. The start of an antidumping investigation may be a rather credible threat of antidumping actions, and firms apparently choose not to take the risk of waiting for the outcome but instead decide to invest at an earlier stage.

A firm's market share in Japan has a positive and significant effect on the decision to invest in the EC or the US: *SHARE5* is positive and has a very low estimated standard error, while *SHARE* is significant at the 5 per cent level. Marginal players in the Japanese market are not as likely to invest as firms which hold more than 5 per cent of the Japanese market, and the likelihood of investment increases the more market shares rise above 5 per cent. The results correspond with the view that the market share variables measure the relative competitiveness of the Japanese firms, and that such competitiveness can be maintained in foreign markets.

In previous work on multinational firms, evidence was found that market leaders are less likely to expand abroad than follower firms with medium market shares. The argument is that, given a dominant presence of the market leader(s), follower firms face the strongest constraints on domestic expansion and will be most inclined to look for expansion abroad (Flowers 1976, Mascarenhas 1986, Hennart and Park 1994). The hypothesis that leading firms are less likely to invest abroad was tested by including an extra variable, $SHARE^2$, in the empirical model. $SHARE^2$ indeed appeared significantly negative while the estimated coefficient of *SHARE* increased compared with the model in Table 6.4.[62] However, the estimated coefficients implied that the effect of market share on investment is increasing up to a level of 60 per cent: market leaders with a market share of up to 60 per cent are still more likely to invest abroad than follower firms.[63] Inspection of the data also reveals that there are several cases where the market leader in Japan was the sole investor in the EC or the US in 1992: Canon in inkjet printers (Italy), Sony in camcorders (France), and Matsushita in vacuum cleaners (Spain).[64] Hence, the hypothesis that follower firms are more likely to invest is not supported by the evidence on Japanese electronics firms. In global industries, market leaders are more likely to have the necessary competence to invest abroad, as well as the largest overseas sales to defend, which gives powerful incentives for DEI.

The expected positive and significant coefficient of *MARKET* confirms that Japanese electronics firms are more likely to invest in the US or the EC if the regional market is relatively large. Regional export intensity (*EXPORT*) is also positive and significant. Firms that are more dependent on the US or EC market are more likely to set up plants there as well. As discussed above, this may be partly connected to relatively strong positions in the EC or US market compared with market shares held in Japan, and may be due partly to the fact that local marketing experience facilitates the start of manufacturing abroad.[65]

The variable *MATURE* has the wrong sign but is not significant. It may be that the measure of product maturity used is inaccurate. It is possible that product cycle effects should be measured at an even more disaggregated level. For example, super density VCRs and wide screen televisions are still largely manufactured in Japan, while conventional VCRs and CTVs are manufactured abroad. The measure of maturity used—the number of years since the start of production in Japan—does not take into account such technology upgrading of products. On the other hand, the explanation may be that the product cycle effect does not apply to a great extent to Japanese investments in developed countries such as the US and the EC, but pertains more to investments in South-East Asia. There are several relatively mature products with very few Japanese investments recorded in the US and the EC (e.g. radio cassette recorders, refrigerators, calculators), but substantially more in South-East Asia.[66] While there may be a tendency to transfer the production of mature products to South-East Asia, the transfer of production to the US or the EC appears more related to trade policy measures.

The dummy variable *DEPENDENT* has the expected negative sign but is not significant. Dependent firms in a vertical business group supplying the core firm (usually on an OEM basis) are, *ceteris paribus*, not significantly less likely to set up a plant abroad. Since dependent firms tend to be less export oriented and rarely hold large market shares in Japan, it is conceivable that investment considerations are sufficiently well explained by the export and market share variables.

The dummy variable *EUROPE* has a negative sign but the coefficient is not significant. If controlled for all other factors such as trade policy measures, Japanese firms are, if anything, less likely to set up manufacturing plants in the EC. The greater incidence of manufacturing investment (see Table 6.3) must be attributed to higher EC tariffs and stricter antidumping and other trade policy measures targeting Japanese electronics firms.[67]

Finally, the market share and market size variables are likely to have a different effect on the decision to invest abroad when firms are faced with trade policy measures compared with a situation of free trade. The analytical model in Section 6.3 posited that a marginal cost advantage of overseas production over export is a necessary condition for DFI. If this condition is not met, even competitive firms selling in large foreign markets will not find it profitable to invest. In the case of trade policy measures such as antidumping, the marginal costs of exporting increases such that the necessary condition for DFI is more likely to be met. This implies that, in the presence of trade policy measures, firm-specific advantages (reflected in market shares) and the size of the foreign market are more closely related to investment decisions. To test this prediction, a sub-sample was selected of trade policy cases: observations for which one (or more) of the variables *AD*, *VER*, *HIFIQUOTA*, and *PCTARIFF* were assigned the value 1. The model was estimated for this sub-sample with the trade policy variables omitted. As predicted, all the estimated coefficients and the calculated magnitude of effects (see below) in the trade policy model were greater than in the full-sample model.[68]

6.5.1 Magnitude of Effects

The coefficients estimated with the logit model cannot be readily interpreted in terms of the magnitude of effects on DFI decisions. Based on the estimates, the effects of changes in the explanatory variables on the probability that firms invest in the US or the EC were calculated. Table 6.5 presents the results for the significant explanatory variables.[69] Overall, the trade policy dummies have strong effects on the probability that firms will set up manufacturing plants. In industries where VERs have been negotiated, the probability of DFI is 38 per cent points higher. The retaliatory

Table 6.5 Magnitude of effects: percentage point changes in the probability that a firm has set up a manufacturing plant as a result of changes in the explanatory variables

Switch in dummy variables	
SHARE5	44
VER	38
AD (US)	22
AD (EC)	41
PCTARIFF	45
HIFIQUOTA	40
Ratio variables: 10 percentage point increase	
SHARE	5
EXPORT	4
MARKET	5
TARIFF	21
Sample mean	0.23

Notes: The effects are based on derivatives calculated in the sample mean.

tariff for personal computers in the US and the national quota for hi-fi equipment in the EC are estimated to have similar effects on DFI, with a probability increase of 45 and 44, respectively. Antidumping actions in the US increase the probability of DFI by 22 percentage points, but antidumping actions in the EC have roughly twice that effect (a 41 percentage point increase). The probability of investment is also higher in industries with high conventional tariffs. If tariffs are increased by 10 percentage points, say from 4 to 14 per cent (comparable to the difference between US and EC tariffs in consumer electronics), the probability of DFI increases by 21 percentage points.

The probability of DFI is 44 percentage points higher for firms with a Japanese market share greater than 5 per cent. Among the top firms, market dominance also matters. For every 10 percentage point increase in market share, the probability of DFI increases by 5 percentage points. Effects of a similar magnitude are calculated for regional exports over sales (*EXPORT*) and the share of the regional market as a percentage of Triad markets (*MARKET*). Although the effects of *SHARE*, *EXPORT*, and *MARKET* may appear small compared with the other calculated effects of the dummy variables, the actual effects can be substantial considering the greater variation in the variables. For instance, dominant firms which supply more than half of the Japanese market (such as Canon in inkjet printers) are 20 per cent more likely to invest abroad.

6.5.2 Possible Extensions

The empirical analysis still leaves room for improvement. Although the fact that significant effects were estimated for market share and regional export intensity does not suggest strong biases resulting from their measurement in 1990–1992, the analysis can be refined by using historical market share and export data, in particular for products with a longer overseas manufacturing history. In addition, overseas marketing and manufacturing experience facilitating the decision to invest abroad could be more accurately measured, for instance by measuring the number of years since the establishment of the first subsidiary in EC and US markets. Measures of transport cost, ignored in the analysis, could be included, as well as some measure of setup costs for assembly plants if these differ across products. More important, the fact that Japanese market shares may be a less reliable indicator for competitiveness in US and EC markets remains a potential problem. Here a possible extension of the analysis would be to include indicators of Japanese industries' overall competitiveness such as estimates of Japanese industries' world market share. Extensions of the empirical analysis along these lines are envisaged. However, given the substantial and significant effects of trade policy variables in the present model, it appears unlikely that the findings are reversed.

6.6 Conclusions and Implications

The empirical results suggest that antidumping as well as other trade policy measures in the EC and the US have substantially increased the incidence of manufacturing investment by Japanese electronics firms in the two regions. The relatively large number of plants set up in the EC is to be attributed to higher tariff walls and more frequent antidumping measures, in combination with an antidumping system which provides much greater incentives for tariff jumping DFI than the antidumping system functioning in the US. The notion that Japanese firms' investment in the US and the EC can be characterised as the transfer of production of relatively mature products to overseas manufacturing plants, a process in which trade policy measures only play a minor additional role (Thomsen 1993, Ozawa 1991), is not supported.

This raises the question whether antidumping actions targeting imports from other countries and industries have had similar effects on DFI. At least in theory, the existence of antidumping laws gives firms incentives for DFI. As discussed in Chapter 1, antidumping laws disallow a range of business actions which are usually not punishable under domestic competition laws. This disparity between restrictions on international and domestic transactions will encourage firms to internationalise production rather than rely on exports to serve foreign markets. DFI will be more likely if the firms facing antidumping threats possess technological or competitive advantages that can be transferred abroad, and if the manufacturing process is of the assembly type such that manufacturing operations can be relocated abroad at a relatively low cost. Both are characteristics of Japanese firms in the electronics industry,[70] but there is evidence that the relationship between DFI and antidumping has not been limited to Japanese electronics firms. Similar patterns of DFI have been observed for several other Japanese industries, such as excavators and hydraulic shovels, ball bearings, and machine tools (see e.g. Strange 1993). In addition, there is abundant evidence that South Korean firms have been responding to frequent antidumping actions in the US and in particular the EC by setting up local manufacturing plants (McDermott 1992). Japanese and South Korean firms alone accounted for over 20 per cent of US antidumping actions initiated against imports from non-communist countries in the 1980s; the corresponding figure for the EC was close to 25 per cent.[71] Moreover, investments may increasingly be undertaken in anticipation of, or to avert, future antidumping actions.[72] All this suggests that the tariff jumping response to antidumping threats may be an important feature of contemporary antidumping practice.

At least two common perceptions concerning the effects of antidumping may have to be altered. First, antidumping measures do not restrict trade volumes as much as is suggested by import figures (Messerlin 1989), as a decline in imports may be matched by increases in foreign firms' overseas production. Antidumping actions in such cases work as import substituting instruments but can provide only limited relief from foreign competition to the petitioning industry.

Second, antidumping measures are not very effective in acting against international price discrimination. Once the targeted firms are producing abroad, they are unaffected by antidumping measures and will be able to continue their pricing strategies. Although antidumping authorities have adapted antidumping law and practice to deflect tariff jumping DFI which aims at circumventing antidumping orders, no effective measures are possible against firms setting up integrated production facilities and firms investing in anticipation of future antidumping measures. Moreover, if there is a situation of anti-competitive conduct by exporting firms which are able to sustain dumping by relying on a 'sanctuary market' in their home country, antidumping actions are likely to hit the wrong firms. The empirical results suggest that it is precisely the firms with dominant positions in the home market, i.e. those firms that benefit most from the privileged access to a 'sanctuary market', that will be able to avoid the effects of antidumping actions through tariff jumping DFI. Smaller players in the home market are less likely to be able to afford the fixed cost of foreign investment, and will have to pay antidumping duties (in the EC system) or increase prices above those of dominant firms (in the US system).

There are more reasons why small firms generally will be harmed more by antidumping actions than large firms. As noted above, the cost of co-operation with antidumping authorities and legal representation are a greater burden to small firms. Costs may be high compared with export revenues and may lead smaller firms to withdraw from the market. Antidumping measures are also biased against new entrants (often smaller firms) which face the highest duty in both the US and EC antidumping systems.[73] All these asymmetric effects of antidumping actions on large and small firms are likely to result in increased concentration and reduced competitive dynamics in the industry under antidumping schemes.

It is rather surprising that both the empirical and theoretical literature concerned with the determinants and effects of antidumping law and practice have largely ignored the possibility that antidumping actions induce direct foreign investment. The challenge for theoretical research, which until now has focused on price and quantity adjustment strategies of foreign firms in the presence of actual and threatened antidumping actions, is to allow for responses in the form of overseas investment. The task for future empirical work is to establish the effects of antidumping measures as well as antidumping threats on world-wide investment patterns.

APPENDIX 6.1

Data Sources and Data Construction

This appendix describes the selection and construction of data used in the empirical analysis and the data sources that were used. For convenience, data sources are referred to in capital letter acronyms. The list of data sources is provided at the end of this appendix.

A6.1.1 Selection of Manufacturers

Japanese manufacturers of the 35 products included in the dataset were identified by examining two data sources. YANO lists Japanese market shares for the top firms for a broad range of products and also includes listings of smaller players (with no market share given). An extensive listing of producers, including privately held firms, in the electronics industry by product is also provided in DKK1, DKK2, and DKK3. Firms listed in one of the above two sources were included in the dataset, except for the most minor unlisted firms in DKK2 and DKK3. It was confirmed that all Japanese exporters mentioned in the antidumping investigations (CEC1, FEDREG) were included in the list. One exception was made for the Seiko group in the case of watch production. Although two group firms (Seiko Epson and Seiko Denshi Kogyo) produce watches in Japan, the core firm Hattori Seiko has centralised control over watch sales. The Seiko group was considered as one 'company' in this case, with market share and overseas investment assigned to Hattori Seiko.

A6.1.2 Manufacturing Investments in the EC and US

It was determined whether the identified firms had set up a manufacturing line for the product in the US or the EC and whether the plant was in operation in 1992. Most relatively well known data sources on Japanese investments, such as TOYOKEI1, JETRO1, and JETRO2, often contain only limited or sometimes inaccurate data on the product lines manufactured in Japanese subsidiaries. JEI, on the other hand, is rather comprehensive and provides useful product line data for Japanese plants in the US in 1990. The identification of product-specific manufacturing investments in Europe was possible in most cases by drawing on two specialised electronics industry data sources: DKK4 and EIAJ1. Both these sources organise investments by product line, while DKK4 is the most comprehensive source with the most detailed product classification. DKK4, EIAJ1, and JEI data were cross-checked with JETRO1, JETRO2, and TOYOKEI1, and with information on overseas plants provided in data books describing Japanese electronics firms: DODWELL, DEMPA, and DKK1–3. In case of contradictory information, most credence was assigned to JEI and DKK4, while for the other sources confirmation by at least one other source (or in selected cases financial reports or newspaper articles) was required.

DFI data in Europe in principle cover EFTA investments as well, but no manufacturing plants for the 35 products were identified in EFTA countries. DFI data in the US cover Canada and Mexico. All firms manufacturing products in Canada also did so in the US, but in three cases firms operated manufacturing plants in Mexico but not in the United States. Since these plants (the so-called 'maquiladoras') are often being managed from the US subsidiary and are likely to be serving the US market, they were counted as US manufacturing investments.

In a few cases, manufacturing subsidiaries were controlled by two or more Japanese firms, usually when a core firm (Matsushita Electric, Alps Electric) owned a stake in a subsidiary jointly established with group firms (e.g. Kyushu Matsushita Electric and Alpine, respectively). Here the group firm was taken as the investor. Where the core firm was listed separately as manufacturer in Japan, both group and core firm were assigned the investment.

In an examination of the various data sources on Japanese manufacturing investments in the US and the EC, no divestments could be found until 1992. After 1992 some plant relocations to Mexico were recorded in the US, while several plant closures took place in the EC.

Plants acquired through acquisitions could be identified in JEI, TOYOKEI1, and additional data presented in Chapter 1. Acquisitions were excluded from the analysis, with the exception of cases where Japanese firms entered US or EC markets through both acquisition and greenfield investment. Examples of the latter are Mitsubishi Kasei in microdisks (acquisition of Verbatim in the US), Fujitsu in personal computers (acquisition of Pocqet Computer in the US), and Matsushita in CTVs (acquisition of Quasar in the US).

A6.1.3 Market Shares in Japan

Market share data were taken from YANO. This source lists market shares of the top firms for a broad range of products. Usually market shares of at least the top four or five firms are specified, and in several cases the list is extended to the top 10 firms. In the case of walkmans and calculators, data were used from NIKKEI, which also provides Japanese market share data, but for a much smaller range of products. The data for pager market shares were taken from DODWELL (1993), and in a few selected cases additional data for specific firms could be added from BIS. For the majority of products, market share data are based on shipments in Japan, including imports from (Japanese) assembly plants abroad. For other products, mostly in office machines and computer peripherals, market share data are based on total shipments from Japanese factories (including exports but excluding imports). The latter data may be less reliable if there are important differences in the extent to which individual Japanese firms transfer production abroad or rely on exports. This could introduce a negative correlation between market shares and DFI. However, a weaker performance of the market share variables in the case of total shipment data could not be detected.

The market share data are for 1991 or 1990, except for pagers (1992), PBXs (1989), and inkjet printers (1993). PBX market share data are combined from data on small telephone systems and small PBXs (less than 300 lines), to focus on business telephone systems that were targeted in the US antidumping case. In case of inkjet printers, the market was still underdeveloped in 1991, and 1993 market shares give a better representation of Japanese firms' relative competitiveness.

Based on the available information, it was possible to determine which firms identified as producers had a market share greater than 5 per cent (the *SHARE5* variable) and if so what this market share was (*SHARE*).

A6.1.4 Regional Exports

Data on exports per region were taken from DKK1–3, which is based on company financial reports and separate surveys under privately held firms. Where data were not available in this source, individual firms' financial reports were examined (MOF). In a few cases, export data for privately held firms could be added from DEMPA. Export data are for fiscal year 1992. Regional export data reported in company statements usually refer to Europe and North America. Europe includes Eastern European countries and North America includes Canada, but these additions are not expected to add substantially to exports (probably about 5–10 per cent), or to differ systematically across firms.

A6.1.5 Market Size

At the micro level adopted in the analysis, there are no systematic data available on sales in Japan, the US, and Europe. A large number of data sources had to be examined to assemble the market size data required. EIAJ 2 provided systematic world demand data for seven consumer electronics products. ELSEVIER also provides electronics that would market data but often not on a sufficiently disaggregated level. The ELECTRONICS journal (1991) provided comparable data on sales in Japan, the US, and the five largest European markets for a range of products. Here figures for the European market as a whole were calculated by multiplying market size of the five largest economies with the ratio of total European sales over sales in the five largest economies for the product group as provided by ELSEVIER. CD-ROM data bases such as COMPUSELECT and PREDICAST1 provided systematic data on sales in world markets for a number of products as well, drawing on trade journals. For other products, again, market data for Japan, the US, and Europe had to be gathered from different sources. YANO, NIKKEI, and DEMPA provided data on sales in Japan, EUROMON1 on European sales, and PREDICAST2 and EUROMON2 on US sales. In a few isolated cases, market size data could be found in journals or newspapers (e.g. EBUSINESS or the *Financial Times*).

Market size data are for the US and Western Europe (EC and EFTA) in 1990 or 1991. Market size data for North America as a whole would have been preferable, considering that US plants may also serve the Mexican and Canadian markets, but such data were available for only a limited number of products. Since US electronics markets make up for roughly 90 per cent of the North American market and this ratio does not differ substantially across products, the use of US market data is not likely to bias the results. In case of pagers, data are for the installed base because data on pager sales were not available. In case of HDDs, sales data for all external storage systems were used, and in case of laser and inkjet printers, market sales for all computer printers. For walkmans, the market size of portable radio cassette recorders was taken. If market size data were available in units, such data were preferred over value data. The latter may vary substantially owing to exchange rate changes which will make them less representative. In order to construct an indicator of market size which is comparable across products, *MARKET* was calculated as the share of the Western European or US market of the total 'Triad' market (US, Western Europe, and Japan). *MARKET* data are presented in Table A6.1.

A6.1.6 Trade Policy Measures

Tariff data were taken from CEC2 and USITC. Tariffs are pre-Uruguay Round tariffs. In the EC case, tariffs applying after 1986 were taken. The two-year temporary increase in the CD player tariff was not included. Data on antidumping cases were taken from their original sources: CEC1 and FEDREG. Data on quantitative restrictions in the EC were drawn from GATT1, GATT2, and KOSTECKI.

A6.1.7 Dependent Firms

Data on the membership of vertical business groups were drawn from TOYOKEI2 and DKK1–3. Firms were classified as dependent firms (*DEPENDENT*) if they were partially or wholly owned by a core firm and if they were considered member of the core firm's *keiretsu*, if the core firm was one of their major clients, and if the core firm itself was listed as manufacturer of the product. Data on major clients were drawn from TOYOKEI3 and DKK1–3. An exception to the above rule was made in case of Aiwa (controlled by Sony), which is known to be run as an independent firm.

A6.1.8 Maturity of Products

The variable *MATURE* was measured as the number of years since the product was included in MITI's production statistics (MITI). The variable is divided by 100 to scale it in a way similar to the other independent variables. In a few cases (such as printers) where MITI's classification was not sufficiently disaggregated, the first year of production or sales mentioned in YANO was taken. For a number of consumer electronics products, the first year of production thus recorded could be compared with information on the year of development of the product in KOSEN. The lag between development and inclusion in production statistics varied between two and four years. Data for HDDs and FDDs are for 3.5 inch drives. The data on the first year of production are presented in Table A6.1.

Table A6.1 Share of the EC and US markets as a percentage of the 'Triad' market, and first year of production recorded in Japanese statistics

Product	Year of first production	Share EC market	Share US market
Audio and video equipment			
CRT CTVs	1962	41	42
LCD CTVs	1986	25	24
Projection CTVs	1988	2	84
VCRs	1979	41	39
Camcorders	1987	44	37
Headphone stereos	1985	37	50
Radio cassette players	1968	37	50
Stereo sets	1973	31	28
CD players	1984	49	38
Laser disk players	1984	10	25
Car audio	1969	43	39
Audio tapes	1968	36	28
Video tapes	1979	33	36
Home electrical and electronic equipment			
Microwave ovens	1969	38	46
Refrigerators	1954	46	32
Washing machines	1954	46	29
Airconditioners	1957	9	28
Vacuum cleaners	1956	46	37
Communication equipment			
Mobile phones	1984	29	53
Pagers	1979	12	62
Facsimiles	1974	32	39
Telephone switching systems (PBX)	1982	49	41
Computers and peripherals			
PCs	1981	40	51
Workstations	1984	34	52
FDDs	1984	24	61
HDDs	1985	36	40
Dot matrix printers	1980	41	43
Laser printers	1984	30	55
Inkjet printers	1986	30	55
3.5 microdisks	1984	31	55
Other office machines			
Calculators	1968	30	46
Copiers	1970	36	53
Typewriters	1957	64	28
Precision machinery			
Watches	1954	46	39
Cameras	1955	35	40

Data Sources

BIS

BIS Mackintosh, 1991, *La Distribution des Produits D'Electronique Grand Public au Japon (The Distribution of Consumer Electronics in Japan)*, Report prepared for Simavelec, August 12, 1991.

CEC1

Commission of the European Communities, *Official Journal of the European Communities*, various issues.

CEC2

Commission of the European Communities, 1994, Integrated Tariffs of the European Communities (TARIC), *Official Journal of the European Communities Annex*, C 141A, Vol. 31.

COMPUSELECT

Compuselect, CD-ROM Database.

DEMPA

Dempa, 1990–1994, *Japan Electronics Buyers' Guide*, Dempa Publications, Tokyo.

DKK1

Denshi Keizai Kenkyuujo, 1993a, *Denshi Kiki Buhin Meikah Risuto: Joujou Kigyou Hen (Directory of Electronics Equipment and Components Manufacturers: Listed Firms)*, Publication No. 653, Denshi Keizai Kenkyuujo, Tokyo.

DKK2

Denshi Keizai Kenkyuujo, 1993b, *Denshi Kiki Meikah Risuto: Hijoujou Kigyou Hen (Directory of Electronics Equipment Manufacturers: Unlisted Firms)*, Publication No. 668, Denshi Keizai Kenkyuujo, Tokyo.

DKK3

Denshi Keizai Kenkyuujo, 1993c, *Denshi Buhin Meikah Risuto: Hijoujou Kigyou Hen (Directory of Electronics Components Manufacturers: Unlisted Firms)*, Publication No. 642, Denshi Keizai Kenkyuujo, Tokyo.

DKK4

Denshi Keizai Kenkyuujo, 1993d, Kaigai Seisan Shinshutsu Kigyou Joukyou: Ichiran Kunibetsu to Hinmokubetsu (Foreign Production: Overview by Country and Product), *Denshi Jouhou*, October 1994, Publication No. 673, Denshi Keizai Kenkyuujo, Tokyo.

DODWELL

Dodwell, 1988, 1993, *The Structure of the Japanese Electronics Industry*, 2nd and 3rd editions, Dodwell Marketing Consultants, Tokyo.

EBUSINESS

Electronics Business, various issues.

EIAJ1

Nihon Denshi Kikai Kougyoukai (Electronic Industries Association Japan), 1989–1994, *Kaigai Houjin Risuto (List of Overseas Affiliates)*, EIAJ, Tokyo.

EIAJ2

Nihon Denshi Kikai Kougyoukai (Electronic Industries Association Japan), 1992, *AV 7 hinmoku Sekai Juuyou Yousoku (Word Demand for Seven AV Products)*, EIAJ, Tokyo.

ELECTRONICS

Electronics, 1990 and 1991, various issues.

ELSEVIER

Elsevier Science Publishers, 1992–1995, *Yearbook of World Electronics Data*. Vol. 1: *West Europe*; Vol. 2: *America, Japan & Asia Pacific*, Elsevier Science Publishers, Amsterdam.

EUROMON1

Euromonitor, 1991–1993, *Consumer Europe*, Euromonitor Publications, London.

EUROMON2

Euromonitor, 1992, *Consumer USA*, Euromonitor Publications, London.

FEDREG

United States Federal Register, available on the LEXUS database.

GATT1

General Agreement on Tariffs and Trade (GATT), 1993, *Trade Policy Review Mechanism: European Communities*, Report by the Secretariat, Geneva.

GATT2

General Agreement on Tariffs and Trade (GATT), 1988, *Developments in the Trading System, October 1987–March 1988*, Report by the Secretariat, Geneva.

JEI

Japan Economic Institute, *Japanese Manufacturing Investments in the United States*, Washington, DC.

JETRO1

Nihon Boeki Shinkoukai (Japan External Trade Organisation), various years, *Zai Ou Nikkei Seizougyou Keiei no Jittai 1–8 (The Current Management Situation of Japanese Manufacturing Enterprises in Europe, Reports 1–8)*, JETRO, Tokyo.

JETRO2

Nihon Boeki Shinkoukai (Japan External Trade Organisation), various years, *Zai Bei Nikkei Seizougyou Keiei no Jittai 1–8 (The Current Management Situation of Japanese Manufacturing Enterprises in the United States, Reports 1–8)*, JETRO, Tokyo.

KOSEN

Kosen, Saburo, 1992, *Kaden Gyoukai (Consumer Electronic Business)*, Sangyoukai Shirisu No. 606, Kyouikusha Shinsho, Tokyo.

KOSTECKI

Kostecki, Michael M., 1989, Electronics Trade Policies in the 1980s, *Journal of World Trade*, 23, 17–35.

MITI

Tsuushou Sangyoushou (MITI), various years, *Kikai Toukei Nenpyou (Yearbook of Machinery Statistics)*, Tokyo.

MOF

Oukurashou (Ministry of Finance), various years, *Yuukashouken Houkokusho Souran (Company Financial Reports)*, Oukurashou Insatsukyoku, Tokyo.

NIKKEI

Nihon Keizai Sangyou Shinbun (Japan Industrial Journal), 1993, *Shijou Senyuuritsu 1993 (Market Shares 1993)*, Nihon Keizai Shinbunsha, Tokyo.

PREDICAST1

Predicast, CD-ROM Database.

PREDICAST2

Predicast, *Predicast Forecast*, 1990–1991.

TOYOKEI1

Touyou Keizai Shinpousha, 1987–1994, *Kaigai Shinshutsu Kigyou Souran (Directory of Japanese Multinational Corporations)*, Tokyo.

TOYOKEI2

Touyou Keizai Shinpousha, 1990, *Nihon no Kigyou Guruupu (Japanese Corporate Groups)*, Tokyo.

TOYOKEI3

Touyou Keizai Shinpousha, 1991, *Kigyou Keiretsu Souran (Directory of Japanese Industrial Groups)*, Tokyo.

USITC

United States International Trade Commission, 1995, *Harmonised Tariff Schedule of the United States*, USITC Publication 2831, Washington DC.

YANO

Yano Keizai Kenkyuujo, 1989–1995, *Nihon Market Share Jiten (Japan Market Share Handbook)*, Mitsutomosha, Tokyo.

APPENDIX 6.2

Acquisitions of EC and US Firms

Table A6.2 lists Japanese electronics firms' acquisitions of US and EC firms by product. Only those cases are included where Japanese firms entered into manufacture of the product solely through the take-over of an existing manufacturing plant. The table shows 21 entries through acquisitions. In only four cases did the Japanese firm hold a market share greater than 5 per cent in Japan.

APPENDIX 6.3

Predictive Power of the Model

One way of assessing the goodness fit of the empirical model is to compare the estimated probabilities of the dependent variable (DFI or no DFI) with the probabilities obtained if the effects of the explanatory variables are ignored. Observations are then classified on the basis of this comparison: whether the model predicts better than a prediction obtained by chance.[74]

In Table A6.3 the 929 observations are classified by comparing the predicted probabilities for 'DFI' and 'no DFI' with the sample frequencies (predictions obtained by chance) for these cases, 0.23 and 0.77, respectively. For instance, of the 212 actual plant establishments, the model predicts a probability of DFI greater than the 'base value' of 0.23 in 177 cases, while the predicted probability is below this threshold value in 35 cases. The model improves the predictions based on the 'base model' in 83 per cent of the cases. The comparable improvement rate is lower for 'no DFI' cases, at 74 per cent.

Table A6.2 Entry in the US and the EC through acquisition only

Japanese firm	Product	Japanese Market share	Acquired firm	Year
EC acquisitions				
Minolta	Copiers	—	Develop Dr Eisbein (G)	1986
Mitsubishi Chemical	Microdisks	9	Verbatim (US)*	1989
Mitsubishi Electric	PCs	—	Apricot (UK)	1990
Fujitsu	PCs	11	ICL (UK)	1991
Mitsubishi Electric	Workstations	—	Apricot (UK)	1990
Fujitsu	Workstations	9	ICL (UK)	1991
Hitachi Koki	Dot matrix printers	—	Dataproducts (US)*	1990
US acquisitions				
Shinko Kogyo	Airconditioners	—	Brod & McClung-Pace Co.	1990
Clarion	CD players	—	McIntosh Laboratory Inc.	1990
Konica	Facsimiles	—	Konica Imaging Inc.	1987
Hitachi Koki	Laser printers	—	Dataproducts Inc.	1990
Olympus	Laser printers	—	Delphax Systems	1990
Kanda Tsushin Kogyo	PBX	—	Kanam Tec Corp.	1992
Clarion	Stereo sets	—	McIntosh Laboratory Inc.	1990
Matsushita	Vacuum cleaners	26	Matsushita Floor Care Co.	1990
Kubota	Workstations	—	Kubota Pacific Computer Inc.	1992
Matsushita	Workstations	—	Solbourne Computer Inc.	1988
Canon	Workstations	—	Next Inc.	1989
Hitachi Koki	Dot matrix printers	—	Dataproducts Corp.	1990

Note: — = market share in Japan smaller than 5%.
* Take-over of existing EC manufacturing plant of the US firm.

Sources: see Appendix 6.1.

Table A6.3 Predictive power of the model: number of observations for which the probability of predicted state is greater than the sample mean

	Actual		Total
	DFI	No DFI	
*Predicted**			
DFI	177	183	
No DFI	35	534	
Total	212	717	929
% improvement	83	74	

*Estimated probability of DFI greater than 0.23; estimated probability of no DFI greater than 0.77.

NOTES

1. Sony, however, was the only Japanese firm not found to be dumping.
2. The OMA concluded a separate investigation under Section 201 of the 1974 US Trade Act.
3. The reason for the withdrawal is not clear. What may have played a role is that, since the most important exporters were not found to be dumping, an injury finding was unlikely. It is also conceivable, as Prusa (1992b) notes in an analysis of withdrawn antidumping petitions, that US industry had come to an understanding with Japanese firms.
4. The US Department of Commerce uses the term 'fair value'.
5. Salvatore (1989), in a time series analysis of US antidumping actions, finds that the 1979 change in the law had a significantly positive effect on the number of antidumping actions taken.
6. Important changes in antidumping law occurred again in 1994–1995 when the US and the EC implemented the new Uruguay Round Code on antidumping into their respective antidumping legislation. See e.g. Bourgeois *et al.* (1995).
7. See the discussion in Section 1.3.
8. To some extent, the relatively large number of negative injury findings may be related to the lack of screening of antidumping petitions in the US. According to the GATT code, petitions should contain 'sufficient' evidence of injurious dumping before an investigation can be initiated. Horlick (1990) however notes that virtually all petitions lead to a formal investigation in the US. In the EC, the (undisclosed) pre-selection of antidumping petitions appears stricter, although Bellis (1990: 48) suggests that the standard enforced tends to be low.
9. It is apparent that in several cases Japanese exporters followed a price adaptation strategy in response to US antidumping actions. In the electric typewriter

case, Silver Seiko's initial duty of 14.91 per cent in 1980 was reduced to 3.8 per cent in 1981, and in the LCD CTV case, Citizin's duty of 17.07 per cent in 1989 was reduced to 1.26 per cent in 1990. As one would expect in such cases, neither company invested in the US.

10. A refund claim is a very complex procedure in the EC and often may take more than a year. If importers–distributors are related to exporters (as is common in case of Japanese electronics firms), special restrictions apply which make it almost impossible to receive a refund, and interest is never refunded (Bellis 1990: 61). A review may take even longer than a refund procedure and where lower dumping margins are found lower duties apply only to future exports. In practice, almost no refund procedures or reviews are initiated. The CD player case is one exception: two small Japanese CD player manufacturers, Accuphase and Asahi Corporation, were granted refunds and a review of the case was later initiated partly as a response to the companies' concerns (Strange 1993: 444).
11. Horlick (1990: 129) estimates the cost of co-operation with a review in US antidumping cases at 50,000 US dollars at least. The cost of co-operation in the initial investigation is likely to be higher than this. Note that in the US antidumping system the costs are recurrent, since petitioners or exporters may ask for a review every year.
12. An example is Towa Sankiden, a minor Japanese exporter of electric typewriters, which withdrew from the market and shut down its typewriter plant altogether after being confronted with dumping duties (Denshi Keizai Kenkyuujo 1994a: 584). In the EC televisions broadcasting camera case, Matsushita, an insignificant player in the EC broadcasting camera market, did not co-operate and received a duty of 96.9 per cent. Matsushita subsequently stopped exporting to the EC (personal communication with a Matsushita manager, July 1994).
13. Here one example is the pager case in the US. Matsushita failed to co-operate properly with the investigation and received a duty of 109 per cent. By the time the antidumping order was issued, the firm had stopped exporting pagers and was serving the US market from its US plant. (See Horlick 1990: 156, and 'Certain High Capacity Pagers From Japan: Preliminary Results of Administrative Review of Antidumping Duty Order', published in the US Federal Register, dated 25 July 1984.)
14. The US did commit itself to the introduction of a 'sunset clause' in its antidumping law when it signed the new Uruguay Round Code on Antidumping in 1994.
15. Antidumping actions can be revoked if the exporter shows no exports or no sales at less than 'fair value' (no dumping) for two years, and if there is no likelihood of resumption of dumped exports (Horlick 1990: 129). The latter condition is of course difficult to establish, and in practice it is almost impossible to get a revocation as long as the US petitoners oppose. For instance, in the CTV case several Japanese firms had not been exporting for at least five years, but revocation was not granted because there was judged to be a possibility the firms would start exporting LCD televisions in future at less than 'fair value.'
16. As noted above, exporters can ask for an annual review to reduce duties. On the other hand, US petitioners can ask for a review if they think duties are likely to increase, for instance if exporters do not increase prices in full in case of currency appreciation (Horlick 1990). Substantial duty increases have been

recorded after the 1985 yen appreciation: the duties for electric typewriters were below 10 per cent in 1985 but increased for several firms to above 60 per cent in 1987. Similar but less pronounced increases in duties are recorded in the CTV case.

17. This would indicate that the large, integrated firms invariably get higher dumping margins than the smaller Japanese firms. Van Marion (1992) indeed notes that the largest Japanese consumer electronics manufacturer, Matsushita, usually has one of the highest margins in US and EC antidumping cases in which it is involved. However, he attributes this to Matsushita's greater capacity to dump based on the firm's high domestic market share.
18. In theory, the antidumping authorities may also use prices on other export markets to derive the 'normal value'. In practice, however, the EC invariably uses the fully allocated cost calculation of the 'fair value' (Van Bael and Bellis 1990: 302). In the US, 60 per cent of all antidumping cases are decided on the basis of the fully allocated cost measure, but the DOC also uses export market price data if such data are judged to be reliable (Horlick 1990: 145).
19. Bellis (1990: 69–75) and Bell (1987) note that the EC Commission's methodology has been consistent to the extent that it adds to the 'normal value' an amount for indirect selling and administrative expenditures of distributors. The justification is that 'normal' value is to be calculated *as if* sales were made on the home market. The methodology to determine 'reasonable' profit margins also changed in major antidumping cases involving Japanese firms, to the effect that profit margins of 47 per cent (typewriters), 14.6 per cent (copyers), and 37 per cent (printers) were obtained, whereas previously the profit margins used had not surpassed 10 per cent.
20. Horlick (1990: 119–120). For instance, in the case of DRAMs from Japan, DRAMs etched in Japan but assembled in third countries were included in the antidumping measures.
21. For instance, it determined that electric typewriters assembled by Brother in Taiwan and exported to the EC fell within the scope of the antidumping action concerning typewriters from Japan because the assembly operations in Taiwan were not sufficient to confer Taiwanese origin on the products (Van Bael and Bellis 1990: 225).
22. See Vermulst and Waer (1990) and Chapter 1 for further discussion of the use of rules of origin in the EC. Another case where the adoption of a new rule of origin is likely to have been related to antidumping actions against Japanese firms is the DRAM rule of origin adopted in 1989.
23. Rules of origin can be used by Customs to determine the origin of products and to levy duties if the products fall within the scope of an antidumping order. Yet where 'insubstantial' operations are performed within the EC, EC-assembled goods do not pass external EC borders and rules of origin are ineffective.
24. See Koulen (1990). This may have been in part in response to the 1983 pager case. In the latter case, the antidumping order was not extended to subassemblies and NEC set up an assembly plant in the US in response to the antidumping action. Motorola (the petitioner) in theory had the choice of filing a new antidumping complaint for the subassemblies and components but could not do so since it imported most components from Malaysia itself (Horlick 1990: 154).

25. The Commission had apparently used this power only once until 1988 (Bellis 1990).
26. Examples are the 1989 audiocassettes case and the 1995 decision on the copier case review, as discussed in Chapter 1.
27. This is stressed by Horlick (1990). Moore (1992) did find that the likelihood of an affirmative ITC decision increases if the case involves the constituency of Senators in the Oversight Committee for the ITC, but this result did not appear robust.
28. A comparative empirical investigation of the determinants of antidumping decisions in the US and the EC confirmed that political, non-technical, factors played a much more important role in the injury decision in the EC than in the US (Tharakan and Waelbroeck 1994). Most empirical studies of US ITC decisions find that, while political factors such as the size of the industry and penetration of non-dumped imports play a role, economic criteria consistent with the antidumping code tend to be dominant (e.g. Baldwin and Steagall 1993, DeVault 1993a, Moore 1992).
29. The ITC investigation has been conducted in secret until the 1988 Trade and Competitiveness Act changed this situation.
30. An illustrative example is the case of flat panel displays (FDPs). High duties were levied on the imports of such displays in 1991 after positive dumping and injury determinations, despite protests by US manufacturers of laptop computers that the price increases of FDPs would make assembly of laptop computers in the US unprofitable. It was only two years later, in June 1993, after continued pressure from the computer industry, that the antidumping measure was cancelled. See Hart (1993) for a discussion of the FDP antidumping case.
31. In particular, where local competitors have established a reputation for aggressive use of trade policy instruments, the threat of antidumping actions will be strong. In the EC, Philips has filed 11 out of 19 EC antidumping petitions against Japanese electronics firms during 1982–92. US semiconductor and telecommunications manufacturer Motorola has taken active recourse to trade policy measures in US (antidumping actions for pagers and mobile phones, Section 301 actions for mobile phone equipment) and also in the EC (antidumping actions for DRAMS and mobile phones). As for the EC, the Japanese Electronics Industries Association in the late 1980s used the following rule of thumb: expect EC trade policy measures against Japanese firms if they have 50 per cent of the market, the product is relatively technology intensive, and EC firms are not very competitive (Flamm 1990: 277).
32. Japanese firms may have to set export prices high to be certain that dumping margins, as calculated by the DOC or the EC Commission, will be negligible, while raising prices may not be an option in the case of vigorous price competition (for instance from South Korean or Taiwanese firms).
33. In a few cases, however, Japanese manufacturing plants established *before* antidumping actions have been involved in antidumping actions. Here antidumping petitions were specifically brought against assembled products as well as components. In the US microdisk case, imports of coated media by Hitachi Maxell, which was assembling microdisks from coated media imported from Japan at the time of the investigation, were included in the antidumping action. In the EC audiocassette case the investigation initially included the tape

component, but the case against the tapes was eventually dropped (see Chapter 1).

34. See Leipziger and Shin (1991) and Feinberg and Hirsch (1989) for cross-industry analysis of the occurrence of antidumping petitions. Lee and Swagel (1994) examine the political and economic determinants of protection and its effects on trade flows simultaneously for a large number of countries, but do not include antidumping measures.
35. See also Strange (1993: 211), where it is noted that the Commission suggested the change while there was no indigenous EC producer to protect.
36. No tariffs were imposed since an agreement was reached, but Yano Keizai Kenkyuujo (1994a) reports that Japanese firms took this threat into account in their investment decisions.
37. *Yomiuri Shimbun and Kyodo News*, 30 April 1991. The Japanese newspaper reported that Japanese firms were drawing up plants to accommodate such moves.
38. The EC Commission feared the diversion of exports to the EC. Prior surveillance implies that all imports require the presentation of a certificate of origin.
39. Winters (1994b), however, finds that EC import prices often increase and import volumes decrease following surveillance measures.
40. The one plant in the US was acquired by Clarion, a marginal player in the home CD player market. See also Appendix 6.2.
41. An indication of the role of national restrictions may be that, of the 9 firms with plants in Europe, 5 set up manufacturing bases in France, and one in Spain (Denshi Keizai Kenkyuujo 1994a).
42. Besides the likely role of US antidumping measures, it is also important to note that the US is by far the largest market for projection CTVs. See Appendix 6.1.
43. See also Horlick (1990: 156).
44. Here at least 3 firms—market leader Casio, Sharp, and Citizen—apparently opted to increase prices to bring down dumping duties in the first review. After relatively high dumping duties were imposed in 1988–1989 in the first assessment of dumping, Casio's duty was brought down to 0.5 per cent in 1989, Sharp's was reduced from 30.76 to 4.76 per cent in 1989, while Citizen's was reduced from 17.07 to 1.26 per cent in 1990. It is possible that the initiation of an antidumping investigation concerning LCD displays in August 1990 discouraged investment in LCD CTVs in the US.
45. Price and quantity adaptation of foreign firms to (anticipated) antidumping measures are analysed in Reitzes (1993), Leidy and Hoekman (1990), Webb (1992), and Staiger and Wolack (1992), among others. The possibility of foreign investment is not taken into account in these studies.
46. Plants are established in Mexico but not in the US for radio cassette recorders, stereo sets, and watches. These plants are thus counted as investments in the 'US'.
47. An exception is the inclusion of flexible disk drives (FDDs) and hard disk drives (HDDs), which can only partly be regarded as final products. This is not likely to be a problem because Japanese firms' sales of FDDs and HDDs for assembly into computers mostly takes place on arm's length markets.
48. The logit model can be derived from profit maximisation in a discrete choice model (DFI or not) under suitable assumptions concerning the distribution of a

stochastic (unmeasured) term in the profit function (Cramer 1991, Foundation for Economic Research 1988, Head, Ries, and Swenson 1995).

49. In addition, it is assumed that the industries can be considered international oligopolies such that each firm is at least a potential competitor in Japan, the US, and the EC. This assumption appears not too restrictive for the products considered in the analysis: in most cases, the main EC and US competitors are multinational enterprises themselves. The position of Japanese firms *vis-à-vis* foreign firms is also likely not to differ markedly between the EC and the US, given that most major US firms have operations in the EC and vice versa (e.g. Motorola is manufacturing in the EC, and Philips and Thomson have major operations in the US). All of these potential problems could have been solved by using EC and US market share data, but unfortunately systematic market share data are available in the public domain only in Japan.
50. See van Marion (1992) and Chapter 2.
51. In the US CTV case, most firms invested after the OMA was concluded, as discussed in Section 6.2.1. In the 1983 EC VCR case, the VER almost preceded the official announcement of the antidumping investigation. Note that in the case of VCRs in the EC there was a second antidumping case targeting only two Japanese producers, Funai and Orion. To take this into account, the *AD* and *AD_EUROPE* variables were assigned the value 1 for these two producers only.
52. Here the VER negotiated by UK industry combined with national quota in France, Italy, and Spain and restrictive PAL licences formed export barriers. For convenience, and because the UK measure had a most appreciable effect on DFI (Strange 1993), these measures are grouped under the 'VER' heading.
53. To be precise, *MATURE* is the number of years since the product was first recorded in MITI's production statistics, divided by 100. See Appendix 6.1.
54. Since overseas production subsidiaries are often multi-product firms, data on capitalisation are not easily used to test for systematic differences in setup costs at the product level. Moreover, no capitalisation data are available for more than half of the 35 products because of the absence of DFI.
55. See Chapter 5 and also Belderbos and Sleuwaegen (1996), Head, Ries, and Swenson (1995), and Kimura and Pugel (1995).
56. Yamawaki (1993), in an empirical analysis of the determinants of Japanese firms' acquisitions in the US and the EC, finds that firms are more likely to enter markets through acquisitions if they do not own competitive advantages. The results in Chapter 9 also suggest that acquiring local firms' expertise in R&D is an important motive for Japanese electronics firms' acquisitions.
57. See Appendix 6.2 for the list of acquisitions. The acquiring Japanese firm held a market share greater than 5 per cent in only four cases. Note that acquisitions are defined as cases where the *sole* entry in the EC or the US is through takeovers. Where a Japanese firm acquired a US or EC firm but set up its own manufacturing plant as well, the argument concerning firm-specific capabilities does not hold.
58. The inclusion of acquisitions as a separate category in a multinomial logit model was attempted but did not produce any significant results, owing to the small number of observations.
59. The fact that various products tend to be manufactured in the same overseas manufacturing subsidiary usually makes it impossible to determine when a new

product line has been added, although the start of production for the first product line can be proxied by the establishment year of the manufacturing subsidiary.

60. No withdrawals occurred according to the various data sources on Japanese DFI. In one case, Silver Seiko 'withdrew' from typewriter production in the EC, but the firm had consigned production to a local firm only. After 1992, however, divestments did occur, particularly in the EC, mainly because of prolonged unfavourable market conditions in Europe. For instance, Kyocera ceased laser printer production in France, YE Data ceased FDD production in the UK, Shintom ceased VCR production in Germany, and Star closed its dot matrix printer plant in the UK. See Section 2.4.5 for details.
61. An analysis of the predictive power of the model is provided in Appendix 6.3.
62. The estimated coefficients were: 0.152 (*SHARE*) – 0.0022 $(SHARE)^2$; both coefficients were significant at the 1 per cent level. The change in specification did not have an appreciable effect on the other estimated coefficients, with the exception of a reduced effect for *SHARE5*.
63. There is only one case in the sample where market share exceeds the 60 per cent threshold: Canon holds a 64 per cent market share in inkjet printers. Although Hennart and Park (1994) in their analysis of the determinants of Japanese foreign investment in the US conclude that median market shares are most likely to be associated with DFI, it appears that their findings are in fact broadly similar. Their estimates imply that the probability of investment is increasing up to a market share of around 50 per cent, a level that would not usually be considered 'median'. It should be noted, however, that Hennart and Park use a crude measure of market share: total sales of the firm over total sales of listed firms in broad industry groups. It is possible that their findings are more representative of the effect of firm *size* on investment, since large diversified firms such as Hitachi and Toshiba will invariably end up as market leaders.
64. Two counter-examples are the absence of investments by market leaders Matsushita (airconditioners) and TEAC (FDDs). In both cases the firms are supplying US and EC markets from large plants in South-East Asia.
65. Omitting the *EXPORT* variable had very little effect on the estimated coefficients and significance of the other variables, while it reduced the fit of the model.
66. According to Nihon Denshi Kikai Kougyoukai (1992a), 28, 18, and 5 plants, respectively.
67. It was also tested whether, apart from the general environment in the EC represented by *EUROPE* and the EC-specific antidumping variable *AD_EUROPE*, there were other differences in DFI decisions for the two regions. A model was estimated which included interactive terms of *EUROPE* with all explanatory variables. Comparing the loglikelihood of this estimation with the loglikelihood reported in Table 6.4 and applying the χ^2 test, the hypothesis that all the additional interactive terms were jointly not significantly different from zero could not be rejected.
68. All variables that were significant in the full-sample model were also significant in the trade policy model, with the exception of *SHARE*, which had a *t*-ratio of 1.8. The effects on the probability to invest abroad, as calculated by derivatives

examined in the sample mean, were on average twice the effects in the full-sample model presented in Table 6.5.

69. The estimated effects presented in Table 6.5 are the derivatives of the probability of DFI with respect to the explanatory variables, calculated in the sample mean. The t-ratios of the derivatives are the same as those of the coefficients. See Foundation for Economic Research (1988) and Maddala (1983) for details.
70. In capital and scale intensive industries the high cost of setting up efficient plants abroad may be prohibitive, and (threats of) antidumping actions may induce different responses. An example is the steel industry, where Japanese firms have chosen to give technological assistance, and consign production, to US steel makers. Japanese firms now operate six such joint ventures in the US, apparently because frequent use of the antidumping instrument by US firms made an exporting strategy unfeasible. In 1994, Nippon Steel took a 10 per cent equity stake in a subsidiary of Oregon Steel (CF&I) which will produce rail steel with assistance of the Japanese firm. Nippon Steel cited the need to deflect US antidumping charges: CF&I earlier had filed an antidumping petition against rail steel imports from Japan (*Financial Times*, 21 July 1994).
71. Calculations based on data provided in Van Bael and Bellis (1990: 20) and Baldwin and Steagall (1993).
72. There is some evidence that the threat of antidumping action continues to play an important role in investment decisions in the 1990s. For instance, Fujitsu and NEC shifted production of asynchronous transfer mode (ATM) switches to plants in Texas and Oregon, respectively, explicitly stating the need to head off trade friction (antidumping actions) in the US (*Nikkei Weekly*, 27 June 1994).
73. The rationale for assigning the highest duty to exporters not involved in the investigation is to encourage co-operation. Under EC rules, if a new entrant is not dumping, it still has to pay the highest ('residual') duty for a year. After this period, the entrant can apply for a refund, but this has been a complicated and time-consuming procedure. In the US, a new entrant has to make a cash deposit based on the highest duty. If the firm is not found dumping on shipments during the first year, the deposit is reimbursed with interest.
74. Classifying observations by ascertaining whether predicted probabilities are greater than 0.5 (following the 'maximum probability rule'), as is also done frequently in binomial logit, would lead to biased results when applied in the present model, given that the sample frequency of DFI at 0.23 is considerably below 0.5.

7

DFI and Export: Substitutes or Complements?

7.1 Introduction

The relationship between direct foreign investments (DFI) and exports by multinational enterprises (MNEs) is not one that is firmly established in the empirical and theoretical literature. In the theory of international involvement of firms (e.g. Hirsch 1976, Dunning 1981, Caves 1982), exports and local production are alternatives for a single-product firm. If a firm is endowed with sufficient firm-specific assets to overcome the inherent difficulties associated with operating a plant abroad, and if locational advantages warrant foreign production, the firm will substitute local production for exports.

However, there are several reasons why export substitution might be limited or absent. First, if the foreign manufacturing plant in country B serves as an export platform to country C, these manufacturing operations are clearly not substituting for exports to country B. Second, local manufacturing may have important demand enhancing effects by decreasing variable costs (e.g. by avoiding transport costs), facilitating marketing and design specifically geared to the market, and creating local goodwill and customer loyalty. Transfer of production may in this way be accompanied by increased demand, leading to export growth. Third, if the production process can be separated into stages and only assembly activities are transferred abroad, increased demand for locally assembled products leads to increased exports of components, partly offsetting export substitution at the final product level. Fourth, goodwill and consumer loyalty generate 'spillovers' to other exportable products manufactured by the firm, such that multi-product firms experience less overall export substitution. Fifth, if DFI occurs through the acquisition of a local firm in the foreign country, this may lead to restructuring of the local firm's activities involving increased sourcing of parts and final goods from the acquiring firm. The acquirer could, for example, make use of brand names, distribution networks and exclusive ties with customers to increase its own exports.

The above considerations may explain why empirical studies generally have been inconclusive on the issue of substitution between exports and DFI. The difficulty in obtaining data on activities of multinational enterprises has moreover limited empirical research to analysis of US and Swedish firms. In Lipsey and Weiss (1981, 1984) a positive effect of US firms' foreign production on US exports is found, both in regressions across countries and across firms. In Swedenborg (1979) a negative effect of foreign production by Swedish MNEs on exports to independent overseas distributors is reported, while intra-firm exports to overseas affiliates were complementary to foreign production. Blomström, Lipsey, and Kulchycky (1988) did not find support for export substitution in Swedish industries, but found significantly negative effects of foreign production on exports for several US industries.

In this chapter, the empirical analysis is extended to the relationship between exports and DFI by Japanese firms focusing on the electronics industry. The experience of Japanese firms might differ from those of US and Swedish MNEs because the surge in Japanese DFI since the mid-1980s was to an important extent a reaction against restrictions on exports to North America and Europe. Several empirical studies have found trade protection to affect significantly the cross-industry pattern of Japanese DFI.[1] Chapter 1 examined the close connection between the timing of Japanese electronics firms' plant establishments in the EC and antidumping actions, and the analysis in Chapter 6 confirmed that a substantial share of Japanese electronics firms' DFI in the US and Europe has been induced by trade policy measures. To the extent that Japanese DFI has been 'tariff-jumping', i.e. responding to barriers to export or the expectation that these will arise, it is not a managerial decision based on a search for lower production costs or demand-enhancing effects of manufacturing investment. This may be true particularly for Japanese firms, since a specific feature of the international operations of Japanese firms has been that they have managed very well to create customer loyalty by investing in extensive distribution networks abroad, which take care of marketing and after sales service.[2] Tariff jumping DFI also implies that production will be mainly serving the local market: indeed, roughly 98 per cent of sales by Japanese electronics manufacturing plants in Europe and North America were within the region.[3] These factors suggest that Japanese DFI in the electronics industry may be characterised by relatively strong trade substitution effects.[4]

This chapter tests the hypothesis that Japanese DFI in EC electronics manufacturing in the second half of the 1980s has substituted for exports. Two complementary analyses are performed. Analysis at the *product* level examines the development in exports and DFI following trade policy measures, and compares DFI and export patterns in Europe and the US. An econometrical analysis at the *firm* level examines the determinants of exports to Europe in 1989 by 86 Japanese electronics firms and the effect of Japanese firms' investment in EC manufacturing on export intensity. The results give broad support for the export substitution hypothesis, although some evidence is found of a partly offsetting increase in components exports.

The remainder of this chapter is organised as follows. Section 7.2 presents the product level analysis of exports and DFI. Section 7.3 discusses empirical and theoretical considerations concerning export behaviour at the firm level. Section 7.4 presents the model and data used in the firm level analysis, and Section 7.5 presents estimation results. Section 7.6 concludes.

7.2 Product Level Analysis: DFI and Exports

Investment patterns as well as EC and US trade policy measures targeting Japanese electronics firms were described in detail in Chapters 1 and 6. This section extends the analysis by examining the relationship between trade policy, DFI, and exports for a number of electronics goods. In Section 7.2.1 the development of Japanese exports to the EC and production capacity of Japanese plants in the EC is examined for four products that have been subject to antidumping duties. In Section 7.2.2 patterns of plant establishments, exports, and trade policy measures across products are compared for the EC and the US.

7.2.1 EC Trade Policy, Japanese Exports, and Local Manufacturing

The available evidence on the relationship between trade policy measures, exports, and local manufacturing is presented for four major Japanese export goods: VCRs, microwave ovens, plain paper copiers, and CD players.

Figure 7.1 illustrates the case of VCRs. It sets out on a time scale the number of Japanese manufacturing plants in the EC, the volume of Japanese firms' EC production, the volume of exports to the EC, and VCR sales in the EC, for the years 1982 and 1985–1989. The first Japanese plants were set up in 1982 at the time the VER was negotiated. The number of plants increased to 14 in 1985 and again to 22 at the time of the antidumping investigation in 1987. The major Japanese exporters were not affected by the 1987 antidumping action, which targeted only two minor Japanese firms (Funai and Orion). While total market volume in the EC rose to 10.1 million units in 1989, the volume of exports decreased from 4 million units in 1982–1983 to 2.8 million units, and EC production by Japanese firms continuously increased to 5.6 million units. Thus, increases in Japanese firms' VCR sales were covered by local production, resulting in substitution

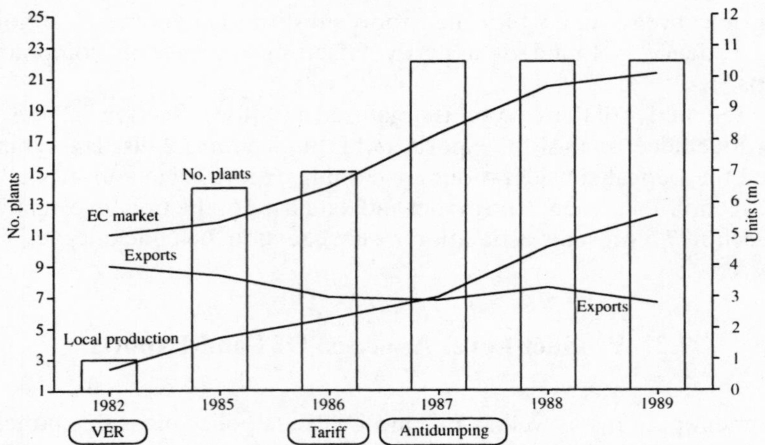

Figure 7.1 Japanese manufacturing plants, local production, and exports to the EC: VCRs

Sources: Belderbos (1994), Euromonitor (1991), Watanabe (1988), Dempa (1990b), Nihon Kaihatsu Ginkou (1989), Appendix 1.3.

of local production for exports in terms of *market share*. Substitution in absolute terms was less strong, given the comparatively small decrease in the level of VCR exports.

Figure 7.2 presents the evidence for the case of microwave ovens. The number of Japanese microwave oven plants in the EC rose to nine after the EC Commission initiated an antidumping investigation in 1987. From that year, exports declined from 1.5 million to 800,000 units, while total market demand in the EC reached 7.8 million units in 1989. Local production rose to approximately 1.3 million units in 1989 (Dempa 1990a), when the antidumping petition was eventually withdrawn. These figures suggest that export substitution took place while actual duties were never levied.[5] Figure 7.2 also shows the development in exports of magnetrons, the most technologically advanced component of microwave ovens, which has been developed by Japanese firms. Exports rose from 0.7 million units in 1985 to 3.2 million units in 1989. Although part of the Japanese magnetron exports is supplied to EC firms, the export trend suggests that the growth in local assembly activities stimulated demand for magnetrons imported from Japan. In later years, however, the growth in magnetron exports abated[6] under the influence of Japanese firms' investment in EC magnetron manufacturing plants. Sanyo, a major producer of microwave ovens, established a magnetron plant in the UK in 1988, and Matsushita followed suit by establishing a UK plant in 1990.

Substitution of exports by local production is apparent also in the copier industry (Figure 7.3). The number of Japanese plants rose to 11 after the start of the antidumping investigation in 1985, and local production of copiers reached an estimated 650,000 units in 1989. Exports, on the other hand, declined from 840,000 to 470,000 from 1985 to 1989.

The European CD player market has been growing rapidly to approximately 7.8 million units in 1989 (Figure 7.4). Japanese exports peaked at 3.2 million units in 1988, the year after an antidumping investigation was initiated, and subsequently declined to 2 million units in 1990. In contrast, local production increased to at least 1 million units in 1988.[7]

7.2.2 *Trade Policy, Exports, and Japanese DFI: A Comparison with the US*

The effects of trade barriers on exports and foreign production can be further uncovered by comparing the trade and investment relation between Japan *vis-à-vis* the EC on the one hand, and the US on the other. The EC and the US are the two most important export markets for Japanese electronics goods, and Japanese firms can be assumed to follow similar export and investment strategies in both regions in the absence of trade policy measures. As discussed in Chapter 6, for some products parallel trade policy measures have been taken against Japanese electronics exports by the EC and the US, while for other products important differences in trade regimes are apparent.

Table 7.1 illustrates the effects of trade policy measures through a

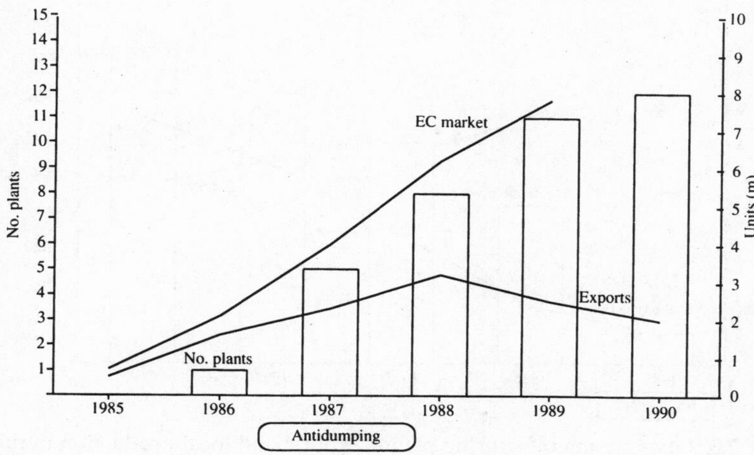

Figure 7.2 Japanese manufacturing plants and exports to the EC: microwave ovens
Sources: see Figure 7.1.

comparison of exports and local production of CTVs and VCRs. Whereas trade restrictions have severely affected Japanese CTV exports to both the US and the EC, trade barriers for VCR exports have occurred only in the EC. The table shows that in 1987 about half of all Japanese VCRs sold in the EC were produced in Japanese manufacturing plants located in the EC, whereas Japan's vast market share in the United States was predominantly accounted for by exports. In case of CTVs, the ratio between local production and Japanese exports was roughly equal in the US and EC, with local production almost five times the volume of exports. This suggests that trade restrictions in the EC have been a factor of importance in reducing imports from Japan and increasing Japanese firms' local production in the VCR industry. Barring import protection and DFI, it is likely that exports to the EC would have been more like US levels.

A further indication of the relationship between trade policy, DFI, and exports is provided by Table 7.2. This table presents data on the volume of Japanese exports, the number of manufacturing plants, and trade policy measures in the EC and the US for a number of electronics products. The ratio of exports to the EC to exports to the US (column (3)) shows the relative importance of the EC as a market for Japanese exports. Comparison with the EC–US market size ratio (column (4)) indicates where exports are lower than one would expect based on total sales in the market. The products are ranked by the EC–US export ratio. The bottom row includes data on the value of all electronics exports to the EC and the US.

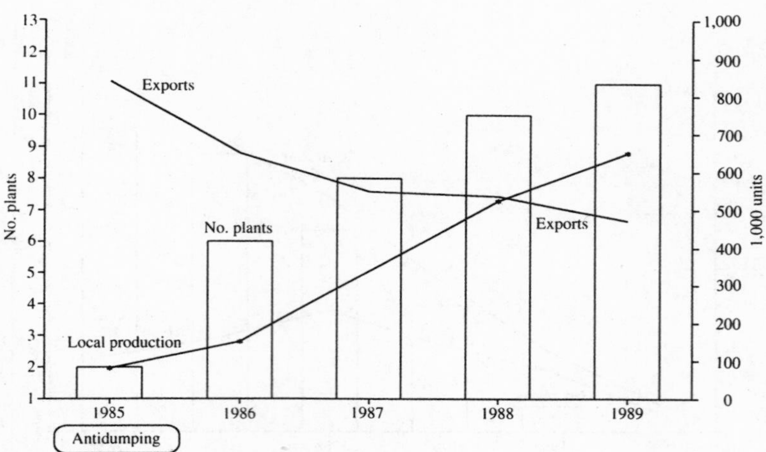

Figure 7.3 Japanese manufacturing plants, exports and local production in the EC: plain paper copiers

Sources: Belderbos (1994), JETRO (1986a–1991a), Watanabe (1988), Dempa (1990b: App. 1.3).

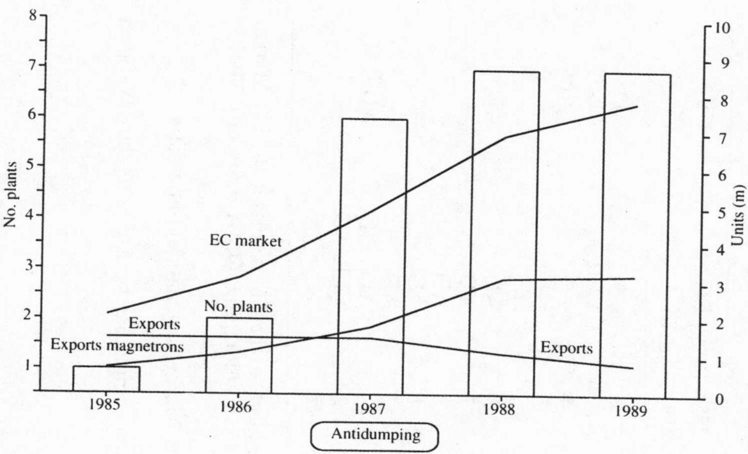

Figure 7.4 Japanese manufacturing plants and exports to the EC: CD players
Sources: see Figure 7.1.

Table 7.1 Local production and exports of VCRs and CTVs by Japanese firms in 1987: the EC and the US compared

	No. of CTVs (m)		No. of VCRs (m)	
	EC	US	EC	US
Total market	16.1	19.6	8.2	11.0[a]
Exports (% of market)	0.5 (3)	1.4 (7)	2.9 (35)	10.0[a] (91)
Local production (% of market)	2.2 (14)	5.8 (30)	3.0 (37)	0.2 (2)

[a]1988.

Sources: Belderbos (1994), Nihon Kaihatsu Ginkou (1989), Euromonitor (1991), JETRO (1989a).

Total Japanese electronics exports to the EC amounted to 72 per cent of electronics exports to the US in 1990. This ratio is lower than the EC–US market size ratio (0.85), which may be related to stricter EC trade policy measures in the electronics sector as a whole. To some extent this is reflected in the investment pattern: although the EC electronics market is smaller, the figures on the aggregate number of manufacturing plants are comparable (140 in the EC and 141 in the US). The relationship between trade policies, DFI, and exports is much more apparent from the data on individual products. The highest EC–US export ratios (the top rows of the

Table 7.2 Japanese firms' exports and DFI in 1990 compared for the EC and the US

Product	Exports (1,000 units)			Market size	No. of plants		Trade policy	
	EC (1)	US (2)	ratio (3)	ratio (4)	EC (5)	US (6)	EC (7)	US (8)
PBX[a]	3,320	1,370	2.42	1.18	1	6	—	AD
CTVs	313	167	1.87	0.99	15	11[b]	VER	AD/OMA
PCs[c]	356	190	1.87	0.78	2	4	—	Tariff
Facsimiles	1,111	1,017	1.09	1.09	5	3	—	—
Camcorders[d]	4,058	3,841	1.06	1.19	0	0	—	—
Microwave ovens[d]	449	487	0.92	0.83	6	3	AD	AD
Copiers	456	726	0.62	0.68	11	3	AD	—
Dot printers	2,855	6,242	0.46	0.97	10	2	AD	—
CD Players	2,198	4,955	0.44	1.29	10	1	AD	—
Audiocassettes[e]	8,200	18,500	0.44	1.27	4	3	AD	—
Integrated circuits[f]	1,138	2,627	0.43	0.46	7	12	AD/OMA	AD/OMA
VCRs	3,171	8,610	0.37	1.05	16	2	VER/AD	—
All electronics[g]	24,603	34,131	0.72	0.85	140	141		

Notes: Products are ranked by the relative importance of exports to the EC. Export ratio is exports to the EC/exports to the US. Market size ratio is volume sales in Europe/volume sales in the US, if not stated otherwise. AD = antidumping, OMA = Orderly Market Arrangement.

[a] Export data are in billion yen (1991) for multi-button and telephone switching equipment. Market size data are in dollars.
[b] Four more plants are located in Mexico and two in Canada.
[c] Export data are for 1989. Temporary 100% tariff levied in 1987 as a retaliation for non-compliance by Japan to the US–Japan semiconductor agreement.
[d] Export figures are for 1991.
[e] Export figures are in kilograms for 1991.
[f] Export and market size data (1992) are in million dollars.
[g] Export and market size (1992) data in million dollars. Export data include precision machinery and office machines.

Sources: Belderbos (1995c), Elsevier Science Publishers (1995), Nihon Denshi Kikai Kougyoukai (1992a), JETRO (1991a), Japan Tariff Association (1991), Dempa (1991a–1992a), Appendix 6.1.

table) are found for products that have been targeted only by US trade policies (PBXs, PCs), products for which exports to both markets have been restricted (CTVs, microwave ovens), or products for which no overt trade policy measures have been taken in either the EC or the US (facsimiles, camcorders). The lowest EC–US export ratios are found for products that have been targeted by EC trade policies (copiers, dot printers, CD players, audiocassettes, VCRs). There is one exception to this rule—integrated circuits—but here the low EC–US export ratio is fully explained by the fact that the EC market is considerably smaller.

In all cases where Japanese exports have been targeted by trade policy measures in the EC only, export ratios are below market size ratios. Except for copiers, the differences are substantial. For instance, in case of CD players, while the EC market is almost 30 per cent larger than the US market, the EC–US export ratio is only 44 per cent.[8] That is: exports to the EC are about a third of what one would expect based on the size of the market. Similarly, in the two cases where US trade policies have restricted Japanese exports (PBXs and PCs), export ratios are substantially higher than market size ratios. In the two cases where no trade measures have been taken (facsimiles and camcorders), export and market size ratios are very similar.

Table 7.2 also shows that, in all cases of exclusive EC trade policies, the number of EC manufacturing plants is larger than in the US, and vice versa;[9] for instance, the number of PBX manufacturing plants in the US in 1990 reached six, while only one plant was established in the EC. Manufacturing plants are more numerous in the EC for products targeted by EC antidumping: the most illustrative examples are copiers, dot printers, CD players, and VCRs.

The evidence in Tables 7.1 and 7.2 as well as the analysis in Section 7.2.1 suggests that tariff jumping DFI by Japanese electronics firms as a response to EC trade policy measures has resulted in reduced exports from Japan. Hence, the conclusion is that Japanese firms' DFI in the EC electronics industry in the second half of the 1980s, which was closely linked to trade policy measures, has substituted for exports. This conclusion may have to be qualified in two respects. First, the evidence of export substitution is at the final goods level, and DFI is likely to result in increased Japanese exports of components to supply EC plants. However, local content requirements have led Japanese firms to extend manufacturing investment to include components and integrated production, which suggests that there must have been a limit to which increased components exports from Japan have been able to replace exports of final goods.

Second, it is possible that reduced exports from Japan were associated with increased exports from Japanese assembly plants located in South-East Asian countries (e.g. Singapore, Taiwan, Malaysia, and China). While there is some evidence of such circumvention of trade measures (see e.g.

van Marion 1992), subsequent EC antidumping measures and threats of antidumping action against imports from South-East Asian countries have made this response to trade policy measures lose much of its attraction (see Section 1.3.4). There is no evidence that this response has been of great importance in comparison with tariff jumping DFI,[10] and the figures in Section 7.2.1 show that export declines are clearly associated with increased EC production by Japanese firms.

The evidence thus suggests that Japanese manufacturing investment in the EC in the late 1980s has also been substituting for exports at the *firm* level. This hypothesis is tested in Section 7.4. First, Section 7.3 briefly reviews the empirical and theoretical literature on export behaviour.

7.3 Firm Characteristics and Export Behaviour

In order to test whether manufacturing DFI substitutes for exports at the firm level, it is necessary to control for various other factors which are expected to have an impact on the export intensity of firms. Traditional trade theories emphasise the importance of countries' comparative advantages in determining cross-industry patterns of trade. At the firm level, theories of international operations of firms regard exporting as a means of exploiting competitive advantages, such as the possession of technological and managerial skills and marketing capabilities, in overseas markets (Hirsch 1976, Dunning 1981, Caves 1982). These theories predict that firms which possess such competitive advantages will generally be more export intensive. Vernon's product cycle theory predicts a positive relationship between innovative behaviour, product oriented R&D, and exports (Vernon 1979). Recent contributions to the theory of international rivalry between firms operating in oligopolistic markets suggest that a firm's investment in strategic assets such as R&D, marketing, and physical capital, *relative* to other firms, determines market shares at home and abroad (e.g. Yamawaki and Audretsch 1988). One such strategic investment, which only recently has received attention, concerns the establishment of a network of foreign sales subsidiaries to enhance marketing efforts and after sales service abroad (Williamson and Yamawaki 1989).

Several of the above predictions have been empirically tested. However, studies dealing with the analysis of Japanese exports have invariably taken the *industry* as the level of analysis. Yamawaki and Audretsch (1988) found that Japanese export as a share of the US market is well explained by Japanese industries' expenditures on R&D, advertising, and physical capital, relative to US industries. Audretsch, Sleuwaegen, and Yamawaki (1989) found a positive relationship between R&D expenditures and world export shares, while this relationship was strongest in the case of Japan. Yamawaki (1991) found that Japanese industries' investments in distribution networks in the US have promoted exports. The results in Doi (1988) are less conclusive. The export intensity of Japanese industries is found to be positively affected by industry concentration, the importance of subcontracting, and labour intensity, while the effects of R&D and advertising intensity were ambiguous.

Exports at the *firm* level are the subject of analysis in Glejser, Jacquemin, and Petit (1980). For Belgian firms, a positive influence of product differentiation and the presence of overseas sales subsidiaries on export intensity is confirmed. Swedenborg (1979) analyses export intensities of Swedish firms and finds a positive relationship with R&D intensity, labour skill, and economies of scale in the industry.

The theoretical and empirical literature suggests that an empirical model explaining export intensities at the firm level should include firm-specific characteristics which are related to competitive advantages to be exploited in foreign markets, in addition to explanatory factors related to comparative advantages. It should also take into account the effect of investments in overseas distribution networks in supporting exports from the home country. After controlling for these factors, the effect of foreign manufacturing investment can be assessed.

7.4 Firm Level Analysis: Empirical Model and Data

The empirical model relates the propensity of Japanese electronics firms to export to Europe[11] to a set of structural features of the firm and its environment following the arguments in the previous section. The dependent variable divides exports to Europe by total sales during fiscal year 1988 (the year ending March 1989) and is related to a vector explanatory variable X with coefficients β and a constant term α, according to the following logistic relationship:

$$(1) \quad \frac{\text{Exports to Europe}}{\text{Sales}} = \frac{\exp[\alpha + \beta X]}{1 + \exp[\alpha + \beta X]}$$

Through a simple transformation, i.e., taking the *log of the odds*, we get:

$$(2) \quad \log EXPODD = \log\left(\frac{\text{Exports to Europe}}{\text{Sales} - \text{exports to Europe}}\right) = \alpha + \beta X$$

As the transformed dependent variable is no longer restricted within the interval (0,1), equation (2) can in principle be estimated with ordinary least squares.

Among the structural features of the firm, R&D intensity (*RDINT*, i.e. R&D expenditures divided by value added), marketing intensity (*MARKINT*, i.e. direct and indirect sales costs divided by turnover), and human resource intensity (*HUMRES*, i.e. wage costs of white collar workers divided by total wage costs) are all expected to be positively related to *EXPODD*.[12] The capital–labour cost ratio (*CAPLAB*, i.e. the value of total depreciable capital divided by total wage costs) is likely to reflect the use of different technologies with different levels of capital intensity across firms. A high *CAPLAB* is expected to stimulate exports, as it represents an advantage for those firms that are using capital, Japan's relatively abundant factor, more intensively. Moreover, a high *CAPLAB* will in many cases also reflect aggressive investment in new production plants and automation associated with economies of scale and gains in productivity.[13] In order to take specific industry effects into account, a set of six industry dummies controls for the effects of market size, industry environment, and industry-wide locational factors.

The model is then extended to take account of the growing investments of Japanese firms in Europe. A simple recursive model is posited to relate exports to manufacturing investments. Exports are assumed to react with a certain time lag to the establishment of manufacturing plants abroad. In order to capture the DFI–export succession in the model, data were collected on the number of EC manufacturing subsidiaries for each firm at the end of 1985 and 1988. These numbers provide a measure of the level of EC manufacturing investment just before the end of fiscal year 1988 (ending March 1989) and the growth in manufacturing activities over the years 1985–1988 in which a substantial number of antidumping petitions were filed. In the recursive model, exports measured at the end of the first quarter of 1989 are related to Japanese manufacturing investments made before the end of 1988. Since the dependent variable reflects the relative orientation of Japanese exports towards Europe, The DFI variable has to be scaled accordingly. The explanatory variable *MANF88* divides the number of manufacturing subsidiaries in the EC by the total number of consolidated subsidiaries in Japan as well as abroad. *MANF88* thus becomes a measure of the importance of manufacturing activity in Europe relative to the firm's worldwide activities. This type of scaling has the advantage that *MANF88* is only weakly correlated with the structural explanatory variables in the model.

It is also necessary to control for Japanese firms' investments in distribution networks in the EC which serve to support exports from Japan. A dummy variable, *DIST88*, which takes the value 1 if the firm operated a subsidiary engaged in distribution activities in the EC at the end of 1988, effectively splits the sample of firms into two groups: those with an active presence in the EC, and those without such a presence.[14]

The specific characteristics of inter-firm relationships in Japan suggest controlling for another factor: whether the firm is engaged in components production for a 'core' firm in a vertical *keiretsu*.[15] Subcontractor firms within vertical *keiretsu* are likely to show export behaviour that differs from independent firms. If subcontractor firms are tied to the domestic operations of the core firm, they will be less export-intensive. On the other hand, if the core firm has invested in EC assembly plants, subcontractors can easily redirect components sales to supply the core firm in the EC. To test whether this effect has occurred, a dummy variable, *AFFEXP* (affiliated exporter), is included. *AFFEXP* takes the value 1 if the firm is a components subcontractor in a vertical *keiretsu* and if the core firm operated an EC manufacturing plant at the end of 1988.

The model is estimated using data on Japanese firms classified in the electronics or precision machinery industries and listed at Japanese stock exchanges. A broad measure of the electronics sector is used which includes firms manufacturing copiers, cameras, and measuring equipment, besides consumer electronics, semiconductors, components, telecommunications equipment, and computers. Out of an initial selection of 200 listed firms, 86 firms could be qualified as having positive exports to Europe on the basis of the information available. The relatively small sample can nevertheless be considered as representative since it excludes mostly minor firms and non-exporters but includes most major exporters such as Matsushita, Hitachi, Toshiba, Sony, Canon, and Sharp. To be precise, fiscal year 1988 exports to Europe by the firms in the sample added up to 2.2 trillion yen (17 billion dollars), 65 per cent of total Japanese exports to Europe in the 'electrical machinery', 'precision machinery', and 'office machinery' sectors.[16]

7.5 Firm Level Analysis: Estimation Results

The estimation results for equation (2) are presented in Table 7.3. The estimation method used is ordinary least squares, with the standard deviations of estimated parameters corrected for heteroscedasticity using the method suggested in White (1980). The variables related to firm-specific intangibles assets are all taken in natural logarithms.

Regression I shows the results of the model with direct investment variables excluded. The empirical results are in line with the a priori expectations: *RDINT*, *MARKINT*, *HUMRES*, and *CAPLAB* all have positive coefficients significantly different from zero. High R&D as well as marketing expenditures measure competitive advantages of firms, and these stimulate exports. Firms that are more capital and human resource intensive benefit from Japan's comparative advantages and also show a higher export intensity. The coefficient for *AFFEXP* is positive and significantly different

Table 7.3 Regression results explaining exports to Europe by 86 Japanese electronics firms

Dependent variable: log *EXPODD*	Regression I	Regression II	Regression III	Regression IV
log *RDINT*	0.47**	0.35**	0.30**	0.29**
	(3.54)	(3.24)	(2.78)	(2.71)
log *MARKINT*	0.28*	0.19	0.20	0.17
	(2.00)	(1.56)	(1.57)	(1.39)
log *CAPLAB*	0.65**	0.47*	0.54**	0.50*
	(3.13)	(2.43)	(2.77)	(2.56)
log *HUMRES*	0.70**	0.64**	0.67**	0.67**
	(2.96)	(3.30)	(3.49)	(3.49)
AFFEXP	1.01*	1.38**	1.40**	1.39**
	(2.50)	(3.73)	(3.66)	(3.70)
DIST88		0.94**	1.00**	0.95**
		(4.00)	(4.47)	(4.23)
MANF88		–0.39		
		(–0.44)		
MANF85			1.57*	1.84*
			(2.11)	(2.45)
MANFGROW[a]			–2.65**	–2.70**
			(–3.61)	(–3.56)
ACQUIS				0.74**
				(3.23)
Constant and industry dummies				
Constant	–2.50**	–3.29**	–3.26**	–3.24**
	(–3.49)	(–4.88)	(–5.00)	(–4.90)
CONSUM	1.97**	1.85**	1.80**	1.81**
	(3.35)	(3.21)	(3.30)	(3.27)
OFFCOMP	1.70**	1.75**	1.70**	1.65**
	(3.27)	(3.39)	(3.49)	(3.31)
TELCOM	0.37	0.80	0.74	0.73
	(0.59)	(1.42)	(1.38)	(1.33)
COMPO	0.23	0.27	0.17	0.12
	(0.44)	(0.53)	(0.34)	(0.25)
AUTOM	0.78	0.75	0.65	0.63
	(1.28)	(1.36)	(1.27)	(1.21)
MEDICAL	0.95	0.99	0.83	0.74
	(1.66)	(1.87)	(1.63)	(1.39)
Observations	86	86	86	86
Adjusted R^2	0.49	0.53	0.59	0.60

[a] excludes acquisitions in regression IV.

Remarks: see Appendix 7.1 for the definition of the variables. Hetereoscedasticity-corrected asymptotic *t*-ratios in parentheses; * = significant at the 0.05 level, ** = significant at the 0.01 level.

from zero, implying that subcontractor firms' exports to Europe cannot solely be explained by the firm-specific structural features related to competitive advantages. The explanation must be that subcontractors have become affiliated exporters, exporting components to their parent firms' manufacturing plants in the EC. These sales are more akin to a form of intra-firm trade and do not require local distribution activities.[17] The estimated fixed industry effects imply that firms producing consumer electronics goods and office machines are exporting relatively more to Europe. This will reflect the size of the EC market as well as the strength of Japanese firms *vis-à-vis* European firms in these industries. Although trade restrictions have been more prevalent as well in office machines and consumer electronics, the European exports of firms in these industries remained well above average.

Regressions II–IV show the estimation results when variables related to direct investment in manufacturing and distribution are included. In regression II, *MANF88* is negatively signed, which points to export substituting direct investment, but the coefficient is not significantly different from zero. *DIST88*, the variable indicating whether the firm operates a distribution subsidiary in the EC, has the expected positive sign and is significant at the 1 per cent level. This corresponds with the finding in Yamawaki (1991) that Japanese investment in distribution promotes exports from Japan. The fact that the estimated variance of the coefficient *MARKINT* becomes wider in regression II is partly related to a relatively strong correlation between *DIST88* and *MARKINT*.[18] *MARKINT* includes not only the cost of advertising but also the direct costs of maintaining a sales force and repair and warranty services. Firms that operate an extensive distribution network in Japan tend to have high sales cost intensities and it is this behaviour that Japanese firms have been adopting abroad as well (Williamson and Yamawaki 1989).

The insignificant coefficient of *MANF88* is puzzling. The analysis in Section 7.2 suggested that the escalation of trade restricting measures after 1985 did trigger new Japanese investments in Europe which were substituting for exports from Japan. In order to refine the analysis, the variable *MANF88* was decomposed into two components: the number of manufacturing subsidiaries at the end of 1985 divided by the number of consolidated subsidiaries at the time, *MANF85*, and the growth in the number of manufacturing subsidiaries in 1985–1988, again divided by the number of consolidated subsidiaries, *MANFGROW*.[19] This decomposition makes it possible to test whether or not there has been a shift in regime around 1985 with respect to the effects of DFI. *MANFGROW*, which is associated with the rise in import barriers in the EC, is expected to have the most pronounced negative effect on exports from Japan.

Regression III tests for the regime shift in 1985, with *MANF88* split up into *MANF85* and *MANFGROW*. The changes in the regression results are remarkable. The goodness of fit of the regression improves markedly. *MANF85* is significantly positive, while *MANFGROW* is negatively signed and significant at the 1 per cent level. These results do lend support to the hypothesis that Japanese electronics firms' manufacturing DFI in the EC in the second half of the 1980s has been substituting for exports. Firms that added manufacturing plants during 1985–1988 had significantly lower export intensities in 1989. In contrast, a relative stronger manufacturing position in the EC in 1985 has a positive effect on export intensity. One explanation is that manufacturing activity in 1985 concentrated on simple assembly activities, with the Japanese plants often putting together kits imported from Japan. The measure of manufacturing activity used, the number of subsidiaries with manufacturing operations, does not measure the size or extent of integration of manufacturing activity.[20] In later years, local content measures induced integrated Japanese production in Europe. This worked to limit offsetting increases in the export of components and strengthened export substitution, although the results suggest that components exports did grow at the subcontractor level.

Regression IV is similar to regression III but extends the model to include one more factor related to Japanese DFI which is likely to influence export intensities: whether the Japanese firm set up greenfield manufacturing plants or acquired an existing EC firm. As earlier noted, entry through acquisition is expected to have more ambiguous effects on exports. The acquired firm will not produce goods that are perfect substitutes for the exports of the acquirer. Indeed, there is evidence that Japanese firms are more likely to choose entry through acquisition if investment is diversifying (Hennart and Park 1992, Yamawaki 1993). Also, the acquired firm may possess brand names, distribution networks, and exclusive ties with customers, which all could be used by the acquiring firm to increase exports from Japan. The acquisition may also lead to a restructuring of activities involving the sourcing of components or final products from the acquiring firm. Although acquisitions have played only a very minor role in the investments of Japanese electronics firms in the EC in the 1980s,[21] it is useful to correct for these possible effects. In regression IV, acquisitions are excluded in *MANFGROW* and a separate dummy *ACQUIS* is included, which takes the value 1 if the Japanese firm acquired an EC firm during 1985–1988. *ACQUIS* has a positive effect on export intensity and is significant at the 1 per cent level, while the coefficient of *MANFGROW* becomes slightly more negative. Japanese firms that acquired EC firms thus show distinctly different export behaviour, all things equal, than firms that invested in greenfield plants.

7.6 Conclusions

This chapter has examined the relationship between Japanese electronics exports to Europe and Japanese firms' investments in manufacturing and distribution activities in the EC in the second half of the 1980s. Analysis at both the product and the firm level support the hypothesis that Japanese manufacturing investment has substituted for exports from Japan. Analysis at the product level shows that EC trade policy measures were followed by a decline in Japanese exports and a commensurate increase in Japanese firms' EC manufacturing capacity. Comparison of product level export and investment patterns in the US and the EC shows that manufacturing investment is associated with trade policy measures and has led to reduced exports from Japan.

Export substitution is also confirmed by an econometrical analysis of 86 Japanese electronics firms' exports to Europe in 1989. Controlling for industry- and firm-specific characteristics which are expected to influence export intensity, as well as for the presence of Japanese firms in the EC in 1985, the growth in the number of manufacturing subsidiaries in the EC during 1985–1988 is found to have a significantly negative effect on Japanese firms' exports to Europe. Exports to Europe are significantly higher for firms that invested in distribution subsidiaries in the EC and for firms that increased market access by acquiring an EC firm. In line with theoretical predictions, export intensity is found to be higher for firms with higher R&D intensities, higher direct and indirect marketing intensities, and higher capital and human resource intensities.

Inter-firm relationships between Japanese firms also play a role in export behaviour. Subcontractor firms in a vertical *keiretsu*, of which the 'core' firm operates manufacturing plants in the EC, are found to export relatively more to Europe. This suggests that affiliated exporters were able to expand exports by supplying components to the EC assembly plants of the core firms. While manufacturing investment has substituted for exports (final goods as well as components) of the investing firms, export substitution has been less if measured at the level of the vertical *keiretsu*.

The finding that Japanese manufacturing DFI has substituted for exports contrasts to an important extent with previous empirical results for American and Swedish DFI reported in Lipsey and Weiss (1981, 1984), Swedenborg (1979), and Blomström, Lipsey, and Kulchycky (1988). This can be attributed to the fact that Japanese DFI has for a substantial part been a response to EC trade policy measures and trade policy threats, as seen in Chapter 6. Such tariff jumping DFI is undertaken to bypass trade barriers, and is less motivated by possible merits of overseas production such as reductions in manufacturing costs or enhanced marketing functions.

This reduces the scope for demand increases and export growth. The results suggest that the motives for DFI as well as the mode of entry into foreign markets are of crucial importance for the relationship between DFI and exports.

APPENDIX 7.1

Variable Definitions, Means, and Standard Deviations

Table A7.1 presents a list of variable definitions, means, and standard deviations of the variables included in Table 7.3.

Table A7.1 Variable definitions, means, and standard deviations

Symbol	Definition of variable	Mean (standard deviation)
EXPODD	Exports to Europe/(Sales – exports to Europe), fiscal year 1988 (year ending March 1989)	0.109 (0.147)
RDINT	R&D expenditures/Value added, fiscal years 1986–1988	0.206 (0.157)
MARKINT	(Direct and indirect sales costs)*100/Sales, fiscal years 1986–1988	4.249 (3.234)
CAPLAB	Gross fixed depreciable capital/Total labour costs, fiscal years 1986–1988	1.048 (0.521)
HUMRES	Non-manufacturing (white collar) labour costs/Total labour costs, fiscal years 1986–1988	0.358 (0.160)
AFFEXP	Dummy variable, =1 if the firm is a member of a vertical *keiretsu* and sells components to the 'core' firm, which operated one or more manufacturing plants in the EC by 31 December 1988	0.081 (0.275)
DIST88	Dummy variable, =1 if the firm had established a subsidiary which engaged in distribution activities in the EC by 31 December 1988	0.547 (0.500)
MANF88	Number of the firm's EC subsidiaries with manufacturing operations by 31 December 1988/Number of consolidated subsidiaries of the firm in fiscal year 1988	0.055 (0.104)
MANF85	Number of the firm's EC subsidiaries with manufacturing operations by 31 December 1985/Number of consolidated subsidiaries of the firm in fiscal year 1985	0.033 (0.087)

Table A7.1 (*Continued*)

Symbol	Definition of variable	Mean (standard deviation)
MANFGROW	Increase through 1986–1988 in the number of the firm's EC subsidiaries with manufacturing operations/Number of consolidated subsidiaries of the firm in fiscal year 1985; excludes acquisitions in regression IV	0.037 (0.087)
ACQUIS	Dummy variable, =1 if the firm acquired an EC-based manufacturing firm in the years 1986–1988	0.035 (0.185)
CONSUM	Dummy variable, =1 if the firm's major line of business is consumer electronics	0.140 (0.349)
OFFCOMP	Dummy variable, =1 if the firm's major line of business is office machines and computers	0.163 (0.371)
TELCOM	Dummy variable, =1 if the firm's major line of business is telecommunications	0.093 (0.292)
COMPO	Dummy variable, =1 if the firm's major line of business is electric or electronic components	0.314 (0.467)
AUTOM	Dummy variable, =1 if the firm's major line of business is factory automation and control equipment	0.105 (0.308)
MEDICAL	Dummy variable, =1 if the firm's major line of business is medical and scientific equipment	0.128 (0.308)
HEAVY	Dummy variable, =1 if the firm's major line of business is heavy electrical equipment	0.058 (0.235)

APPENDIX 7.2

Data Sources

Information on sales, exports, direct and indirect sales costs, value added, fixed depreciable assets, and total and non-manufacturing labour costs in Japanese fiscal years 1986, 1987, and 1988 were all taken or calculated from Nihon Kaihatsu Ginkou Setsubi Toushi Kenkyuujo (1986–1989). The information in this database is based on unconsolidated financial reports of firms listed at Japanese stock exchanges; consolidated financial figures are not available in detail in Japan. Data on R&D expenditures were taken from Touyou Keizai (1986d–1990d). The share of European exports in total exports was drawn from Dempa (1990b) and in some cases from company financial reports. Information on EC subsidiaries (number, distribution or manufacturing, acquisition or greenfield) was taken from Touyou Keizai (1985a–1992a). The number of subsidiaries is measured at December 1985 and December 1988. Information on membership of vertical *keiretsu* was taken from Touyou Keizai (1990c). The latter information was combined with information on the most important client firms available from Touyou Keizai (1991b) and with information on manufacturing subsidiaries of the parent firm from Touyou Keizai (1988a–1992a). Finally, firms were classified into seven industries based on sales by product group in Nihon Kaihatsu Ginkou Setsubi Toushi Kenkyuujo (1989) and Touyou Keizai (1990d).

NOTES

1. See e.g. Kimura and Pugel (1995), Drake and Caves (1992), Kogut and Chang (1991), and Sleuwaegen and Yamawaki (1992) for DFI in the US, and Heitger and Stehn (1990) for DFI in the EC.
2. See Williamson and Yamawaki (1989) on this issue. Chapter 1 provides figures on Japanese electronics firms' DFI in EC distribution.
3. Calculations based on Nihon Tsuushou Sangyoushou (1991: 200–211), show intra-regional sales of Japanese electronics manufacturing subsidiaries at 97 per cent for North America and 98 per cent for Europe in the fiscal year ending March 1990 (see also Chapter 1). This is in contrast to an important extent with Japanese DFI in Asia, which has been attracted by lower labour costs and is often of the export-platform type (see also Urata 1991, 1992): intra-regional sales reached only 54 per cent here.
4. See also Wakasugi (1994a), where it is argued that export substitution has been important in the car and electronics industries.
5. The finding that antidumping cases and not necessarily antidumping duties have significant effects on EC imports is corroborated by a more systematic analysis of EC antidumping policy in Messerlin (1989).
6. In 1990 magnetron exports only reached 1.4 million units, less than half the volume in 1989; see Appendix 1.3.
7. This figure is an estimate based on available information on plant capacities of individual Japanese firms. See Appendix 1.3.
8. Exports to the EC will also be lower if Japanese firms' market share in the EC is relatively low because of stronger competition from EC producers. Preferably, exports should be related to total sales by Japanese firms in the EC or US market (as in Table 7.1) but the latter data are not available. Since production

of the electronics goods listed in Table 7.2 tends to be dominated by global firms and transatlantic DFI is important (e.g., Philips too is a major player in the US consumer electronics market), the market size figures may still be reliable benchmarks.

9. See also Chapter 6 on the relationship between DFI and trade policy measures in the US and the EC.
10. Figures in MITI's survey among Japanese multinationals show that exports to Europe from Asian subsidiaries of Japanese electronics MNEs amounted to only 3 per cent of the parent firms' direct exports to Europe in 1990 (Nihon Tsuushou Sangyoushou 1991).
11. European export data include exports to EFTA and Eastern European countries as well as exports to EC countries. The latter account for 90 per cent of Japanese electronics exports to Europe (JETRO 1989a).
12. A listing of variables with definitions, means, and standard deviations is provided in Appendix 7.1 and data sources are given in Appendix 7.2.
13. Some observers see this as a major contributing factor to Japanese firms' competitive strength; see e.g. Abegglen and Stalk (1985).
14. Including the ratio of the number of sales subsidiaries to the total number of consolidated subsidiaries did not give any robust results. This is probably due to the poor information such a ratio conveys. Some firms have established sales subsidiaries in each EC country but only have a small number of employees working in these, while other firms let the manufacturing subsidiary handle distribution and do not operate separate sales subsidiaries.
15. Firms are considered subcontractors (1) if they belong to a vertical *keiretsu*, (2) if they produce electronic components, and (3) if their 'core' or parent firm is also a major client.
16. Exports in those sectors amounted to 26 billion dollars according to JETRO (1989a).
17. In Chapter 5 evidence was found that subcontractors in Japanese vertical *keiretsu* are also more likely to invest abroad if the parent firms have set up extensive manufacturing networks there. Among the eight affiliated exporters in the sample, however, no firm had set up subsidiaries in the EC by 1989.
18. The correlation coefficient is 32 per cent.
19. This specification follows from taking the *relative* growth in the number of manufacturing subsidiaries and weighing this growth ratio with *MANF85* to take the relative importance of EC manufacturing subsidiaries in 1985 into account. Thus, $MANFGROW = ((ESUB88 - ESUB85)/ESUB85)*(ESUB85/CONSUB85) = (ESUB88 - ESUB85)/CONSUB85$, where *ESUB* stands for the number of EC manufacturing subsidiaries and *CONSUB* for the number of consolidated subsidiaries.
20. The number of manufacturing subsidiaries as a measure of manufacturing activity also introduces a measuring error which might bias the coefficient of *MANF85* upwards: in practice, several subsidiaries with manufacturing activities are also engaged in distribution activities. In 1985, with manufacturing operations rather limited, the fact that those subsidiaries manufactured or assembled electronics goods was probably less important than the fact that they were engaged in sales activities. Based on the information available, it was possible to distinguish two groups of manufacturing subsidiaries: those with

manufacturing activities only, and those with both manufacturing and sales activities. A test was performed splitting *MANF85* into these two components. The coefficient for production-cum-sales subsidiaries turned out to be significantly positive, while the coefficient for manufacturing subsidiaries was negatively signed but insignificant.

21. In fact, in the sample only three firms increased their manufacturing activity in the EC through acquisitions. This obviously calls for caution in interpreting the effect of *ACQUIS* in regression IV. Japanese acquisitions of European electronics firms have become much more common since 1989 (see Chapter 1).

8

Local Content Requirements and Local Procurement

8.1 Introduction

The rapid rise in Japanese firms' investment in the European Community (EC) since the mid 1980s has inspired an increasing number of studies analysing its determinants and effects.[1] Much attention has focused on the relationship between inward investment and the formation of the Single Market and accompanied threats of discriminatory action against imports from non-EC countries. The prevailing view is that the Single Market initiative and actual trade policy measures such as VERs and antidumping actions have brought forward Japanese investments, but the debate on whether the level of investment has been affected is still ongoing.[2] The evidence presented in Chapter 6 brought some clarity on this issue. Trade policy measures did substantially increase Japanese investment in the EC electronics industry.

With the debate on the relationship between import barriers and Japanese investment, other policy measures with a potentially important impact on Japanese trade and investment have not received due attention: local content requirements for Japanese firms' manufacturing operations in the EC. Although neither the EC Commission nor national governments have legislated formal local content requirements, a range of such requirements existed in the late 1980s and these often singled out Japanese manufacturers. The main local content requirements affecting Japanese electronics firms were described in Chapter 1. For example, local content requirements were informally negotiated in the context of a VER, were negotiated between national or local authorities and Japanese investors as a condition for investment subsidies, and were included in an anti-circumvention clause in antidumping law. Moreover, the remaining national quota for Japanese imports transformed rules of origin into content requirements which needed to be cleared for a free circulation of Japanese goods within the EC.

The theoretical analysis in Chapter 4 suggested that the economic effects of local content requirements crucially depend on the response elicited from the firms involved and the mode of competition on components markets. No study has yet emerged in which the actual effects of EC local content requirements are assessed. This is an empirical issue of obvious importance, but a systematic analysis requires the collection of detailed information on procurement changes and the structure of components industries.

This chapter attempts to answer part of the empirical question by examining how Japanese firms have responded to local content requirements in the late 1980s. It does so by analysing detailed data on procurement and sales activities in 1990 by Japanese manufacturing subsidiaries in the EC in two vertically related industries, consumer electronics and electronic components. These industries are responsible for a sizeable share of trade and investment by Japanese firms and have been targeted by a range of local content requirements in the EC. Through a comparison with procurement and sales patterns of Japanese subsidiaries in North America, where local content requirements have been much less prominent, an assessment is made of the effects of local content requirements.

The plan of the chapter is as follows. Section 8.2 provides an overview of local content requirements for Japanese firms in the EC in the 1980s with an emphasis on the electronics industry, and argues that local content requirements have been less stringent in the United States. Section 8.3 describes the survey data on Japanese electronics firms and presents the findings concerning procurement and sales behaviour. The final section draws conclusions and discusses implications of the findings.

8.2 Local Content Requirements in the EC and North America

Local content requirements aimed at Japanese firms' manufacturing subsidiaries have been particularly widespread in the EC. Although neither the EC Commission nor national governments have imposed formal local content requirements, a range of *de facto* content measures have targeted Japanese firms in the 1980s. Pressures to increase local content reached a peak towards the end of the 1980s in response to Japanese investments in EC assembly operations. This section reviews the most important local content measures affecting Japanese firms' manufacturing activities in the EC, in particular those in the electronics sector.[3] A comparison with local content requirements in the US suggests that these requirements have been much less stringent there. Prima facie evidence for the importance of such differences is provided by the results of a survey among Japanese electronics subsidiaries in the EC and North America.

8.2.1 Local Content Requirements in the EC

Five types of local content requirements for foreign manufacturers in the EC can be distinguished.

First, there is *negotiated* local content, applying mostly to larger manufacturing investments. A firm wishing to invest in an EC country may be confronted with local content requests by the local government, as part of broader arrangements including land acquisition and subsidies. These local content requests are usually informal and undisclosed, but the available information suggests that such requests can be frequent and demanding. In a 1992 survey by the Japan External Trade Organisation (JETRO) among Japanese manufacturing affiliates in Europe, more than a quarter of such Japanese firms stated that they were confronted with local content requests by local governments when considering investments in Europe. For electronic machinery producers this was 44 per cent, and for automobile producers 78 per cent (JETRO 1992b: 77)[4]. As for automobiles, it is known that Nissan promised authorities in the United Kingdom that its Sunderland automobile plant would eventually reach 80 per cent local content as part of a broader agreement between Nissan and the UK government. In the electronics industry, the UK government reportedly requested that Japanese colour television producers reach 70 per cent local content (Burton and Saelens 1987).

Second, informal local content requirements have been negotiated at the Community level as part of a broader agreement on export restrictions. In 1982, the EC Commission negotiated a voluntary export restraint for Japanese video cassette recorders (VCRs) through MITI. In the same year, however, several Japanese firms had set up manufacturing plants in the EC. The VCR agreement stipulated that such Japanese manufacturing plants in the EC should reach a local content level of 25 per cent of value added in 1984 rising to 45 per cent in 1985, for shipments by these plants not to be counted in the quota.[5]

Third, a similar but much more powerful linkage of trade restrictions and local content rules came into effect in June 1987 with the 'screwdriver' amendment to EC antidumping law.[6] Since the early 1980s, EC firms had stepped up antidumping actions against Japanese imports and the EC Commission had imposed antidumping duties on such products as electronic scales, copying machines, and machine tools. In most cases, however, Japanese firms chose to avoid paying the duties by setting up manufacturing operations for these products in the EC. As mentioned in Chapter 1, the major Japanese exporters had typically established such subsidiaries at the time of the final antidumping decision, between one and two years after the start of an investigation. Some of the manufacturing plants were involved in only the simplest assembly tasks, putting together knock-down kits imported from Japan; hence the term 'screwdriver' plants. In 1987, after some intensive lobbying by EC firms, the Commission responded by amending its antidumping legislation to make it potentially applicable to Japanese manufacturing plants as well. The new rule stipulated in general terms that firms that had been target of antidumping actions and had reacted by setting up assembly plants in the EC were required to procure at least 40 per cent of the value of components used in assembly from countries other than the home country. If firms did not clear the requirement, antidumping duties were to be levied on products assembled in the EC.

In practice, the amendment was administered as a local content requirement for Japanese firms manufacturing in the EC. It has been invoked seven times, and all cases concerned Japanese products assembled in the EC: electronics scales, electronic typewriters, copying machines, dot matrix printers, video tape recorders, numerically controlled machine tools, and ball bearings (Van Bael and Bellis 1990). All of these cases were finally settled through undertakings by which individual Japanese firms agreed to reduce dependence on imports from Japan and to increase the local content of EC production. It has to be noted that the 40 per cent non-Japanese parts requirement, which in practice was interpreted by Japanese firms as a 40 per cent *European* content requirement, was rather stringent. Japanese firms could not count assembly and overhead costs as European content; the 40 per cent rule applied to the assembled parts only. There is at least one case reported of a European firm—in fact, a complainant in the antidumping case—that would not have been able to pass the 40 per cent test.[7]

The requirement was also stricter than existing EC *rules of origin*, rules that determine which nationality should be given to a product when it enters the EC (Vermulst and Waer 1990). Rules of origin gain importance when trade policy measures are country- or firm-specific, as is the case with antidumping policy or national quotas. The basic EC rule of origin, dating from 1968, takes as the country of origin of a product the country where the 'last substantial manufacturing process' is carried out. The ambiguity of this definition can lead to different standards applied by the various national customs services, and this has led the EC commission to adopt several product-specific rules of origin. For instance, for CTVs and printed circuit boards, the definition implies that a minimum of 45 per cent of value added has to be generated in the exporting country if a product is to be considered as originating in that country. This requirement in practice, but not by law, also applies to VCRs (Vermulst and Waer 1990). Rules of origin were used by the Commission to establish circumvention by Japanese firms through assembly in, and exports from, third countries.[8] However, in the case of circumvention through the assembly of products within the EC, the Commission chose to set the stricter 40 per cent requirement to supersede the existing rules of origin. The difference in local content standards between the antidumping legislation and rules of origin implied that Japanese manufacturing operations which would not constitute circumvention if conducted in, say, Taiwan, could still be considered mere 'screwdriver' activities if conducted in the EC.

The antidumping actions against assembly plants increased demand for EC-made components such as printed circuit boards, power supply units, tuners, capacitors, magnetic heads, and the like. This was an important reason for Japanese producers of such components, integrated manufacturers as well as independent components manufacturers, to establish or extend manufacturing activities in the EC. It was crucial that such components produced in the EC by Japanese firms could be considered 'European' and not 'Japanese', since only 'European' components could be used by Japanese producers of final goods subject to antidumping to reach a sufficient level of non-Japanese content. In most cases, the Commission used rules of origin to determine whether components should be considered of European origin. This implied, for instance, that Japanese producers of printed circuit boards in the EC had to reach a European content of 45 per cent of value added in order to be able to sell their products to Japanese final goods producers subject to local content requirements. This in turn implied that Japanese producers of ICs in the EC which were selling to these circuit board producers had to make sure that their ICs were considered of European origin. Hence, local content rules cascaded upstream to components and ultimately sub-components and ICs.

After the EC Commission had invoked the anti-circumvention amendment seven times, in May 1990 a GATT panel ruled against the antidumping amendment. The panel agreed with the complaining Japanese government that duties and content requirements were applied in a discriminatory way to Japanese producers within the EC, violating GATT rules. The EC Commission has not invoked the law since, although the Commission confirmed that existing undertakings would remain in force. The Commission also stated that it would seek a satisfactory anti-circumvention regulation in the framework of the Uruguay Round of GATT negotiations. The events may not have convinced Japanese firms that local content requirements will not affect their EC activities in some form in future.[9]

Fourth, through a combination of factors, Japanese firms manufacturing products in the EC have been required to reach a certain local content for these products to be freely traded within the EC. Until 1993, a range of national quotas were administered for Japanese imports, most with special permission granted by the EC Commission under Article 115 of the EC's Treaty of Rome. The best known example is those of cars, where Italy, Spain, Portugal, and France remained a strict quota on Japanese imports. In the electronics sector, quotas were in effect for colour televisions (Spain, Italy, France), video tape recorders (Spain), and audio products (Italy, France), among others. EC-produced Japanese cars and electronics were excluded from these import quotas only if they could be considered 'European' and not Japanese. In practice, this was determined at customs by applying the EC's rules of origin.

Hence, if Japanese producers of colour televisions and video tape recorders in, say, the UK wanted to export freely to countries maintaining quotas on Japanese imports, they were tied to a 45 per cent value added local content rule. Restrictions on intra-EC trade of UK-produced Japanese cars became most apparent in 1988, when Nissan started exporting its UK-produced Bluebird car to France. Although Nissan claimed that its cars reached 60 per cent European content, France argued that the Nissan cars could not be considered to be of European origin and should be included in its informal import quota for Japanese cars. Italy and Spain took the same position and included their UK imports in their quota. The lack of an unambiguous product-specific rule of origin for cars made the issue difficult to resolve. France claimed that the Nissan cars could be considered European only if the local content of the UK-produced cars reached 80 per cent of value added, but there was no legal basis for this argument. In 1989, pressure from the UK and the EC Commission, which did not want to introduce new restrictions on intra-EC trade, forced France and Italy to retreat and accept the cars as European.[10] The episode clearly illustrates the pressure mounting on Japanese firms to reach 'satisfactory' levels of local content.

Not only national governments, but also the EC Commission itself has attempted to use rules of origin to influence trade and investment by Japanese firms. The Commission has used its power to issue product-specific rules of origin twice, in 1989 and 1990, to target Japanese firms. In July 1989 a new origin for ICs was adopted, stating that the country of origin is the one where the etching of silicon wafers takes place. This new rule mainly affected the operations of Japanese firms, which were still under investigation in an antidumping case concerning DRAM and EPROM memory chips.[11] At the time, the major Japanese manufacturers operated IC plants in the EC, but these plants mostly engaged in assembly, packaging, and testing. Without the new rule of origin, EC-assembled ICs would be considered of European origin, and antidumping duties could have been avoided by increasing EC assembly activities. In addition, as noted above, Japanese IC manufactures had to make sure that their ICs could be labelled 'European' to satisfy demand from Japanese manufacturers of products such as copiers and printed circuit boards in the EC. In response to all these pressures, all major Japanese manufacturers (NEC, Fujitsu, Hitachi, Toshiba, and Mitsubishi) announced plans to extend their EC operations to include wafer etching or to establish new integrated plants.[12]

Fifth, public procurement practices in the EC may favour 'European' products over foreign ones. EC regulations on public procurement in the telecommunications and energy sectors allow governments to favour domestic offers notwithstanding that foreign firms offer to supply at a lower price. The maximum price differential is small, though, at 3 per cent. Products manufactured in the EC by foreign firms can qualify for preferential treatment if at least 50 per cent of value added is generated within the Community. This has given foreign firms additional incentives to increase local content in particular in the telecommunications industry, where as much as 90 per cent of sales may be to the public sector (Flamm 1990).

8.2.2 Local Content Requirements in North America

In the US, measures taken to increase the local content of Japanese manufacturing plants have arguably had a much smaller impact on Japanese firms' trade and investment. State authorities are likely to include local content requirements in negotiations with Japanese investors, in particular in the case of large scale investments such as automobile plants. There have also been local content requirements linked to trade restrictions. An informal local content requirement of 40 per cent of value added was reportedly agreed within the framework of the 1978 orderly market arrangement by which Japanese manufacturers of CTVs agreed to limit exports to the US.[13] In some antidumping cases involving Japanese exports, i.e. cellular mobile telephones, duties were jointly levied on assembled products and subassemblies (see also Chapter 6). This restricted the possibility of Japanese firms' jumping the antidumping levies by investing in simple assembly operations in the US. Since the signing of the 1988 Omnibus Trade Act, antidumping measures can automatically be extended to include components (see Vermulst and Waer 1990). Although such measures can force Japanese investors to procure parts locally, the anti-circumvention clause is substantially less strict than the 40 per cent requirement in the EC 'screwdriver plant' legislation.

In the 1988 Canada–US free trade agreement, rules of origin took a prominent position. A range of product-specific rules of origin determining whether goods qualify for duty free intra-regional trade were introduced. In case of automobiles, for instance, the origin rule states that the local (North American) content should reach 62.5 per cent of value added. Most of the specific rules of origin were taken over by the North American Free Trade Agreement (NAFTA) (see also Lloyd 1993). However, such rules of origin have not affected Japanese firms' operations in North America to the same extent as in the EC, because both manufacturing investments and the market for Japanese products are heavily concentrated in the United States and intra-regional trade is much less important than in the EC.

Last, state and local governments in the US may favour products of US origin over goods of foreign origin in public procurement decisions; such practices are often laid down in 'buy American' acts.

8.2.3 Effects of Local Content Requirements

Prima facie evidence of the differences in the reach of local content measures facing Japanese electronics manufacturers in the EC compared with

Table 8.1 Japanese electronics subsidiaries in the EC and North America: reasons for increase in local content in 1989–1990 (%)

	EC	North America
(1) Local content increase	49	23
(2) Reasons for increase		
Local content requirements	48	4
Cost effectiveness	29	48
(3) Causes of local content increase		
Increased production by local components suppliers	10	17
Increased quality of local components due to technical assistance given to local firms	5	4
Increased procurements from local Japanese firms	29	30
Increased local production by the firm itself	14	30
Increased local production by related firms	5	9

Note: Percentages of subsidiaries answering affirmatively; multiple answers are possible. Percentages under (2) and (3) are for firms that increased local content.

Source: Nihon Tsuushou Sangyoushou (1991).

North America is provided in Table 8.1. The table lists responses of Japanese electronics firms to questions concerning procurement in the fiscal year 1989 (the year ending March 1990) MITI survey. Asked if their subsidiaries had increased procurements of local components and materials, the answer was affirmative for almost half of the EC subsidiaries but for less than a quarter of North American subsidiaries. Asked to give the major reasons for recent increases in local procurement, almost half of the EC subsidiaries but only 4 per cent of North American subsidiaries cited local content requirements. In contrast, local content was increased in 48 per cent of North American subsidiaries because this strategy was judged more cost effective, whereas the corresponding figure for EC subsidiaries was 29 per cent. These responses suggest that local content requirements have played an important role in increasing the local content of Japanese subsidiaries in the EC. Subsidiaries in North America, on the other hand, apparently have decided to increase procurement only when doing so reduced costs.

The Japanese firms were also asked to indicate the causes of the increase in local content. The answers give some indication of the strategies Japanese firms follow to increase local content. Several strategies can be distinguished, not all of which are included in MITI's questionnaire: increasing procurements of components from local producers (which may necessitate the provision of technical assistance to local firms); integrating manufacturing operations to include components production; inviting related firms and subcontractors within the vertical *keiretsu* to manufacture components abroad; increasing procurements from independent Japanese components producers in the EC (which have often been supplying the firms in Japan as well); and establishing joint ventures with local firms to manufacture components (see also Yamazawa 1991).

The figures in Table 8.1 suggest that, in both the EC and North America, procurement from local components suppliers is less important than procurement from group firms or independent Japanese components manufacturers. In particular, few firms reported that they had chosen to provide technical assistance to local suppliers in order to facilitate increased procurements of components (5 per cent of EC subsidiaries and 4 per cent of North American subsidiaries). Relatively often mentioned are increased components production by the firm itself (14 per cent of EC subsidiaries and 30 per cent of North American subsidiaries) and procurements from locally established independent Japanese manufacturers (29 and 30 per cent, respectively). The importance of procurement from independent Japanese components suppliers in the EC has also been suggested in Chapter 1, where it was seen that Japanese components manufacturers, including Alps Electric, Murata Electric, and Kyocera, substantially expanded manufacturing employment in the EC in the second half of the 1980s.

It cannot be inferred from the survey results in Table 8.1 whether stricter local content requirements in the EC have led Japanese firms to adopt specific procurement strategies. None of the causes of local content increases distinguished in the questionnaire appears more important for EC subsidiaries. The questionnaire furthermore lacks clear and comprehensive categories and does not investigate the quantitative importance of each procurement strategy. Differences in procurement behaviour are better analysed by examining actual procurement and sales data of the Japanese subsidiaries.

8.3 Procurement and Sales by Japanese Electronics Firms in the EC and North America

Procurement and sales behaviour of Japanese manufacturing subsidiaries is examined for two vertically related industries: the consumer electronics industry and the electronic components industry.[14] The analysis uses unpublished data from the 1989 MITI survey among Japanese multinational enterprises. The MITI survey received valid responses from 72 per cent of foreign subsidiaries. All foreign subsidiaries in which Japanese firms have a capital stake of at least 10 per cent are included.[15] Table 8.2 gives the number of, and total sales by, Japanese manufacturing subsidiaries responding to the survey, classified in the consumer electronics and elec-

Table 8.2 Japanese consumer electronics and electronic components manufacturing subsidiaries in North America and the EC: sales and number of subsidiaries

	North America		EC	
	Sales (bn yen)	No. of subs.	Sales (bn yen)	No. of subs.
Consumer electronics	1,498	19	684	34
Electronic components	278	23	101	22

Source: Nihon Tsuushou Sangyoushou (1991).

tronic components industries and active in the EC or North America.
Sales of 19 consumer electronics subsidiaries in North America totalled 1,498 billion yen, more than double the 684 billion yen worth of consumer electronics goods sold by 34 subsidiaries in the EC. Calculated at March 1990 exchange rates (159 yen per dollar), sales amounted to 9.4 and 4.3 billion dollars, respectively. Subsidiaries in the electronic components industry registered much lower total sales at 278 billion yen in North America and 101 billion yen in the EC. The figures show that EC subsidiaries are considerably smaller in scale than their North American counterparts. This is due to the traditional fragmentation of the EC market, which has induced Japanese firms to set up production plants for similar products in several EC countries. The evidence in Chapter 1 showed that Japanese firms have later moved towards rationalisation and a closer integration of their EC activities.[16]

The firms responding to the MITI survey were asked to give information for each subsidiary on the geographical distribution of sales, and the value and geographical distribution of procurements of components and materials. The questionnaire also asked firms to distinguish between intra-group transactions and arm's length trade with independent suppliers and customers. This information allows for an assessment of the relative importance of procurements from local companies versus procurements from firms within the vertical *keiretsu*.[17] Since procurements in the definition of the MITI survey include purchases of components and materials but not those of machinery and tools, it is possible to use procurement and sales data to calculate local value added in the subsidiaries. Based on these data, a fairly accurate picture of the value added chain can be obtained: the location of value added activities and whether these activities are controlled by the same 'core' firm. In addition, since Japanese electronic components producers also supply Japanese consumer electronics firms, additional information on intra-group components deliveries can be obtained by looking at the sales pattern of Japanese components manufacturing subsidiaries.

Not all subsidiaries produced valid answers to all questions relating to sales and procurements, and a selection of subsidiaries with sufficient information was made. Subsidiaries responsible for on average 60–70 per cent of industry sales could be included in the selection.[18] The results of the analysis of sales and procurements by the selected subsidiaries are presented in Figures 8.1–8.4, which depict the structure of sales and procurements for the two groups of subsidiaries in North America and the EC, respectively. The value of sales by the subsidiaries is set at 100; the figures show how this sales value is marketed by region and how the sales value is distributed over value added generated within the manufacturing subsidiaries, and procurements.

8.3.1 Procurement and Sales by North American Subsidiaries

Figure 8.1 shows the structure of regional and intra-group sales and procurements of Japanese consumer electronics manufacturing subsidiaries in North America. North American subsidiaries exclusively service the North American market: 99 per cent of sales go to the local market (the US or Canada, whichever country the subsidiary is established in) and 1 per cent is exported to the rest of North America (Canada when the subsidiary is established in the US, or vice versa). Intra-group sales to dependent wholesalers is limited to 1 per cent of sales. The latter result is puzzling, since Japanese electronics firms are well known to have invested extensively in wholesale distribution networks in the United States (Yamawaki 1991, Williamson and Yamawaki 1989). It is possible that the low level of reported intra-group sales is due to the fact that North American subsidiaries combine production and wholesale activities. Where such subsidiaries also import finished products from Japan, calculated value added ratios may be biased downwards and imports from Japan upwards, and caution should be exercised in interpreting the results.[19]

More than half the value of sales (53 per cent) of North American subsidiaries is embedded in the procurement of components from Japan, all of which are intra-group procurements from the parent firm or affiliated components suppliers in Japan. This finding corresponds with the conclusion in Graham and Krugman (1990) that Japanese manufacturing subsidiaries in the United States are in general strongly dependent on supplies of components from their home country. North American procurements amount to 12 per cent of sales value, of which 2 per cent are procurements from related components suppliers established in North America. Procurement from Asia is also important (8 per cent), while the manufacturing operations of the subsidiaries themselves add the remaining 26 per cent of sales value. The figures imply a North American content of 39 per cent, of which 11 per cent is added by unrelated local components manufacturers. In

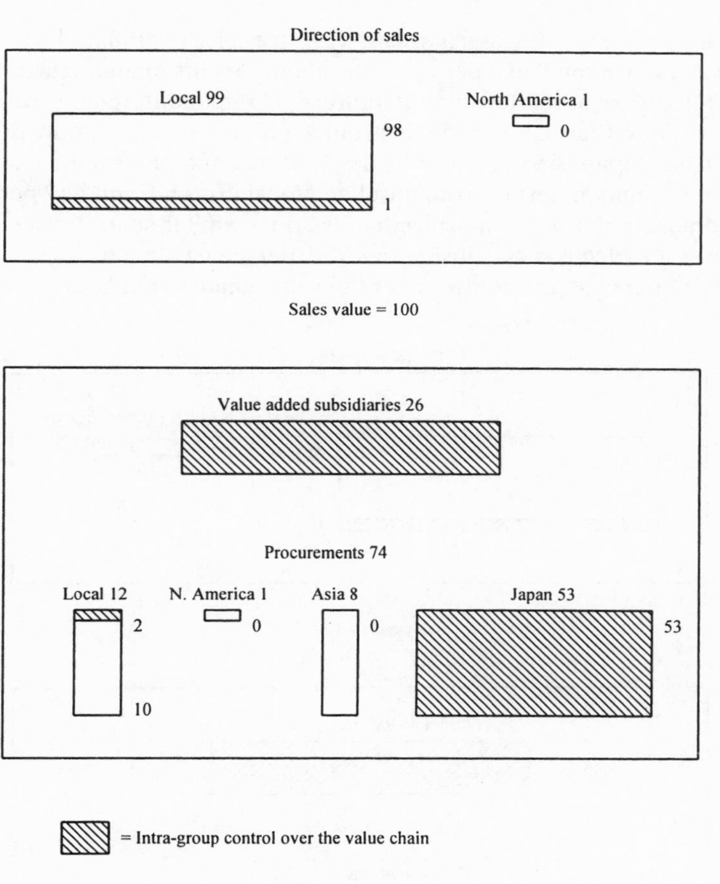

Figure 8.1 Structure of regional and intra-group sales and procurements of Japanese consumer electronics manufacturing subsidiaries in North America, 1990

Source: calculations based on Nihon Tsuushou Sangyoushou (1991).

general, the involvement of unrelated firms in the supply chain is limited, with the Japanese firm controlling 81 per cent of transactions on a value basis (26 per cent value added, 53 per cent intra-group procurements from Japan, and 2 per cent local intra-group procurements).

Figue 8.2 shows the structure of procurements and sales of Japanese electronic components manufacturing subsidiaries in North America. Most of the sales are marketed in North America (97 per cent); 2 per cent of sales are exports to Japan. Intra-group sales (captive sales to affiliated electronics subsidiaries) are small at 4 per cent: most components manufacturers sell at arms' length to unrelated manufacturers. Components plants rely even more strongly than consumer electronics plants on intra-group procurements from Japan (65 per cent of sales value), while procurements of sub-components and materials from unrelated local firms are small (7 per cent). Components manufacturing subsidiaries add a similar share to sales value as consumer electronics subsidiaries (26 per cent). In all, local content reaches 34 per cent and control over the value chain extends to 93 per cent.

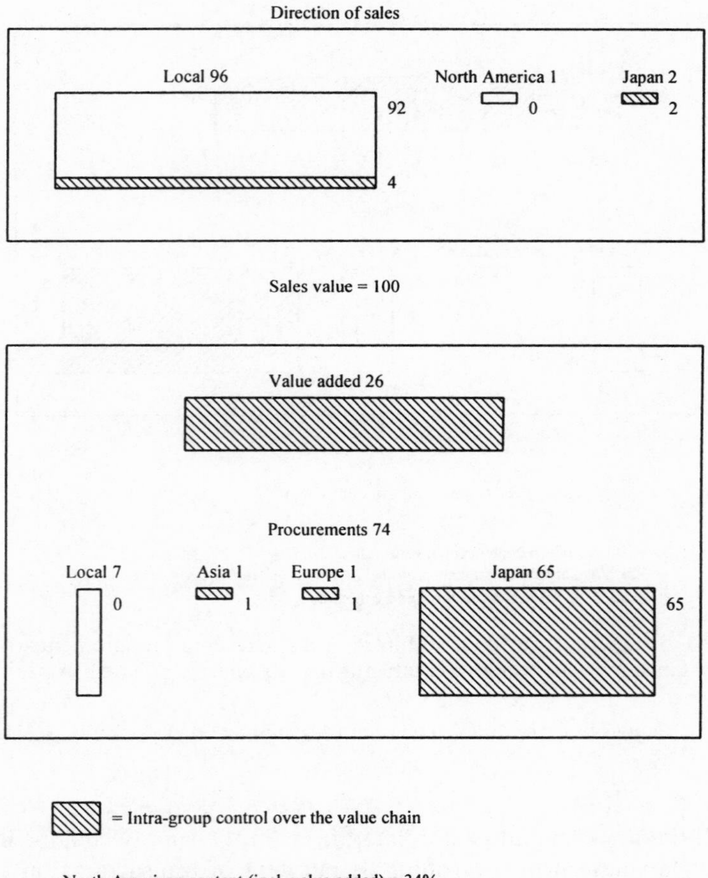

Figure 8.2 Structure of regional and intra-group sales and procurements of Japanese electronic components manufacturing subsidiaries in North America, 1990

Source: calculations based on Nihon Tsuushou Sangyoushou (1991).

8.3.2 Procurement and Sales by EC Subsidiaries

Figure 8.3 shows the structure of sales and procurements of Japanese consumer electronics manufacturing subsidiaries in the 12 countries of the European Community. As with North American subsidiaries, almost all sales are to the regional market: 77 per cent of sales goes to the country where the subsidiary is established and 22 per cent to other European countries. Sales to other regions (Asia and Japan) account for only 2 per cent. A relatively large share of sales is intra-group: 20 out of 77 per cent in case of local sales, and 19 out of 22 per cent for sales to other Europe. The high share of intra-group sales to other European countries is likely to be due to the establishment of separate distribution subsidiaries in each European country.

Procurement behaviour shows characteristics that are clearly distinct from North American subsidiaries. Only roughly one third of sales value can be attributed to procurements of components from Japan, while procurements from the country of investment and other European countries reaches 35 per cent of sales value. EC subsidiaries are also less reliant on procurements from Asia, which amount to only 2 per cent of sales value. Value added is 5 percentage points higher than in case of North American subsidiaries, at 31 per cent. This brings the European content of Japanese consumer electronics manufacturing operations to 66 per cent, substantially higher than in North America.

However, Figure 8.3 also shows that high local content ratios are not accompanied by substantial procurements from local components suppliers. One third of local procurements (4 out of 11 per cent) and the major share of procurements from Europe (19 out of 23 per cent) are intra-group transactions. Procurements from unrelated European firms account for only 12 per cent of sales, similar to the 11 per cent found for North American subsidiaries. Total control over the value chain is even higher than in North America at 88 per cent.

Another point of caution in interpreting the above results should be noted. It is possible that intra-group procurements from other countries include procurements from central procurement and distribution centres operated by the Japanese firms, which in turn may have purchased the components from independent suppliers. Such a procurement strategy will artificially raise the reported share of intra-group procurements and control over the value chain. It is known that such international procurement offices are operated by most large Japanese firms in Singapore (Nihon Tsuushou Sangyoushou 1990: 136), such that the figures for intra-group procurements from Asia are likely to be biased. However, these intra-group procurements from Asia are not important quantitatively and it is much less evident that procurement offices are important in European activities. The fact that intra-group sales of Japanese electronics components manufacturers in the EC are similarly important (see Figure 8.4)

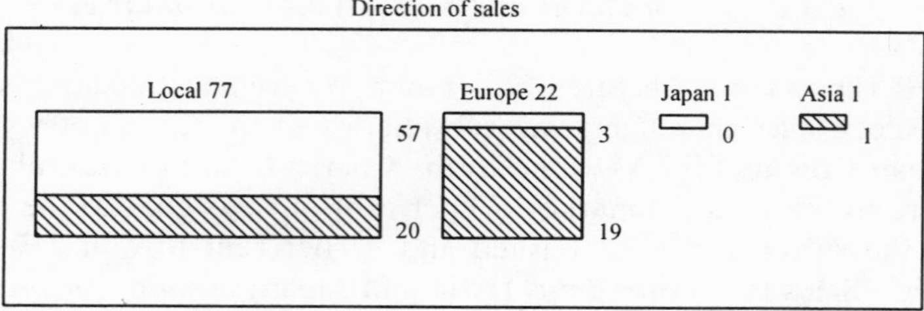

Sales value = 100

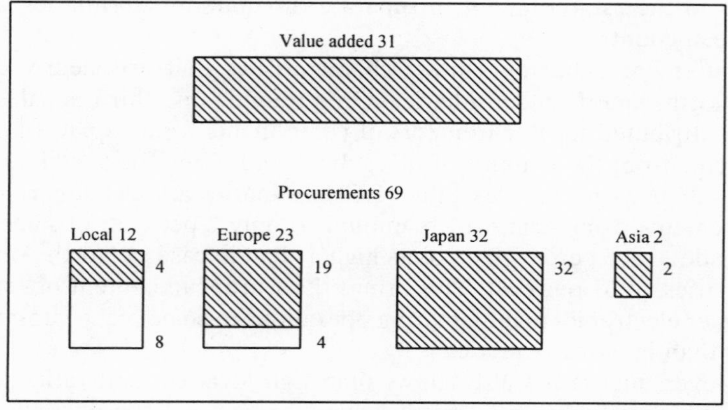

= Intra-group control over the value chain

- European content (incl. value added) = 66%
- European content provided by non-controlled firms = 12%
- 88% of the value chain controlled by the group

Figur 8.3 Structure of regional and intra-group sales and procurements of Japanese consumer electronics manufacturing subsidiaries in the EC, 1990

Source: calculations based on Nihon Tsuushou Sangyoushou (1991).

is consistent with an important role of EC intra-group procurement.

Sales of Japanese electronic components manufacturing subsidiaries in the EC (Figure 8.4) are to an important extent the mirror image of procurements by consumer electronics subsidiaries. Most of the sales in the EC are intra-group (18 out of 37 per cent for local sales and all sales to other European countries). This is consistent with the suggestion that many Japanese electronic components manufacturing plants have been set up to supply components to assembly plants of the same *keiretsu* firms. The

European content of components (52 per cent) is substantially higher than for North American subsidiaries. This European content is added almost solely by the subsidiaries themselves (49 per cent). Virtually all materials and subcomponents are supplied by group firms in Japan (45 per cent of sales value), while procurements in Europe are small (3 per cent). Independent local suppliers of materials are responsible for only 2 per cent of sales value, while Japanese firms' control over the value chain reaches 96 per cent.

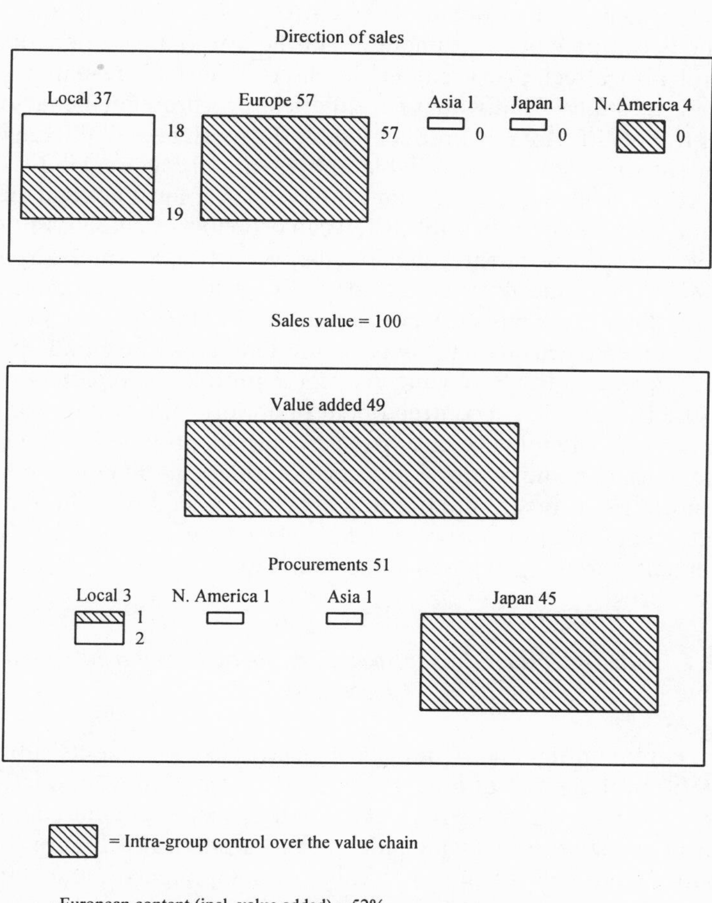

Figure 8.4 Structure of regional and intra-group sales and procurements of Japanese electronic components manufacturing subsidiaries in the EC, 1990

Source: calculations based on Nihon Tsuushou Sangyoushou (1991).

8.3.3 The Response to Local Content Rules

Besides local content rules, differences in procurement behaviour are also related to a number of other factors. Procurement behaviour depends on the particular consumer electronics products or electronic components manufactured in the Japanese subsidiary, since it will be more cost effective to procure locally for some products than for others. The degree of experience in local manufacturing is important since establishing links with local suppliers generally takes time, in particular if it concerns complex components for which product quality is essential.[20] The competitiveness of the indigenous components manufacturers in the different components industries will also affect procurement decisions. The best research strategy would be to analyse individual subsidiaries' procurement behaviour and control for such factors as product line and experience. Unfortunately, in the present study, data are available only on a more aggregated level.

Nevertheless, given the important differences in local content rules and the prima facie evidence in Table 8.1, it can probably be safely assumed that differences in procurement behaviour between North American and EC subsidiaries are primarily related to strict EC local content rules. Comparison of the figures for North America and the EC then suggests that Japanese consumer electronics firms have predominantly responded to local content requests in the EC by increasing the production of components in-house and by inviting subcontractors in their vertical *keiretsu* to manufacture in the EC. The reliance on Japanese components could even be higher if the increasing manufacturing presence of independent components suppliers in the EC is taken into account. The conclusion must be that European components suppliers have not benefited much from EC local content requirements targeting Japanese electronics firms.

8.3.4 Intra-Group Transactions and Local Content in Consumer Electronics

The procurement figures for Japanese electronic components subsidiaries show that local content of final goods production as conventionally measured, i.e. the sum of local value added and procurements of components, can easily overstate actual value added generated locally. Figure 8.4 shows that only 52 per cent of the sales value of components manufactured by Japanese subsidiaries in the EC is generated in the region. An estimate of the actual local content of consumer electronics production is obtained by subtracting from the 66 per cent in Figure 8.3 the non-European content (48 per cent) of intra-group procurements in Europe (4 + 19 per cent). This reduces the local content ratio by 11 per cent to 55 per cent. This exercise shows that in many cases it is necessary to look at the entire value chain and the nature of vertical transactions to obtain an accurate picture of local content and the contribution of manufacturing investments to local economies.

8.4 Conclusions and Implications

Japanese electronics firms have been confronted with a number of *de facto* local content requirements in the European Community in the second half of the 1980s. This contrasts to an important extent with the situation in the United States, where local content requirements have been less strict. These policy differences correspond with marked differences in the sales and procurement behaviour of Japanese firms' manufacturing subsidiaries in the US and EC. Local content (value added and local procurements) of Japanese firms' operations in the consumer electronics and electronic components industries in the EC is substantially higher than local content of comparable North American operations. This higher local content ratio in the EC is achieved predominantly by increased integration of manufacturing operations and increased intra-group procurements from EC components plants established by the same firm or by subcontractors within the same vertical *keiretsu*. In contrast, there is no evidence of a greater involvement of independent components suppliers in the EC in the supply chain of Japanese firms. These findings suggest that EC components producers have not benefited much from local content requirements imposed on Japanese firms.

The analysis shows the strong preference of Japanese electronics firms to keep control over components manufacturing while investing abroad. This reliance on Japanese components may reflect factors such as the technological superiority of Japanese components, the desire to maintain close control over quality and design of components, and the importance of long term supplier–client relationships between Japanese firms (Sako 1992). The relationships with subcontractors and long-standing suppliers are part of an organisation of production characterised by 'lean production' methods, just in time deliveries of components, and joint development of components for new products. Since this type of production management may constitute a competitive advantage of Japanese electronics firms, firms faced with local content measures have pursued a strategy to transfer the system abroad (Dunning and Gittelman 1992, Caves 1993). The empirical results in Chapter 5 confirmed this role of inter-firm relationships within vertical *keiretsu* in the process of Japanese firms' internationalisation.

The behaviour of Japanese firms does suggest that supply chains are relatively closed to foreign firms. A similar preference for Japanese suppliers has been reported for machinery procurements by Japanese manufacturing subsidiaries in Australia (Kreinin 1992).[21] Long term supplier–client relationships by their nature are difficult to break for EC components producers, even when the firms are able to compete on price and quality. An increasing dominance of Japanese firms in final product markets will almost automatically lead to falling demand for EC components producers, in the absence of efforts to integrate EC suppliers in the supply chain of Japanese firms. It is conceivable that EC local content requirements have actually worsened the sales prospects of European components producers. The involvement of new components producers in the supply chain usually takes time and effort. Components producers need to learn to manufacture to the specification of the Japanese firms, are often required by Japanese firms to upgrade quality control (which European clients traditionally carry out themselves), and may first be involved in design-in projects for new models before delivery of components can start. The time pressure put on Japanese firms to increase local content may have forced them to transfer components production to the EC and integrate production, in order to increase local content quickly without loss of reliability. After components production has been set up, it becomes unlikely that in future the firm will shift to European suppliers.

This all suggests that local content requirements and Japanese firms' responses have not helped to develop the indigenous EC components industry. For components industries characterised by competition between small and medium sized companies, increased procurement from EC suppliers accompanied by technical assistance of Japanese firms would have benefited the EC electronics industry. In this respect, the information available on the efforts by Japanese firms to include European components manufacturers in supply chains is not encouraging. It was shown that only 5 per cent of Japanese electronics subsidiaries reportedly increased local content after providing technical assistance to local firms. Similarly, in the 1993 JETRO survey among Japanese manufacturers in Europe, only 12 per cent of Japanese electronics producers indicated that they provided some form of (technical) assistance to local suppliers (JETRO 1993b).

The above arguments do not imply that the investment response to local content requirements did not have a positive effect on the EC electronics industry. In particular, where Japanese components manufacturers have a technological advantage, and where components industries are oligopolistic, investment by Japanese firms increases manufacturing capability and competition in the components industry and helps to avoid price increases associated with local content requirements. To the extent that increased EC components manufacturing is less cost effective for Japanese firms, it follows from the analysis in Chapter 4 that local content requirements may have 'raised rivals' costs' and assisted EC final goods producers.

However, the question whether and to what extent EC local content requirements on average have provided benefits to the EC economy can only be answered after more detailed analysis of procurement changes and developments in the various components markets.

APPENDIX 8.1

Selection of Subsidiaries

Procurement and sales data by region and type (intra-group or arm's length) are not available for all subsidiaries in the MITI survey. Manufacturing subsidiaries with sufficient information were selected from the full sample of subsidiaries reporting to the MITI survey by the Institute for International Trade and Investment (Kaigai Boueki Toushi Kenkyuujo) in Tokyo. Table A8.1 gives the number of subsidiaries selected and the sales value of the subsidiaries. Both the number of subsidiaries and the value of sales are also expressed as percentages of the figures for all subsidiaries (coverage ratio). The coverage ratio of the sample in terms of total sales ranges from 92 per cent for electronic components subsidiaries in North America to 48 per cent for the electronic components industry in the EC, while the coverage for the consumer electronics industry in both regions is about 70 per cent. The sales and procurement characteristics (regional distribution and type) of the selected firms compared well with those of the whole group of subsidiaries, and the selection appeared representative for the full sample.

Table A8.1 Selected consumer electronics and electronic components manufacturing subsidiaries in North America and the EC: sales and number of subsidiaries

	North America		EC	
	Sales (bn yen)	No. of subs.	Sales (bn yen)	No. of subs.
Consumer electronics	972	12	504	24
Coverage (%)	(65)	(63)	(74)	(71)
Electronic components	256	19	49	13
Coverage (%)	(92)	(57)	(48)	(59)

Source: calculations based on Nihon Tsuushou Sangyoushou (1991).

NOTES

1. An incomplete listing is: Sachwald (1995), Mason and Encarnation (1994), Thomsen (1993), Strange (1993), Balasubramanyam and Greenaway (1992), Williamson and Yamawaki (1991), Heitger and Stein (1990), Kume and

Totsuka (1991), Micossi and Viesti (1991), Nicolaides and Thomsen (1991), Thomsen and Nicolaides (1991), and Yamazawa (1991).

2. Several studies claim that the evidence suggests an important impact of trade barriers on the size of Japanese manufacturing investment in the EC (e.g. Balasubramanyam and Greenaway 1992, Heitger and Stein 1990, Kume and Totsuka 1991), while others, notably Thomsen and Nicolaides (1991) and Thomsen (1993) disagree.
3. The overview in this section is rather comprehensive and partly overlaps with the description of EC local content requirements in Section 1.3.3.
4. Such requests seem to have become more rather than less frequent since the late 1980s. Three years earlier (in the 1989 JETRO survey), 17 per cent of Japanese firms answered in the affirmative, while the percentages for automobile and electronic equipment manufacturers were 35 and 31 per cent, respectively.
5. Within the framework of the same agreement, Japanese firms promised to limit exports to the EC of cathode ray tubes, the component that can make up 40 per cent of a television's value. See also Tyson (1992: Chapter 6).
6. EC legislation Council Regulation No. 1761/87, published in the *Official Journal of the European Communities*, 26 June 1987. See Ishikawa (1990) for a discussion.
7. This concerned the copier plant of Rank Xerox in the UK (Vermulst and Waer 1990).
8. In 1986, exports of electronic typewriters by the Japanese firm Brother from its Taiwan plant were considered of Japanese origin because the activities in Taiwan did not constitute a 'substantial transformation' and thus did not confer Taiwanese origin (Vermulst and Waer 1990: 73). Consequently, antidumping duties on Brother typewriters from Japan were extended to Brother typewriters from Taiwan.
9. See also 'A Little Local Difficulty' and 'A Spark of Life', *Far Eastern Economic Review*, 18 May 1989.
10. See Ishikawa (1990) for a discussion of the events.
11. Eventually, the case was settled through an undertaking which established minimum prices for Japanese IC exports to the EC.
12. It is estimated that cumulative investment in Japanese IC manufacturing plants in the EC amounted to 3 billion ECUs by 1991. See CEC (1991b: 12–15), Furlotti (1991), and *Electronics Business*, 17 September 1990: 79. Those US firms that had no wafer etching facilitates in the EC followed a similar investment strategy.
13. See Graham and Krugman (1990). Procurement of cathode ray tubes by Japanese television manufacturing plants in the US was also affected by antidumping cases against the exports of these tubes from Japan.
14. The consumer electronics and electronic components sectors between them are responsible for more than two thirds of total sales by Japanese manufacturing subsidiaries in the electronics ('electrical machinery') industry.
15. This low threshold is not likely to affect the results appreciably, since only 2 per cent (EC) and 4 per cent (North America) of subsidiaries in the electronics industry are minority owned.
16. Another reason for the small scale of EC subsidiaries is that differences in legal systems of the various EC countries have led to the establishment of separate

subsidiaries as legal entities (*houjin*) in major EC countries, while in the US one legal entity can suffice. While a US subsidiary of a major Japanese electronics firm often operates more than one manufacturing plant, this is less likely to be the case for EC subsidiaries. Therefore, the difference in size of the legal entities (*houjin*) does not necessarily imply a difference in size at the *plant level*.

17. Information on procurements in horizontal, bank-centred *keiretsu* is not available in the survey, nor is information on procurements from unrelated but Japanese-affiliated companies.
18. Sales and procurement data based on these selections were prepared by Kyoko Imada at the Institute of International Trade and Investment.
19. Japanese electronics subsidiaries' characteristics are further examined in Belderbos (1995a). It is suggested that, while there is a classification problem for subsidiaries combining distribution and manufacturing, the problem is rather similar in the EC and the US. This implies that the comparison of US and EC subsidiaries is not likely to be affected.
20. A survey among Japanese multinationals in the EC (Arcos *et al*. 1995) suggests a gradual use of indigenous suppliers.
21. Kreinin (1992) finds that machinery orders by Japanese manufacturing subsidiaries in Australia usually are not open for competitive bids but are directly issued at affiliated firms or long-standing suppliers in Japan; this is not the case for European and American subsidiaries in Australia.

9

Overseas Research and Development

9.1 Introduction

There is growing interest among both researchers and policy makers in the internationalisation of research and development activities by multinational enterprises (MNEs). This is to an important extent due to the perception that the internationalisation of R&D is progressing rapidly, as a result of a broader trend towards the 'globalisation' of business. It is also related to an increasing awareness of the importance of innovation and the development of high technology industries for the long term competitiveness and economic growth of countries. Since MNEs' R&D activities can make an important contribution to the science and technology infrastructure of countries, the location of such R&D facilities is of obvious concern to both home and host countries.

R&D by Japanese multinationals is interesting in this respect. On the one hand, Japanese firms clearly lag behind European and North American firms in the internationalisation of R&D (e.g. Cantwell 1989, Patel and Pavitt 1991, Patel 1995). It is conceivable that Japanese firms have a greater tendency to centralise R&D at home because of the particular characteristics of industrial organisation and innovation in Japan. Japanese firms' R&D activities are strongly co-ordinated with marketing departments and manufacturing operations while co-development in supplier networks is also important. These features may favour the centralisation of R&D in Japan, where the pilot factory and suppliers are located and where new products are tested on a highly sophisticated Japanese market.[1] On the other hand, recent evidence shows that Japanese firms have increased overseas R&D activities rapidly in the late 1980s and early 1990s.[2] The question arises whether the low degree of R&D internationalisation of Japanese firms is merely a corollary of their relatively late emergence as multinationals, or a structural characteristic related to R&D management and industrial organisation in Japan.

This chapter addresses this question by analysing the determinants of Japanese electronics firms' overseas R&D activities. The analysis uses firm level data for 1992 contained in MITI's *Basic Survey of Foreign Investment* (Nihon Tsuushou Sangyoushou 1994), the only systematic data source on overseas R&D by Japanese firms. Two empirical models are estimated. At the *parent* firm level, it is investigated whether difference in electronics firms' overseas R&D ratios (the share of foreign R&D expenditure in total R&D expenditure of the firm) can be explained by differences in the degree of internationalisation of the firms. This analysis is complemented by an analysis of the R&D intensity of individual *subsidiaries* of Japanese electronics firms, which also takes into account the role of subsidiary and country characteristics in overseas R&D. Preceding the empirical analysis, some peculiarities of the MITI data are discussed.

The remainder of this chapter is organised as follows. Section 9.2 briefly discusses the main themes in the literature on overseas R&D by multinational enterprises. Section 9.3 briefly reviews Japanese overseas R&D in general. Section 9.4 describes the data on overseas R&D by Japanese electronics firms as contained in MITI's 1992 *Basic Survey*. Section 9.5 presents the results of econometrical analysis of the determinants of foreign R&D, and Section 9.6 concludes.

9.2 Determinants of Overseas R&D

The literature on the internationalisation of research and development distinguishes between several types of foreign R&D conducted by MNEs (e.g. Pearce 1989, Casson 1991).

First, most MNEs adopt a geographical decentralisation of development activities, to be able to adapt products to particular demands and regulations in local markets. Foreign development activities support foreign marketing and after sales service as well as foreign manufacturing activities: they follow from an increased reliance on overseas sales and production. Empirical studies of the determinants of overseas R&D invariably find that the degree of internationalisation of firms and industries is an important determinant of the foreign R&D ratio.[3] Adaptive R&D activities usually do not require strong co-ordination with home based R&D departments. If the local development centre has built up sufficient expertise, the centre's activities may be upgraded to involve the development of new products for the local markets as well. In general, the initiation and further upgrading of overseas R&D functions is found to be an evolving process. Empirical research highlights the importance of experience in manufacturing and R&D activities for the development of subsidiaries' R&D. Thus, firms that have internationalised production very fast tend to lag behind in the internationalisation of R&D (Granstrand, Hakanson, and Sjölander 1993).

Second, and more fundamentally, large MNEs are increasingly seen to adopt a global innovation strategy, involving a close co-ordination of worldwide R&D activities and an active management of the geographical allocation of R&D resources. Foreign research centres of the firm may be given the extended mandate to develop new products for the global market place, with home and other laboratories focusing on different technologies and products. Furthermore, firms in high technology industries may establish R&D centres engaging in basic and applied research abroad to utilise specific strengths of the science bases of various countries.

Empirical research has not fully supported the notion of a rapid increase in internationalisation of R&D activities. Patel (1995) and Cantwell (1992a) have shown that, while the importance of foreign R&D by the world's largest enterprises is increasing, this increase on average has not been large throughout the 1980s. Moreover, foreign R&D is most important in *relative* terms (as a percentage of total R&D activities of the firms) in low technology industries such as food and building materials. In these industries adaptation and development of products for local markets is more important than basic and applied research. High technology industries such as computers and electronics, with stronger links to the science base, tend to have R&D activities relatively concentrated in the home country, although in *absolute* terms their foreign R&D activities may contribute significantly to R&D activities in host countries.

9.3 Overseas R&D by Japanese Firms

The empirical literature shows Japanese MNEs as standing out in terms of an exceptionally low degree of R&D internationalisation. Patel (1995) calculates that, for the 139 largest Japanese MNEs, only 1 per cent of US patenting is based on R&D conducted in foreign laboratories during 1985–1990; this compares with 8 per cent for US MNEs and 40–60 per cent for MNEs from smaller countries such as the UK, Sweden, Switzerland, and the Netherlands. Cairncross (1994) notes that by 1989 R&D expenditures of foreign firms in Japan were still higher than R&D expenditure of Japanese firms abroad.[4]

There is, however, evidence that the internationalisation of R&D has been promoted seriously by Japanese MNEs in the 1990s. A survey among R&D managers in the world's largest MNEs in 1989 reported that Japanese MNEs, more than US or European MNEs, saw an increased emphasis on a globally integrated R&D network as an important part of future R&D strategy (Casson 1991). It is suggested that the fact that Japanese MNEs are relative 'latecomers' in internationalisation of R&D may even facilitate a more rational tailoring of R&D strategy to the requirements of the era of global competition (Papanastassiou and Pearce 1994). Papanastassiou and Pearce (1995) examine various data sources and find that, while the share of overseas R&D has remained relatively low, the absolute increase in Japanese firms' foreign R&D activities has been remarkable. US Department of Commerce data on R&D expenditure of Japanese firms in the United States show a rapid rise in the late 1980s. R&D expenditure by Japanese affiliates increased from 307 million dollars in 1987 to 770 million dollars in 1989 and 1,215 million dollars in 1990 (US Department of Commerce 1993).

Recent surveys among Japanese manufacturers in Europe also show a marked increase in R&D activities by Japanese firms (JETRO 1990b, 1995b). The number of R&D facilities rose from 73 in 1990 to 292 in 1994 (almost a quadrupling), while the number of manufacturing plants rose from 516 to 720 (a 40 per cent increase). Most of the R&D facilities are linked to manufacturing plants or sales subsidiaries. They monitor local technological developments and provide technical support for manufacturing and marketing, which can extend to product adaptation and development for the local market. However, the 264 R&D facilities in 1994 also include 71 stand-alone laboratories, of which a considerable number are engaged in basic and applied research. Japanese firms appear to be keen to utilise local distinctive scientific and educational traditions and tend to pursue a strategy of developing liaison links with local universities rather than contracting out specific R&D tasks (Casson 1991).

The rise in Japanese firms' overseas R&D has also stimulated empirical work on the determinants of internationalisation. Odagiri and Yasuda (1996) examined the determinants of overseas R&D both at firm and industry level. Firm level analysis looked at the number of overseas subsidiaries that engaged in R&D or software development for 254 parent firms in manufacturing industries in 1990. Industry level analysis focused on aggregate data from the 1989 MITI survey among Japanese MNEs. The results showed that overseas R&D activities are more important for firms and industries that are more dependent on overseas markets and have higher overseas manufacturing ratios. The results also indicated differences in the motives for R&D in Western industrialised countries on the one hand, and Asian countries on the other. Japanese firms exporting more technology to Western countries than they import (in terms of number of licenses) were significantly *less* likely to set up an R&D facility there. This suggests that technology sourcing is an important motive for overseas R&D, in particular for those firms that are lagging behind Western firms in technological capabilities. However, the opposite was true for R&D in South-East Asia: here Japanese firms were more likely to engage in R&D the greater their apparent technological advantage *vis-à-vis* local firms. This finding is consistent with a greater importance of search for lower R&D costs as the motive for R&D in South-East Asia.

Wakasugi (1994b) analysed original data on 195 Japanese electronics manufacturing subsidiaries in MITI's 1989 *Basic Survey*. He examined the likelihood that these subsidiaries spent a positive amount on R&D. R&D

activity in these subsidiaries was found to be positively related to subsidiary size and negatively related to the dependence on imports of components (and with that, technology and design) from Japan. The number of years the subsidiary had been operating (experience effect) and the profitability of the subsidiary in 1989 were not found to have significant effects. Characteristics of the parent firm were not included in the analysis.

The econometrical analysis in Section 9.5 builds on the analysis of both Odagiri and Yasuda (1996) at the parent firm level, and Wakasugi (1994b) at the subsidiary level. A major advantage of the analysis in this chapter is that detailed firm-level data from MITI's *Basic Survey* could be used. Both parent firm characteristics and characteristics of firms' overseas subsidiaries could be combined in the analysis to get an accurate picture of global R&D activities. Before turning to the empirical analysis, the next section describes MITI's *Basic Survey*.

9.4 Overseas R&D by Japanese Electronics Firms in MITI's *Basic Survey* for 1992

Adopting a broad definition of the electronics industry, MITI's *Basic Survey* for 1992 covers 233 parent firms classified in the following electronics-related industries: office machines (7), consumer appliances (51), communication equipment (19), computers (11), parts (62), other electrical equipment (40), medical equipment (11), optical equipment (10), clocks (5), and other precision equipment (17). These parent firms operated 1,420 foreign subsidiaries in March 1993, according to the survey data. Each firm was asked about R&D expenditure of the parent firm in Japan as well as R&D expenditure, R&D employees, R&D laboratories, and the purposes of R&D in each overseas subsidiary.

According to the data published in the MITI survey report (Nihon Tsuushou Sangyoushou 1994), the 233 Japanese firms spent a total of 2,471 billion yen on R&D in Japan in 1992, while foreign R&D amounted to 76.5 billion yen. These data imply a foreign R&D ratio (foreign R&D as a percentage of worldwide R&D) of 3.0 per cent. However, the published MITI data are a simple aggregation of individual firms' R&D figures and are not corrected for non-response. Analysis of the original firm-level data reveals that the R&D questions are answered for only a minority of overseas subsidiaries. Out of the total of 1,420 subsidiaries, 1,064 (75 per cent) do not list a figure for R&D expenditure, 253 (18 per cent) report no R&D, and only 103 subsidiaries (7 per cent) report positive R&D.[5] While it appears that for a large number of subsidiaries a non-response is likely to indicate the absence of R&D activities, this is certainly not the case for all subsidiaries, and overseas R&D is substantially under-reported.[6] Since the

Table 9.1 Overseas and domestic R&D, sales, and employment for parent firms with sufficient R&D information

Industry	No. of firms	R&D (m yen)							Sales (m yen)		Employees	
		Asia	Europe	N-Amer.	Other	Total overseas	Japan	Overseas ratio	Japan	Overseas ratio	Japan	Overseas ratio
Consumer electronics	9	127	0	0	0	127	8,264	1.5	467,190	12.3	14,450	20.5
Communication equipment	4	0	0	1	0	1	4,418	0.0	180,695	6.6	4,415	7.8
Computers	2	0	0	1	0	1	46,990	0.0	1,093,514	1.7	4,674	17.2
Parts	12	81	0	3,055	2	3,138	27,022	10.4	581,634	28.5	14,564	51.2
Other electrical equipment	10	17	0	5	0	22	3,525	0.6	187,027	6.3	3,556	25.6
Optical equipment	2	0	0	0	0	0	2,466	0.0	35,359	9.2	1,456	8.3
Clocks	1	0	0	0	0	0	1,657	0.0	26,291	1.2	734	4.6
Other precision equipment	3	27	650	64	0	741	12,697	5.5	199,013	15.6	5,464	18.4
Total	43	252	650	3,126	2	4,030	107,039	3.6	2,770,723	12.1	49,313	31.8

Source: calculations based on Nihon Tsuushou Sangyoushou (1994).

MITI surveys are the only source available on overseas R&D expenditure by Japanese firms, the published figures have nevertheless been cited (Cairncross 1994, Belderbos 1995c).

Since there is no reliable way to ascertain whether a non-response is indicative of no R&D expenditure, the only solution to the problem is to limit the analysis to firms and subsidiaries for which sufficient information is available. At the parent firm level, a selection was made of electronics firms with complete data on both domestic and overseas R&D. Of the 233 parent firms, only 43 could be regarded as fully responding firms. This selection excludes most large MNEs operating a substantial number of subsidiaries abroad, because such firms unfortunately failed to report R&D expenditure for at least some of their overseas subsidiaries. The selection includes a relatively large number of firms operating only one or a handful of subsidiaries with no R&D functions abroad.[7] Overseas R&D expenditure is moreover concentrated in a relatively small number of firms in the sample: only 15 firms engage in overseas R&D, and the top 3 firms are responsible for almost 90 per cent of all R&D expenditures. The over-representation of small, less internationalised firms in the sample requires caution in drawing conclusions for overseas R&D by the Japanese electronics industry as a whole.

Key data on R&D, sales, and employment for the 43 firms are presented in Table 9.1. Most R&D expenditure is carried out in the United States (3.1 billion yen), and least in Asia (252 million yen). The foreign R&D ratio for the firms is 3.6 per cent. This is higher than the uncorrected figure of 3.0 per cent reported for the full sample. Given that the selection of 43 firms is biased towards the inclusion of firms without overseas R&D activities, the actual figure for the full sample is likely to be substantially higher than the reported figure. For the 43 firms in the sample, the ratio is highest for the parts and components sector (10.4 per cent). This is also the industry with the highest overseas employment ratio (51.2 per cent) and overseas sales ratio (28.5 per cent). There appears to be a correlation between the importance of internationalisation and overseas R&D. In the next section, the existence of such a relationship will be tested empirically.

9.5 The Determinants of Oversease R&D: Empirical Analysis

Section 9.5.1 presents the empirical analysis of the determinants of overseas R&D for the 43 selected parent firms. Section 9.5.2 examines R&D activities at the subsidiary level while taking into account parent firm characteristics. The latter analysis has the advantage that it allows for a much broader selection of firms including large MNEs.

9.5.1 The Overseas R&D Ratio

Which factors determine overseas R&D spending by Japanese electronics firms? This section presents the results of empirical analysis of overseas R&D by the 43 electronics firms for which reliable data are available. The data allow for analysis of the extent of overseas R&D and accurate measurement of the degree of internationalisation of firms in terms of sales and value added in overseas subsidiaries. The dependent variable in the empirical analysis is the share of overseas R&D in worldwide R&D expenditure, the foreign R&D ratio (*RDRAT*). Since *RDRAT* is restricted in the interval [0,1], Tobit analysis is used to related *RDRAT* to the following independent variables:

SALRAT sales of overseas subsidiaries over parent firm sales plus sales of overseas subsidiaries (the overseas sales ratio);
VARAT value added of overseas manufacturing subsidiaries over parent firm value added plus value added of overseas manufacturing subsidiaries (the overseas production ratio);
VASAL value added of overseas subsidiaries over total sales of overseas subsidiaries;
EXPER number of months since the establishment of the parent firm's first subsidiary abroad;
RDINT parent firm's R&D expenditure in Japan over parent firm sales;
SALES parent firm sales.

SALRAT and *VARAT* test the product adaptation hypothesis. *SALRAT* measures the degree of internationalisation in terms of sales. Previous research has indicated that one characteristic of Japanese electronics firms' internationalisation is extensive investments in distribution activities to take care of promotion, after sales service, and feedback of information on local markets (see Chapters 1 and 7). The function of such service and distribution subsidiaries may also includes R&D to keep track of local technological developments and provide technical support for marketing and after sales service.[8] If overseas R&D follows overseas manufacturing, to provide technical support to overseas manufacturing operations and to adapt products and processes to local conditions, then *VARAT*, the overseas production ratio, should be positively related to *RDRAT*. Since *SALRAT* and *VARAT* are strongly correlated, an alternative way to test the importance of overseas manufacturing is to include *SALRAT* in conjunction with *VASAL*. *VASAL* measures the relative importance of overseas manufacturing (value added) compared with overseas sales, and is expected to have an additional effect on the overseas R&D ratio. *EXPER*, the length of time the firm has operated subsidiaries abroad, is a proxy for the experience effect in overseas R&D (see Granstrand, Hakanson, and Sjölander 1993). *EXPER* is expected to have a positive sign. *RDINT* measures the R&D intensity of the parent firm. As noted in Section 9.2, across *industries*, R&D intensity is found to be negatively related to the overseas R&D ratio. The explanation is that in R&D intensive industries, firms tend to concentrate R&D activities at home, since there will be stronger linkages with the Japanese science base and the industries will face greater diseconomies of dispersion of R&D activities. Across *firms* in the same industry, however, these effects will be less powerful. Moreover, it may be that the most R&D intensive firms have reaped the economies of scale in domestic R&D and have developed the most distinctive R&D internationalisation strategies (Pearce 1989). These firms may be more active in overseas R&D. The sign of *RDINT* can therefore not a priori be determined. *SALES* is included to test whether, apart from internationalisation and experience factors, larger firms tend to do more R&D abroad. Larger firms may have a greater pool of managerial and financial resources facilitating the establishment of overseas R&D facilities. A positive effect is expected.

Table 9.2 shows the results of Tobit analysis. Model I shows that the coefficient for the overseas value added ratio, *VARAT*, has the expected positive sign but is not significantly different from zero. Model II shows that overseas R&D is better explained by the overseas sales ratio, *SALRAT*, which has a positive coefficient significant at the 5 per cent level. The variable indicating the relative importance of value added in overseas sales, *VASAL*, has the expected positive sign but is not significant. Together, these results indicate that overseas R&D is related more to the importance of sales on overseas markets and concomitant investments in distribution and after sales service, than to overseas manufacturing activities. This may however be particular to the sample of relatively small and less internationalised firms.

The experience variable *EXPER* included in model III has a positive and significant effect on *RDRAT*. Firms that took the first step towards internationalisation earlier have higher overseas R&D ratios, even after controlling for the degree of internationalisation. However, *SALRAT* becomes statistically insignificant from zero in regression III. This is due to multicollinearity between *SALRAT* and *EXPER* (the correlation coefficient between these two variables is 33 per cent and significant), but it also indicates that the effect of *EXPER* is relatively robust. *RDINT* and *SALES* in models IV and V do not have a significant effect on *RDRAT*.

As mentioned earlier, the results in Table 9.2 may be affected by sample selection bias: the firms in the sample are relatively small and two thirds of the firms do not perform any R&D abroad. In order to obtain additional insight into the determinants of overseas R&D, an analysis restricted to firms that actually engage in overseas manufacturing and R&D was conducted. Although the number of observations is very small (14), the subsample may give a somewhat better representation of overseas activities of

Table 9.2 Tobit analysis of the overseas R&D ratio (*RDRAT*) of 43 electronics firms

	Model				
	I	II	III	VI	V
VARAT	0.12				
	(1.39)				
SALRAT		0.37**	0.24	0.24	0.28*
		(2.30)	(1.51)	(1.53)	(1.67)
VASAL		0.07			
		(0.62)			
EXPER			0.04**	0.04**	0.04*
			(2.04)	(2.03)	(1.73)
RDINT				–0.14	
				(–0.20)	
SALES					0.10
					(0.93)
Constant	–7.17**	–12.59**	–15.22**	–14.93**	–15.70**
	(–2.31)	(–2.13)	(–3.00)	(–2.86)	(–3.02)
Tobit σ	11.27**	10.69**	10.24**	10.24**	10.27**
	(4.96)	(5.02)	(5.08)	(5.08)	(5.07)
Observations	43	43	43	43	43
Log likelihood	–71.9	–70.0	–67.9	–67.9	–67.4

Notes: *t*-ratios within parentheses; * = significant at 10%, ** = significant at 5% level.

Japanese electronics multinationals. The dependent variable, *RDRAT*, now does not assume the value zero, and ordinary least squares regression can be used after a logarithmic transformation of *RDRAT*. Consider the following model:

$$(1)\quad RDRAT = \frac{ORD}{ORD + JRD} = \frac{\exp[\alpha + \beta \log(X)]}{1 + \exp[\alpha + \beta \log(X)]}$$

where *ORD* is overseas R&D, *JRD* is R&D expenditure by the parent firm in Japan, α is a constant, and X is a vector of independent variables with coefficients β. The specification in (1) ensures that *RDRAT* correctly falls in the interval (0,1). The logarithm of the independent variables is taken to maintain the linearity between *RDRAT* and the independent variables. The logarithm of the odds ratio, *ORD* over *JRD*, becomes:

$$(2)\quad \log(ORDJRD) = \log\left(\frac{ORD}{JRD}\right) = \alpha + \beta \log(X)$$

The coefficients α and β can be estimated by ordinary least squares regression of equation (2). The regression results are presented in Table 9.3. The results again confirm the importance of the overseas sales ratio and the experience effect. This time *SALRAT* is highly significant while *EXPER* is significant at the 10 per cent level. A major difference with the results in Table 9.2 is that *VASAL*, indicating the relative importance of overseas manufacturing activities, is significantly positive. This suggests that the insignificance of overseas manufacturing in the 43-firm sample may indeed be a peculiarity of sample selection, with a considerable number of firms in the earlier stage of internationalisation. Firm size (*SALES*) is not significantly different from zero, while *RDINT* has a negative sign but again fails to reach significance. The explanatory power of regression I is relatively large with an adjusted R^2 of 77 per cent. The fit of the model improves slightly if *SALES* is omitted in regression II. The basic results of regression I do not change with the omission of *SALES* or *RDINT* (not shown).

The results confirm the importance for overseas R&D of overseas sales and manufacturing as well as experience in operating subsidiaries abroad. These conclusions are in line with previous empirical results for US and Swedish MNEs (Pearce 1989).[9] The robustness of these results should be

Table 9.3 Regression analysis of log (*ORDJRD*): 14 electronics firms

	Regression	
	I	II
SALRAT	2.23**	2.35**
	(5.11)	(6.47)
EXPER	1.81*	1.64*
	(1.94)	(1.93)
VASAL	2.78**	2.89**
	(2.91)	(3.23)
RDINT	−0.77	−0.89
	(−1.15)	(−1.44)
SALES	−0.17	
	(−0.60)	
Constant	−22.02**	−23.51**
	(−3.16)	(−3.78)
Observations	14	14
Adjusted R^2	0.77	0.79

Notes: All independent variables are in logarithms, *t*-ratios are in parentheses; ** = significant at 5% level, * = significant at 10% level.

tested by extending the analysis to a greater number of Japanese MNEs and to MNEs in other industries. The next section tries to shed more light on the process of overseas R&D through an analysis of R&D activities at the subsidiary level.

9.5.2 The R&D Intensity of Foreign Subsidiaries

In which foreign subsidiaries do Japanese electronics firms perform R&D? Analysis of R&D expenditure at the subsidiary level has the advantage that, for a relatively large number of subsidiaries including a number of subsidiaries of large MNEs, information on R&D expenditure is available. The analysis can thus be more representative for overseas R&D by the Japanese electronics industry as a whole. Furthermore, analysis at the subsidiary level can take into account the effect of location on R&D and the characteristics of the subsidiaries' establishment (greenfield, acquisition, joint venture), and can relate R&D directly to experience at the subsidiary level.

Relating R&D intensity to subsidiary characteristics is useful only if explanatory variables are comparable across subsidiaries. This implies that stand-alone R&D subsidiaries cannot be included, since variables such as sales do not have a clear meaning here. Although some overseas R&D is performed in sales subsidiaries, combining sales and manufacturing subsidiaries in one empirical model is also likely to present major problems (e.g. the interpretation of sales and value added is different in the two types of subsidiaries). Given these considerations, the present analysis is limited to R&D performed in manufacturing subsidiaries. Since stand-alone R&D subsidiaries are not included, the focus of the analysis is necessarily on R&D for sales and manufacturing support, directed at product adaptation and development for local markets. The analysis cannot deal with the determinants of basic R&D abroad.

Among a total of 577 manufacturing subsidiaries, 113 had sufficient data on R&D intensity and other variables. The characteristics of the 113 subsidiaries in terms of average sales and distribution over regions are comparable with those of the larger group of 577 manufacturing subsidiaries. About half of the 113 subsidiaries in the sample spent a positive amount on R&D while the other half reported zero R&D expenditure.[10] As for the location of the subsidiaries, 39 are located in developed countries (North America, Western Europe, and Oceania) and 74 in developing countries (of which the large majority are in the NIEs and ASEAN countries).

The dependent variable in the empirical analysis is the R&D intensity of overseas manufacturing subsidiaries, R&D expenditure as a percentage of subsidiary sales, *S_RDINT*. Tobit analysis is used to relate *S_RDINT* to the following independent variables:

S_EXPER number of months since the establishment of the subsidiary (not valid for subsidiaries controlled by the parent through acquisitions or capital participation);
S_VASAL value added of the subsidiary as percentage of subsidiary sales;
S_SALES sales of the subsidiary;
RDINT parent firm's R&D expenditure in Japan over parent firm sales;
ACQUIS dummy variable with value 1 if the parent firm assumed control over the subsidiary by acquiring an existing local firm;
PARTCAP dummy variable with value 1 if the parent firm assumed (partial) control over the subsidiary by participation in capital of an existing local firm;
JV dummy variable with value 1 if the subsidiary was established as a joint venture with a local partner and the parent in 1992 maintained only a minority share in the subsidiary.

The experience variable *S_EXPER* is expected to have a positive sign. *S_EXPER* is measured only for subsidiaries that were newly established, either as greenfield plants or as joint ventures. This is because, in case of establishment through capital participation or acquisitions, the establishment time of the subsidiary is the date of purchase and will not reflect the production experience of the subsidiary.[11] *S_VASAL*, value added over sales, indicates the degree to which the subsidiary has integrated manufacturing operations and is expected to be positively related to *S_RDINT*. *S_SALES* has a positive sign if high sales values are required to justify investments in R&D, given the existence of economies of scale in R&D activities. *RDINT* is expected to have a positive sign. If R&D intensity in Japan reflects the complexity and innovativeness of a firm's products and the importance of product adaptation and development, the R&D intensity of foreign activities will be positively related to R&D intensity in Japan.[12] *ACQUIS* and *PARTCAP* will have a positive sign if overseas firms are acquired in part for their technological expertise. In addition, existing R&D activities are often maintained after acquisition even when such activities are not contributing sufficiently to the acquiring firms' R&D strategy, owing to the difficulties in rationalising R&D functions (see e.g. Hakanson 1992, Hewitt 1980). *JV* is expected to have a negative sign. Japanese firms may be reluctant to conduct R&D activities jointly with a local partner, given the difficulties in distributing the rewards of such R&D and the possibility of leakage of technological information. In particular, when the subsidiary is minority owned, the hypothesis is that lack of full control over the subsidiaries' activities makes a commitment to R&D less likely. The analysis further includes dummy variables for the location of the subsidiary—North America, Europe, NIEs (including Singapore), ASEAN countries (excluding Singapore), and Oceania—to control for locational factors influencing R&D decisions.

The results of Tobit analysis are presented in Table 9.4. *RDINT* has a positive effect on the R&D intensity of Japanese electronics firms' subsidiaries abroad; *RDINT* is significantly different from zero at the 10 per cent level in model I and at the 5 per cent level in model II. Those firms that are more R&D intensive in Japan are also more likely to operate relatively R&D intensive overseas subsidiaries, controlling for other subsidiary characteristics.[13] *S_EXPER* has the expected positive sign and is significant. In contrast with the findings in Wakasugi (1994b), manufacturing experience does have an important effect on R&D activities in Japanese electronics firms' subsidiaries abroad. Subsidiary size *S_SALES* and the degree of manufacturing integration *S_VASAL* have the expected positive sign but do not have a statistically significant effect on *S_RDINT*. The estimation results with *S_SALES* omitted, in model II, are largely unchanged.

Of the three dummy variables describing the establishment mode of the subsidiaries, *ACQUIS* and *PARTCAP* both have the expected positive sign. R&D intensity is significantly higher in subsidiaries in which Japanese firms assumed (partial) control through acquisition or capital participation than in greenfield subsidiaries. This effect is stronger for acquisitions leading to full control over the overseas company (*ACQUIS*), than for acquisitions of a share of the company's stock (*PARTCAP*). The results suggest that the acquisition of technological capabilities is an important reason for overseas acquisitions by Japanese electronics firms,[14] a finding that is consistent with previous empirical results on Japanese overseas investment (Kogut and Chang 1991) and the findings in Odagiri and Yasuda (1996). Given the importance of experience in building up R&D functions overseas, acquisitions may be the only way for Japanese MNEs to 'catch up' swiftly in terms of internationalisation with European and US MNEs. The third establishment mode variable, *JV*, has a positive sign but is not significant. There is no evidence that Japanese electronics firms are less inclined to engage in R&D in minority owned joint ventures, relative to greenfield plants.

Besides parent firm and subsidiary characteristics, R&D intensity is also affected by locational factors. All things equal, R&D intensity is significantly higher in subsidiaries in North America than in subsidiaries in developing countries (excluding ASEAN countries and NIEs). Although the other differences between locations are not statistically significant, the size of the coefficients appears to follow the level of general economic development and expertise in electronics technology. The highest coefficient is for North America, followed by Western Europe, NIEs, ASEAN countries, and other developing countries.[15]

It is conceivable that R&D in subsidiaries in developing countries is affected differently by the explanatory factors from R&D in subsidiaries in industrialised countries. Separate estimations of model I for the two groups

Table 9.4 Tobit analysis of electronics subsidiaries' R&D intensity (*S_RDINT*)

	Model	
	I	II
RDINT	0.20*	0.21**
	(1.81)	(2.02)
S_EXPER	0.010**	0.014**
	(2.70)	(2.73)
S_SALES	0.01	
	(0.38)	
S_VASAL	0.035	0.032
	(1.39)	(1.34)
ACQUIS	8.80**	8.73**
	(5.14)	(5.16)
PARTCAP	4.34**	4.32**
	(2.49)	(2.48)
JV	1.20	1.21
	(0.94)	(0.95)
North America	4.67**	4.82**
	(2.10)	(2.35)
Western Europe	3.23	3.29
	(1.44)	(1.47)
Oceania	–0.74	–0.40
	(–0.17)	(–0.10)
NIEs	2.21	2.23
	(1.09)	(1.11)
ASEAN	1.15	1.18
	(0.50)	(0.52)
Constant	–8.42**	–8.34**
	(–3.17)	(–3.16)
Tobit σ	3.61**	3.59**
	(10.77)	(10.82)
Observations	113	113
Log likelihood	–191.2	–191.8

Notes: *t*-ratios are in parentheses; * = significant at 10% level, ** = significant at 5% level. The omitted establishment mode is 'Greefield plants' and the omitted region is 'Other developing countries'.

of subsidiaries generally did not show important differences in behaviour. The variable *ACQUIS* did not play a role in developing countries because acquisitions are almost absent here, but *PARTCAP* was positive and significant. *S_EXPER* was not significant in the model for industrialised countries, but the estimated coefficient was roughly equal to the coefficient for *S_EXPER* in the model for developing countries. It is possible that the experience effect can not be estimated with precision for industrialised countries because of the generally recent establishment of subsidiaries.[16]

9.6 Conclusions

This chapter has analysed data from MITI's *Basic Survey* among Japanese multinational firms in 1992 to examine the determinants of overseas R&D activities by Japanese firms in the electronics industry. Although MITI's survey is potentially a rich source of data on Japanese firms' overseas R&D activities, the quality of the data is relatively poor, and uncorrected aggregate data based on the survey, as published by MITI, can be misleading. The large number of non-responses forced a limitation of empirical analysis of the determinants of overseas R&D to a small sample of firms for which sufficient data were available.

Analysis at the parent firm level confirmed that the overseas R&D ratio is positively related to the dependence on overseas sales and manufacturing as well as to the degree of experience in operating subsidiaries abroad. Analysis of the R&D intensity of a broader group of 113 individual subsidiaries showed that R&D intensity is higher, the higher is the R&D intensity of the parent firm and the greater is the operating experience of the subsidiary. R&D intensity is also higher in subsidiaries located in industrialised countries and in subsidiaries that have come under the control of Japanese firms through capital participation or acquisition. The latter result confirms previous empirical findings that Japanese firms' overseas acquisitions are in part motivated by technology acquisition.

The results are consistent with the hypothesis that Japanese electronics firms lag behind in R&D internationalisation mostly because of the firms' relatively late internationalisation. The findings suggest that acquisitions by Japanese firms play an important role in the process of enhancing their R&D capabilities and 'catching up' with US and European MNEs in R&D internationalisation.

NOTES

1. See Odagiri (1992) and Odagiri and Yasuda (1996) on this argument and a discussion of the evidence.

2. See Papanastassiou and Pearce (1995). See also Chapter 1 on the growth in Japanese electronics firms' R&D facilities in Europe.
3. See Hewitt (1980) and Hirschey and Caves (1981) for early empirical studies on US firms' overseas R&D. Pearce (1989: Chapter 3) and Granstrand, Hakanson, and Sjölander (1993) provide surveys of the empirical literature.
4. However, this conclusion is based on analysis of aggregate data on overseas R&D in MITI's *Basic Survey*, which substantially under-reports overseas R&D. See Section 9.4.
5. See Belderbos (1995b) for a more detailed discussion of R&D data in the MITI survey.
6. An indication of the degree of under-reporting can be obtained by comparing US Department of Commerce data on Japanese affiliates' R&D expenditure with the MITI data on R&D expenditure in the US. The aggregate MITI data show R&D expenditure in the US of 35.6 billion yen in fiscal year 1989, which amounts to 225 million dollars at the exchange rates used in the MITI survey. The latter amount is less than a third of the 770 million dollars in R&D reported by the US Department of Commerce in calendar year 1989.
7. In fact, 11 parent firms in the sample operate sales and service subsidiaries abroad, but do not have an overseas manufacturing base.
8. Eight per cent of overseas R&D by the 43 firms is conducted in subsidiaries classified in the distribution sector.
9. Odagiri and Yasuda (1996), however, find mixed support for the effect of experience on overseas R&D.
10. The reliability of the data on R&D was cross-checked by comparing the data with the available information on R&D employment and R&D type in 1992 and, where subsidiaries could be matched, with R&D activities as reported in the 1989 *Basic Survey*. Several subsidiaries reporting zero R&D in 1992 had to be omitted from the analysis for various reasons: although they reported zero R&D, they also reported the type of R&D activities or a positive number of R&D employees, or they reported a significant R&D expenditure in 1989. The exercise suggests that in some cases firms erroneously report zero R&D expenditure where R&D expenditure information is in fact not available.
11. This specification is a refinement of the experience variable in Wakasugi (1996b), who did not distinguish between newly established and acquired firms. *S_EXPER* was entered separately for subsidiaries established through acquisitions and capital participation but this variable did not have any significant effect on *S_RDINT*.
12. As noted above, R&D intensive firms may on the other hand have a stronger tendency to concentrate R&D in Japan. However, while this argument predicts a negative correlation between the overseas R&D ratio and the parent firm R&D intensity, it does not necessarily imply a negative correlation between parent firm R&D intensity and absolute R&D expenditure or R&D intensity overseas.
13. *RDINT* will also reflect R&D intensity of the sub-sector(s) of the electronics industry the parent firm is active in. Inclusion of subsidiary industry dummies to control for such variation in R&D intensity and other factors across sub-sectors did not however give any robust results.
14. More than a quarter of total R&D spending in the 113 subsidiaries in the sample

was in acquired firms, a figure that also points to the importance of technology acquisition.

15. The only exception is Oceania, but here the coefficient is based on just one observation.
16. De Arcos *et al.* (1995) found no significant effect of experience on R&D activities for a small sample of Japanese MNEs' subsidiaries in Europe. They argue that the explanation should be sought in a shift in investment strategy by Japanese firms. Whereas manufacturing activities in the 1970s and 1980s were mostly assembly operations and involved little R&D, more recent investments in the late 1980s and 1990s have focused on integrated manufacturing and have been more R&D intensive.

10

Conclusions

This book has dealt with various aspects of the internationalisation of Japanese electronics firms and the role of trade policies in shaping Japanese firms' trade and investment behaviour. This final chapter summarises the main conclusions and points out broader implications of the findings. Three themes are distinguished. Section 10.1 reviews the factors behind the internationalisation of Japanese electronics firms. Section 10.2 discusses the objectives and effects of EC trade policies targeting Japanese electronics firms. Section 10.3 summarises the conclusions on the role of antidumping in combating 'unfair' trade and anti-competitive behaviour and stresses the need for reform of antidumping and antitrust law and practice. Finally, some comments are offered on the future of EC trade policy and Japanese DFI in the electronics industry.

10.1 The Internationalisation of Japanese Electronics Firms: Are Japanese Multinationals Different?

Are Japanese multinationals different? The analysis in this book suggests that they are not in most important respects.

10.1.1 Firm-specific Capabilities

The main factors behind the internationalisation of Japanese electronics firms are similar to those known to be important for US and European multinationals. The rise of Japanese electronics firms as major exporters to, and investors in, the US and EC is strongly based on technological and managerial capabilities that give a competitive edge in foreign markets. Firm-level exports as well as direct foreign investment (DFI) are significantly related to technological capabilities based on investments in research and development, investments in productivity increasing plants and equipment, marketing skills, and the availability of human resources. A direct measure of individual firms' competitiveness relative to other Japanese firms—market share in Japan at the product level—is also strongly related to DFI. Although Japanese firms are lagging behind Western multinationals in the appointment of local managers to their overseas subsidiaries and the internationalisation of research and development activities, the evidence suggests that this is mostly related to Japanese firms' late internationalisation and lack of experience in multinational business. Since the late 1980s, Japanese electronics firms have rapidly increased overseas R&D and have made progress in the 'localisation' of management in overseas subsidiaries.

10.1.2 DFI and Trade Policies

The internationalisation of Japanese electronics firms does reveal a number of characteristics which appear to set it apart from the experience of Western multinationals. Although the role that import barriers and discriminatory government procurement played in attracting US electronics firms' investment to the EC in the 1960s and 1970s is well documented, the extent to which Japanese electronics firms' investments, in particular in the EC, have been shaped by trade policies may be unique. Tariffs, voluntary export restraints (VERs), and a range of antidumping measures have all worked to encourage Japanese electronics firms to invest in the EC. Such policies have not only accelerated investment that would have taken place in any case, but they have also increased Japanese manufacturing investment substantially above the level it would otherwise have reached.

The importance of this 'tariff jumping' motive for Japanese DFI has important consequences. DFI is more likely to substitute directly for exports of the (final) products targeted by trade policy measures. On the other hand, manufacturing investment is also more likely to be limited to assembly-type operations dependent on imported components. Empirical analysis revealed important export substituting effects of Japanese electronics firms' manufacturing investment, a result that differs from the ambiguous findings on export substitution in studies of US and Swedish multinationals. Reliance on imported components certainly was a characteristic of Japanese electronics plants just after establishment, but local content (defined as value added of the plants plus the value of components bought in the EC) has rapidly increased and reached relatively high levels in the early 1990s. Again, this trend has been importantly influenced, if not forced, by EC policies, i.e. local content rules and idiosyncratic changes in rules of origin.

10.1.3 DFI in South-East Asia

Another remarkable feature of the internationalisation of Japanese electronics firms is the pattern of DFI in South-East Asia. The determinants of the decision by Japanese electronics firms to start manufacturing operations in South-East Asia differ markedly from the determinants of foreign investment in North America and Europe. While firm-specific capabilities based on technological and marketing skills are a prerequisite for manufacturing investment in North America and Europe, such firm capabilities, apart from the availability of human resources, are not a factor for DFI in South-East Asia. These findings suggest that cumulative economic ties between Japan and South-East Asia and the relative absence of strong firms competing locally have reduced the barriers Japanese firms face in expanding in the region.

Another factor of importance in Japanese DFI in South-East Asia are inter-firm linkages within vertical and horizontal business groups or *keiretsu*. Member firms of bank-centred horizontal business groups are less liquidity constrained in DFI decisions than independent firms, apparently because the former can draw on finance from the main bank for investment projects in South-East Asia. Member firms' DFI in the region is also encouraged if other group members and the group trading firms have established manufacturing and trade networks in the region. Likewise, subcontractor firms within manufacturer-centred vertical business groups are more likely to invest in South-East Asia if the 'core' firm has established networks of plants in the region. These findings suggest that long term trade relationships between Japanese firms are maintained and replicated abroad. Inter-firm trade linkages, along with accompanied information exchange and financial assistance, facilitate expansion abroad, and may help smaller firms and firms lacking strong capabilities to become multinational.

The findings are consistent with the hypothesis of the rise of a trade and investment bloc in South-East Asia in which the trade and manufacturing networks of the larger Japanese multinationals play an important role. The role of smaller and less competitive Japanese firms as manufacturers in South-East Asia is also consistent with the observations made on Japanese investment in the 1970s by Kojima (1978) and Ozawa (1979). However, the characteristics of Japanese DFI within the Asian trade and investment bloc may not be dissimilar to the features of European and North American firms' DFI in their respective regional blocs, the European Union and NAFTA. The final verdict on the 'uniqueness' of Japanese investment in Asia must await thorough examination of determinants of DFI within Western regional trading blocs.

10.1.4 Keiretsu and Internationalisation

Vertical business groups, but not horizontal business groups, emerge as a factor of importance in trade and investment behaviour of Japanese electronics firms in North America and Europe as well. On the one hand, exports to Europe are higher for subcontractors in vertical business groups in cases where the 'core' firm has established a manufacturing plant there. In this case supply linkages with the 'core' firm provide export opportunities for dependent firms in Japan. On the other hand, subcontractor firms are also found to follow the 'core' firm in investing in EC and US manufacturing plants in order to supply the 'core' firm with locally produced components. Such investments took place in response to the EC's local content requirements imposed on Japanese electronics firms. The evidence on Japanese overseas subsidiaries' procurement behaviour generally shows a preference to keep control over components production abroad, either through in-house production or through procurement from long-standing Japanese suppliers. The relationships with subcontractors and long-standing suppliers are part of an organisation of production characterised by 'lean production' methods, just-in-time deliveries of components, and joint development of components for new products. This type of production management is widely seen as constituting a competitive advantage of Japanese electronics firms, and firms faced with local content measures have pursued a strategy to transfer the system abroad.

If Japanese multinationals are to be found 'different', it must be in the role of long term trade links, in particular with member firms of *keiretsu*, and the way these relationships influence trade and investment behaviour abroad. Yet again, inter-firm linkages such as long-term supplier links are also present in Western industries, and the apparent differences could also be a matter of degree (Sako 1992). Only comparative investigation of the role of inter-firm linkages in DFI and trade by Western firms can provide a definitive answer here.

10.2 EC Trade Policies: Protecting EC-Owned or EC-Based Industries?

The formation of the Single Market with the implementation of Lord Cockfield's White Paper provoked intense debate on the possibility that the establishment of the Single Market in 1992 would be accompanied by higher external trade barriers. The analysis in this book has shown that for Japanese electronics firms, the feared 'fortress Europe' had actually materialised in the late 1980s.

The EC has taken a range of trade policy measures since the early 1980s to protect the electronics industry, often specifically targeting Japanese firms. The EC maintains much higher tariffs on most electronics imports than the US and Japan, and tariffs were increased for CD players (temporarily) and VCRs. A voluntary export restraint was negotiated for Japanese VCRs in 1983. The most important instrument of trade policy has undoubtedly been antidumping. A wave of antidumping actions, concentrated in the second half of the 1980s, targeted Japanese electronics firms and often led to the imposition of duties. When the Japanese firms appeared to respond by investing in EC manufacturing operations in order to bypass antidumping measures, the EC amended its antidumping law to make it applicable to Japanese assembly plants as well. The so-called 'screwdriver plant' amendment was effectively administered as a (relatively strict) local content rule. It was invoked seven times during 1987–1990. All cases involved Japanese firms, and five cases targeted electronics products. Besides antidumping actions, the EC has used changes in rules of origin with the apparent objective of altering the trade environment in favour of EC firms. In 1989, a new rule of origin for integrated circuits essentially forced Japanese firms to establish integrated production in EC plants.

10.2.1 Strategic Trade Policies

The application of strategic trade policy models to EC trade policies provides a number of insights into the rationale for such policies and their potential merits. The strategic trade policy literature emphasises that in imperfectly competitive (oligopolistic) industries where excess returns can be earned, and where economies of scale or dynamic economies of 'learning by doing' are important, free trade does not necessarily lead to optimal outcomes. Countries can improve economic welfare by assisting domestic firms to commit to aggressive behaviour which increases their share of sales and profits in world markets. Trade policies such as import tariffs become a 'rent shifting' instrument, increasing the export costs of foreign firms and helping domestic firms to increase profits as a result. Domestic economic welfare increases if tariff revenue and the increase in domestic firms' profits more than compensate for the loss in consumer welfare as a result of the ensuing price increases. Strategic trade policies are likely to be more effective if (dynamic) economies of scale are present, since increased sales will allow domestic firms to lower production costs and increase long term competitiveness. Furthermore, trade and industrial policies will have beneficial effects if development of the domestic industry has beneficial 'spillover' effects on other industries, such as perceived in high technology industries.

There is however a string of important qualifications attached to the above case for strategic policies. The effects of strategic trade policies depend crucially on industry structure and on the strategic interactions between firms. Scope for welfare improving policies is not the rule but rather the exception. The effective implementation of policies requires access to an elaborate set of information on industry characteristics and firm strategies which is usually not available to governments. Although empirical studies of strategic trade policies have calculated positive welfare effects, it is also clear that the quantitative effects have typically been small. Probably the most important qualification concerns the 'beggar thy neighbour' character of strategic trade policies: in almost all cases, policies improve domestic welfare only at the cost of harming foreign countries' interests. If competing countries pursue similar policies or directly retaliate, all countries will be worse off compared with the free trade situation.

10.2.2 EC Policies as Rent Shifting Devices

To what extent can EC policies be seen as 'rent shifting' devices, assisting EC-owned firms in competition with Japanese rivals? Both antidumping duties and local content requirements targeting foreign-owned firms can be seen as 'raising rivals' cost' strategies, improving the competitive position of EC firms by increasing the costs of Japanese rivals.

Analysis shows that tariff policy is less effective as a profit shifting instrument if Japanese firms can 'jump' the tariff by investing in the EC. If the objective is to protect EC firms, the first best policy would be to inhibit Japanese investment. If this is not a feasible policy, the preferable solution is to set the tariff as low as necessary in order to avoid 'tariff jumping DFI'. To be sure, tariffs that induce DFI can still assist domestic firms if EC assembly increases the costs of Japanese firms (which is likely to have been the case), but the 'raising rivals' cost' effects are necessarily smaller. There is also one important prerequisite for tariffs or antidumping duties to have welfare improving effects. EC firms should not lag behind foreign firms too much in terms of competitiveness and market share: if they do, they will not be able to benefit much and any profit increases will be outstripped by greater costs to consumers.

Local content requirements associated with the EC's 'screwdriver plant' amendment are a logical extension of tariff policy in cases where tariffs or antidumping duties induce DFI. Local content rules will increase the costs of components sourcing for the EC manufacturing plants of Japanese firms or raise the setup costs of Japanese plants as they have to generate more value added. This raises investment barriers and may discourage firms from investing in the EC, enhancing the 'raising rivals' cost' effect of antidumping actions. In practice, however, the 'screwdriver plant' amendment worked to increase the costs of established Japanese plants rather than to deter Japanese DFI. Analysis of local content rules for foreign-owned firms shows that profit shifting and welfare effects in this case crucially depend on the structure of EC components industries. If EC components industries are oligopolistic, local content requirements push up components prices and may actually reduce profits and market share of EC electronics firms.

Confronting strategic trade policy analysis with the empirical evidence on EC trade policies and developments in the EC electronics industry, it becomes clear that EC policies have been less than effective in reaching a major objective of strategic trade policies: protecting EC firms. This is not to say that EC trade policies have not been instigated to protect 'European champions' such as Philips and Thomson in consumer electronics, and Olivetti in office machines. The extent of protection offered to some EC firms is remarkable. Philips, the Dutch consumer electronics group, was involved in 11 out of 19 antidumping petitions filed against Japanese firms during 1982–1992. EC antidumping law and practice have been changed on several occasions to increase their effectiveness as a weapon against Japanese firms. Japanese firms were targeted by antidumping even in cases where their production capacity in the EC matched or surpassed EC firms' production. Clearly, EC policies have discriminated against Japanese firms in favour of EC rivals.

However, the investment response to antidumping reduced the effectiveness of antidumping duties and local content requirements. The empirical evidence shows that Japanese firms reacted to the latter by producing components in-house at EC factories, inviting subcontractors in the *keiretsu* to invest in the EC, and procuring components from independent Japanese components producers in the EC. Japanese firms' DFI in both final goods and components manufacturing will have enabled them to limit the 'raising rivals' cost' effect of the EC policies.

Indeed, the available evidence on developments in the EC electronics industry in the late 1980s and early 1990s suggests that EC electronics firms have not benefited much from EC policies. In most cases EC electronics firms have not been able to increase their competitiveness, EC production volumes, or EC market shares. On the contrary, in a number of industries (CD players, electric typewriters, and VCRs), EC firms eventually transferred production to South-East Asia, which left the EC with a predominantly Japanese-owned manufacturing base. Antidumping may rather have postponed EC firms' rationalisation and the ultimate transfer of production to lower cost locations. Since, in most industries targeted by antidumping measures, Japanese firms have commanding market shares in the EC, it is likely that the 'raising rivals' costs' measures have brought more harm to EC consumers than benefits to EC producers. As welfare improving rent shifting policies, EC policies are likely to have failed.

The evidence on procurement behaviour by Japanese firms also indicates that local content requirements have largely failed to promote components manufacturing by EC firms. Paradoxically, the requirements may have *reduced* sales of EC components suppliers to Japanese electronics firms. Since successful involvement of new components suppliers in the supply chain involves time and effort, the time pressure put on Japanese firms to increase local content is likely to have spurred transfer of components production to the EC in order to comply with the rules without loss of reliability and quality. Here policies encouraging supply links between EC suppliers and Japanese assemblers would have been much more effective than local content rules which do not specify the source of local procurements.

10.2.3 Developing an EC-Based Electronics Industry

It has been suggested that the EC has used the antidumping instrument and rules of origin to address its 'Japan problem': the advance of Japanese firms in high technology markets of the EC, the relative weakness of EC firms, and the increasing bilateral trade deficit. Trade barrier induced Japanese investment has indeed reduced, or at least stemmed the increase in, the EC's electronics trade deficit with Japan. Yet EC trade policies had relatively poor results with respect to protecting the position of EC firms. What EC policies certainly have done is to help create a Japanese-owned electronics industry in the EC.

It is clear that EC policies, while initially conceived as protecting 'European champions', have evolved to include the broader objective of maintaining electronics manufacturing capability with much less concern for ownership.[1] It is apparent that antidumping measures have been used opportunistically to attract Japanese investment and strengthen the EC electronics industry with Japanese manufacturing skills and technology. More value has been attached to the potential positive spillover effects of development of high technology electronics manufacturing, and less to the narrow 'rent shifting' objective of strategic trade policy. In most of the antidumping decisions in electronics there have been references to the high technology character of the industries and the importance of linkages between components and final goods manufacturing. In a number of cases it was clear that the most important effect of antidumping action would be to increase the manufacturing activity of Japanese firms in the EC. The most illustrative example is the decision to extend antidumping duties on copier imports from Japan in 1995. The main reason offered by the EC Commission for extension of duties as in the interest of the EC was to maintain Japanese firms' manufacturing activities in the EC (which otherwise could be transferred to South-East Asia) and the positive linkage with the EC components industry (where Japanese firms are important producers as well).

Improving the domestic manufacturing base by encouraging inward investment has of course been central to industrial policy in the United Kingdom since the early 1980s. The UK has also been the main beneficiary of antidumping induced Japanese investments, which may have prevented it from opposing the increased use of the antidumping instrument in the

1980s. France, which traditionally had a hostile attitude towards Japanese inward investment, changed its stance in 1984 and has been encouraging Japanese firms since then. Owing to various regional investment incentive schemes, Japanese firms have been able to get substantial subsidies for their manufacturing investments.

The evolving policy emphasis on attracting Japanese investment arguably had positive effects on the EC electronics industry. Employment in Japanese manufacturing subsidiaries rose fourfold to about 80,000 people in 1991, and skill levels of the jobs provided have risen. There is evidence that EC firms have been able to emulate Japanese style production and management practices successfully. Joint production and R&D with EC firms in joint ventures is a minor but important part of Japanese investment, facilitating technology transfer where Japanese firms have built up engineering and product quality advantages. Japanese firms have stepped up R&D and design activities in the EC and are appointing more local managers, although Japanese subsidiaries started from a low base in the late 1980s.

There is one important caveat in this positive assessment of trade barrier induced inward investment. To the extent that DFI decisions are a response to trade barriers, manufacturing in the EC will not be cost-effective and will reduce allocative efficiency in the global industry. Although it has been argued that Japanese manufacturing investment in the EC has evolved from a second best to a first best strategy (Ozawa 1991), it cannot be doubted that in the absence of trade policy measures at least part of Japanese manufacturing in the EC would be undertaken more cost effectively at Japanese or South-East Asian plants. Protection of the EC industry has often been extended by antidumping actions against imports from South-East Asian countries such as Korea, Taiwan, and China, this time also benefiting Japanese manufacturers in the EC. Virtually all output of Japanese manufacturing plants in the EC is sold on EC markets. For the EC industry as a whole, extra-EC exports as a percentage of EC production have been declining. While trade policy measures have supported the EC electronics industry, there is no guarantee that this industry will be competitive on world markets and viable in the absence of trade barriers.

10.3 Antidumping and Antitrust

A country may protect a domestic industry by imposing dumping duties on imports if the imports are found to be dumped, i.e. sold at a price below the price in the home country of the exporter or below full production cost, and if dumped imports cause some form of 'injury', e.g. a decline in sales or profitability, to the domestic industry. The most common justification given for antidumping actions is that they counter foreign firms' low cost pricing strategies which are sustained through subsidisation with profits reaped on a 'sanctuary market' at home. Foreign firms may have privileged access to a 'sanctuary market' because of government regulations and private entry barriers. Since domestic firms do not have the same strategic option, dumping is considered 'unfair' competition and puts domestic firms at a disadvantage. A clear rationale for intervention arises if dumping by foreign firms is 'predatory': if foreign firms make strategic losses on exports in order to induce exit of domestic firms and to establish dominance in the market. Once this dominance is established, it may be exploited to charge higher prices.

A large number of studies have looked at the legal and economic aspects of antidumping law and practice (e.g. Finger 1992, Van Bael and Bellis 1990, Jackson and Vermulst 1990, Boltuck and Litan 1991, Tharakan 1991b). The prevailing view is that antidumping does more harm than good. In practice, a much too wide range of foreign firms' behaviour is punishable by antidumping action. Biases in price calculations and comparisons, as well as a flexible interpretation of the causal linkage between dumping and injury, make antidumping more akin to a projectionist device: if import competing industries are faced with declining profitability or sales, they stand a good chance of receiving antidumping protection. Recent analysis has also shown that antidumping may be used by the petitioning firms to force foreign firms to engage in anti-competitive price and sales arrangements (e.g. Prusa 1992a). The analysis in this book has emphasised a number of features and consequences of antidumping which until now have not received due attention.

10.3.1 Antidumping and Tariff Jumping DFI

It was shown that the response of Japanese firms to EC (and to a lesser extent US) antidumping actions has predominantly been to invest in local manufacturing plants in order to avoid the effects of antidumping measures. Generally, the fact that an antidumping scheme is in place in export markets gives incentives to firms to produce abroad rather than to rely on exports from the home country. Antidumping law disallows pricing strategies for exported goods that are allowed in the host economy if transactions do not cross borders. The risk of antidumping actions is substantial given the frequency of temporary currency overvaluations to which firms with established market positions based on investments in distribution and marketing would not normally want to react by increasing prices commensurably.[2] Moreover, antidumping action may always be a risk if exports increase and local firms are losing market share, given the biases in dumping and injury calculations. All this would suggest that tariff jumping DFI is not limited to Japanese electronics firms but is a much more common response to actual as well as threatened antidumping actions. This will in particular be the case if antidumping targets foreign firms with competitive advantages and financial resources which enable the firm to invest abroad, and if firms are active in assembly type industries where manufacturing operations can be transferred abroad at relatively low cost.

Tariff jumping DFI has been observed for several other Japanese industries, such as machine tools, ball bearings, and hydraulic shovels. There is also abundant evidence that South Korean firms have set up EC manufacturing plants as a response to VERs and antidumping measures. Japanese and South Korean firms alone are responsible for 20–25 per cent of EC and US antidumping actions. Clearly, tariff jumping DFI in response to antidumping may be an important feature of contemporary antidumping practice. The question arises to what extent global trends in DFI in the 1980s and the increased popularity of antidumping actions in the same period are not only correlated but also causally related. This calls for systematic empirical research on the relationship between DFI, trade, and antidumping for a broader range of countries and industries.

10.3.2 The Effects and Ineffectiveness of Antidumping

If the DFI response to antidumping is important, then at least two common perceptions concerning antidumping may have to be altered. First, antidumping measures do not restrict foreign firms' trade as much as import figures suggest (e.g. Messerlin 1989), as imports are replaced by local production. Second, antidumping is not effective in acting against international price discrimination or below cost pricing by foreign firms. Once foreign firms are producing in the host economy, there is not much to prevent them from continuing to sell at prices below prices in the host country or below full production costs.

The latter fact undermines the effectiveness of antidumping actions in reaching a central objective: to shield domestic firms from the pricing strategies of foreign firms made possible by anti-competitive conduct abroad. Antidumping actions by definition can only act on *trade flows*, while effective policies dealing with consequences of overseas market conditions in international industries should focus on the behaviour of *firms*. The latter approach is taken by antitrust policy. However, antitrust policy does not take sufficiently into account the international linkages between markets and spillovers of anti-competitive conduct abroad.

An example of the limitations of national antitrust policies is given by the case of Japanese–US rivalry in the CTV industry in the 1960s and early 1970s. A 'sanctuary market' existed for Japanese CTV manufactures in Japan, arising from import barriers and Japanese firms' control over the distribution system. The seven Japanese CTV producers apparently cartelised the home market, set high prices in Japan, and sold CTVs at much lower prices in the US. Analysis shows that dumping in relationship with cartelisation of the Japanese market could have had negative consequences for US firms as well as, ultimately, US consumers. This conclusion is not based on the assumption of strategic loss making by Japanese firms in the US market (prices covered variable costs), but is consistent with profit maximising behaviour of Japanese firms. It is the spillover of anti-competitive conduct in Japan to the US market that had negative consequences for competition in the US. US antitrust action proved ineffective in this case. The charge brought by US producers in 1974, that Japanese firms were conspiring to drive US firms out of the market (the *Matsushita* v. *Zenith* case), was eventually dismissed by the US Supreme Court in 1986.

Once the potential DFI response is taken into account, another disturbing effect of antidumping actions must be considered: not only are antidumping actions ineffective, they are also likely to hit the wrong firms. Empirical results for DFI decisions by Japanese electronics firms suggest that precisely the firms with dominant market positions in Japan, i.e. those that benefit most from privileged access to a 'sanctuary market' if such a market exists, will be able to avoid paying duties by investing abroad. Smaller players in the market, on the other hand, will not be able to afford the cost of setting up foreign plants and so will be forced to pay the dumping duties. In addition, the legal cost of co-operation with antidumping authorities are a relatively greater burden to small exporters, while antidumping procedures raise important barriers to new entrants by assigning them the highest duties. The asymmetric effects of antidumping actions between large and small firms is likely to have negative consequences in terms of increased industry concentration and reduced competitive dynamics, an effect that apparently has not been sufficiently recognised.

10.3.3 Antidumping as Strategic Trade Policy?

A salient feature of antidumping which deserves more emphasis is the substantial difference between the antidumping systems of the EC and the US. In the US system, exporters can avoid paying duties in response to an affirmative antidumping decision by increasing export prices, but in the EC dumping duties are fixed for a period of five years.[3] Under the EC system, foreign firms do not have strong incentives to increase prices and the DFI response is much more attractive, as is confirmed by empirical analysis of Japanese DFI in the US and the EC. There are other differences, too. The EC has discretion in determining the level of antidumping duties as long as they are below the calculated dumping margin, while in the US dumping duties can by law only be set equal to the dumping margin. In the EC, antidumping actions can formally be taken only if they are in the 'Community interest', a concept not precisely defined in antidumping law, but in practice implying that protection of EC industries should not bring undue costs to user industries and consumers. No such general interest clause is present in US antidumping law. Generally, in the EC system there is considerably more discretion to decide on antidumping actions, while the US system is more technical and rules based.

It is interesting to observe that a number of characteristics of the EC antidumping system in particular may make antidumping a more suitable instrument of strategic trade policy than traditional instruments such as tariffs or export subsidies. The most important problem with the implementation of strategic trade policies is the lack of information available. However, an antidumping administration may be uniquely place to formulate policies since foreign firms are required to submit detailed information on costs, profits, production, and sales. Antidumping measures also have the necessary policy flexibility, particularly if compared with conventional tariffs. Antidumping actions can be targeted at specific countries or even specific firms within a country, and the level of dumping duties is firm-specific. Authorities may also decide to strike a deal with foreign firms which commits the firms to certain pricing and sales behaviour ('undertakings') instead of levying duties. The discretion in the EC system in terms of the determination of duties provides the EC with more opportunities to formulate specific policies.

On the other hand, the capacity of the EC to implement strategic trade policies under the guise of antidumping law can easily be overestimated. Although EC antidumping law has undoubtedly been applied flexibly to target Japanese firms, the discretion built into the EC system has also allowed individual member states to influence antidumping decisions in order to protect their own interests. Political influence in the antidumping procedures, arising from the fact that a majority[4] of member states has to approve each definitive antidumping decision, is likely to lead to compromise solutions and to inhibit the formulation of 'optimal' policies.

If antidumping is considered a tool of strategic trade policy, the potentially negative welfare consequences are also directly apparent. One of the central results of strategic trade policy analysis is that, while unilateral policies can be welfare improving, retaliation by other countries leads to welfare losses for all. The GATT Antidumping Code allows all signatories to use the antidumping instrument and so provides GATT member countries with the possibility of retaliation if their firms are targeted by antidumping abroad. Japan is yet to use its antidumping law against imports from the EC or US. But it is apparent that countries such as Brazil and Mexico have retaliated against US and EC antidumping actions by taking antidumping measures against US and EC imports. This development has certainly driven the move towards more transparent and less biased procedures, resulting in the new GATT Antidumping Code negotiated in the Uruguay Round.

10.3.4 Antidumping and Antitrust: Reform?

The conclusions on antidumping must be added to a long list of potentially harmful effects of antidumping practice. It is not argued here that there is no legitimate cause for concern about 'unfair' trade and 'sanctuary markets' abroad, in particular if they involve anti-competitive practices. But taking potential DFI responses into account, antidumping is not even a second best option to counter potentially harmful effects of foreign firms' behaviour, and may actually make matters worse. A fundamental problem is also that antidumping actions can never address the source of the problem, which lies in industry conditions abroad. First best policies address the problems in the foreign market that lead to dumping. The solution, then, must be found in co-ordination and harmonisation of antitrust rules and enforcement.

Current antitrust law cannot deal adequately with spillovers of anti-competitive conduct abroad. Although the US Department of Justice announced in April 1992 that anti-competitive behaviour abroad affecting US exporters would be subject to US antitrust litigation, such extra-territorial application of domestic antitrust law will necessarily conflict with the authority of antitrust administrations abroad. The way forward is co-operation between different countries to achieve a greater degree of harmonisation of antitrust laws and implementation and to remove clear incompatibilities. The GATT Uruguay Round has further reduced tariff and non-tariff barriers and has brought improvements in the harmonisation of discriminatory standards and government procurement. Certainly, anti-competitive behaviour which constitutes barriers to trade should now be high on the agenda of the World Trade Organisation.

In an ideal world, international antitrust would deal adequately with anti-competitive conduct and 'sanctuary markets' abroad, which would remove the need for antidumping. To the extent that import competing industries will require a form of protection against a surge in imports, temporary import relief could be granted by invoking a safeguard clause. In contrast to antidumping, safeguard actions are not justified because they counter 'unfair' trade, and countries invoking the clause would have to provide compensation to the affected exporting countries, which would avoid over-extensive use of the instrument.

Most observers are pessimistic that antitrust harmonisation can be achieved in the near future, and the prospect for abolishing antidumping is judged even less bright (e.g. Finger and Fung 1993). It can only be emphasised that a stronger commitment to a harmonisation of antitrust laws and practices is necessary and will have the important advantage that current over-extensive use of the antidumping instrument can then be avoided. In fact, the failure of US anti-trust to deal with anti-competitive behaviour in the *Matsushita* v. *Zenith* case left US firms no choice but to take recourse to trade protection. Partly as a response, US antidumping laws were tightened and the US position on a tougher antidumping code was eventually adopted in the 1979 GATT Code. The failure of antitrust to deal with the international dimension of anti-competitive behaviour has in a way caused the current antidumping malaise.

There are signs that the prevailing view of antidumping among governments is changing. The new Antidumping Code appears less biased against foreign firms, and it is conceivable that future rounds of negotiations in the WTO will at least further tighten the conditions for the use of the antidumping instrument. In the EC, it has appeared increasingly difficult to convince a majority of member states of the rationale for antidumping measures, as some recent decisions show.[5] Increased opposition by a number of member states to the frequent use of antidumping may limit the use of antidumping in the EC even without any formal change to antidumping law.

10.4 What's Next?

The rapid increase in Japanese electronics firms' DFI in the late 1980s and early 1990s, which was the main focus of this book, was a unique phenomenon and is not likely to be repeated. The steep rise in the value of the yen and the extremely low cost of finance in Japan were features particular to the late 1980s. The ensuing surge in Japanese DFI was to a large extent a belated effort to reduce reliance on exports and internationalise production. In the EC, the Single Market has now been established. Trade measures targeting Japanese firms in the 1980s, such as national quotas, local content rules, VERs, and the discretionary use of rules of origin, are either abolished or severely restricted in use by the new Uruguay Round GATT code.

A few factors have not changed. The yen remains a strong currency, and increasing competition in electronics markets from producers in the NIEs, in particular South Korea, has forced Japanese firms to relocate manufacturing capacity to lower-cost locations. DFI flows have been recovering after a strong decline in the aftermath of the collapse of the 'bubble economy'. However, DFI as well as trade has strongly been re-focused on South-East Asia. Where DFI has consistently outpaced DFI in Europe in recent years. Within South-East Asia, the share of Japanese DFI in China has shown a remarkable increase. A recent survey among a large number of Japanese electronics firms showed that during 1994–1995 almost three quarters of new investment projects and manufacturing consignment projects in South-East Asia went to China, up from about 20 per cent in 1990–1991 (see Denshi Keizai Kenkyuujo 1995).

What also remains is the threat of antidumping actions against Japanese firms' exports, as is illustrated by a number of recent antidumping cases initiated in the EC. However, for a number of reasons, antidumping is likely to be less of a problem for Japanese firms than before. As Japanese firms have become established as producers in the EC, antidumping actions in electronics have increasingly focused on imports from other South-East Asian countries, often to the benefit of Japanese firms. The threat of antidumping action is also reduced as EC firms themselves have further internationalised production and relocated manufacturing activity to South-East Asia. In addition, increasing opposition to antidumping measures among member states may tighten the conditions for use of the antidumping instrument in the near future.

The Japanese manufacturing presence in the EC is still growing towards the second half of the 1990s, but the pace of growth has slowed down markedly and divestments have become a common phenomenon as well. Japanese firms are expected to continue investing in the EC at this slower pace, in some cases in response to antidumping actions or antidumping threats. They are also expected steadily to increase R&D activities in the EC and elsewhere to support their manufacturing and marketing activities and to cope with a coming shortage of scientists and engineers in Japan. As Japanese subsidiaries become more established producers, they will increasingly be seen as 'insiders' comparable to US electronics manufacturers in the EC, and judged less on the basis of their ownership. Some Japanese R&D centres in the EC have now been granted EC R&D subsidies, which suggests that the prevailing view of Japanese firms as 'outsiders' is changing.[6] Arguably, Japanese firms will definitively have passed the 'insider' test once they have successfully filed their first EC antidumping petition against imports from third countries.

NOTES

1. A policy of actively encouraging inward DFI also has its proponents in the US, for example, Robert Reich, currently Labour Secretary in the Clinton Administration (Reich 1990). EC policies towards Japanese firms appear to have had an important influence on the discussion concerning inward DFI and the broader debate on industrial policy in the US; see Sharp (1995).

2. As is pointed out in the literature on 'exchange rate pass through' and 'pricing to market' behaviour; see e.g. Froot and Klemperer (1989) and Knetter (1993).
3. The US system is also called a 'duty-avoidance' system, in contrast to the EC 'duty payment' system.
4. Prior to the accession of Sweden, Austria, and Finland in 1994, this was a qualified majority.
5. In the 1995 microwave oven case and the 1995 copier case review, the Council of Ministers voted in favour of antidumping actions with only an 8 to 7 majority (see Chapter 1). In two other recent cases, antidumping measures proposed by the EC Commission were actually rejected. In the case of Gum Rosin from China, the Commission decided to terminate the investigation without imposing measures, because there was no qualified majority of member states to approve antidumping measures (see *Official Journal of the European Communities*, 12 February 1994). In the recent case of powdered activated carbon from China, a majority of member states apparently indicated a willingness to vote against definitive measures, so duties lapsed with the expiry of the provisional measures (see Tim Jones, 'Antidumping "Sea Change" as Carbon Duties are Lifted', *European Voice*, 15 February 1996).
6. Sony Germany has won approval from the EC to participate in three high technology projects sponsored by the EC, one of which is a joint effort with Ericsson and Siemens to develop next generation mobile telecommunications terminals. NEC has been granted subsidies to develop image and voice processing integrated circuits with a UK venture firm. See *Nikkei Weekly*, 5 February 1996.

REFERENCES

Abegglen, James C., and George Stalk, 1985, *Kaisha: The Japanese Corporation*, Basic Books Publishers, New York.

Abo, Tetsuo, 1994, Sanyo's Overseas Production Plants, in: Helmut Schütte, ed., *The Global Competitiveness of Asian Firms*, Macmillan, London.

Alcocella, Nicola, 1992, Trade and Direct Investment within the EC: The Impact of Strategic Considerations, in: John Cantwell, ed., *Multinational Investment in Modern Europe*, Edward Elgar, Aldershot.

Aliber, Robert Z., 1970, The Theory of Direct Foreign Investment, in: Charles P. Kindleberger (ed.), *The International Corporation*, MIT Press, Cambridge, MA, and London.

Aoki, Masahiko, 1988, *Information, Incentives, and Bargaining in the Japanese Economy*, Cambridge University Press, Cambridge.

Aoki, Masahiko, ed., 1984, *The Economic Analysis of the Japanese Firm*, North Holland, Amsterdam.

Audretsch, David B., 1989, *The Market and the State: Government Policy towards Business in Europe, Japan, and the United States*, Harvester Wheatsheaf, Brighton.

Audretsch, David B., and Maryann P. Feldman, 1994, *R&D Spillovers and the Geography of Innovation and Production*, Wissenschaftszentrum Berlin for Sozialforschung Discussion Papers FSIV 94-2, Wissenschaftszentrum Berlin.

Audretsch, David B., and Hideki Yamawaki, 1988, R&D Rivalry, Industrial Policy, and US–Japanese Trade, *Review of Economics and Statistics*, 70, 438–447.

Audretsch, David, B., Leo Sleuwaegen, and Hideki Yamawaki, 1989, The Dynamics of Export Competition, in: David B. Audretsch, Leo Sleuwaegen, and Hideki Yamawaki, eds., *The Convergence of International and Domestic Markets*, North-Holland, Amsterdam, 211–245.

Bael, Ivo van, 1995, The 1994 Anti-Dumping Code and the New EC Anti-Dumping Regulation, in: Jacques H. J. Bourgeois *et al.*, eds., *The Uruguay Round Results: A European Lawyers' Perspective*, European Interuniversity Press and College of Europe, Brussels.

Balasubramanyam, V. N., and David Greenaway, 1992, Economic Integration and Foreign Direct Investment: Japanese Investment in the EC, *Journal of Common Market Studies*, 30, 175–193.

Baldwin, Robert E., 1991, ed., *Empirical Studies of Commercial Policy*, University of Chicago Press, Chicago.

Baldwin, Robert E., ed., 1988, *Trade Policy Issues and Empirical Analysis*, University of Chicago Press, Chicago and London.

Baldwin, Richard E., and Paul R. Krugman, 1988, Market Access and International Competition: A Simulation Study of 16K Random Access Memories, in: Robert C. Feenstra, *Empirical Methods for International Trade*, MIT Press, Cambridge, MA, and London.

Baldwin, Robert E., and Jeffrey W. Steagall, 1993, An Analysis of Factors Influencing ITC Decisions in Antidumping, Countervailing Duty and Safeguard Cases, National Bureau of Economic Research Working Paper No. 4282, Cambridge, MA.

Batzer, Erich, and Helmut Laumer, 1989, *Marketing Strategies and Distrubution Channels for Foreign Companies in Japan*, IFO Institute for Economic Research, Munich, Federal Republic of Germany.

Bayard, Thomas E., and Kimberly Ann Elliott, 1994, *Reciprocity and Retaliation in US Trade Policy*, Institute for International Economics, Washington, DC.

Beghin, John C., and C. A. Knox Lovell, 1993, Trade and Efficiency Effects of Domestic Content Protection: The Australian Tobacco and Cigarette Industries, *Review of Economics and Statistics*, 75, 623–631.

Beghin, John C., and Daniel A. Sumner, 1992, Content Requirements with Bilateral Monopoly, *Oxford Economic Papers*, 44, 306–316.

Belderbos, René A, 1995a, A Note on the Classification of Manufacturing and Sales Subsidiaries in the Basic Surveys 1989 and 1992: Implications for Procurement Analysis and the Foreign Production Ratio, in: Kokusai Boueki Toushi Kenkyuujo (Institute for International Trade and Investment), *Kaigai Jigyou Katsudou Kihon Chousa Deita nado ni Motozuku Bunseki Kenkyuu (Analysis of the Basic Surveys on Direct Foreign Investment)*, Tokyo.

Belderbos, René A, 1995b, Overseas R&D by Japanese Electronics Multinationals, in: Kokusai Boueki Toushi Kenkyuujo (Institute for International Trade and Investment), *Kaigai Jigyou Katsudou Kihon Chousa Deita nado ni Motozuku Bunseki Kenkyuu (Analysis of the Basic Surveys on Direct Foreign Investment)*, Tokyo.

Belderbos, René A., 1995c, The Role of Investment in Europe in the Globalization Strategy of Japanese Electronics Firms, in: Frédérique Sachwald, ed., *Japanese Firms in Europe*, Harwood, Luxembourg, 89–168.

Belderbos, René A., 1994, On the Advance of Japanese Electronics Manufacturers in the EC: Companies, Trends, and Trade Policy, in: Helmut Schütte, ed., *The Global Competitiveness of the Asian Firm*, Macmillan, Basingstoke, 203–231.

Belderbos, René A., 1993, Tariff Jumping DFI and Export Substitution: The Case of Japanese Electronics Firms in Europe, in: Alan Bird, ed., *Association of Japanese Business Studies Best Paper Proceedings: 6th Annual Meeting*, Columbia University, New York.

Belderbos, René A., 1992, Large Multinational Enterprises Based in a Small Economy: Effects on Domestic Investment, *Weltwirtschaftliches Archiv*, 128, 543–557.

Belderbos, René A., and Peter Holmes, 1995, An Economic Analysis of Matsushita Revisited, *Antitrust Bulletin*, 40, 825–857.

Belderbos, René A., and Leo Sleuwaegen, 1996, Japanese Firms and the Decision to Invest Abroad: Business Groups and Regional Core Networks, *Review of Economics and Statistics*, 78, 214–20.

Belderbos, René A., and Leo Sleuwaegen, 1995, Local Content Requirements and Vertical Market Structure, Mimeograph, Science Policy Research Unit, University of Sussex, forthcoming in *European Journal of Political Economy*.

Belderbos, René A., Clive Jie a Joen, and Leo Sleuwaegen, 1995, *Cascading Contingent Protection and Vertical Market Strucutre*, Discussion Paper Series A No. 310, Institute of Economic Research, Hitotsubashi University, Tokyo, forthcoming in *International Journal of Industrial Organization*.

Bell, Alasdair, 1987, Anti-Dumping Practice of the EEC: The Japanese Dimension, *Legal Issues of European Integration*, 2, 1–31.

Bellis, Jean-François, 1990, The EEC Antidumping System, in: John H. Jackson and Edwin A. Vermulst, eds., *Antidumping Law and Practice: A Comparative Study*, Harvester Wheatsheaf, New York, 41–98.

Bhagwati, Jagdish, *et al.*, 1987, Quid Pro Quo Foreign Investment and Welfare: A Political-Economy-Theoretic Model, *Journal of Development Economics*, 27, 127–138.

Blair D., *et al.*, 1991, An Economic Analysis of Matsushita, *The Antitrust Bulletin*, 36, 355–381.

Blomström, Magnus, Robert E. Lipsey, and Ksenia Kulchycky, 1988, US and Swedish Direct Investment and Exports, in: R. E. Baldwin, ed., *Trade Policy Issues and Empirical Analysis*, University of Chicago Press, Chicago.

Boltuck, Richard, and Robert Litan, eds., 1991, *Down in the Dumps: Administration of the Unfair Trade Laws*, Brookings Institution, Washington.

Boltuck, Richard, Joseph F. François, and Seth Kaplan, 1991, Down in the Dumps: The Economic Implications of the Administration of the US Unfair Trade Laws, in: Richard Boltuck and Robert Litan, 1991, eds., *Down in the Dumps: Administration of the Unfair Trade Laws*, Brookings Institution, Washington, 152–199.

Borrus, Michael, Laura D'Andrea Tyson, and John Zysman, 1986, Creating Advantage: How Government Policies Shape International Trade in the Semiconductor Industry, in: Paul R. Krugman, ed., *Strategic Trade Policy and the New International Economics* MIT Press, Cambridge, MA, and London.

Bourgeois, Jacques H. J., *et al.*, 1995, *The Uruguay Round Results: A European Lawyer's Perspective*, European Interuniversity Press and College of Europe, Brussels.

Bowen, Harry, 1991, Consumer Electronics, in: David Mayes, ed., *The European Challenge: Industry's Response to the 1992 Programme*, Harvester Wheatsheaf, Brighton.

Brander, James, and Paul R. Krugman, 1983, A Reciprocal Dumping Model of International Trade, *Journal of International Economics*, 15, 313–321.

Brander, James A., and Barbara Spencer, 1987, Foreign Direct Investment with Unemployment and Endogenous Taxes and Tariffs, *Journal of International Economics*, 22, 257–279.

Brander, James A., and Barbara Spencer, 1984, Tariff Protection and Imperfect Competition, in: Henryk Kierzkowski, ed., *Monopolistic Competition and International Trade*, Clarendon Press, Oxford.

Brander, James A., and Barbara J. Spencer, 1983, International R&D Rivalry and Industrial Strategy, *Review of Economic Studies*, 50, 707–722.

Bronckers, Marco C. J. E., 1995, WTO Implementation in the European Community: Antidumping, Safeguards, and Intellectual Property, *Journal of World Trade*, 29, 73–95.

Buckley, Peter, 1985, The Economic Analysis of Multinational Enterprise: Reading versus Japan, *Hitotsubashi Journal of Economics*, 26, 117–124.

Buckley, Peter, and Marc Casson, 1981, The Optimal Timing of Foreign Direct Investment, *Economic Journal*, 91, 75–82.

Buckley, Peter, and Robert D. Pearce, 1981, Market Servicing by Multinational Manufacturing Firms: Exporting versus Foreign Production, *Managerial and Decision Economics*, 2, 229–246.

Buigues, Pierre, and Alexis Jacquemin, 1994, Foreign Direct Investment and Exports to the European Community, in: Mark Mason and Dennnis Encarnation, eds., *Does Ownership Matter? Japanese Multinationals in Europe*, Oxford University Press, Oxford and New York, 163–199.

Buigues, Pierre, and Alexis Jaxquemin, 1989, Strategies of Firms and Structural Environments in the Large Internal Market, *Journal of Common Market Studies* 28, 53–67.

Bulow, Jeremy I., John D. Geanakoplos, and Paul D. Klemperer, 1985, Multimarket Oligopoly: Strategic Substitutes and Complements, *Journal of Political Economy*, 93, 488–511.

Bürgenmeyer B., and J. L. Mucchielli, 1991, *Multinationals and Europe 1992*, Routledge, New York.

Bürger, Peter, and Holger Green, eds., 1991, *Japanische Investitionen in Europa 1990 (Japanese Investments in Europe 1990)*, Deusche Industrie- und Handeslkammer in Japan, Tokyo.

Burton F. N., and F. H. Saelens, 1987, Trade Barriers and Japanese Foreign Direct Investment in the Colour Television Industry, *Managerial and Decision Economics*, 8, 285–293.

Cairncross, David, 1994, Location of R&D Centres in the UK by Japanese Enterprises, in: Nigel Campbell and Fred Burton, eds., *Japanese Multinationals: Strategies and Management in the Global Kaisha*, Routledge, London and New York.

Campbell, Nigel, and Fred Burton, 1994, *Japanese Multinationals: Strategies and Management in the Global Kaisha*, Routledge, London and New York.

Cantwell, John, ed., 1992a, *Multinational Investment in Modern Europe*, Edward Elgar, Aldershot.

Cantwell, John, 1992b, The Internationalisation of Technological Activity and its Implications for Competitiveness, in: O. Granstrand, Lars Hakanson, and S. Sjolander, eds., *Technology Management and International Business: Internationalization of R&D and Technology*, John Wiley, Chichester, 79–95.

Cantwell, John, 1989, *Technical Innovations in Multinational Corporations*, Basil Blackwell, Oxford.

Casson, Mark, ed., 1991, *Global Research Strategy and International Competitiveness*, Basil Blackwell, Oxford and Cambridge, MA.

Casson, Mark, 1987, *The Firm and the Market: Studies on Multinational Enterprise and the Scope of the Firm*, Basil Blackwell, Oxford.

Caves, Richard E., 1993, Japanese Investment in the United States: Lessons for the Economic Analysis of Foreign Investment, *The World Economy*, 16, 279–300.

Caves, Richard E., 1982, *Multinational Enterprise and Economic Analysis*, MIT Press, Cambridge, MA.

Caves, Richard E., and Masu Uekusa, 1976, *Industrial Organization in Japan*, Brookings Institution, Washington.

Cawson, Alan, and Peter Holmes, 1991, The New Consumer Electronics, in: Christopher Freeman, Margaret Sharp, and William Walker, eds., *Technology and the Future of Europe: Competition and the Global Environment in the 1990s*, Pinter, London.

Cawson, Alan, *et al.*, 1990, *Hostile Brothers: Competition and Closure in the European Electronics Industry*, Clarendon Press, Oxford.

Cheng, Leonard, 1988, Assisting Domestic Industries under International Oligopoly: The Relevance of the Nature of Competition to Optimal Policies, *American Economic Review*, 78, 746–758.

Coase R. H., 1937, The Nature of the Firm, *Economica*, 4, 386–405.

Commission of the European Communities (CEC), 1990, 1991a, 1992, 1993, 1994, *Panorama of EC Industry*, Luxembourg.

Commission of the European Communities (CEC), 1991b, *The European Electronics and Information Technology Industry: State of Play, Issues at Stake and Proposals for Action*, DG XIII.

Corden W. M., 1974, *Trade Policy and Economic Welfare*, Oxford University Press, Oxford.

Cramer J. S., 1991, *The Logit Model: An Introduction for Economists*, Edward Arnold, London.

Dalton, Donald H., and Phyllis A. Genther, 1991, *Japanese Direct Investment in US Manufacturing*, US Department of Commerce, Washington.

Davidson, Carl, Steven J. Matusz, and Mondechai E. Kreinin, 1987, Analysis of Performance Standards for Direct Foreign Investments, *Canadian Journal of Economics*, 18, 876–890.

Davies, Stephen W., and Bruce R. Lyons, 1988, Theories of Horizontal Multinational Enterprise, Paper presented at the ADRES Conference on 'Dynamiques de Marches et Structure Industrielle', University of Paris-I, 3–5 November 1988.

Davies, Stephen W., and Anthony J. McGuinness, 1982, Dumping at less than Marginal Cost, *Journal of International Economics*, 12, 169–182.

Davies, Stephen, *et al.*, 1988, *Economics of Industrial Organisation*, Longman, London and New York.

de Arcos, Luisa, *et al.*, 1995, *Innovative Capability, Embeddedness, and the Contribution of Foreign Firms to Innovation in their Host Regions*, Report to the SPRINT Programme of the European Commission.

Dei, Fumio, 1990, A Note on Multinational Corporations in a Model of Reciprocal Dumping, *Journal of International Economics*, 29, 161–171.

Dei, Fumio, 1985, Voluntary Export Restraints and Foreign Investment, *Journal of International Economics*, 19, 305–312.

Dempa, 1990a–1992a, *Japan Electronics Almanac*, Dempa Publications, Tokyo.

Dempa, 1986b–1992b, *Japan Electronics Buyers' Guide*, Dempa Publications, Tokyo.

Denshi Keizai Kenkyuujo, 1995, Kaigai Seisan Shinshutsu Kigyou Joukyou: Shinshutsu, Genkyou, Tettai Nado (Foreign Production: Advance, Current Situation, and Withdrawals), *Denshi Jouhou*, November 1995, Publication No. 696, Denshi Keizai Kenkyuujo, Tokyo.

Denshi Keizai Kenkyuujo, 1994a, Kaigai Seisan Shinshutsu Kigyou Joukyou: Shinshutsu, Genkyou, Tettai Nado (Foreign Production: Advance, Current Situation, and Withdrawals), *Denshi Jouhou*, April 1994, Publication No. 664. Denshi Keizai Kenkyuujo, Tokyo.

Denshi Keizai Kenkyuujo, 1994b, Kaigai Seisan Shinshutsu Kigyou Joukyou: Shinshutsu, Genkyou, Tettai Nado (Foreign Production: Advance, Current Situation, and Withdrawals), *Denshi Jouhou*, October 1994, Publication No. 673, Denshi Keizai Kenkyuujo, Tokyo.

Denshi Keizai Kenkyuujo, 1993a, *Denshi Kiki Buhin Meikah Risuto: Joujou Kigyou*

Hen (Directory of Electronics Equipment and Components Manufacturers: Listed Firms), Publication No. 653, Denshi Keizai Kenkyuujo, Tokyo.

Denshi Keizai Kenkyuujo, 1993b, *Denshi Kiki Meikah Risuto: Hijoujou Kigyou Hen (Directory of Electronics Equipment Manufacturers: Unlisted Firms)*, Publication No. 668, Denshi Keizai Kenkyuujo, Tokyo.

Denshi Keizai Kenkyuujo, 1993c, *Denshi Buhin Meikah Risuto: Hijoujou Kigyou Hen (Directory of Electronics Components Manufacturers: Unlisted Firms)*, Publication No. 642, Denshi Keizai Kenkyuujo, Tokyo.

Denshi Keizai Kenkyuujo, 1993d, Kaigai Seisan Shinshutsu Kigyou Joukyou: Ichiran Kunibetsu to Hinmokubetsu (Foreign Production: Overview by Country and Product), *Denshi Jouhou*, July 1993, Publication No. 646, Denshi Keizai Kenkyuujo, Tokyo.

Destler I. M., 1992, *American Trade Politics*, Institute for International Economics, Washington.

Detrouzos, Michael L., Richard K. Lester, and Robert M. Solow, 1989, *Made in America: Regaining the Productive Edge*, MIT Press, Cambridge, MA.

DeVault, James M., 1993a, Economics and the International Trade Commission, *Southern Economic Journal*, 60, 463–478.

DeVault, James M., 1993b, The Impact of the US Unfair Trade Laws: A Preliminary Assessment, *Weltwirtschaftliches Archiv*, 129, 735–751.

Dick, Andrew R., 1993a, Strategic Trade Policy and Welfare, *Journal of International Economics*, 35, 227–249.

Dick, Andrew R., 1993b, Japanese Antitrust: Reconciling Theory and Evidence, *Contemporary Policy Issues*, 11, 50–61.

Dick, Andrew R., 1991, Learning by Doing and Dumping in the Semiconductor Industry, *Journal of Law and Economics*, 34, 133–159.

Dicken, Peter, 1988a, *Global Shift: Industrial Change in a Turbulent World*, Paul Chapman, London.

Dicken, Peter, 1988b, The Changing Geography of Japanese Foreign Direct Investment in Manufacturing Industry: A Global Perspective, *Environment and Planning*, 20, 633–653.

Didier, Pierre, 1990, EEC Antidumping: The Level of Trade Issue after the Definitive CD Player Regulation, *Journal of World Trade*, 24, 103–109.

Dixit, Avinash, 1986, Comparative Statics for Oligopoly, *International Economic Review*, 27, 107–122.

Dixit, Avinash, 1980, The Role of Investment in Entry-Deterrence, *Economic Journal*, 90, 95–106.

Dixit, Avinash, and Gene M. Grossman, 1986, Targeted Export Promotion with Several Oligopolistic Industries, *Journal of International Economics*, 21, 233–249.

Dixit, Avinash K., and Albert S. Kyle, 1985, The Use of Protection and Subsidies for Entry Promotion and Deterrence, *American Economic Review*, 75, 139–152.

Dixon, Huw, 1988, Oligopoly Theory Made Simple, in: Stephen Davies *et al.*, eds., *Economics of Industrial Organisation*, Longman Group, London and New York.

Dodwell, 1993, *The Structure of the Japanese Electronics Industry*, 3rd edition, Dodwell Marketing Consultants, Tokyo.

Dodwell, 1989, *Industrial Groupings in Japan*, Dodwell Marketing Consultants, Tokyo.

Dodwell, 1988, *The Structure of the Japanese Electronics Industry*, 2nd edition, Dokwell Marketing Consultants, Tokyo.

Doi, Noriyuki, 1991, Aggregate Export Concentration in Japan, *Journal of Industrial Economics*, 39, 433–438.

Doi, Noriyuki, 1988, Concentration, Subcontract, and Exports in Japanese Manufacturing Industries, *Managerial and Decision Economics*, 9, 109–117.

Drake, Tracey A., and Richard E. Caves, 1992, Changing Determinants of Japan's Foreign Investment in the United States, *Journal of the Japanese and International Economies*, 6, 228–246.

Dunning, John H., 1986, *Japanese Participation in British Industry*, Croom Helm, London.

Dunning, John H., 1981, *International Production and the Multinational Enterprise*, London.

Dunning, John H., and Michelle Gittelman, 1992, Japanese Multinationals in Europe and the United States: Some Comparisons and Contrasts, in: Michael W. Klein and Paul J. J. Welfens, eds., *Multinationals in the New Europe and Global Trade*, Springer-Verlag, Berlin.

Dunning, John H., and Robert D. Pearce, 1985, *The World's Largest Industrial Enterprises*, Gower, Aldershot.

Dunning, John H., and Peter Robson, eds., 1988, *Multinationals and the European Community*, Basil Blackwell, Oxford.

Eaton, Jonathan, and Gene Grossman, 1986, Optimal Trade and Industrial Policy under Oligopoly, *Quarterly Journal of Economics*, 101, 383–406.

Eaton, Jonathan, and Akiko Tamura, 1994, Bilateralism and Regionalism in Japanese and US Trade and Direct Foreign Investment Patterns, *Journal of the Japanese and International Economies*, 8, 478–510.

Elsevier Science Publishers, 1992–1995, *Yearbook of World Electronics Data, i, West Europe; ii, America, Japan & Asia Pacific*, Elsevier, Amsterdam.

Elzinga, Kenneth G., 1989, Collusive Predation: Matsushita versus Zenith, in: John E. Kwoka and Lawrence J. White, eds., *The Antitrust Revolution*, Scott Foresman, Glenview, IL.

Elzinga, Kenneth G., and David E. Mills, 1989, Testing for Predation: Is Recoupment Feasible? *Antitrust Bulletin*, 34, 869–892.

Ethier, W. J., 1986, The Multinational Firm, *Quarterly Journal of Economics*, 101, 805–833.

Euro-JERC Research Center, 1990, *Japanese Presence in Europe*, Catholic University of Louvain.

Euromonitor, 1989–1993, *Consumer Europe*, Euromonitor Publications, London.

European Association of Consumer Electronics Manufacturers (EACEM), 1990, *Consumer Electronic Industrial Plants in Europe by Far-East Manufacturers*, fifth edition, Brussels.

Eurostat, 1985–1990, *Harmonized External Trade Statistics*, Eurostat, Luxembourg.

Eymann, Angelika, and Ludger Schuknecht, 1992, Antidumping Enforcement in the European Community, in: J. Michael Finger, ed., *Antidumping: How It Works and Who Gets Hurt*, University of Michigan Press, Ann Arbor, MI, 221–240.

Feenstra, Robert C., 1989, ed., *Trade Policies for International Competitiveness*, University of Chicago Press, Chicago.

Feinberg, Robert M., and Barry T. Hirsch, 1989, Industry Rent Seeking and the Filing of 'Unfair Trade' Complaints, *International Journal of Industrial Organiza-*

tion, 7, 325–340.

Feinberg, Robert M., and Seth Kaplan, 1990, Fishing Downstream: The Political Economy of Effective Administered Protection, *Canadian Journal of Economics*, 26, 150–158.

Finger J. Michael, ed., 1992, *Antidumping: How It Works and Who Gets Hurt*, University of Michigan Press, Ann Arbor, MI.

Finger J. Michael, and K. C. Fung, 1993, *Will GATT Enforcement Control Antidumping?* Policy Research Working Paper 1232, Trade Policy Division, Policy Reseach Department, World Bank, Washington.

Flam, Harry, 1994, EC Members Fighting about Surplus: VERs, FDI, and Japanese Cars, *Journal of International Economics*, 36, 117–131.

Flamm, Kenneth, 1990, Semiconductors, in: Gary Hufbauer, ed., *Europe 1992: An American Perspective*, Brookings Institution, Washington.

Flath, David, 1993, Shareholdings in the Keiretsu, Japan's Financial Groups, *Review of Economics and Statistics*, 75, 249–257.

Flath, David, 1988, Vertical Restraints in Japan, *Japan and the World Economy*, 1, 187–203.

Flath, David, and T. Nariu, 1989, Returns Policy in the Japanese Marketing System, *Journal of Japan and the International Economies*, 3, 49–63.

Flowers, Edward B., 1976, Oligopolistic Reactions in European and Canadian Direct Investment in the United States, *Journal of International Business Studies*, 7, 43–55.

Foundation for Economic Research of the University of Amsterdam, 1988, *Manual Logit-JD*, University of Amsterdam, Amsterdam.

Franko, Lawrence G., 1983, *The Threat of Japanese Multinationals: How the West can Respond*, John Wiley, Chichester.

Froot, Kenneth A., 1991, *Japanese Foreign Direct Investment*, Working Paper No. 3737, National Bureau of Economic Research, Cambridge, MA.

Froot, Kenneth A., and Paul D. Klemperer, 1989, Exchange Rate Pass Through When Market Share Matters, *American Economic Review*, 79, 637–654.

Fukao, Kyoji, and Koichi Hamada, 1994, International Trade and Investment under Different Rates of Time Preference, *Journal of the Japanese and International Economies*, 8, 22–52.

Fukao, Kyoji, Toshiyasu Izawa, Morio Kuninori, and Toru Nakakita, 1994, R&D Investment and Overseas Production: An Empirical Analysis of Japan's Electric Machinery Industry Based on Corporate Data, *BOJ Monetary and Economic Studies*, 12, 1–60.

Fung K. C., 1992, Some International Properties of Japanese Firms, *Journal of the Japanese and International Economies*, 6, 163–175.

Fung K. C., 1991, Characteristics of Japanese Industrial Groups and their Potential Impact on US–Japan Trade, in: R. Baldwin, ed., *Empirical Studies of Commercial Policy*, University of Chicago Press, Chicago.

Furlotti, Marco, 1991, Japanese Foreign Direct Investment in the Electronic Industry and the European Community, unpublished MA dissertation, Hitotsubashi University.

General Agreement on Tariffs and Trade (GATT), 1994, *Final Act Embodying the Results of the Uruguay Round of Multilateral Trade Negotiations*, GATT Secretariat, Geneva.

General Agreement on Tariffs and Trade (GATT), 1993, *Trade Policy Review*

Mechanism: European Communities, Report by the Secretariat, Geneva.

General Agreement on Tariffs and Trade (GATT), 1988, *Developments in the Trading System, October 1987–March 1988*, Report by the Secretariat, Geneva.

Genther, Phyllis A., and Donald H. Dalton, 1992, *Japanese-Affiliated Electronics Companies: Implications for US Technology Development*, US Department of Commerce, Washington.

Glejser, Herbert, Alexis Jacquemin, and Jean Petit, 1980, Export in an Imperfect Competition Framework: An Analysis of 1,446 Exporters, *Quarterly Journal of Economics*, 94, 507–524.

Gold, David, Persa Eonomou, and Telly Tolentino, 1991, Trade Blocs and Investment Blocs: The Triad in Foreign Direct Investment and International Trade, Paper presented at the annual meeting of the Academy of International Business, Miami, 19 October 1991.

Goto, Akira, 1982, Business Groups in a Market Economy, *European Economic Review*, 19, 53–70.

Goto, Akira, and Kazuyuki Suzuki, 1989, R&D Capital, Rate of Return on R&D Investment, and Spillover of R&D in Japanese Manufacturing Industries, *Review of Economics and Statistics*, 71, 555–564.

Graham, Edward M., and Paul Krugman, 1990, *Foreign Direct Investment in the United States*, Institute for International Economics, Washington.

Granstrand, Ove, Lars Hakanson, and Sören Sjölander, 1993, Internationalization of R&D: A Survey of Some Recent Research, *Research Policy*, 22, 413–430.

Greenaway, David, 1989, Why Are We Negotiating on TRIMs? Paper presented at a conference on 'Global Protectionism', Lehigh University, Bethlehem, PA, 22 and 23 May 1989.

Greenhut, Melvin L., and Hiroshi Ohta, 1976, Related Market Conditions and Interindustrial Mergers, *American Economic Review*, 68, 267–277.

Gregory, Gene, 1986, *Japanese Electronics Technology: Enterprise and Innovation*, John Wiley, Chicester.

Grossman, Gene M., 1981, The Theory of Domestic Content Protection and Content Preference, *Quarterly Journal of Economics*, 68, 584–603.

Grubaugh, Stephen G., 1987, Determinants of Direct Foreign Investment, *Review of Economics and Statistics*, 69, 149–152.

Gruenspecht, Howard K., 1988, Dumping and Dynamic Competition, *Journal of International Economics*, 25, 225–248.

Hakanson, Lars, 1992, *Locational Determinants of Foreign R&D in Swedish Multinationals*, in: Ove Granstrand, Lars Hakanson, and Soren Sjolander, eds, *Technology Mangement and International Business, Internationalization of R&D and Technology*, John Wiley, Chichester, 97–115.

Hakanson, Lars, and Robert Nobel, 1993, Determinants of Foreign R&D in Swedish Multinationals, *Research Policy*, 22, 397–411.

Hart, Jeffrey A., 1993, The Anti-dumping Petition of the Advanced Display Manufacturers of America: Origins and Consequences, *World Economy*, 16, 85–109.

Head, Keith, John Ries, and Deborah Swenson, 1995, Agglomeration Benefits and Location Choice: Evidence from Japanese Manufacturing Investments in the United States, *Journal of International Economics*, 38, 223–247.

HEC Eurasia Institute, 1989, *Corporate Challenges for Japan and Europe 1992*, HEC Eurasia Institute, Jouy-en-Josas.

Heitger, Bernhard, and Jürgen Stein, 1990, Japanese Direct Investments in the EC: Response to the Internal Market 1993, *Journal of Common Market Studies*, 29, 1–15.

Helou, Angelina, 1991, The Nature and Competitiveness of Japan's Keiretsu, *Journal of World Trade*, 25, 99–313.

Helpman, Elhanan, 1985, Multinational Corporations and Trade Structure, *Review of Economic Studies*, 52, 443–457.

Helpman, Elhanan, and Paul Krugman, 1989, *Market Structure and Trade Policy*, MIT Press, Cambridge, MA, and London.

Helpman, Elhanan, and Paul Krugman, 1985, *Market Structure and Foreign Trade*, MIT Press, Cambridge MA, and London.

Hennart, Jean-François, 1991, The Transaction Costs Theory of Joint Ventures: An Empirical Study of Japanese Subsidiaries in the United States, *Management Science*, 37, 483–497.

Hennart, Jean-François, 1982, *A Theory of Multinational Enterprise*, University of Michigan Press, Ann Arbor, MI.

Hennart, Jean-François, and Young-Ryeol Park, 1994, Location, Governance, and Strategic Determinants of Japanese Manufacturing Investments in the United States, *Strategic Management Journal*, 15, 419–436.

Hennart, Jean-François, and Young-Ryeol Park, 1992, Greenfield versus Acquisition: The Strategy of Japanese Investors in the United States, Faculty Working Paper 92-0179, Bureau of Economic and Business Research, University of Illinois at Urbana-Champaign.

Herander, Mark G., and J. Brad Schwartz, 1984, An Empirical Test of the Impact of the Threat of US Trade Policy: The Case of Antidumping Duties, *Southern Economic Journal*, 51, 59–79.

Hewitt, G., 1980, Research and Development Performed Abroad by US Manufacturing Multinationals, *Kyklos*, 33, 308–326.

Hindley, Brian, 1990, *Foreign Direct Investment: The Effects of Rules of Origin*, Institute of International Affairs Discussion Paper No. 40, London.

Hindley, Brian, 1988, Dumping and the Far East Trade of the European Community, *The World Economy*, 11, 445–464.

Hirsch, Seev, 1976, An International Trade and Investment Theory of the Firm, *Oxford Economic Papers*, 28, 258–270.

Hirschey, Robert C., and Richard E. Caves, 1981, Internationalisation of Research and Transfer of Technology by Multinational Enterprises, *Oxford Bulletin of Economics and Statistics*, 42, 115–130.

Hodder, James E., 1991, Is the Cost of Capital Lower in Japan? *Journal of the Japanese and International Economies*, 5, 86–100.

Hoekman, Bernard M., and Michael P. Leidy, 1992, Cascading Contingent Protection, *European Economic Review*, 36, 883–892.

Hoekman, Bernard M., and Petros C. Mavroidis, 1994, Antitrust-Based Remedies and Dumping in International Trade, Paper presented at the JETRO Fifth Global Contribution Seminar, 12–17 June, Tokyo.

Hoekman, Bernard M., and Petros C. Mavroidis, 1993, Competition, Competition Policy and the GATT, *Journal of World Trade*, 17, 121–150.

Hollander, Abraham, 1987, Content Protection and Transnational Monopoly, *Journal of International Economics*, 23, 283–297.

Holmes, Peter, and Alan Cawson, 1993, *Study on Consumer Electronics Prices: Final Report*, International Economics Research Centre, University of Sussex.

Holmes, Peter, René Belderbos, and Alasdair Smith, 1992, Strategic Trade and 'Unfair' Business Practices in Global Information Technology and Electronics Markets: Problems and Policy Responses, Report prepared for the European Commission (DGXIII), University of Sussex.

Hood, Neil, and Stephen Young, 1987, Inward Investment and the EC: UK Evidence on Corporate Integration Strategies, *Journal of Common Market Studies*, 25, 193–206.

Horaguchi, Haruo, 1992, *Nihon Kigyou no Kaigai Chokusetsu Toushi: Ajia he no Shinshutsu to Tettai (Direct Foreign Investment by Japanese Firms: Investment and Divestment in Asia)*, Toukyou Daigaku Shuppankai, Tokyo.

Horiye, Yasuhiro, 1987, Export Behaviour of Japanese Firms, *BOJ Monetary and Economic Studies*, 5, 33–104.

Horlick, Gary N., 1990, The United States Antidumping System, in: John H. Jackson and Edwin A. Vermulst, eds., *Antidumping Law and Practice: A Comparative Study*, Harvester Wheatsheaf, New York, 99–166.

Horst, Thomas, 1972, Firm and Industry Determinants of the Decision to Invest Abroad: An Empirical Study, *Review of Economics and Statistics*, 54, 258–266.

Horstman, Ignacius J., and James R. Markusen, 1989, Firm-Specific Assets and the Gains from Direct Foreign Investment, *Economica*, 56, 41–48.

Horstman, Ignacius J., and James R. Markusen, 1987, Strategic Investments and the Development of Multinationals, *International Economic Review*, 28, 109–121.

Horstman, Ignacius J., and James R. Markusen, 1986, Up Your Average Cost Curve: Inefficient Entry and the New Protectionism, *Journal of International Economics*, 20, 225–249.

Hoshi, Takeo, Anil Kashyap, and David Scharfstein, 1992, Corporate Structure, Liquidity, and Investment: Evidence from Japanese Industrial Groups, *Quarterly Journal of Economics*, 107, 33–60.

Humbert, Marc, and Jean-Louis Perrault, 1991, *La Globalisation de l'Industrie Electronique (The Globalisation of the Electronics Industry)*, Université de Rennes.

Ishikawa K., 1990, *Japan and the Challenge of Europe 1992*, Royal Institute of International Affairs, Pinter Publishers, London.

Jackson, John H., and Edwin A. Vermulst, eds., 1990, *Antidumping Law and Practice: A Comparative Study*, Harvester Wheatsheaf, New York.

Jacquemin, Alexis, 1989, International and Multinational Strategic Behaviour, *Kyklos*, 42, 495–513.

Japan External Trade Organisation (JETRO), 1985a–1992a, *White Paper on International Trade*, Tokyo.

Japan External Trade Organisation (JETRO), 1989b–1995b, *Survey of European Operations of Japanese Companies in the Manufacturing Sector*, Tokyo.

Japan Fair Trade Commission, 1992, *The Outline of the Report on the Actual Conditions of the Six Major Corporate Groups*, Tokyo.

Japan Fair Trade Commission, 1991, *Japanese Competition Law*, Tokyo.

Japan Industrial Structure Council, 1993, *1993 Report on Unfair Trade Policies by Major Trading Partners: Trade Policies and GATT Obligations*, JETRO, Tokyo.

Japan Tariff Association, 1991, *Japan Exports and Imports: Commodity by Country*, Tokyo.

Jensen, Michael C., 1986, Agency Costs of Free Cash Flow, Corporate Finance, and Takeovers, *American Economic Review*, 76, 323–329.

Jie a Joen, Clive, Leo Sleuwaegen, and René A. Belderbos, 1995, Local Content Requirements, Cooperative Bargaining, and Direct Foreign Investment, Paper presented at the 24th EARIE Conference, Juan les Pins, 3–6 September 1995.

Jones, Ronald W., and Anne O. Krueger, eds., 1990, *The Political Economy of International Trade*, Basil Blackwell, Cambridge, MA.

Jorde T. M., and M. A. Lemley, 1991, Summary Judgment in Anti-Trust Cases: Understanding *Monsanto* and *Mastsushita*, *Antitrust Bulletin*, 36, 271–323.

Judge, George G., *et al.*, 1985, *The Theory and Practice of Econometrics*, John Wiley, Chicester.

Jun, Kwang W., Frank Sader, Haruo Horaguchi, and Hyuntai Kwak, 1994, *Japanese Foreign Direct Investment*, Policy Research Working Paper 1213, World Bank, Washington, DC.

Kaburagi, Shinji, 1992, 1991 Nendou no Wagakuni no Kaigai Chokusetsu Toushi Doukou (Trends in Japanese DFI in Fiscal Year 1991), *Kaigai Toushi Kenkyuushohou*, 11, 110–130.

Karp, Larry S., and Jeffrey M. Perloff, 1989, Estimating Market Structure and Tax Incidence: The Japanese Television Market, *Journal of Industrial Economics*, 37, 225–239.

Keizai Chousa Kyoukai, 1990, *Keiretsu no Kenkyuu (Research on Industrial Groupings)*, 30, Tokyo.

Kester, Carl, 1991, *Japanese Takeovers*, Harvard Business School Press, Boston, MA.

Kierzkowski, Henryk, ed., 1984, *Monopolistic Competition and International Trade*, Clarendon Press, Oxford.

Kikai Shinkou Kyoukai Keizai Kenkyuusho (Machinery Promotion Assiociation, Economic Research Institute), 1992, *Kigyou no Takokusekika ni Tomonau Kokusashuushi he no Eikyou ni Kansuru Toukei Kenkyuu Houkokusho (Research Report on transactions Related to the Multinationalization of Firms)*, Tokyo.

Kikai Shinkou Kyoukai Keizai Kenkyuusho (Machinery Promotion Association, Economic Research Institute), 1989, *Nichi-Ou Kikai Kougyou no Kyouzon Kyouei (Co-existence and Co-prosperity of the Japanese and European Machinery Industry)*, Tokyo.

Kimura, Yui, 1994, Japanese Direct Investment in the European Semiconductor Industry, in: Mark Mason and Dennis Encarnation, eds., *Does Ownership Matter? Japanese Multinationals in Europe*, Oxford University Press, Oxford and New York, 293–327.

Kimura, Yui, 1989, Firm-Specific Strategic Advantages and Foreign Direct Investment Behavior of Firms: The Case of Japanese Semiconductor Firms, *Journal of International Business Studies*, 20, 296–314.

Kimura, Yui, and Thomas A. Pugel, 1995, Keiretsu and Japanese Direct Investment in US Manufacturing, *Japan and the World Economy*, 7, 481–503.

Kindleberger, Charles P., and David B. Audretsch, 1983, *The Multinational Corporation in the 1980s*, MIT Press, Cambrige, MA, and London.

Klein, Michael W., and Paul J. J. Welfens, eds., 1992, *Multinationals in the New Europe and Global Trade*, Springer-Verlag, Berlin.

Knetter, Michael M., 1993, International Comparisons of Pricing-to-Market Behavior, *American Economic Review*, 83, 473–486.

Knickerbocker, Frederick T., 1973, *Oligopolistic Reaction and Multinational Enterprise*, Harvard University Press, Cambridge, MA.

Kogut, Bruce, and Sea-Jin Chang, 1991, Technological Capabilities and Japanese Foreign Direct Investment in the United States, *Review of Economics and Statistics*, 73, 400–413.

Kogut, Bruce, and Sea-Jin Chang, 1996, Platform Investments and Volatile Exchange Rates: Japanese Direct Investment in the US by Japanese Electronic Companies, *Review of Economics and Statistics*, 78, 221–231.

Kojima, Kiyoshi, 1985, Japanese and American Direct Investment in Asia: A Comparative Analysis, *Hitotsubashi Journal of Economics*, 26, 1–35.

Kojima, Kiyoshi, 1978, *Direct Foreign Investments: A Japanese Model of Multinational Business Operations*, Croom Helm, London.

Kokusai Kakaku Kouzou Kenkyuujo (Research Institute for International Price Mechanism), 1992, *Naigai Kakakuka Mondai he no Shuuapurouchi to Kakaku Hikaku Houhou no Kenkyuu (The Problem of Domestic and Foreign Price Differentials: Various Approaches to Compare Prices)*, Kokusai Kakaku Kouzou Kenkyuujo, Tokyo.

Komiya, Ryutaro, 1987, Japan's Foreign Direct Investment: Facts and Theoretical Considerations, Discussion Paper 87-F-13, University of Tokyo.

Kostecki, Michael M., 1989, Electronics Trade Policies in the 1980s, *Journal of World Trade*, 23. 17–35.

Koulen, Mark, 1990, Some Problems of Interpretation and Implementation of the GATT Antidumping Code, in: John H. Jackson and Edwin A. Vermulst, eds., *Antidumping Law and Practice: A Comparative Study*, Harvester Wheatsheaf, New York, 366–371.

Kreinin, Mondechai E., 1992, How Closed is Japan's Market? Additional Evidence, *Journal of World Trade*, 26, 529–542.

Kreps D., and J. Scheinkman, 1983, Quantity Precommitment and Betrand Competition Yield Cournot Outcomes, *Bell Journal of Economics*, 14, 326–337.

Krishna, Kala, and Motoshige Itoh, 1988, Content Protection and Oligopolistic Interactions, *Review of Economic Studies*, 55, 107–125.

Krugman, Paul, ed., 1991, *Trade with Japan: Has the Door Opened Wider?* National Bureau of Economic Research, University of Chicago Press, Chicago and London.

Krugman Paul, 1986a, Introduction: New Thinking about Trade Policy, in: Paul Krugman, ed., *Strategic Trade Policy and the New International Economics*, MIT Press, Cambridge, MA, and London.

Krugman, Paul, ed., 1986b, *Strategic Trade Policy and the New International Economics*, MIT Press, Cambridge, MA, and London.

Krugman, Paul, 1984, Import Protection as Export Promotion: International Competition in the Presence of Oligopoly and Economies of Scale, in: Henryk Kierzkowski, ed., *Monopolistic Competition and International Trade*, Clarendon Press, Oxford.

Krugman, Paul, and Alasdair Smith, eds., 1994, *Empirical Studies of Strategic Trade Policy*, University of Chicago Press, Chicago and London.

Kume, Gorota, and Keisuke Totsuka, 1991, Japanese Manufacturing Investment in the EC: Motives and Locations, in: Masaru Yoshitomi, ed., *Japanese Direct Investment in Europe*, Sumitomo-Life Research Institute and the Royal Institute of International Affairs, Avebury, Aldershot.

Lakeman, Pieter, 1991, *100 Jaar Philips: De Officieuze Biografie (Philips' Hundred Years: The Unofficial Biography)*, Lakeman Publishers, Amsterdam.

Lall, Sanjaya, 1980, Monopolistic Advantages and Foreign Involvement by US Manufacturing Industry, *Oxford Economic Papers*, 32, 102–122.

Lall, Sanjaya, 1979, The International Allocation of Research Activity by US Multinationals, *Oxford Bulletin of Economics and Statistics*, 41, 313–331.

Lawrence, Robert Z., and Charles L. Schultze, 1990, *An American Trade Strategy: Options for the 1990s*, Brookings Institution, Washington.

Lee, Jong-Wha, and Phillip Swagel, 1994, *Trade Barriers and Trade Flows across Countries and Industries*, National Bureau of Economic Research Working Paper No. 4799, Cambridge, MA.

Leidy, Michael P., and Bernard M. Hoekman, 1990, Production Effects of Price and Cost Based Anti Dumping Laws under Flexible Exchange Rates, *Canadian Journal of Economics* 23, 873–895.

Leipziger, Danny M., and Hyun Ja Shin, 1991, The Demand for Protection: A Look at Antidumping Cases, *Open Economies Review*, 2, 27–38.

Levinsohn, James A., 1989, Strategic Trade Policy when Firms can Invest Abroad: When are Tariffs and Quotas Equivalent? *Journal of International Economics*, 27, 129–146.

Lipsey, Robert E., and Merle Yahr Weiss, 1984, Foreign Production and Exports of Individual Firms, *Review of Economics and Statistics*, 66, 304–308.

Lipsey, Robert E., and Merle Yahr Weiss, 1981, Foreign Production and Exports in Manufacturing Industries, *Review of Economics and Statistics*, 63, 488–494.

Lloyd, P. J., 1993, A Tariff Substitute for Rules of Origin in Free Trade Areas, *World Economy*, 16, 699–713.

Long Term Credit Bank of Japan (LTCB), 1989, *Entry in the Internal Market of the European Community by Japanese Manufacturers*, LTCB, Tokyo.

Lopes-de Silanes, Florencio, James R. Markusen, and Thomas F. Rutherford, 1993, *Anti-Competitive and Rent-Shifting Aspects of Domstic Content Provisions in Regional Trade Blocks*, NBER Working Paper No. 4512. Cambridge, MA.

Lowe, Jeffrey H., and Raymond J. Mataloni Jr, 1991, US Direct Investment Abroad: 1989 Benchmark Survey Results, *Survey of Current Business*, October, 29–55.

Mackintosh I., 1986, *Sunrise Europe: The Economics of Information Technology*, Basil Blackwell, Oxford.

Mackintosh International, 1985, *The European Consumer Electronics Industry*, Office for Official Publications of the European Communities, Luxembourg.

Mackintosh-BIS, 1991, *La Distribution des Produits D'Electronique Grand Public au Japon (The Distribution of Consumer Electronics in Japan)*, Report prepared for Simavelec, 12 August 1991.

Maddala G. S., 1983, *Limited-Dependent and Qualitative Variables in Econometrics*, Cambridge University Press, Cambridge.

Mann, Catherine L., 1990, *Determinants of Japanese Direct Investment in US Manufacturing Industries*, Federal Reserve Board, Washington.

Mascarenhas, Briance, 1986, International Strategies of Non-Dominant Firms, *Journal of International Business Studies*, 17, 1–25.

Mason, Mark, and Dennis Encarnation, eds., 1994, *Does Ownership Matter? Japanese Multinationals in Europe*, Oxford University Press, Oxford and New York.

McCalman, James, 1988, *The Electronics Industry in Britain: Coping with Change*, Routledge, London and New York.

McCulloch, Rachel, 1988, Japanese Investment in the United States, Paper presented at the 10th Annual Middlebury College Conference on Economic Issues, April 1988.

McDermott, Michael C., 1992, The Internationalization of the South Korean and Taiwanese Electronics Industries: The European Dimension, in: Stephen Young and James Hamill, eds., 1992, *Europe and the Multinationals: Issues and Responses for the 1990s*, Edward Elgar, Aldershot.

McGee, J., 1958, Predatory Pricing: The Standard Oil (NJ) Case, *Journal of Law and Economics*, 23, 137–169.

Messerlin, Patick A., 1990, Anti-Dumping Regulations or Pro-Cartel Law? The EC Chemical Cases, *World Economy*, 13, 465–492.

Messerlin, Patrick A., 1989, The EC Anti-Dumping Regulations: A First Economic Appraisal, 1980–1985, *Weltwirtschaftliches Archiv*, 125, 563–587.

Micossi, Stefano, and Gianfranco Viesti, 1991, Japanese Direct Manufacturing Investment in Europe, in: L. Alan Winters and Anthony J. Venables, eds., *European Integration: Trade and Industry*, Cambridge University Press, Cambridge.

Milgrom, Paul, and John Roberts, 1990, New Theories of Predatory Pricing, in: Giacomo Bonano and Darco Brandolini, *Industrial Structure and the New Industrial Economics*, Oxford University Press, Oxford, 112–137.

Ministry of International Trade and Industry (MITI), 1990, *White Paper on Small Business 1990*, MITI, Tokyo.

Moore, Michael O., 1992, Rules or Politics? An Empirical Analysis of ITC Anti Dumping Decisions, *Economic Inquiry*, 30, 449–56.

Morita, Akio, 1987, *Made in Japan*, Fontana/Collins, London.

Morris, Jonathan, Max Munday, and Barry Wilkinson, 1994, *Working for the Japanese: The Economic and Social Consequences of Japanese Investment in Wales*, Athlone Press, London and Atlantic Highlands, NJ.

Motta, Massimo, 1992, Multinational Firms and the Tariff Jumping Argument: A Game Theoretical Analysis with some Unconventional Conclusions, *European Economic Review*, 36, 1557–1571.

Nakakita, Toru, and Shujiro Urata, 1991, Industrial Adjustment in Japan and its Impact on Developing Countries, Paper presented at the conference on 'Industrial Adjustment of Developed Countries and its Impact on Developing Countries', Ajia Kenkyuujo, Tokyo, 1–2 February 1991.

Nakatani, Iwao, 1984, The Economic Role of Financial Corporate Grouping, in: Masahiro Aoki, ed., *The Economic Analysis of the Japanese Firm*, North Holland, Amsterdam, 227–258.

National Consumer Council, 1990, *International Trade and the Consumer: Consumer Electronics and the EC's Anti-Dumping Policy*, National Consumer Council, London.

Nicolaides, Phedon, 1992, Predatory Behaviour, Mimeograph, European Institute of Public Administration, Maastricht.

Nicolaides, Phedon, and Stephen Thomsen, 1991, Can Protectionism Explain Direct Investment? *Journal of Common Market Studies*, 6, 636–643.

Nihon Boueki Shinkoukai (Japan External Trade Organisation), 1985a–1992a, *Tsuushou Hakusho (White Paper on International Trade)*, JETRO, Tokyo.

Nihon Boueki Shinkoukai (Japan External Trade Organisation), 1991b, *Sekai to Nihon no Kaigai Chokusetsu Toushi (The World's and Japan's Foreign Direct Investments)*, JETRO, Tokyo.

Nihon Boueki Shinkoukai (Japan External Trade Organisation), 1985c–1995c, *Zai Ou Nikkei Seizougyou Keiei no Jittai (The Current Management Situation of Japanese Manufacturing Enterprises in Europe)*, JETRO, Tokyo.

Nihon Chouki Shinyou Ginkou (Long Term Credit Bank of Japan), 1990, *EC Tougou: EC no tai Nichi Senryaku to Nihon Kigyou no Taiou (The Unification of the EC Market: EC Strategies towards Japan and the Response of Japanese Firms)*, Chougin Chousha Geppou, July 1990.

Nihon Denshi Kikai Kougyoukai (Electronic Industries Association Japan, EIAJ), 1989a–1992a, *Kaigai Houjin Risuto (List of Overseas Affiliates)*, EIAJ, Tokyo.

Nihon Denshi Kikai Kougyoukai (Electronic Industries Association Japan, EIAJ), 1991b, 1992b, *Minseiyou Denshi Kiki Deitashuu (Consumer Electronics Databook)*, EIAJ, Tokyo.

Nihon Denshi Kikai Kougyoukai (Electronic Industries Association Japan, EIAJ), 1989c, *1989 ni Okeru Denshi Kougyou no Doko (1989 Report of the Electronics Industry)*, EIAJ, Tokyo.

Nihon Kaihatsu Ginkou (Japan Development Bank), 1989, *Kyuuninen EC Tougou to Wagakuni seigyou no Mondai: Jidousha to Denshi meikah no Taiou (The 1992 EC Unification and the Problems faced by our Country's Industries: The Case of the Automobile and Electronics Industries)*, Nihon Kaihatsuginkou Chousa No. 131, Tokyo.

Nihon Kaihatsu Ginkou (Japan Development Bank), 1988, *Douki Hajimeru Wagakuni Kigyou no Kaigai Kenkyuu Kaihatsu (Factors behind the Start of R&D Activities Abroad by Japanese Firms)*, Nihon Kaihatsuginkou Chousa No. 115, Tokyo.

Nihon Kaihatsu Ginkou Setsubi Toushi Kenkyuujo (Japan Development Bank Investment Research Institute), 1986–1989, *Kigyou Zaimu Deita (Corporate Financial Data)*, Tokyo.

Nihon Kaihatsu Ginkou Setsubi Toushi Kenkyuujo (Japan Development Bank Investment Research Institute), various years, *Renketsu Kigyou Zaimu Deita (Consolidated Corporate Financial Data)*, Tokyo.

Nihon Keizai Sangyou Shimbun (Japan Industrial Journal), 1993, *Shijou Senyuuritsu 1993 (Market Shares 1993)*, Nihon Keizai Shimbunsha, Tokyo.

Nihon Keizai Shimbunsha (Japan Economic Journal), 1993, *Renketsu Kaisha Nenkan (Yearbook of Consolidated Accounts)*, Tokyo.

Nihon Kikai Yushutsu Kumiai (Japan Machinery Export Council), 1992, *Kikai Yushutsu Shijou Kankyou Seibi Taisaku Suishin Chousa Houkokusho (Report on Developments in Policies Dealing with Localization in Machinery Export Markets)*, Nihon Kikai Yushutsu Kumiai, Tokyo.

Nihon Kousei Torihiki Iinkai (Japan Fair Trade Commission), 1992, *Nihon no Dairoku Kigyou Shuudan (The Six Major Japanese Corporate Groups)*, Touyou Keizai Shinpousha, Tokyo.

Nihon Okurashou (Japan Ministry of Finance), various years, *Yuukashouken*

Houkokusho Souran (Company Financial Reports), Oukurashou Insatsukyoku, Tokyo.

Nihon Okurashou (Japan Ministry of Finance), 1991, *Zaisei Kinyuu Tokei Geppou (Financial Investment Statistics Monthly)*, No. 476, December 1991.

Nihon Soumuka Tokeikyoku (Japan Management and Co-ordination Agency, Statistics Bureau), 1990, *Kagaku Gijutsu Kenkyuu Chousa Houkoku (Report on the Survey of Research and Development in Japan)*, Nihon Tokei Kyoukai Rengoukai, Tokyo.

Nihon Tsuushou Sangyoushou (Japan Ministry of International Trade and Industry), Sangyou Seisakukyoku (Research and Statistics Department), 1991, 1994, *Kaigai Toushi Tokei Souran (Basic Survey on Foreign Direct Investment)*, Okurashou Insatsukyoku, Tokyo.

Nihon Tsuushou Sangyoushou (Japan Ministry of International Trade and Industry), Sangyou Seisakukyoku (Research and Statistics Department), 1990, 1992, 1993, 1995, *Wagakuni Kigyou no Kaigai Jigyou Katsudou (Report on the Foreign Activities of Japanese Corporations)*, Okurashou Insatsukyoku, Tokyo.

Nihon Yushutsunyuu Ginkou (Japan Export-Import Bank), Research Institute on Overseas Investments, 1989, *Chokusetsu Toushi no Kyuuzou to Keiei no Guroubaruka (The Sudden Increase in Direct Investments and the Globalization of Management)*, Nihon Yushutsunyuu Ginkou, Tokyo.

Nonaka, Ikujiro, and Shigemi Yoneyama, 1991, The Semiconductor Industry: Organization and Strategy for 1M DRAM Development, Nomura School of Advanced Management, Tokyo.

Odagiri, Hiroyuki, 1992, *Growth through Competition, Competition through Growth: Strategic Management and the Economy in Japan*, Clarendon Press, Oxford.

Odagiri, Hiroyuki, and Tatsuo Hase, 1989, Are Mergers and Acquisitions Going To Be Popular in Japan Too? *International Journal of Industrial Organization*, 7, 49–72.

Odagiri, Hiroyuki, and Hideto Yasuda, 1996, *The Determinants of Overseas R&D by Japanese Firms: An Empirical Study at the Industry and Company Levels*, Institute of Socio-Economic Planning Discussion Paper Series No. 594, Tsukuba University.

Ohmae, Kenichi, 1985, *Triad Power: The Coming Shape of Global Competition*, Free Press, New York.

Oliver, Nick, and Barry Wilkinson, 1992, *The Japanization of British Industry: New Developments in the 1990s*, Basil Blackwell, Oxford and Cambridge, MA.

Ordover, J. A., A. O. Sykes, and R. D. Willig, 1983, Unfair International Trade Practices *Journal of International Law and Politics*, 323–337.

Ozawa, Terutomo, 1992, Cross-Investments between Japan and the EC: Income Similarity, Technological Congruity and Economies of Scope, in: John Cantwell, ed., *Multinational Investment in Modern Europe*, Edward Elgar, Aldershot.

Ozawa, Terutomo, 1991, Japan in a New Phase of Multinationalism and Industrial Upgrading: Functional Integation of Trade, Growth, and FDI, *Journal of World Trade*, 25, 43–60.

Ozawa, Terutomo, 1979, *Multinationalism, Japanese Style: The Political Economy of Outward Dependency*, Princeton University Press, Princeton, NJ.

Papanastassiou, Marina, and Robert D. Pearce, 1995, The R&D Activitities of Japanese Multinationals in Europe, in: Frédérique Sachwald, ed., *Japanese Firms in Europe*, Harwood Academic Publishers, Luxembourg, 265–310.

Papanastassiou, Marina, and Robert D. Pearce, 1994, The Internationalisation of Research and Development by Japanese Enterprises, *R&D Management*, 24, 155–165.

Patel, Pari, 1995, Localized Production of Technology for Global Market, *Cambridge Journal of Economics*, 19, 141–153.

Patel, Pari, and Keith Pavitt, 1991, Large Firms in the Production of the World's Technology: An Important Case of 'Non-Globalization', *Journal of International Business Studies*, 22, 1–22.

Penrose, Edith, 1990, 'Dumping', 'Unfair' Competition and Multinational Corporations, *Japan and the World Economy*, 2, 181–187.

Pearce, Robert D., 1989, *The Internationalisation of Research and Development by Multinational Enterprises*, Macmillan, Basingstoke.

Pearce, Robert D., and Satwinder Singh, 1990, *The Internationalisation of Research and Development by Multinational Enterprises: A Firm-Level Analysis of Determinants*, Discussion Papers in International Investment and Business Studies, Series B, Vol. III, No. 145, University of Reading.

Pitelis, Christos, and Roger Sugden, eds., 1990, *The Nature of the Transnational Firm*, Routledge, London and New York.

Porter, Michael E., 1986, Changing Patterns of International Competition, *California Management Review*, 28, 9–41.

Potjes, Jeroen C. A., 1993, *Empirical Studies in Japanese Retailing*, Thesis Publishers, Amsterdam.

Prusa, Thomas J., 1992a, Why Are So Many Anti-Dumping Petitions Withdrawn? *Journal of International Economics*, 33, 1–20.

Prusa, Thomas J., 1992b, The Selection of Antidumping Cases for ITC Determination, in: Robert Baldwin, ed., *Empirical Studies of commercial Policy*, University of Chicago Press, Chicago.

Pugel, Thomas A., 1987, Limits of Trade Policy toward High Technology Industries: The Case of Semiconductors, in: Ryuzo Sato and Paul Wachtel, *Trade Friction and Economic Policy*, Cambridge University Press, Cambridge.

Pugel, Thomas A., 1981, The Determinants of Foreign Direct Investment: An Analysis of US Manufacturing Industries, *Managerial and Decision Economics*, 2, 220–228.

Pugel, Thomas A., Erik S. Kragas, and Yui Kimura, 1996, Further Evidence on Japanese Direct Investment in US Manufacturing, *Review of Economics and Statistics*, 78, 208–213.

Rapp, William V., 1976, Firm Size and Japan's Export Structure: A Microview of Japan's Changing Export Competitiveness since Meiji, in: Hugh Patrick, ed., *Japanese Industrialization and its Social Consequences*, University of California Press, Berkeley.

Rasmussen, Eric, 1989, *Games and Information*, Basil Blackwell, Oxford and New York.

Ray, Edward John, 1989, The Determinants of Foreign Direct Investment in the United States, 1979–1985, in: Robert C. Feenstra, ed., *Trade Policies for International Competitiveness*, University of Chicago Press, Chicago, 53–83.

Ray, Edward John, 1977, Foreign Direct Investment in Manufacturing, *Journal of Political Economy*, 85, 283–297.

Reich, Robert, 1990, Who is Us, *Harvard Business Review*, 68, 53–64.

Reitzes, James D., 1993, Antidumping Policy, *International Economic Review*, 34, 745–63.

Richardson J. David, 1990, The Political Economy of Strategic Trade Policy, *International Organization*, 44, 107–135.

Richardson, Martin, 1993, Content Protection with Foreign Capital, *Oxford Economic Papers*, 45, 103–117.

Richardson, Martin, 1991, The Effects of a Content Requirement on a Foreign Duopsonist, *Journal of International Economics*, 31, 143–155.

Sachwald, Frédérique, ed., 1995, *Japanese Firms in Europe*, Harwood, Luxembourg.

Sako, Mari, 1992, *Prices, Quality, and Trust: Inter-Firm Relations in Britain and Japan*, Cambridge University Press, Cambridge.

Salinger, Michael A., 1988, Vertical Mergers and Market Foreclosure, *Quarterly Journal of Economics*, 103, 345–356.

Salop, Steven C., and David T. Scheffman, 1983, Raising Rivals' Costs, *American Economic Review Proceedings*, 73, 267–271.

Salvatore, Dominick, 1989, A Model of Dumping and Protectionism in the United States, *Weltwirtschaftliches Archiv*, 125, 763–781.

Sanekata, Kenji, 1992a, The Enforcement of Competition Policy in Japan: Its Socio-Politico Background and Enforcement System, Mimeograph, University of Hokkaido.

Sanekata, Kenji, 1992b, Competition Policy and Trade Friction in Japan: How a Sleeping Watchdog Began Biting, Mimeograph, University of Hokkaido.

Sazanami, Yoko, 1992, Globalization Strategy of Japanese Manufacturing Firms and its Impact on Trade Flows Between Europe, Asia and North America, Mimeograph, Keio University.

Sazanami, Yoko, 1989, Trade and Investment Patterns and Barriers in the United States, Canada, and Japan, in: Robert M. Stern, 1989, *Trade and Investment Relations among the United States, Canada, and Japan*, University of Chicago Press, Chicago and London, 91–126.

Scheffman, David T., 1992, The Application of Raising Rivals' Costs Theory to Antitrust, *The Antitrust Bulletin*, 37, 187–206.

Scherer F. M., and David Ross, 1990, *Industrial Market Structure and Economic Performance*, third edition, Boston, MA, Houghton Mifflin.

Schwartzman, David, 1993, *The Japanese Television Cartel*, Michigan University Press, Ann Arbor, MI.

Senker, Jacqueline, 1991, Information Technology and Japanese Investment in Europe, *Futures*, 815–827.

Shapiro, Carl, 1989, Theories of Oligopoly Behaviour, in: Richard Schmalensee and Robert D. Willig, *Handbook of Industrial Organization*, North Holland, Amsterdam.

Sharp, Margaret, 1995, Trade and Technology Policies: The Influence of European Programmes on the Emergent Industrial Policy of Clinton's America, in: David Mayes, ed., *The Evolution of Rules for the Single European Market*, Office for Official Publications of the European Communities, Luxembourg.

Shibagaki, Kazuo, Malcolm Trevor, and Tetsuo Abo, eds., 1989, *Japanese and*

European Management: Their International Adaptability, University of Tokyo Press, Tokyo.

Sleuwaegen, Leo, and Hideki Yamawaki, 1992, Foreign Direct Investment and Intra-Firm Trade: Evidence from Japan, in: A. Koekkoek and L. Mennes, eds., *International Trade and Global Development*, Routledge, London.

Smith, Alasdair, 1987, Strategic Investment, Multinational Corporations and Trade Policy, *European Economic Review*, 31, 89–96.

Solis, Mireya, 1994, The Political Economy of Capital Outflows in Japan: Government Policy towards Japanese Outward Investment, Mimeograph, Waseda University.

Spencer, Barbara J., and Ronald W. Jones, 1992, Trade and Protection in Vertically Related Markets, *Journal of International Economics*, 32, 31–55.

Stahl, D. O. 1988, Bertrand Competition for Inputs and Walrasian Outcomes, *American Economic Review*, 78, 373–387.

Staiger, Robert W., and Frank A. Wolak, 1992, The Effect of Domestic Antidumping Law in the Presence of Foreign Monopoly, *Journal of International Economics*, 32, 265–87.

Stegemann, Klaus, 1991a, EC Anti-Dumping Policy: Are Price Undertakings a Legal Substitute for Illegal Price Fixing? *Weltwirtschafliches Archiv*, 127, 268–297.

Stegemann, Klaus, 1991b, Settlement of Anti-Dumping Cases by Price Undertakings: Is the EC More Liberal than Canada? in: Paul Tharakan, ed., *Policy Implications of Anti-Dumping Measures*, North Holland, Amsterdam and New York.

Stegemann, Klaus, 1989, Policy Rivalry among Industrial States: What Can We Learn from Models of Strategic Trade Policy? *International Organization*, 43, 73–100.

Strange, Roger, 1993, *Japanese Manufacturing Investment in Europe: Its Impact on the UK Economy*, Routledge, London and New York.

Suzuki, Kazuyuki, 1993, R&D Spillovers and Technology Transfer among and within Vertical Keiretsu Groups: Evidence from the Japanese Electrical Machinery Industry, *International Journal of Industrial Organization*, 11, 573–591.

Swedenborg, Birgitta, 1979, *The Multinational Operations of Swedish Firms: An Analysis of Determinants and Effects*, Industrial Institute for Economic and Social Research, Stockholm.

Takaoka, Hirobumi, 1991, *The Results of a Survey on Global Management and Overseas Direct Investment*, Export–Import Bank of Japan, Research Institute of Overseas Investment, Tokyo.

Takaoka, Hirobumi, and Takanori Satake, 1991, Report on Results of Fiscal Year 1990 Foreign Direct Investment Survey, *EXIM Review*, 11, 2–25.

Tharakan, P. K. M., 1991a, The Political Economy of Anti-Dumping Undertakings in the European Communities, *European Economic Review*, 35, 1341–1359.

Tharakan, P. K. M., ed., 1991b, *Policy Implications of Antidumping Measures*, North Holland, Amsterdam.

Tharakan P. K. M., and Jaen Waelbroeck, 1994, Antidumping and Countervailing Duty Decisions in the EC and in the US: An Experiment in Comparative Political Economy, *European Economic Review*, 38, 171–193.

Thomsen, Steven, 1993, Japanese Direct Investment in the European Community: The Product Cycle Revisited, *World Economy*, 16, 301–315.

Thomsen, Steven, and Phedon Nicolaides, 1991, *The Evolution of Japanese Direct Investment in Europe: Death of a Transistor Salesman*, Royal Institute of International Affairs, London.

Tirole, Jean, 1989, *The Theory of Industrial Organization*, MIT Press, Cambridge, MA.

Todd, Daniel, 1990, *The World Electronics Industry*, Routledge, London and New York.

Touyou Keizai, 1985a–1995a, *Kaigai Shinshutsu Kigyou Souran (Directory of Multinational Enterprises)*, Touyou Keizai Shinpousha, Tokyo.

Touyou Keizai, 1991b, *Kigyou Keiretsu Souran (Directory of Japanese Industrial Groups)*, Touyou Keizai Shinpousha, Tokyo.

Touyou Keizai, 1990c, *Nihon no Kigyou Guruupu (Japanese Corporate Groups)*, Tokyo.

Touyou Keizai, 1985d–1992d, *Japan Company Handbooks*, Tokyo.

Trevor, Malcolm, ed., 1987, *The Internationalization of Japanese Business: European and Japanese Perspectives*, Campus Verlag, Frankfurt am Main.

Tyson, Laura D'Andrea, 1992, *Who's Bashing Whom? Trade Conflict in High-Technology Industries*, Institute for International Economics, Washington.

Tyson, Laura D'Andrea, 1990, Managed Trade: Making the Best of the Second Best, in: Robert Z. Lawrence and Charles L. Schultze, 1990, *An American Trade Strategy: Options for the 1990s*, Brookings Institution, Washington.

United Nations Centre on Transnational Corporations (UNTC), 1991, *World Investment Report 1991*, New York.

United States Department of Commerce, Office of Business Analysis, 1993, *Foreign Direct Investment in Research and Development in the United States*, Washington.

United States International Trade Commission (USITC), 1993, *Foreign Trade Barriers*, Washington.

United States International Trade Commission (USITC), 1990, *Japan's Distribution System and Options for Improving US Access*, Washington.

Urata, Shujiro, 1992, Japanese Foreign Direct Investment and Its Impact on Foreign Trade in Asia, Mimeograph, Waseda University.

Urata, Shujiro, 1991, The Rapid Increase of Direct Investment Abroad and Structural Change in Japan, in: Eric D. Ramstetter, ed., *Direct Foreign Investment in Asia's Developing Economies and Structural Change in the Asia-Pacific Region*, Westview Press, Boulder, CO.

Van Bael, Ivo, 1990a, Lessons for the EEC: More Transparancy, Less Discretion, and, At Last, A Debate? in: John H. Jackson and Edwin A. Vermulst, eds., *Antidumping Law and Practice: A Comparative Study*, Harvester Wheatsheaf, New York, 405–408.

Van Bael, Ivo, 1990b, EEC Anti-Dumping Law and Procedure Revisited, *Journal of World Trade*, 24, 5–23.

Van Bael, Ivo, and Jean-François Bellis, 1990, *Anti-Dumping and Other Trade Protection Laws of the EEC*, second edition, CCH Editions, Bicester.

van Marion, M. F., 1992, *Liberal Trade and Japan: The Incompatibility Issue in Electronics*, Ph.D. thesis, University of Groningen.

van Wolferen, Karel, 1989, *The Enigma of Japanese Power*, Macmillan, London.

Venables, Anthony J., 1985, Trade and Trade Policy with Imperfect Competition: The Case of Identical Products and Free Entry, *Journal of International Econ-*

omics, 19, 1–19.

Vermulst, Edwin A., 1990, The Antidumping Systems of Australia, Canada, the EEC, and the USA: Have Antidumping Laws Become a Problem in International Trade? in: John H. Jackson and Edwin A. Vermulst, eds., *Antidumping Law and Practice: A Comparative Study*, Harvester Wheasheaf, New York, 425–466.

Vermulst, Edwin, and Paul Waer, 1990, European Community Rules of Origin as Commercial Policy Instruments, *Journal of World Trade*, 24, 55–99.

Vernon, Raymond, 1979, The Product Cycle Hypothesis in a New International Environment, *Oxford Bulletin of Economics and Statistics*, 41, 255–267.

Vives, Xavier, 1989, Cournot and the Oligopoly Problem, *European Economic Review*, 33, 503–514.

Vousden, Neil, 1987, Content Protection and Tariffs under Monopoly and Competition, *Journal of International Economics*, 23, 263–282.

Wakasugi, Ryuhei, 1994a, Is Japanese Foreign Direct Investment a Substitute for International Trade? *Japan and the World Economy*, 6, 45–52.

Wakasugi, Ryuhei, 1994b, On the Determinants of Overseas Production: An Empirical Study of Japanese FDI, Discussion Paper 94–2, Faculty of Economics, Yokohama National University.

Watanabe, Soitsu, 1990, Kaigai Toushi no Kyuukakudai to Guroubalu Keiei no Shinten: Kaigai Chokusetsu Toushi Ankeito Chousa Kekka Houkoku (The Sudden Rise in Foreign Investments and Developments in Global Management: Results of a Survey on Foreign Direct Investment), *Kaigai Toushi Kenkyuushohou*, 16, 4–47.

Watanabe, Soitsu, 1988, Trends of Japan's Direct Investment in Europe, *EXIM Review*, 9, 43–97.

Webb, Michael, 1992, The Ambiguous Consequences of Anti Dumping Laws, *Economic Inquiry*, 30, 437–48.

Weinstein, David E., 1992, Competition and Unilateral Dumping, *Journal of International Economics*, 32, 379–388.

Weinstein, David E., and Yishay Yafeh, 1993, Japan's Corporate Groups: Collusive or Competitive? An Empirical Investigation of Keiretsu Behavior, Mimeograph, Harvard University.

West, Philip, and Frans A. M. Alting von Geusau, eds., 1987, *The Pacific Rim and the Western World: Strategic, Economic, and Cultural Perspectives*, Westview Press, Boulder, CO, and London.

White, Halbert, 1980, A Heteroscedasticity-Consistent Covariance Matrix Estimator and a Direct Test for Heteroscedasticity, *Econometrica*, 48, 817–838.

Williamson, Peter J., and Hideki Yamawaki, 1991, The Japanese Distribution Network in Europe: Ready and Waiting for the Single Market? Mimeograph, London Business School.

Williamson, Peter J., and Hideki Yamawaki, 1989, Export Strategy and the Pattern of Japanese Involvement in US Marketing, Distribution and Service, Mimeograph, London Business School.

Winters, L. Alan, 1994a, The EC and Protection: The Political Economy, *European Economic Review*, 38, 596–603.

Winters, L. Alan, 1994b, Import Surveillance as a Strategic Trade Policy, in: Paul Krugman and Alasdair Smith, eds., 1994, *Empirical Studies of Strategic Trade Policy*, University of chicago Press, Chicago and London, 211–234.

Wolf, Bernard M., 1977, Industrial Diversification and Internationalization: Some Empirical Evidence, *Journal of Industrial Economics*, 26, 177–191.

Yamaichi Shouken Keizai Kenkyuujo (Yamaichi Research Institute), 1991, *Sangyou no Subete (Industry Yearbook)*, Yamaichi Shouken, Tokyo.

Yamamura, Kozo, 1986, Caveat Emptor: The Industrial Policy of Japan, in: Paul Krugman, ed., *Strategic Trade Policy and the New International Economics*, MIT Press, Cambridge, MA, and London, 169–210.

Yamamura. Kozo, and Ulrike Wassmann, 1989, Do Japanese Firms Behave Differently? The Effects of Keiretsu in the United States, in: Kozo Yamamura, ed., *Japanese Investment in the United States: Should We Be Concerned*? Society for Japanese Studies, Washington.

Yamawaki, Hideki, 1994, Entry Patterns of Japanese Multinationals in the US and European Manufacturing, in: Mark Mason and Dennis Encarnation, eds., *Does Ownership Matter? Japanese Multinationals in Europe*, Oxford University Press, Oxford and New York, 91–121.

Yamawaki, Hideki, 1993, International Competitiveness and the Choice of Entry Mode: Japanese Multinationals in the US and European Manufacturing Industries, Paper presented at the Allied Social Science Meetings, Anaheim, January, 1993.

Yamawaki, Hideki, 1992, Location Decisions of Japanse Multinational Firms in European Manufacturing Industries, in: K. Hughes, ed., *European Competitiveness*, Cambridge University Press.

Yamawaki, Hideki, 1991, Exports and Foreign Distributional Activities: Evidence on Japanese Firms in the United States, *Review of Economics and Statistics*, 73, 294–30.

Yamawaki, Hideki, and David B. Audretsch, 1988, Import Share under International Oligopoly with Differentiated Products: Japanese Imports in US Manufacturing, *Review of Economics and Statistics*, 70, 569–579.

Yamazawa, Ippei, 1992, On Pacific Economic Integration, *Economic Journal*, 102, 1519–1529.

Yamazawa, Ippei, 1991, The New Eurpoe and the Japanese Strategy, *Rivista di Politica Economica*, 81, 631–653.

Yannopoulos, George N., 1990, Foreign Direct Investment and European Integration: The Evidence from the Formative Years of the European Community, *Journal of Common Market Studies*, 28, 235–259.

Yano Keizai Kenkyuujo, 1989a–1995a, *Nihon Market Share Jiten (Japan Market Share Handbook)*, Mitsutomosha, Tokyo.

Yano Keizai Kenkyuujo, 1989b, *Kaden Kaigai Seisan: Shinjidai wo Mukaeru Genchi Houjin no Senryaku to Hyouka (Foreign Production of Home Electric Appliances: An Assessment of Recent Foreign Subsidiary Strategies)*, Mitsutomosha, Tokyo.

Yoshitomi, Masaru, ed., 1991, *Japanese Direct Investment in Europe*, Sumitomo-Life Research Institute and the Royal Institute of International Affairs, Avebury, Aldershot.

Young, Stephen, and James Hamill, eds., 1992, *Europe and the Multinationals: Issues and Responses for the 1990s*, Edward Elgar, Aldershot.

Yu, Chwo-Ming Joseph, 1990, The Experience Effect and Foreign Direct Investment, *Weltwirtschaftliches Archiv*, 126, 561–580.

Yu, Chwo-Ming J., and Kiyohiko Ito, 1988, Oligopolistic Reaction and Foreign

Direct Investment: The Case of the US Tire and Textiles Industries, *Journal of International Business Studies*, 19, 449–460.

Zysman, John, 1994, Can Japanese Investment Sustain European Development in Electronics? in: Mark Mason and Dennis Encarnation, eds., *Does Ownership Matter? Japanese Multinationals in Europe*, Oxford University Press, Oxford and New York, 331–362.

INDEX